LOCATING LEARNING:

Ethnographic Perspectives on Classroom Research

edited by

Catherine Emihovich

ABLEX PUBLISHING CORPORATION
NORWOOD, NEW JERSEY

Library of Congress Cataloging-in-Publication Data

Locating learning across the curriculum.
  Bibliography: p.
  Includes index.
  1. Education—Research. 2. Classroom environment—Research. 3. Ob-
servation (Educational method) 4. Educational sociology. I. Emihovich,
Catherine.
LB1028.L58 1989   370.15′23   88-35142
ISBN 0-89391-505-X (cloth)
ISBN 0-89391-577-7 (ppk)

Ablex Publishing Corporation
355 Chestnut Street
Norwood, New Jersey 07648

Table of Contents

SECTION IV. PERSPECTIVES ON COMPUTER LITERACY

Preface

When teaching an introductory course in educational research, I am often asked by students two questions: What is the nature of the research process? and, How can the results be applied to classroom practices? Having spent considerable time thinking about how best to answer these questions, and recognizing the fact that for most students educational research seemed to be a field completely divorced from actual classroom experiences, I was motivated to put this book together. However, my intention is not to discuss research in all its forms, but rather research on classrooms from a set of perspectives grouped under what is broadly termed the ethnographic paradigm, and to show how these perspectives provide knowledge across a wide variety of subjects. Originally, several of the chapters in this book were given as papers at an 1985 AERA symposium, "Ethnographic Perspectives on Locating Learning across the Curriculum;" other authors were added as it became apparent the subject merited a whole book. The final product should not be viewed as a substitution for traditional forms of research. Instead, it should be read as the presentation of perspectives which signal a new voice in the classroom, that of everyday experience, a voice often muffled in the parade of educational reports marching across the terrain.

I would like to thank the authors of this book for their diligent efforts in helping me get this book together, which reflects not only their ideas in individual chapters, but also their ideas as contributed in many conversations I have had with all of them as this book was being completed. I would especially like to thank my colleagues at Florida State, Carolyn Piazza, George Papagiannis, and Cynthia Wallat, for their additional assistance in reading the introduction and contributing comments. Of course, when "thank you's" are in order, one's spouse is always mentioned, but in my case, the assistance of my husband, Ron, extends well beyond spousal duty. His help is appreciated and can never be repaid.

INTRODUCTION
Ethnographic Perspectives on Classroom Research

CATHERINE EMIHOVICH
Florida State University

OVERVIEW

The purpose of this book is to call readers' attention to how ethnographic perspectives frame classroom research, and in this chapter, to provide a few orienting objectives of researchers who have influenced directions in the field of educational ethnography, to sketch further research directions and trends, and to describe what aspects of the ethnographic paradigm these chapters share.

A common beginning in many articles on educational ethnography is to pose the question, What is ethnography? Providing a definitive definition is beyond the scope of this introduction; as Samuel Johnson said, sometimes things get darker through definitions. The risk is real that definitions provide a false sense of security in the belief that, once defined, we "know" what a thing is. My solution to the dilemma of dealing with multiple definitions is editor's choice: to select those that best frame the points made later in the chapters. The definitions thus presented serve this purpose only; readers will find throughout the chapters many references to guide them in learning about those aspects left untouched here.

My first choice begins with Hymes' ideas, one reason being that several chapters draw upon a sociolinguistic model for ethnographies of communication. As Hymes put it:

> In a word, ethnography is inquiry that begins with recognition that one is at work in situations that are indeed massively prestructured, but prestructured by the history and ways among those whom one inquires. At the heart of it is a process of which linguistic inquiry is indeed a model, if we set aside any particular model of grammar, and

1

think of linguistic inquiry in the generic sense as *the interpretation of codes.* (1977, p. 171)

"Interpretation of codes" is a fitting phrase, since for many children, "decoding" what the teacher said becomes their major task in school. As Shirley Heath (1983) beautifully demonstrated in her book, *Ways with Words,* children's language patterns acquired in their home and community affect their use of oral and written language in school, and given differences in social class and ethnic backgrounds, children and teachers may find themselves speaking two different "codes" which neither group fully understands. One of the ethnographer's tasks, then, is to discern what the "codes" are, and to document how understanding (and misunderstanding) are mutually negotiated within specific cultural contexts. In this regard, I note Green and Harker's (1982) point that context is not a given entity like a classroom, but is constructed as part of the interactional process and contributes to the interpretation of meaning. To break the "code," the ethnographer examines contextualization cues (verbal, nonverbal, and prosodic features of conversation) which are "the means by which speakers signal and listeners interpret how semantic content is to be understood and how each sentence [behavior] relates to what precedes or follows" (Gumperz & Tannen, as cited in Green & Harer, 1982, p. 190). A common thread linking several of the chapters is how the discourse patterns help shape the learning of subject matter in diverse areas.

But there is another sense in which an emphasis on language is important, and that is in the choice of language that ethnographers use to describe what they have studied, not just their study of how language functions to create the context. I speak now of the contrast between a personalized language utilizing the narrative form and a more abstract, technical language utilizing mathematics in the statistical sense. The use of a more personal form of language reflects the trend recently noted in several articles (Randall, 1986; Shweder, 1986; Winkler, 1985) of a return to the interpretive mode in the social sciences instead of the dominant quantification mode most commonly found. Randall quotes Clifford Geertz as saying that artificial distinctions between the "humanities" and the "social sciences" were collapsing, and that:

Many social scientists have turned away from a laws and instances ideal of explanation toward a cases and interpretation one, looking less for the sort of thing that connects planets and pendulums and more for the sort that connects chrysanthemums and swords. . . . Analogies drawn from the humanities are coming to play the kind of role in sociological understanding that analogies drawn from the crafts and technology have long played in physical understanding. (1986, p. 31)

This interpretive mode fits perfectly with the concepts being developed in quantum mechanics (a branch of theoretical physics) that the physical world is not a "structure built out of independently existing unanalyzable entities, but rather a web of relationships between elements whose meanings arise wholly from their relationships to the whole" (Zukav, 1979, p. 72). Geertz (1973) himself has alluded to "webs of meaning" present in the "thick description" of ethnographic field notes, and it is this holistic emphasis on data analysis which marks one difference between the ethnographic paradigm and the positivistic paradigm.

Seeing the connection between quantum mechanics and educational research is not that difficult when one realizes that both fields have begun to recognize the importance of two basic tenets: behavior (of either subatomic particles or persons) cannot be analyzed apart from the context in which they were observed, and the observer cannot be divorced from the phenomenon under investigation. The movement away from the positivistic paradigm is not new in educational research; over a decade ago Cronbach (1975) noted that psychologists should observe behavior in relation to the context in which it occurs, and consider giving up a search for causal explanations of behavior by stating the "time has come to exorcise the null hypothesis" (p. 124). Ironically, psychology as a field still clings to use of the "scientific method" to ascertain generalizable laws of human behavior while the method itself is under attack by "hard" scientists, most notably the physicists. The idea that scientists can remain independent from their field of inquiry and objectify reality to see what is *really* there is no longer tenable. As Olson, quoting Heisenberg noted:

The scientific method of analysing, [defining] and classifying has become conscious of its limitations, which rise out of the [condition] that by its intervention science alters and refashions the object of investigation. In other words, method and object can no longer be separated. *The scientific world-view has ceased to be a scientific view in the true sense of the word.* (1971, p. 299)

Most educational researchers derive their models from psychology, and unquestioned adherence to the "scientific method" puts them out of step with the latest evolution as to just what the concept of science is. Ethnography, in contrast, finds much in common with the "new science", and with the field of quantum mechanics in particular. Heisenberg's point meshes very well with the notion that ethnographers cannot separate themselves from the research process; indeed, the ethnographer's self is one of the primary instruments used to collect data. An examination of personal bias is an important aspect of ethnography (LeCompte, 1986), and constitutes one of the new directions in ethnographic research, critical ethnography. As proponents of this field suggest, there needs to be a "commitment to study the character and bases of one's own work practices and their relation to the knowledge such practices produce" (Simon & Dippo, 1987, p. 200). In this context, to use a personalized language makes sense; its very form attempts to preclude a hiding of meaning behind the numbers.

An even stronger case can be made for the fact that a personalized language brings the reader closer to understanding what the ethnographer studied. As the last section of Jay Lemke's chapter makes clear, the cold, technical language of science alienates students, and prevents them from learning that science is, and can be, a warm, human enterprise, and that not all scientific precepts should be accepted unquestioningly. To argue, as many quantitative researchers do, that school practitioners and policy makers would understand research results better if they only had more training in statistics misses the point. Most research literature is written in technical jargon which obscures the reality of everyday classroom life most practitioners and policy makers share. The use of statistics alone is not the problem; it is the lack of interpretation with reference to the context from which they were drawn that becomes the issue. A test score, for example, is an accumulation of meanings (item responses) derived from the researcher's point of view, which may or may not be shared by the participants from whom the scores were obtained. If more quantitative researchers recognized this fact and included a narrative, descriptive language with their statistics, it would provide a more balanced perspective and reach a wider audience.

For these reasons, emphasizing language with respect to the discourse patterns across different subject areas is one of the major themes of the book. But such an examination provides a fairly microscopic view of learning, and if that were the only focus, would neglect another tenet of ethnographic research, that of examining the broader social context in which learning and instruction occurs. A second definition of ethnography then, highlights the holistic aspects of the ethnographic process. As Heath (1982) noted, the "goal of ethnography is to describe the ways of living of a social group, a group in which there is in-group recognition of the individuals living together and working together as a social unit" (p. 34). In traditional ethnographies, the social group was a whole culture, but in educational ethnographies, it can be a school, a classroom, or even a small group of children working on a reading lesson within a classroom. What is critical is to maintain a comparative perspective, whereby the actions of the group are viewed in relation to another group or within the context of a larger frame such as the community structure. As Ogbu (1981) put it, school ethnography needs an "*ethnographic imagination,*" that is, "a good working theory of the social structure of the school and of the wider community in which the school is located" (p. 6). To this criterion I might add that a comparative perspective with reference to a broad domain of literature is also important, as exemplified in Rebecca Barr's chapter.

My choice for a third criterion is a purely personal one, taken from my mentor, Fred Gearing, who defined ethnography as a process of "finding fascination with the commonplace." I chose this one because it exemplifies what I feel is a shared concern among educational ethnographers that the culture of the classroom and the ordinary details of the teachers and students' lives are worth recording. Reading ethnographic accounts allows us to hear the voices from classrooms in a way that other forms of research do not permit—the same voices which are often muffled by the statistical data which many researchers use to speak to their audience of policy makers and school personnel. By paying close attention to what these voices have to say, ethnographic researchers acquire deeper insight into the problems of modern American classrooms. And, as Delamont (1976) observed in her study of two British classrooms, a focus on the "trivia" of everyday classroom life does not preclude a focus on the wider social and economic issues by which classroom events are framed. While many of the chapters describe learning in microscopic detail, these same chapters illustrate how these details are but a microcosm of larger social and psychological issues.

In focusing on these three criteria, the emphasis on language, the broader social context, and the commonplace reality of everyday life in classrooms, I have of course excluded many others. This exclusion was consciously planned, since the following chapters will illuminate further multiple ways researchers can define the dark question, What is educational ethnography? But before turning to an overview of the chapters, I will close by mentioning future trends and directions for research.

FUTURE TRENDS AND DIRECTIONS

Sanday (1979) proposed that ethnographic research is continuously evolving with respect to methods and modes of interpretation, a trend which is evident in the development of two new fields of inquiry: critical ethnography and ethnography as literature. Very briefly I will describe what effect I think these two fields will have on ethnographic research in classrooms.

To summarize the position taken by Simon and Dippo:

> Ethnography as a general term refers to a range of possible procedures for structuring one's experience of a social situation and transforming that experience into a systematic account which renders the social practices of the situation into patterns through which social forms are constructed and maintained. Critical ethnographic work transforms this general procedure into a particular one by supplying it with additional perspectives, principally historical and structural, that alter the ethnographic project toward one which supports an emancipatory as well as a hermeneutic concern. (1987, p. 201)

The authors further state that critical ethnography addresses a range of concerns, such as the "production" of ethnographic data, historical and structural limitations on the ethnographer's understanding of others, the way the discourse frames a point of view, and nature of ethnographic work within specific settings such as university communities.

Although Simon and Dippo do not specifically make this point, I feel their work has special application to the educational scene in the arena of policy making. Ethnographers have been hesitant to enter this arena, fearing that their data would be used to render judgments or evaluations about the appropriateness of a specific learning context, or teaching style, or behavior of certain children. Their reluctance is understandable, since an ethnographer perceived as an evaluator acquires a different role other than the one traditionally assumed in ethnographic research (Emihovich, 1988). However, the very richness of reporting found in most educational ethnographies needs to be brought to the policy makers' attention. At the same time, the ethnographer's willingness to examine critically both the means by which data are collected and the limitations inherent in the research strategies selected throughout the study pave the way for a more intensive and revealing look at classroom practices which may result in policy making decisions which have real and lasting impact on educational reform.

Whether policy makers really want this sort of critical examination is, of course, another question. One reason that educational research as practiced in the dominant mode of quantification and hypothesis testing may be widely accepted is because its purpose is to confirm the existing social order, not to challenge it (Young, 1981). But as critical ethnography matures as a field of inquiry, hard questions will be asked that policy makers cannot afford to ignore as our educational system moves into the 21st century. Some of these questions as they pertain to social studies education are raised by Borman in her chapter, and in the chapters by Bloome, Wallat and Piazza, and Papagiannis, we see how an ethnographic perspective can inform future research and/or policy decisions in the areas of reading, math/science, and computer education.

The field of ethnography as literature stands in stark contrast to mainstream educational research. I almost hesitate to introduce it, because with its use of analogies, metaphors, and other literary devices, it seems to be returning ethnography to the place it still holds in the minds of many positivistic researchers—that of producing "fiction" instead of "facts." The concept is not new; anthropologists have long been aware of the dictum that the "best way to write a compelling ethnography is to lose your field notes" (Shweder, 1986, p. 1). While this prospect appears alarming to many educational and social science researchers, it does not mean a total abrogation of method, nor a denial of the difference between social description and fiction. Instead, this statement reflects Randall's point:

> Questions about whether the social sciences can be "hard science" are not new, but they are being posed in a new way. Two related questions are being posed. How should the social scientist write? And how should social scientists read other societies, cultures or historical periods? (1984, p. 31)

These questions are at the heart of a return to an interpretive mode in the social sciences, and are consonant with the critical ethnographers' point that ethnographic data is "produced" not "discovered" (Simon & Dippo, 1987). And if it is "produced," the means by which the "story" is told merits serious consideration. As James Clifford put it:

> But fictions, in the original sense of something made, something constructed, are serious things, historical collective products that must be analyzed. In anthropology, it is part of the whole process of studying ourselves, our own society, and not merely constructing accounts about other people. (quoted in Randall, 1984, p. 31)

Where does this field fit in with classroom research? While none of the chapters in this book fall under the rubric of ethnography as literature, in some of them we hear an echo of the story waiting to be told, brief excerpts of actual talk that form the basis of classroom narratives constructed from informants' accounts and the analyst's theoretical or interpretive perspective. I believe this field will receive increasing attention as ethnographers ponder the ways in which they construct and reveal meaning in their research.

An added advantage of viewing ethnography as literature is that it will also attract a wider range of authors. Erickson (1986) noted it is not just the ethnographers who have a story to tell, community members have their story too, and the ethnographers can provide a "parallel account in conjunction with community members, thus becoming one among a number of voices in a conversation about the community" (p. 4). Heath (1987) suggested that ethnographic methods can be used to "empower learners" as they realize that the skills of writing and analyzing field notes and conducting interviews are skills which transfer to their daily life, and that there is a relationship between direct experiences and secondary source knowledge by which these experiences are analyzed and reflected upon. In Heath's words, the "researched become the researchers" and when this happens, ethnographic methods may become the bridge by which the community crosses the divide between practice and theory in the educational domain.

What readers of this volume will not learn from these chapters is how to do ethnographic research, although each chapter contains numerous references to methodological works. Instead, what they will gain is a sense of how ethnographic perspectives inform us about the language of learning in diverse disciplines, the broader social context in which learning is embedded, and the policy implications which ensue when an ethnographic perspective on classroom research is taken. While recent reports of the American educational system point out what's wrong (National Commission on Excellence in Education, 1983), and the government issues a pamphlet indicating what works (U.S. Department of Education, 1986), an ethnographer simply poses the question: what is going on in classrooms? By listening to what the participants say, interpreting the responses from an analytic perspective, and translating the analyses into policy objectives, the question, how can education be improved?, can be answered in ways that are more likely to ensure success for all children.

OVERVIEW OF THE CHAPTERS

While each reader develops his or her own interpretation of a text, framing the chapters provides a sense of what to expect. The book begins with the subject of reading, a fitting choice since a recent report indicated that the state of American literacy leaves something to be desired as we draw nearer to the 21st century (Kirsch & Jungeblut, 1986). However, as the chapters in this section make clear, literacy is a far more complex issue than just posing the question, "how well does a student read?" In the chapter by Regina Weade and Judith Green, it is suggested that the study of reading involves multiple dimensions: the student's interaction with the teacher, the type of instructional strategies used to teach reading, and the nature of the text itself. Their view stands in stark contrast to traditional approaches to reading, which view reading as a academic process which can be broken down into discrete components (e.g., phonetics, vocabulary, comprehension) and which overlook both the social and textual demands of reading. What follows from Weade and Green's perspective is that a literacy event cannot be analyzed by a single set of indicators like coding behaviors within "reading;" it must be examined using diverse analytic conceptualizations and tools to locate "reading" within the classroom. Their perspective raises provocative questions as to how teachers will be trained to teach "reading" in the future.

Rebecca Barr, in her chapter, locates reading within the social organization of the classroom, examining such dimensions as instructional arrangements (e.g., small group, total class or individual instruction), peer group learning, and ability grouping. Her comprehensive review of current research in both American and British studies of naturalistic settings illustrates nicely the effect of these different arrangements on students' acquisition of reading skills, providing a more macro perspective to the issues discussed by Weade and Green. Of especial interest is her mention of peer group arrangements, particularly with reference to the fact that little naturalistic documentation exists in the area of reading and language arts. With the advent of computer technology applied in the classroom, allowing for more tutoring and peer learning to take place, research examining the effects of peer group learning in reading instruction from an ethnographic perspective promises to be a new and exciting area for years to come.

David Bloome's chapter introduces a third important factor in locating reading, that of examining the effect of cultural variation.

He refutes the concept of reading as defined within deficit, difference and effectiveness models, and outlines a series of questions which will through their answers lead to a more comprehensive picture of how children's learning to read is influenced by social and cultural processes. Picking up on many of themes articulated by the authors of the previous two chapters, his chapter suggests implicitly the kinds of policy changes needed if this broader concept of reading as a literacy event constructed on multiple levels is to be realized.

The next section of the book is given over to an ethnographic perspective on social studies. Ensuring a literate citizenry is a necessary but not sufficient condition for a democratic society; we also need to prepare students to assume their civic responsibilities. But as the chapter by Linda McNeil makes clear, American schools are failing in this task. Through her analysis of "defensive teaching," we learn that teachers reduce critical issues in American political and social history to rote memorizations which produce a student population alienated from their own traditions. Her proposed solution is that teachers should find ways to "empower" students and make the learning of academic content consonant with their personal experiences; otherwise, the much touted educational reforms will result in even more poorly educated students ill-equipped to face the future.

Catherine Cornbleth, in her chapter, elaborates further on issues raised by McNeil, and examines social studies education from a critical perspective along the lines of the critical ethnographers. Reporting on data gathered from the Pittsburgh Critical Thinking Project (PCTP), she illustrates how a school can successfully engage students and teachers in constructing a curriculum-in-use to facilitate critical thinking. While the success of programs of this type in affecting student learning outcomes remains to be determined, the PCTP program marks an important beginning in shifting attention away from an exclusive focus on standardized test results as the only way to locate learning in social studies.

In her chapter, Kathryn Borman notes the growing use of ethnographic studies to provide a substantive critique of the public school system, and highlights some of the theoretical issues underlying this perspective. She argues persuasively that social studies education needs a critical perspective which questions, among other issues, the production of school knowledge, and the hegemony of cultural interests which promote one particular viewpoint of the appropriate functions of schools in society. Echoing the notion of empowering learners prevalent in the work of McNeil and Heath, Kathryn Borman closes her chapter by citing the work of the KEEP program, which utilizes a cultural focus to transform educational practice for the benefit of Hawaiian children, as a model for American schools.

The third section of the book introduces ethnographic research in a relatively new area for this genre, math and science. For reasons not entirely clear (and which should be the focus of additional research in this area), neither of these two fields have received the same amount of attention as have reading and social studies. Yet, they cannot be overlooked as our society moves into the 21st century, with students' understanding in these areas woefully deficient. In his chapter, Douglas Campbell applies the same sociolinguistic interactional perspective Weade and Green used for reading, with a cross-cultural variation. Examining a math lesson in a Tagalog-speaking village in the Philippines, he found that the learning of math content was embedded in children's understanding of English, and that failing to understand the interconnection between the two impeded children's learning in either content area. As his analysis makes clear, locating math is more than just looking at computations, it also involves how children and teachers talk about math, and mathematical ideas represented by symbols. While his research was conducted in another culture, it has important implications for children's learning of math in this culture when English is also a second language.

What Douglas Campbell does for math, Jay Lemke does for science. His chapter also focuses on talk in science classrooms from a sociolinguistic perspective, and he powerfully documents the fact that science talk, like other specialized languages (Phillips, 1982), can be used as a gatekeeping function to exclude entry of "inappropriate" (read women and minorities, low-ability students) persons into the hallowed halls of science. His chapter underscores the point made earlier in this introduction that a cold, impersonal technical language divorced from personal, everyday speech limits students' understanding of that field, to the ultimate detriment of society, which needs more well-trained people in technical fields. One solution to this problem may lie in changing interactional patterns in classrooms as a way to increase students' interest in science.

In the last chapter in this section, Cynthia Wallat and Carolyn Piazza sketch out policy directions for integrating knowledge from research with decision makers' interests. Of particular interest is their call for new testing directions derived from metaphors for sociolinguistic studies of classroom discourse, which are based on successful problem-solving groups' activities. As they succinctly put it, "more is known than used," and they close by describing some successful efforts to bring researchers and policy makers together to get the "known" used.

The last section of the book examines the role of the new player in the educational ethnographic scene: the computer. Because research in this area is still in its infancy, ethnographic studies are more likely to make an impact sooner than in areas more well covered by traditional research methods. As the chapter by James Heap illustrates, an ethnomethodological approach works well in describing the nature of children's collaborative writing using a computer. His analysis documents the fact that a normative order exists at three levels of collaborative writing: composing, inputting text, and arranging text. The interplay among these three levels as young children work provides a fascinating glimpse into how text is socially constructed, and how children gain a greater understanding of the multiple tasks involved in both oral and written language production.

In the next chapter, Catherine Emihovich looks at the effects of peer collaboration in learning Logo, a computer language designed with young children in mind (Papert, 1980). Contrary to what some would believe, preschool children are able to engage in cooperative learning, albeit in a limited way with the teacher's assistance, and a close look at their language reveals how their understanding of some of the cognitive components of the task increases over time. The ethnographic perspective is combined with a Vygotskian perspective on the role of social interaction in facilitating cognitive development, an area which should receive increased attention in future research studies of children's learning with computers.

The last chapter of this section ends with a comprehensive look by George Papagiannis of the policy issues raised by computer use in the schools. He reviews some of the preliminary findings, and cautions against an uncritical acceptance of computers without first considering the wider sociocultural implications. He ends his chapter on a note which serves to sum up the book as a whole, that no matter what the subject area is, until we fully understand what our enduring goals for education are, we will not be able to implement the reforms which will make these goals possible to achieve. Once identified, an ethnographic perspective may point us in the directions we need to take, but recognizing the "maieutic" potential of any educational innovation is still the researcher and practitioner's first task.

REFERENCES

Cronbach, L.J. (1975). Beyond the two disciplines of scientific psychology. *American Psychologist, 30,* 116–127.

Delamont, S. (1976). *Interaction in the classroom.* London: Methuen.

Emihovich, C. (1988, January). *New roles for evaluators: Collaboration in school improvement.* Talk presented at the Qualitative Research Conference, University of Georgia, Athens, GA.

Erickson, F. (1986). Voices, genre, writers, and audiences. *Anthropology & Education Quarterly, 17*(1), 3–5.

Geertz, C. (1973). *The interpretation of culture.* New York: Basic Books.

Green, J.L., & Harker, J.O. (1982). Gaining access to learning: Conversational, social and cognitive demands of group participation. In L.C. Wilkinson (Ed.), *Communicating in the classroom.* New York: Academic Press.

Heath, S.B. (1982). Ethnography in education: Defining the essentials. In P. Gilmore & A.A. Glatthorn (Eds.), *Children in and out of school.* Washington, DC: Center for Applied Linguistics.

Heath, S.B. (1983). *Ways with words.* Cambridge, England: Cambridge University Press.

Heath, S.B. (1987, April). *Redefining culture: Society, anthropology, and education.* Invited talk at the annual meeting of the American Educational Research Association, Washington, DC.

Hymes, D. (1977). Qualitative/quantitative research methodologies in education: An ethnographic perspective. *Anthropology & Education Quarterly, 8*(3), 165–176.

Kirsch, I., & Jungeblut, A. (1986). *Literacy: Profiles of America's young adults.* (Rep. No. 16–PL–01). Princeton, NJ: National Assessment of Educational Progress.

LeCompte, M. (1987). Bias in the biography: Bias and subjectivity in ethnographic research. *Anthropology & Education Quarterly, 18*(1), 43–52.

National Commission on Excellence in Education. (1983). *A nation at risk: The imperative for educational reform.* Washington, DC: U.S. Government Printing Office.

Ogbu, J.U. (1980). School ethnography: A multilevel approach. *Anthropology & Education Quarterly, 12*(1), 3–29.

Olson, R. (1971). Scientific thought: Key to the Western world-view. In R. Olson (Ed.), *Science as metaphor.* Belmont, CA: Wadsworth Publishing.

Papert, S. (1980). *Mindstorms: Children, computers, and powerful ideas.* New York: Basic Books.

Phillips, S. (1982). The language socialization of lawyers: Acquiring the cant. In G. Spindler (Ed.), *Doing the ethnography of schooling.* New York: Holt, Rinehart, & Winston.

Randall, F. (1984, January 29). Why scholars become storytellers. *New York Times Book Review.*

Sanday, P.R. (1979). The ethnographic paradigms. *Administrative Science Quarterly, 24,* 527–538.

Shweder, R.A. (1986, September 21). Storytelling among the anthropologists. *New York Times Book Review.*

Simon, R.I., & Dippo, D. (1987). On critical ethnographic work. *Anthropology & Education Quarterly, 17*(4), 195–202.

U. S. Department of Education. (1986). *What works: Research about teaching and learning.* Washington, DC: U.S. Government Printing Office.

Winkler, K.J. (1985). Questioning the science in social science: Scholars signal a "Turn to Interpretation." *Chronicle of Higher Education, 30*(17), 5–6.

Young, M.F.D. (1981). Ideology and educational research. In E.B. Gumbert (Ed.), *Poverty, power and authority in education.* Atlanta: Center for Cross-Cultural Research, Georgia State University.

Zukav, G. (1979). *The dancing wu li masters.* New York: Bantam Books.

SECTION I
Perspectives on Reading

CHAPTER ONE

Reading in The Instructional Context: An Interactional Sociolinguistic/ Ethnographic Perspective

REGINA WEADE
University of Florida

JUDITH GREEN
Ohio State University

In the last decade, the study of reading has moved from laboratory settings to examining reading as it occurs in classroom contexts. This move has been facilitated by the development and adaptation of ethnographic and sociolinguistic research. These approaches provide systematic and theoretically principled ways of identifying and exploring "reading" as it occurs in the everyday life of classrooms. The move is not simply one of changing locations, however. In the transition into classroom settings, questions have emerged about what counts as reading in classroom contexts, how instruction influences reading, and what students come to know from participating in reading events that are part of the everyday life in classrooms. In addition, this work raises questions about the reading text, what it is, how it functions, and what is involved in learning from text.

The purpose in this chapter is twofold: (1) To discuss what is meant by an ethnographic and sociolinguistic perspective to the study of reading in everyday classroom events; and (2) To illustrate how such an approach can be used to examine the ways in which instructional processes influence the text read, how reading occurs, the nature of the text, and the outcomes of reading in a classroom context. We will argue that the study of reading as a part of everyday classroom life requires examination of the unfolding and developing interactions of teachers and students with text. As will be argued, in classroom contexts, reading is embedded in and influenced by the instructional strategies of the teacher and students regardless of whether reading is the official purpose of the curriculum (e.g., learning how to read; learning literature) or a vehicle for the curriculum (e.g., reading to learn about something or to complete an assignment).

Defined in this way, reading is a complex process that involves both the intrapersonal and interpersonal contexts of meaning construction (Bloome & Green, 1984; Cazden, 1983). Thus what is needed to examine reading in classroom contexts is a broad definition of reading to guide us in identifying instances of reading as they occur as part of the interactions among participants (e.g., teacher, students, and text). In turn, such a definition requires the use of an approach that provides a systematic, flexible means of locating and examining reading in its various forms and functions.

WHAT IS MEANT BY AN ETHNOGRAPHIC PERSPECTIVE

The first task for those interested in observing and exploring reading in the everyday life of classrooms is to locate "reading." This task may seem simple, for example, just look for students reading books. However, as will be shown below, the task is more complex, and the way in which reading is defined influences what will be identified, observed, recorded, and interpreted.

Recent ethnographic work provides the basis for an operational definition of reading events that enables the ethnographer to locate reading as it occurs in naturally occurring events (e.g., Bloome & Green, 1982; 1984; Griffin, 1977; Heath, 1983; Szwed, 1981; Taylor, 1984). For example, Heath (1983) was able to identify reading and to distinguish it from other types of literacy events by using the following definition that builds on the work of Anderson, Teale, and Estrada (1980):

> Those occasions in which the talk revolves around a piece of writing have been termed literacy events. Anderson, Teale, and Estrada 1980 defines a literacy event as "any action sequence, involving one or more persons, in which the production and/or comprehension of print plays a role" (p. 59). They break literacy events into two types. The first are reading events in which an individual either comprehends or attempts to comprehend a message which is encoded graphically. The second are writing events in which an individual attempts to produce these graphic symbols. (p. 386)

A researcher using this definition can identify a literacy event whenever it occurs and can categorize these events into those that are writing-oriented or those that are reading-oriented events. However, to understand what occurs during the reading event or to examine how it develops requires an analytic perspective that enables the researcher to examine: (a) the ways in which the events function in everyday life, (b) the requirements for participating in the events, (c) the meaning constructed; (d) the types of task demands involved, (e) the types of outcomes produced, (f) the places in which they occurred, (g) the organizational structures of the events, (h) the types of participants, (i) the time of occurrence, (j) the conditions under which they occurred, and (k) the recurrence of the event over time (See Spradley, 1980, for a discussion of domain analysis and a description of semantic relationships that can be used to identify patterns related to reading.) Such a perspective enables the researcher to understand how reading is used and accomplished in everyday life. Once identified and examined, these data can be categorized and taxonomies developed that represent types and functions of reading events and the relationship of these events to other aspects of classroom life among others.

Researchers who have used an ethnographic perspective and approach to study reading in everyday classroom contexts have located reading in a variety of classroom activities (e.g., Bloome, 1981, 1983a; Bloome & Green, 1982, 1984; Cochran–Smith, 1984; Collins, 1983, 1986; Gilmore, 1981; Griffin, 1977; Heap, 1980, 1983a, 1985; Heath, 1983; Hymes, 1981; McDermott, 1976, 1978). From this work, six different types of events in which reading occurs in classrooms can be identified:

1. As an event that is the focus of instruction itself (e.g., formal reading groups; content area reading lesson);
2. As an event embedded in general instructional events (e.g., reading a subject area text, menu, test, blackboard assignment);
3. As an event that is part of informal classroom life (e.g., voluntarily reading a book after assigned work is completed; sitting on the playground reading books);
4. As an event that is part of the hidden world of peer groups (e.g., note reading);
5. As an event that is part of a homework assignment (e.g., an assignment that is completed outside of the classroom itself but is referred to or used during class time);
6. As an event that is specific to the local classroom or to local school settings (e.g., research for the science fair, rules for classroom participation, or rules for reading contests sponsored by the library or a community organization—Burger King among others).

Taxonomies such as this one can be used to compare reading events that occur in different lessons within a classroom as well as lessons across classrooms. Thus, generic aspects of reading in classroom situations can be identified. In addition, situational factors that influence how reading occurs in a given event or classroom can be identified to account for issues of stability and variability within and across events and settings.

An ethnographic perspective, then, is more than a method or set of tools (e.g., participant interviewing, participant observation, field notes, document analysis; Green & Bloome, 1983; Gumperz, 1986; Hammersley & Atkinson, 1985; Heath, 1982; Spindler, 1982). A person with an ethnographic perspective sees the classroom and life in it with a particular conceptual lens, one that is focused on developing an understanding of the everyday life of a social group and what is required to participate appropriately in such life. The ethnographer examines everyday life from the perspective of the participants as reflected in their talk, actions, ways of holding each other accountable, and/or their perceptions (e.g., Erickson & Shultz, 1981; Gumperz, 1982a, 1982b, 1986; Heath, 1982; McDermott, 1976). By observing what participants do, how, when, where, with whom, under what conditions, for what purposes, with what outcomes, the ethnographer is able to identify recurrent patterns of life.

In addition, by examining how participants in a situation work together in concert, or fail to do so, to accomplish the task at hand, the ethnographer is able to examine what participants need to know, predict, produce, and interpret in order to gain access to and participate in the ordinary events of daily life in classrooms (Heath, 1982). Thus researchers who use this perspective ask questions about how events are accomplished through the talk and actions of participants (Cook–Gumperz, 1977; Gumperz, 1982, 1986; Heap, 1983b), how events are organized communicatively (Hymes, 1982), who has access to such events (Collins, 1983; Cook–Gumperz, Gumperz, & Simons, 1981; Gumperz, 1982; Hymes, 1982; McDermott, 1976; Michaels, 1981; 1984), among others. What each researcher seeks to understand is how daily life is organized through the face-to-face interactions of participants, what is required to participate in such life, and what the consequences are of such participation.

To extract patterns of daily life, the ethnographer engages in sustained, over time participant observation so as to be able to examine life through one or more cycles of events. The goal is to obtain a picture of the "whole" of life. However, as Heath (1982) has argued, when the whole of life of a social group cannot be observed, then the decisions about what part of the whole to observe must be made in principled ways (See also Spindler, 1982, for a discussion of the size of the unit observed.) Erickson (1979) provides further clarification that can help the researcher make a principled decision. He argues that the whole that is analyzed is not dependent on size but on the fact that it exists as an analytic whole.

> It is in this sense that ethnographic work is "holistic," not because of the size of the social unit, but because the units of analyses are considered as wholes, whether the whole be a community, a school system, or the beginning of one lesson in a single classroom. (p. 59)

The key, then, is to identify a "whole," a unit that participants see as a whole, and to observe it through a complete cycle of occurrence.

To make such explorations possible, an ethnographer will often make permanent records (e.g., audiotapes, videotapes) to supplement field notes. These records permit in-depth analysis of (1) how events are accomplished and information communicated, (2) factors that support and/or constrain participation, access, and learning, and (3) social and cognitive norms and expectations for participation. In addition, the ethnographer may use participant interviewing and document analysis to obtain the fullest picture possible of daily life, its demands and routines, and to triangulate data. From this data, the ethnographer develops "a" (not "the") grammar of the event. This grammar can also be used to compare the findings in one study with those of others, thus building a broader understanding of everyday life (Mead, 1972) and contributing to the knowledge of about life in educational settings.

INTERACTIVE SOCIOLINGUISTICS AND ETHOGRAPHY OF COMMUNICATION

What is evident in the description of ethnographer presented above is that much of daily life is conducted through the actions of participants. The dominance of communication as a means of carrying out everyday life has led some ethnographers to engage in ethnography of communication, often referred to as microethnography. One of the dominant perspectives within microethnography is the interactive sociolinguistic perspective. Gumperz (1986) captures this perspective well, especially as it applies to educational settings:

The teacher's efforts to organize class settings, set up learning environments, and label and define instructional tasks must be understood. Speakers and hearers depend on each others' good faith in creating such understandings which set the preconditions for effective information transfer. By the above actions, teachers create the conditions that make learning possible.

The interactional sociolinguistic approach focuses on the interplay of linguistic, contextual and social presuppositions which interact to create the conditions for classroom learning. Analysis focuses on key instructional activities that ethnographic observations have shown may be crucial to the educational process. These activities are realized through definable speech events which stand out against the background of everyday conversation; they have characteristics which can be understood and can be described by ethnographers and recognized by participants. Moreover, knowledge of the events and what is accomplished by them is common to groups of people; they are not occasional occurrences but have a place in the daily conduct of affairs of groups. From this perspective language in the classroom can be seen as part of the language of the school setting; characteristics of particular classroom situations of children of different ages are seen to occur regularly as speech routines held together through the daily practices of teacher and students; that is, there are features of these routines which are similar across all classroom contexts and some that vary as schooling progresses. (p. 65)

From the interactive sociolinguistic perspective, the classroom is viewed as a dynamic communicative environment in which the ordinary activities and events of daily life are constructed by participants as they interact. Participation in classrooms is seen as being patterned or routine to a great extent, as requiring the development of a joint perspective on what is occurring, as involving cooperation between and among participants, and as constructed by the participants as they work together to reach the curriculum goals established by the school district (see Cazden, 1986; Edwards & Furlong, 1978; Erickson, 1986; Green, 1983; Heap, 1983b, 1985; Heath, 1983; Stubbs, 1983, for additional premises that undergird the ethnography of communication perspective in educational settings). From this perspective, then, the degree of joint understanding and interpretation of events by participants can influence what occurs, what participants can access (e.g., meaning, types of events), how teachers assess students' display of ability, and what students come to know by participating in the event.

The analysis presented in this chapter involves a sociolinguistic analysis of an everyday event (a review lesson) that is grounded in an ethnographic perspective. It is not, however, a part of an ethnography of classroom life. An interactive sociolinguistic approach along with an ethnographic perspective, we will argue, is appropriate even when a complete ethnography is not the goal for several reasons: First, the questions that were asked required the exploration of the social, academic, and reading requirements for participation of a specific cultural activity (a lesson). Second, the lesson was a definable speech event (a review lesson) that was part of the ordinary life of a social group (the class); and third, the raw data that existed permitted the identification of a routine activity within the classroom across the schoolyear (a grammar test review lesson that occurred in November).

A brief description of the data set will provide further support for the selection of the data analyzed. The raw data were taken from a systematic observational study of classroom management (Evertson, Weade, Green, & Crawford, 1985). The data bank consisted of audiotapes and narrative records of classroom life across the schoolyear (August, September, October, November, and May). Therefore, it was possible to determine that the event selected for microanalysis was a routine or recurrent event. In addition, the data set included, over time, data on a number of other classrooms. These data made the comparison with other lessons for the same classroom and lessons in other classrooms possible (Green & Razinski, 1985). Finally, test data (a school-administered test) and student engagement ratings (Evertson, 1985) provided evidence on traditional measures of effectiveness (Shulman, 1986) that this classroom was a well-managed, learning-oriented classroom (Marshall & Weinstein, in press). This information, while not necessary to the analysis, suggested that the teacher selected could be defined as effective on a specific set of criteria and that there was a high probability that what would be observed during the lesson were learning-oriented teacher–student–text interactions. This latter interpretation was further supported by the selection of the teacher as runner-up for the teacher of the year in her state.

Thus the data selected for analysis were representative of a type of lesson that occurred in this classroom and in classrooms within the larger data set. The teacher selected was described by participants in the field (the district personnel and the state) as an effective teacher. Both of these factors suggested that in the present analysis, we would be able to focus on an analysis of reading in the instructional context with minimal interference of other factors (e.g., management problems).

LOCATING AND ANALYZING READING IN THE
INSTRUCTIONAL CONTEXT

As discussed in the previous section, both the way in which reading is defined and classroom life is viewed influence what will be identified, observed, recorded, analyzed, and interpreted. In this study, reading was defined as both an event and as a process that is part of everyday classroom life. Reading events were identified using the definition discussed previously by Heath (1983) and Anderson, Teale, and Estrada (1980). These instances were considered across lessons, within lessons, for groups of students, and for individuals. Consideration of instances across lessons permitted identificaiton of lessons that specifically involved reading events. Consideration of both the individual's and the group's reading tasks within lessons permitted analysis of the nature of the social and academic demands facing students and teacher as they engaged in reading as part of the everyday life of the classroom. These procedures provided the basis for determining the representativeness of the lesson that was selected for in-depth examination.

While this definition provided a basis for locating reading events and identifying general task demands for reading, it did not provide a way of analyzing what occurred within the lesson, the ways in which what was comprehended contributed to the developing lesson, or the ways in which the social and academic lesson demands influenced what was read and comprehended. To explore these questions, a definition of reading as an interpersonal process was selected. This definition was selected because it permitted analysis of the ways in which teacher's and students' actions and interactions with each other and with the text influenced what was read, how, when, where, in what ways, for what purpose, with what outcome. In addition, this definition was consistent with the view of classroom life as jointly constructed by participants that serves as the framework for this study.

In this study, then reading was viewed as both an intrapersonal process and an interpersonal process (Bloome & Green, 1984; Cazden, 1983). That is, while individuals were seen as interpreting text (graphic symbols), text was also viewed as a product of the interactions among participants (e.g., other students, teachers, the printed symbols). Text, in this sense, included both the graphic symbols on the test and the verbal and nonverbal interactions that comprised the unfolding lesson. The graphic symbols, therefore, were only one contributing factor to lesson construction and to the evolving text (Green, Weade, & Graham, in press). This definition of text as an object to be interpreted and as an unfolding composition led to an exploration of the demands for reading in the lesson, how these demands varied across the lesson, what was "read," and what was text. In other words, exploration of reading as it occurred in and contributed to everyday events of classroom life involved consideration of the social, academic, and reading processes and demands within lessons (e.g., Collins, 1983; Erickson, 1982, 1986; Green & Weade, 1987; Harker, 1988).

DEFINING LESSONS AND EXAMINING READING AS AN INTERPERSONAL PROCESS

To understand the analysis of the reading in the instructional context that is presented below, it is necessary to understand the ways in which instruction and lessons were viewed in this study. From an ethnographic/interactive sociolinguistic perspective, instruction was defined as a dynamic process of communication among participants that is goal-directed. Instructional events were seen as involving co-occurring academic and social demands transmitted through verbal and nonverbal messages and actions of participants (e.g., teacher, students, texts, materials) in a lesson. That is, as teachers and students worked together and interacted with texts or other instructional materials to meet the curricular goals, a variety of academic and social meanings were being jointly constructed. In an academic sense, participants were seen as constructing and interpreting meaning during the ongoing flow of talk and activity. From this flow of activity, students were assumed to be discovering what was to be learned and how learning was to be displayed (Bloome, 1987; Bloome & Theodorou, 1988; Morine–Dershimer, 1985; Puro & Bloome, 1987). This aspect of the lesson is often referred to as the academic task demand (Erickson, 1982; Green & Harker, 1982; Harker, 1988). This task is viewed as developing during the lesson and as including the structure of the content, the nature of the content presented, and the way in which the information is presented and displayed.

In addition, recent work has shown that as academic content is being delivered, the teacher also indicates how the content is to be considered, by whom, in what ways, for what purpose. In other words, as the academic content is being developed by participants, expectations are also signaled that indicate the socially appropriate ways of interacting or "doing" a lesson. This aspect of lesson is referred to as the social participation task structure (cf., Doyle, 1986; Erickson, 1982, 1986; Erickson & Shultz, 1981; Florio & Shultz, 1979; Green & Harker, 1982; Philips, 1972, 1982) and as studenting (Fenstermacher, 1986, 1987). Thus by adopting the view of lessons as including both social and academic task demands, factors that contributed to the construction of lessons can be examined. In addition, by considering the academic and social demands, the nature of the activity and tasks that made up everyday life in classrooms can be identified (e.g., what is meant by reading group, vocabulary drill, sustained silent reading, social studies test, science project discussion, among others). In addition, by considering the academic and social demands within and across lessons that were constructed by participants, a taxonomy of classroom lessons can be constructed and then used to compare lessons across time and across teachers.

Finally, recent work on the role of text in classroom lessons suggested that the ways in which text is used and acted on in a lesson can influence what is comprehended (Bernhardt, 1987; Golden, in press, 1986, 1987; Green, Harker, & Golden, 1986; Harker, 1988). This work suggested the need to consider the ways in which teacher and students interacted with the text and to examine how the talk about text influenced what was comprehended during the lesson. In this way, we were able to explore how the teacher and students mediated the text and thus influenced the development of the lesson. (See also Collins, 1983; 1986; Collins & Michaels, 1986; Green & Weade, 1987, for a discussion of how teacher and students' interactional patterns influence what is learned from text, and Graham, 1986, for a discussion of how these patterns influenced the academic content of and participation in physical education activities in the gym.)

During the present analysis, however, we became aware of an additional set of reading task demands occurring during the lesson. We found that teachers and students interacted not only with each other about the graded test, the text physically present in the lesson, but at times, referred to texts that were not evident in the physical setting (e.g., "I bet you were thinking about rise [not raise] when you were taking the test, and when I graded your papers. . . ."). Thus to examine reading in the instructional context, we needed to consider what was read during lessons, what other texts were reflected in the task in the lesson (the graded grammar test), and how those texts read prior to the lesson influenced what developed in the lesson under construction.

The discussion of the multiple task demands facing students and teachers presented above provides a picture of the complex and dynamic nature of classroom lessons and suggests how reading is both an intrapersonal and interpersonal process. The analysis of the grammar review lesson presented below will further illustrate the complexity of the construction process and will highlight various aspects of the interpersonal processes of reading. In addition, the discussion will demonstrate ways in which such complexity can be systematically examined.

READING IN THE GRAMMAR REVIEW LESSON

Transcription and Mapping

Exploration of lesson construction and the social, academic, and reading demands of the review lesson was undertaken using a sociolinguistic approach to discourse analysis developed by Green and her colleagues (Green, 1977; Green & Harker, 1982; Green & Wallat, 1981; Green, Weade, & Graham, 1988). This approach involved the transcription of the audiotape of the lesson and the development of an expanded transcript using narrative notes made by observers in the classroom to provide contextual information and verify the structure of the tasks. (See Cochran–Smith, 1984; Corsaro, 1982; Mishler, 1984; and Ochs, 1979, for a discussion of transcription procedures and the ways in which transcripts reflect theoretical assumptions about the nature of process.)

Once the transcription was completed, a map of the structure of the developing lesson was constructed. This map represents the thematic development of the lesson and instances of divergence of talk from the themes under construction. The structural maps provide the basis for the exploration of patterns of organization, demands for participation and learning (academic, social, and reading demands), and instances of miscommunication or breaks in expected actions. The former patterns provided an understanding of what was ordinary action and expected performance. The latter patterns were points in the lesson where the expected actions did not occur and a "clash" in expectations occurred (Mehan, 1979). These clash points were places where the smooth or forward progress of the lesson broke down. At such points, what was expected or problems in interpretation became visible (Cook–Gumperz, Gumperz, & Simons, 1981; Green & Weade, 1987; Green, Weade, & Graham, 1988; Mehan, 1979; Michaels & Cook–Gumperz, 1979; Michaels, 1986; Weade & Green, 1986).

Identifying the Organizational Structure

The analysis began by considering what aspect of the day recorded could be defined as "the lesson." Examination of what occurred with whom, when, where, for what purpose, under what conditions, with what outcome indicated that there was a single lesson, a whole event, on the day selected for analysis. That is, the lesson (the whole) occurred during a single class period on a single day. That the lesson was considered to be a whole by participants was reflected in the teacher's talk. For example, when she got to the fourth phase of the lesson, the teacher indicated that she wanted students to speed up their answers so that they could finish on the same day. She also switched approaches in the last phase and read the correct answers to students rather than involving students in the correction process. This switch was done so that the class could get through the review of the text lesson (See Bloome, Theodorou, & Puro in press, for a discussion of procedural display as a means of getting through the lesson.)

From an analytic perspective, then, the lesson was a whole. As indicated in Table 1, the lesson phases followed the structure of the test, which had a five-part structure. That is, the lesson evolved as a series of interrelated phases in which the social, academic, and reading demands placed on students varied by phase. This variation occurred even though the physical structure of the classroom did not vary (i.e., students sat in rows and the teacher remained in front of the class throughout the lesson). The phases, however, were more than literal reproductions of the test. Each phase had its own set of academic, social, and reading demands, and thus was also a whole within the whole.

As described in Table 1, in each part of the lesson students were required to demonstrate their knowledge of verbs in different ways. Across the phases of the lesson, students were required to state the past and past participle for a given verb (Phase 1), name the tense when given a principal part (Phase 2), place the correct tense of the verb in the space provided in the sentence (Phase 3), correct the verb in the sentence, rewriting the sentence if necessary (Phase 4), and identify verbs in a given sentence as either active or passive (Phase 5).

On the surface, this lesson appears simple. The teacher and students were reviewing answers on a test taken on a preceding day that had been subsequently graded and returned. When approached in terms of what the participants were required to know and do in order to respond and participate in the ongoing interactions, however, the complexity of the multiple task demands within and across lesson phases became apparent.

To examine the complexity of lesson construction, the actions and interactions of participants were considered. That is, by considering

Table 1.   Academic, Social, and Reading Demands, by Phase, in a Grammar Review Lesson

Phase	Academic Demand	Social Demand	Reading Demand
1	Name past and past participle of given verb.	Respond when called on (at random).	Read each verb; recognize each as present tense form.
2	Name tense for given verb.	Volunteer by raising hand; respond when called on.	Identify each verb or verb phrase; recognize "helping" verbs as part of verb phrase.
3	Given present tense verb and a sentence without a verb, place verb form in correct tense in the sentence.	Respond when called on (at random).	Read given sentence, placing verb form in *context* of sentence.
4	Given sentence with incorrect verb usage, read the sentence, corrrecting the usage.	Respond when called on (at random); then volunteer another response (more than one correct answer) by raising hand; then respond when called on.	Read sentence to identify incorrect usage, repair usage, then read in correct form.
5	Check paper as T. gives answers, identifying given verbs as active or passive.	Listen as T. gives answers; ask questions at end, if any.	Match word (active/passive) with teacher's dictation.

what occurred, with whom, for what purpose, under what conditions, with what outcome on a moment-by-moment basis, factors that supported and/or constrained lesson construction, individual student participation, and group participation in the social, academic, and reading tasks were identified. In this way, the nature of the inter-personal context of reading was explored. Each set of factors (the social, academic, and text demands) will be considered below. While these factors overlap or are interrelated in the real time of classroom lessons, they will be discussed separately for heuristic purposes. The three analyses are presented in the order in which they were un-dertaken: the social, the academic, and the text.

The Social Participation Requirements of the Review Lesson

The exploration of social requirements of lesson participation laid the foundation for the exploration of the academic task demands and the nature of text that were undertaken during subsequent phases of the analysis. Underlying this approach to analysis is the assumption that while these three aspects of lessons are interrelated, the academic task (the content of what was said and what was read) and the text demands (what to read and how) are embedded in the social/instructional doings of the teacher and students (Bloome & Theodorou, 1988; Erickson, 1982; Green & Harker, 1982; Phillips, 1982). In addition, the social participation demands and actions of participants mediate the academic content of lessons (Golden, 1986, 1987; 1988; Graham, 1986; Green, 1977; Green, Harker, & Golden, 1986; Harker, 1988; Morine–Dershimer, 1985).

The analysis of the social demands of lesson began with an examination of the rules or expectations for participating that were developed within and across the phases of this lesson. Social task demands for the lesson were identified by exploring the maps of the lesson for indicators of who was permitted to talk, about what, in what ways, when, with what outcome. A message-by-message analysis was undertaken of the ways the participants worked with the message and contributions of others, of what was accepted by the teacher and students, of which messages were related to each other, of which involved new information or actions (e.g., tied or related sequences of action), and of the major shifts in activity within and across phases of the lesson.

In the first phase of the lesson, students were to respond orally when called on by name. In giving a response, students were to name the past and past participle of the given verb. They were to say "rose and risen," "lay and lain," or "had and had," and so on, until each verb contained in the items on their test paper had been reviewed. Students and teacher proceeded in an ordered, item-by-item fashion. Thus participants were able to predict the next topic of discussion and to keep their place in the lesson by using the structure of the test.

While the review in this phase proceeded in an ordered sequence from item to item and student to student, it was not an automatic process or a simple script. The teacher asked questions of students about the review items. Some of the questions were directed to other students. At times, students were asked to agree or disagree with the response that had been given by another student. Thus to participate fully, students needed to attend not only to the items being reviewed but also to what others students were saying about these items (Morine–Dershimer, 1985). In addition, the teacher sometimes requested information about how students had arrived at a given response or what a particular word meant, e.g., "lay" in the present tense means "to put or place," not to recline.

In the second phase of the lesson, the social demands shifted as students and teacher began the review of the second section of the test. The expectations for how turns would be distributed changed from calling on students at random to soliciting voluntary answers. Students were to bid for a turn by raising a hand. At the outset of this phase the teacher noted that:

T: This was hard, wasn't it.
I could tell.
Let's just uh get some voluntary answers on this one.
Who got number 1?
Alice? (excerpt from transcript)

Again, as in the earlier phase, students were to give an initial word or single phrase response. Similarly, students were asked to elaborate on each response by responding to a second and sometimes third question about how they had known or figured out the answer. One difference in this phase was that the second question for an item was consistently directed to the student who had volunteered the first response; that is, the teacher did not call on students who had not initially volunteered. The contrast between the pattern set in the first phase of the lesson and the one that became established in the second phase revealed the teacher's sensitivity to the difficulty of the content and level of expectations communicated to students.

In the third phase of the lesson, the teacher signaled yet a third form of response:

T: Write the correct form of the verb
What I'd like to do is
So we'll have one more time to hear these in sentences correctly
Read the sentence with the correct form in it
OK?
We'll start with um
Karen (Excerpt from transcript)

In this phase, the teacher shifted back to calling on students at random as in Phase 1, but the form of response changed to giving the complete sentence rather than individual forms of the verb. Soon after this phase had begun, the teacher added that if she called on someone who happened to have missed the item, the student was to "just say pass and we'll go on to the next person." Once again the teacher demonstrated a sensitivity to students.

As students and teacher proceeded on to the fourth section of the test, the social task demands shifted again. As before, the social demands shifted in accord with the nature of the academic task. In this case, students were to have corrected the verb usage in an incorrectly written sentence. In contrast to previous sections of the test, more than one alternative response was possible. The teacher's announcement of the shift in social demands is evident in Example 1.

While the teacher's statement of general intent was overt, "let's see how you corrected these sentences" (line 908), the way in which turns would be allocated and how students were to proceed was not stated explicitly. Rather, students had to observe what the teacher did and how she interacted with others in order to extract the expected pattern of participation. For example, as the teacher calls on Donna to respond to "number 1" (lines 917–919), she was also signaling that students would be called on by name, to speak one at a time. In addition, they were to read their whole sentence, as opposed to reading just the verb phase. Once a student finished responding, other students were invited to volunteer an alternative sentence (920). To get a turn, however, students were, once again, required to raise a hand for permission to contribute to the lesson. The demands for social participation and performance in this phase of the lesson, then, were more complex than in other phases.

Consideration of the interactions that followed the responses to the first item indicated that at least one student, Keith, had read only part of the expectations. As indicated in line 927, he did volunteer an alternative and his response was given in a "whole sentence" as directed. The teacher's subsequent response, however, indicates that Keith had failed to follow the direction to raise his hand (line 921). By not raising his hand, Keith committed a social error. The teacher responded to this error by not acknowledging Keith's turn and calling on Carolyn to respond.

The teacher's response to Keith whose answer was correct but presented in an inappropriate manner contrasts to her response to Brian's answer that was incorrect yet presented in an appropriate manner (lines 933–950). The teacher accepted Brian's turn but not his use of "got." The difference in teacher responses to these two errors, one social and one academic, provided information to students and observer about the expectations for participation: A response must be given in a socially appropriate way to be accepted; errors

Example 1

907 ALL RIGHT
908 LET'S SEE HOW YOU CORRECTED THESE SENTENCES
909 MOST OF YOU DID A GOOD JOB OF THESE

910 THERE'S A COUPLE OF THINGS WE STILL NEED TO WORK ON A LITTLE BIT THOUGH

911 NOW I THINK WE'VE ALL DECIDED
912 THAT "AIN'T" IS NOT ACCEPTABLE

913 BUT SOME OF US ARE SO USED TO USING "AIN'T"
914 THAT WE REALLY HAVE TO THINK ABOUT AN ALTERNATIVE DON'T WE?

915 WE HAVE TO THINK ABOUT WHAT ELSE IS GOING TO GO IN ITS PLACE
916 AND WRITE IT DOWN ON PAPER

917 WHAT DID YOU PUT FOR NUMBER 1 IN PLACE OF IT?
918 READ YOUR WHOLE SENTENCE
919 DONNA

920 AND IF ANYBODY HAS ANOTHER SENTENCE YOU WANT TO READ US
921 RAISE YOUR HAND

922   Donna: We don't have any money

923 THAT'S A GOOD CHOICE
924 YOU DON'T HAVE ANY MONEY
925 I LIKE THE WAY THAT SOUNDS
926 THAT (Keith says 927 simultaneously with 926)
927   Keith: We have no money
928 SOUNDS GOOD ON YOU

929 RAISE YOUR HAND KEITH (ties to line 927)

930 CAROLYN

931   Carolyn: We haven't got any money.
932 "WE HAVEN'T GOT ANY MONEY" WOULD BE GOOD.

933 ALL RIGHT.
934 BRIAN.

935   Brian: We do not uh got any money.

936 WE DO NOT GOT ANY MONEY.
937   Several: laughter

938   Brian: I mean
939   we do not
940   got any money

(continued)

Example 1 (Continued)

941   ALL RIGHT
942   YOU KNOW WHAT WOULD SOUND GOOD BRIAN?
943   IF YOU CHANGE IT TO "WE DO NOT HAVE ANY MONEY."
944   SEE WE GOT TO BE CAREFUL
945   WE
946   WE HAVE TO BE CAREFUL
947   HOW WE USE GOT
948   DON'T WE?

949   I INCLUDE MYSELF IN THAT TOO
950   Several: laughter

951   OKAY.
952   DOES ANYBODY HAVE ANOTHER ONE?
953   Students: silence (pause)

954   ALL RIGHT
955   WHAT DID YOU DO WITH NUMBER 2?
         FIRST TEACHER PARALLELS WHAT BRIAN SAID
         CHANGES IT
         THEN MAKES MISTAKE
         PARALLELS BRIAN
         THEN MIMICS SELF AND GETS LAUGH

are permitted and corrected but a *faux pas* is not accepted. This example further illustrates the interrelated nature of the social and academic tasks demands and the primacy of the social demands.

The teacher's sensitivity to students is once again displayed in this segment of the lesson. When what occurs in the talk that follows Brian's error is considered, what is visible is the teacher's effort to indicate that the problem is not Brian's alone, but one that all participants must consider and avoid. Analysis of lines 944–951 showed that she made a deliberate error to mimic Brian's, thus turning the problem away from Brian alone and showing her awareness of student feelings.

In the final phase of the lesson, the social demand shifted more dramatically than at any other transition point in the review lesson. Students' opportunities to talk and to participate became highly constrained. The teacher signaled at the outset that they would:

T: Go through these quickly.
     I'll tell you what I think I'll do
     I'm just going,
     We're going to run out of time if I don't.
     Let me tell you the right answer for these
     And then we'll talk about anyone you want to after that.

The teacher then proceeded in a "gunshot" fashion through the remaining items on the test. The social task for students was more constrained than in any other part of the lesson. Her statements indicated that she was concerned with completing the review and not with discussing the items. This procedure suggests that while she was concerned with student knowledge about grammar and with helping them learn about appropriate usage, she was also concerned with time and did not want the lesson to carry over to another day. Thus this phase was constrained by what occurred earlier, in terms of time spent and the teacher's curricular needs to complete the lesson on a single day.

The analysis of the social demands for participation supported the analysis of the general structure of the lesson presented in Table 1 and provided further information about how the lesson was constructed through the talk and actions of the participants. Analysis of the talk and actions of participants showed that the social task demands varied in the grammar review lesson by phase of the lesson. That is, how students were to participate in the lesson (e.g., get a turn to respond; respond to the teacher), engage text, and present information were specific to each phase of the lesson. The requirements were made visible in the talk and actions of teacher and students. A taxonomy of the social task demands is presented in Figure 1.

As illustrated in this figure and described above, requirements for participation were not static across different phases (Ph) of the lesson, but rather varied as the academic task shifted. Lessons were not simple linear events that were rote scripts to be acted out. Rather, expectations for participation were established, modified, suspended, and re-established across the phases of the lesson. To understand the social task demands and to participate appropriately, therefore, it was necessary for students to "read" and interpret the social requirements as they developed for each phase of the lesson. Knowing the correct answer was not sufficient. In fact, students could give an incorrect answer in an appropriate way and still participate and receive feedback, but they could not do the reverse, give a correct answer in a socially inappropriate fashion.

The Academic Tasks and Content of the Review Lesson

The picture of the lesson that has been presented so far is one of a dynamic evolving entity in which lesson is a product of the interactions and conversations of teacher and students. Lesson content,

36

Figure 1: Taxonomy of social demands.

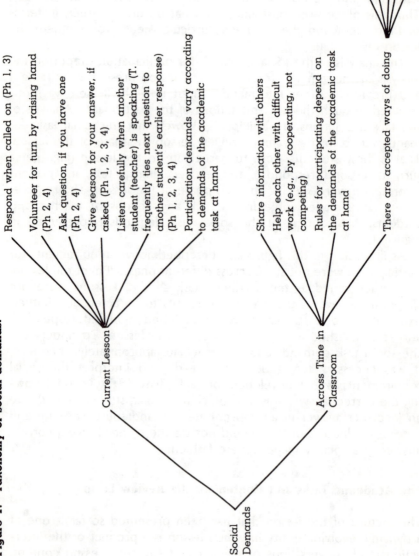

Social Demands

Current Lesson
- Respond when called on (Ph 1, 3)
- Volunteer for turn by raising hand (Ph 2, 4)
- Ask question, if you have one (Ph 2, 4)
- Give reason for your answer, if asked (Ph 1, 2, 3, 4)
- Listen carefully when another student (teacher) is speaking (T. frequently ties next question to another student's earlier response) (Ph 1, 2, 3, 4)
- Participation demands vary according to demands of the academic task at hand
-] Turn-taking is rule-governed (Ph 1, 2, 3, 4, 5)

Across Time in Classroom
- Share information with others
- Help each other with difficult work (e.g., by cooperating, not competing)
- Rules for participating depend on the demands of the academic task at hand
- There are accepted ways of doing

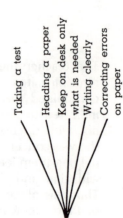
- Taking a test
- Heading a paper
- Keep on desk only what is needed
- Writing clearly
- Correcting errors on paper

therefore, is not a given but rather is signaled in the talk and actions of participants. Academic content evolves on a moment-by-moment, item-by-item basis. Viewed in this way, content is constructed not extracted, is evolving, and is made visible in the actions and interactions of participants. In addition, participants seeking to gain access to the academic content of lesson must continually monitor the topic under construction, what is said or written about the topic, what gets accepted or rejected, and how the teacher and other students work with the information provided. In other words, the students and teacher receive information about what is meant, what is important to know, and how to understand the academic requirements of lessons from the interactions of participants (teachers, students, text, materials).

The constructed and dynamic nature of content can be illustrated if we examine what occurred among the participants in Phase 1 of the lesson. Given both the variable nature of demands across phases of the lesson and the item-by-item structure of the lesson review, the analysis focused on an examination of the talk (themes) that accompanied the review of each item, and the recurrence and development of themes across items. Table 2 provides a summary of the items and the developing themes.

As indicated in this table, the content of the teacher and student talk for the first item that was audible (rise) showed that the teacher told students to use spelling as a strategy to remember when working with this verb. The content of the talk surrounding the next verb (lie) showed a second strategy, focus on meaning. The content of the next verb (be) provided a third strategy, focus on principal parts. This macrolevel analysis of the talk led to the identification of three strategies that students could use to ensure correct responses on a grammar test. These themes were repeated again for item 8, choose (spelling), item 10, swim (principal parts), and item 12, lay (meanings). The talk about the items, then, is part of the evolving lesson text and signals to students what they must know or remember in order to use the verb in question correctly and to complete the test accurately.

The dynamic and responsive nature of the lesson can be further demonstrated if we consider what occurred in Phase 4 of the lesson. In this phase, students were expected to read the sentence and identify the incorrect form of the verb, correct the verb, and rewrite the sentence if needed. In this task, then, a variety of different final sentences were possible. A summary of this phase is presented in Table 3.

Table 2. Content and Theme Distribution by Time
Phase 1

Instructional Sequence Unit (ISU)	Topic	Content Themes Signaled	Length of ISU Interaction Units (IU)	Length of ISU Time (Seconds)
1	(a verb)[a]		2	8.2
2	rise	irregular spelling / verb	2	8.0
3	lie	irregular verb — meanings	9	70.2
4	be	irregular verb — principal parts	7	59.2
5	(procedural	statement: Skip C, she wasn't here)	1	4.8
6	have, has	irregular verb	3	13.2
7	Using have, has in sentences	irregular verb	13	98.6
8	choose	irregular spelling / verb	3	13.1
9	see	irregular verb	1	5.0
10	swim	irregular verb — principal parts	4	24.0
11	drew	irregular verb	1	6.3
12	lay	irregular verb — meanings	7	25.0
13	give	irregular verb	1	4.5
14	bring	irregular verb	8	37.5
15	ring	irregular verb	1	7.1
16	inaudible interaction		1	3.3
17	take	irregular verb	5	30.6
18	drown	regular verb	9	51.9
19	raise	regular verb	9	52.5
20	Questions on part 1	Conclude part 1	1	4.9

[a] Student's response was inaudible. The teacher signaled that the response was correct.

Table 3. Content and Theme Distribution by Time (Phase 4)

Instructional Sequence Unit (ISU)	Topic	Content	Themes Signaled	Length of ISU Interaction Units (IU)	Time (Seconds)
75	ain't	correct the incorrect verb form	"sound" is a clue — think of an alternative — meaning — "sound" is a clue	9	119.2
76	lay	correct the incorrect verb	"sound" is a clue	4	22.8
77	busted	correct the incorrect verb	"feel" is a clue	4	17.0
78	lay	correct the incorrect verb		4	30.2
79	lying	correct the incorrect verb	spelling — meaning	7	43.6
80	drown	correct the incorrect verb	spelling	7	40.7
81	have	correct the incorrect verb		3	13.5
82	lay	correct the incorrect verb	meaning — don't change tense mid-sentence	10	74.2
83	ain't	correct the incorrect verb		3	18.2
84	froze	correct the incorrect verb		3	24.6
85	rose	correct the incorrect verb	don't just add "ed" to irregular verbs	2	13.4
86	ain't	correct the incorrect verb		3	17.5
87	may/can	correct the incorrect verb	meaning	2	10.4
88	rose	correct the incorrect verb	"sound" is not always a good clue	6	53.6
89	saw	correct the incorrect verb		1	6.5

(continued)

Table 3.   Content and Theme Distribution by Time (Continued)
(Phase 4)

Instructional Sequence Unit (ISU)	Topic	Content	Themes Signaled	Length of ISU	
				Interaction Units (IU)	Time (Seconds)
90	may/can	correct the meaning incorrect verb		9	41.9
91	has risen	correct the incorrect verb you	use "up" with "rose" when need to show direction	5	22.5
92	questions?			4	14.8

Examination of the teacher talk (the themes) indicated that she was signaling information to student about their performance on the test and providing them with strategies to avoid errors in the future. For example, for the verb lay (Instructional Sequence Unit 82), the teacher signals that meaning is important and that "you don't change tense mid-sentence." The teacher's talk not only signals what is important for students to know in order to get the correct form of the verb but also shows that she is attempting to fine-tune the information she presents in response to student performance.

This analysis suggested that two different levels of information were provided. First, the items on the test provided a sequential set of themes (test items—verbs) to be read, acted upon, and discussed. Second, the talk about the test items contributed another set of content themes. These themes were also part of the evolving lesson text that was being composed by teacher and students as they reviewed the test itself. While the themes related to the test items could be predicted, those developed in the talk and actions of teacher and students could not be predicted in advance. In addition, when the themes that were developed across phases of the lesson were considered what became evident was the recurrence of themes across phases.

An analysis of the themes signaled in the talk related to these items led to the identification of a series of themes: meaning, sound clues, spelling, don't change tenses mid-sentence, among others. These themes were clues provided for the students to help them complete the local task, for example, the test, and to guide them in future tasks requiring grammatical usage, both spoken and written. Examination of these themes across phases of the lesson and across lessons showed that these themes occurred across phases of the lesson and across lessons (Evertson, Weade, Green, & Crawford, 1985).

Table 4 shows the recurrence of theme within and across phases of the grammar review lesson. These summary data show that spelling was a theme in four of the phases (1, 2, 3, and 4); meaning a theme in three of the phases (1, 3, 4); sound a clue in two phases (3, 4); and principal parts in two phases (2, 3). In addition, the teacher presented algorithm-like grammar rules in various phases. When the themes were explored for unifying or common factors, what became evident was that the themes focused on strategies that students could use to obtain the correct form of the verb and ensure correct usage orally and in writing.

The exploration of themes across phases of the lesson demonstrates further the differentiated nature of the lesson and the complexity of the task facing students. The contrast of academic content across all phases of the lesson led to the development of a taxonomy of academic demands similar to the one on social demands presented above.

The recurrence of themes across phases indicates that the lesson is not merely a literal review of the test in which the correct answers were presented. The lesson was also about the strategies that can be used to ensure correct grammar. In this way, the teacher made the review lesson a dynamic process that moved beyond the oral reproduction of the graded test. To participate in the construction of the lesson, students had to adapt to the differentiated demands that occurred within and across the phases of the lesson, identify the requirements of each phase, and understand the intended outcomes. In addition, the discussion above suggests that the talk about the test is more than a literal reproduction or simple reading of the test. Talk and text are inextricably intertwined in the meaning construction process of this lesson. That is, at times the text is the basis for the production of talk; at other times, it is the outcome of that talk. In addition, the analysis of the talk provided information about how the teacher talk functioned and what purposes it served, for example, to signal what was important to know, to present information to students to help them in future assignments, and to respond to student performance in a helpful way.

The existence of the taxonomy made exploration across lessons possible. When the lessons from the beginning of class were explored, one theme, the spelling theme, was found on the first day of class. Examination of subsequent days showed that this theme and others (e.g., grammar) became recurring themes across lessons observed in August, September, and November.

Table 4. Frequence of Themes by Lesson Phase

Themes	Phases I	II	III	IV	V
Memorize principle parts	4				
Think of the verb in a little sentence	1				
Spelling	4	1	1	2	
Meaning	2		5	5	
Sound is a clue				1	5
Think about principal parts			1	1	
Algorithm-like grammar rules, e.g.:					
present tense + will = future tense		1			
"ing" form = progressive		1			
present participle + "be" verb helper = progressive					1
past participle + "have" = present perfect		1			
"shall have", "will have" = future perfect helpers		1			
past participle + "be" verb helper = passive		7			3
"had" means past perfect		1			
"does," "did" = emphatic		1			
singular verbs end in "s"		1			
Don't change tense mid-sentence				1	
Don't just add "ed" to irregular verbs				1	
Use "up" with "rose" when you need to show direction				1	
Think of an alternative (verb)				1	
When the subject is acted on, the tense is *passive*					2
When the subject acts, the tense is *active*					4
Totals by Lesson Phase	11	18	8	16	10

The existence of the structural maps and summary information also made additional analyses possible. The analysis of theme developed described above suggested the need to consider the different ways in which talk functioned in the lesson. For example, exploration of teacher talk that extended an item indicated that the teacher attempted to fine-tune her talk to student performance and to provide students with strategies for the future. Examination of the teacher's attempts to fine-tune her responses to student performance raised questions about where the information she used as the basis for feedback had originated. Exploration of what was present in the

Figure 2: Taxonomy of academic demands.

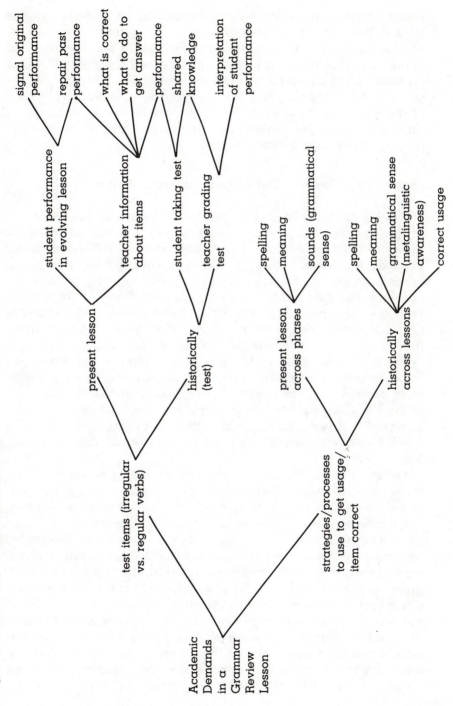

43

lesson under construction led to the conclusion that the teacher used information that was not present in the current lesson. That is, she used information about student performance that was obtained during the grading of the test. This discovery suggested a new question: What was the text used in this lesson? The identification of this question led to further analysis of the lesson and an exploration of the references to texts in the developing lesson. This analysis, in turn, raised new questions about what was involved in the study of reading in the instructional context.

Exploring the Reading Task: Questions about Text

The need to locate reading events was discussed at the beginning of this chapter. In that discussion, a definition based on the work of Heath (1983) and Anderson, Teale, and Estrada (1980) was proposed to guide the identification of reading events. In this definition a general category of literacy events was proposed: "Those occasions in which the talk revolves around a piece of writing have been termed literacy events" (Heath, 1983). These events were defined as "any action sequence, involving one or more persons, in which the production and/or comprehension of print plays a role" (Anderson, Teale, & Estrada, 1980, p. 59). In this definition, a distinction was made between reading events and writing events. Reading events were defined as those events "in which an individual either comprehends or attempts to comprehend a message which is encoded graphically" (Heath, 1983, p. 386). Writing events were those "in which an individual attempts to produce . . . graphic symbols" (Heath, 1983, p. 386).

On the surface, the task of identifying reading events appeared to be straightforward—just look at an instance in which comprehension or decoding of graphic symbols occurred or locate the text. For the present lesson, this meant examining the event(s) in which students were reviewing (comprehending and decoding) the graded test. However, as we analyzed the academic content (the themes), we became aware of statements that referred to a variety of different phases in the life of the test. That is, a different text existed for each phase in the life of the test. The teacher constructed, untaken text; the text being completed by the students; the text constructed as the teacher graded the students' tests; the graded test that was returned to the students during the review lesson; and the text that was being constructed by teacher and students during the review lesson (Golden, 1984, 1987, 1988; Iser, 1980).

Each of these texts involved a different type of literacy event. In addition, some were complex events in which reading and writing co-occurred in interrelated ways. For example, the first phase in the life of the test involved the teacher writing the test. This phase was a writing event as defined above. The second phase was a complex reading-writing event. To participate in the test lesson, students had to read the test and write their answers in academically appropriate ways. The third phase involved the teacher in reading and grading the completed student test. This phase then also involved a complex reading-writing event.

The fourth phase, the first of the two phases in the current lesson, was a reading event, one in which students individually read the graded test as the test was returned. This phase involved a reading event that was accomplished in the intrapersonal context of reading; that is, the individual students read the graded test to themselves. The fifth phase, the phase in which the teacher and students reviewed the corrected student completed test, involved both the intrapersonal context of reading and the interpersonal context. That is, as teacher and students reviewed the test, information was provided in the interpersonal context about how to interpret the test items, what the correct answers to the test were, and how to get correct answers in the future (i.e., spelling, meaning, etc.). Thus in the fifth phase in the life of the test, a new text was constructed, one that included the oral reproduction of test items and the talk about the test. This latter text required students to comprehend the items on the test, the requirements for presenting the information, and the information presented in the talk. This event, then, was not only a reading event, it also involved oral communication and listening comprehension.

Thus what appeared on the surface to be a simple reading event (a review lesson), was a complex reading event, one that included not only the physically present test but also the talk about the test in which the test review was embedded. When the talk about the test was examined in detail, the event was found to be even more complex. Examination of the talk showed that other texts were invoked in the talk. That is, as the teacher and students interacted and worked together to review the test, each referred to earlier phases in the life of the test. The acceptance of the existence and use of these different texts by participants was reflected in their talk and actions. That is, when the actions and talk of the participants were examined, the existence of multiple texts in the lesson could be seen.

The existence of these different texts can be seen in the following examples of teacher talk. At one point in the lesson the teacher made comments about what students were thinking as they completed the test: "I bet you were thinking about rise—rise, rose, risen." In this example she was referring to students' actions as they worked to complete the test. In another example, she indicated that she had observed the fact that "many of you missed that one" while grading the test. These examples indicate the existence and use of different phases in the life of the graded test. These statements indicate prior knowledge of actions based on observation and interpretation (reading) of previous texts. The last example illustrates the dynamic and shifting nature of text used in this lesson. In this example, the teacher indicated that "he tried it when he did it" (referring to the earlier actions of the student who was trying to provide the correct answer to the item during the test); "He tried something else when he told us and that didn't work either" (referring to his present actions in the review lesson that involved reading the original item he had gotten wrong and then trying another answer). The teacher continued, "We'll have to help Mark with this one. Betty, what did you get for this one?" Thus the teacher and the student refer to and use a variety of texts in this single turn or set of exchanges with the individual student and the group.

A Taxonomy of Phases in the Life of the Text in the Review Lesson

By examining the talk and actions of participants during the lesson for indications of reference to the text that was physically present, to previous texts connected with the review lesson, and to possible factors that contributed to the errors that students made, the stages in the life of the text were identified. A taxonomy of these phases is presented in Figure 3.

As indicated, each phase is related to a different reading of the text. Each text was read by a specific person(s) (teacher, individual student, teacher–student group), for a particular purpose (make a test, take a test, review the graded test, reconstruct the taken/graded test during the review lesson), and in a particular time and place (before the lesson in which the test was taken, in the test lesson on a previous day, and during the lesson under construction).

Underlying this taxonomy and the preceding discussion is the view that reading is a process of constructing meaning, not extracting meaning. In addition, reading is seen as a process of text construction both in the intrapersonal and interpersonal contexts. Thus each time a person reads a text or a text is read, it is a new text. Viewed in

Figure 3: Taxonomy of text and text interpretation.

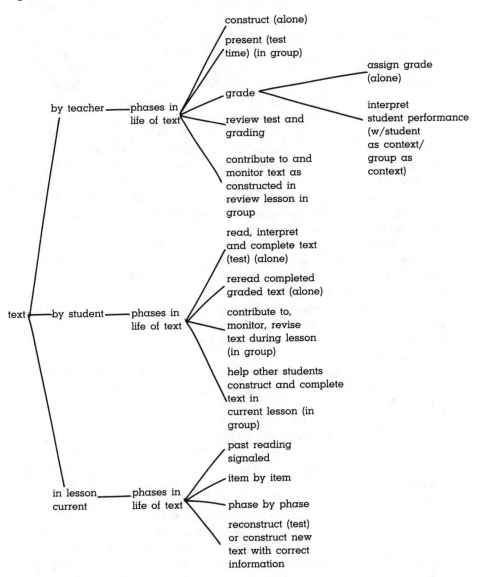

this way, the text that was used in the review lesson was not the original text constructed by the teacher (text 1), or the text read by the students during the test (text 2), or the text graded by the teacher (text 3). While the text used in the lesson was the graded text, this text was not the final text; for as students and teacher reviewed the test, they constructed a new text. This new text contained the printed items on the original test, the students' written responses, the teacher's grading marks and comments, and the teacher and student talk and comments about the items that arose during the review lesson that was being constructed. As indicated in Figure 1, the texts that were visible in the review lesson varied in terms of who read them, for what purposes, under what conditions; with what outcomes.

In addition, the existence of multiple texts and the interrelated nature of the oral–writing–reading dimensions of an event suggests the need to reconsider the definition of literacy in instructional contexts. While it may be possible to identify the primary focus of an event as writing (production or encoding of graphic symbols), as reading (comprehension or decoding of graphic symbols), or as an oral event (production of speech), in the ordinary events of the classroom life, these three types of events are often intertwined and co-occurring. Thus in classrooms, the relationship of literacy and oracy (Tannen, 1982, 1984) needs to be considered. In addition, the ways in which the talk about text and the talk to construct text influences what occurs, what participants experience, what meanings are constructed, and the actions that will be taken among others must be considered when we examine reading in the classroom. The existence of the multiple texts in the talk of the lesson suggests that it is naïve to observe only the visible print as a means of identifying reading events.

The argument that multiple texts existed and were reflected in a lesson also suggests the need to re-examine the notion of analytic whole discussed in an earlier part of this chapter. While the lesson was an analytic whole on one level (it occurred on a single day and was bounded by naturally occurring unit of time), the discussion above indicates the need to consider the historical ties to previous lessons. That is, there is a link between the current lesson and previous lessons (Barr, 1987; Green & Harker, 1982). Therefore, while a lesson may be analytic whole that is bounded in time and can stand alone, the related nature of information across lessons suggests that past lessons need to be considered. When data from previous lessons are not available for independent analysis, the issue of how the past history of the class influences or is visible in the present lesson must be considered. As indicated above, information related to earlier lesson(s) can be extracted from the current lesson by exploring what is being asserted and referred to in the task that is being constructed by teacher and students. (See Frederiksen, 1975, 1981; Green & Harker, 1982; Harker, 1988, for systematic ways of examining the propositional content of lessons.)

CONCLUSION

The analysis presented in this chapter focused on an exploration of reading as it occurred in an everyday lesson in a ninth-grade English class. The purpose of this analysis was to explore what could be learned about the factors involved in the study of reading in classroom contexts using a sociolinguistic and ethnography of communication perspective. From this perspective, reading was defined as an interpersonal as well as an intrapersonal process. Reading events were examined by exploring what happened, with whom, for what purpose, when, under what conditions, with what outcome on a moment-by-moment basis.

The analysis of reading in the everyday context of the English class provided a picture of lesson construction as a complex process, one in which social, academic, and text demands contributed to what occurred and what students learned. What appeared to be a simple review lesson on the surface, a lesson guided by the structure of the test being reviewed, was found to be a complex, dynamic event. For example, in the lesson selected, reading was a means of generating and obtaining information about the items being discussed and about the individual's performance on the test (correct and incorrect answers). As such, the reading event contributed to what occurred and helped structure the interactions between teacher and students.

While the test helped to contribute to the structure of what occurred on a general level, analysis of the moment-by-moment interactions of teacher and students with each other and with the text (test) provided a picture of a complex set of factors that influenced what occurred, with whom, for what purpose, with what outcome. Three sets of demands were identified: social task demands, academic task demands, and text demands. Analysis of the social task demands showed that the lesson was a differentiated event composed of five phases. Each phase required that students participate and present information in specific ways. The teacher distributed turns to students based on a variety of factors. Some phases of the lesson followed the structure of the test on an item-by-item basis with students being called on randomly. Other phases of the lesson involved student volunteers based on the teacher's perception of the difficulty of the items and the students' accuracy on the items. Still others involved the students' listening as the teacher read the answers since time was running out and the lesson was not yet completed. In addition, when a student made an error, the teacher responded in ways that indicated that she was trying to build a cooperative environment among students and that she was sensitive to student feelings.

The social task structure was also closely related to the academic task structure. Students and teacher reviewed the test on an item-by-item basis. Thus the academic task was embedded in the social task structure. However, even though the test structure influenced what occurred, the academic task involved more than a simple re-production of the test items. Analysis of the talk and actions of participants led to the identification of a series of recurrent strategies that students were to use to obtain the correct response in future lessons. These themes were found across phases of the lesson and across lessons in August, September, November, and May. The re-current nature of these strategies (meaning, use sound, and spelling) indicate that they were critical elements of the curriculum. That is, the teacher's actions over time suggest that the curriculum involved both the items being tested and presented in class and the strategies that could be used to obtain correct usage.

The recurrent nature of certain aspects of lessons overtime indi-cates that curriculum is more than what is planned and the items on the formal written tasks. Curriculum also involves the recurrent themes developed in the talk between teacher and students about text. Curriculum viewed in this way is jointly constructed by teacher and students as they work together to accomplish the everyday tasks that make up life in classrooms. Curriculum, then, is directly related to the meanings constructed during lessons (Weade, 1987).

Examination of the meanings constructed and the factors that contributed to the construction of meanings lead to questions about the text. Specifically, exploration of the talk in the lesson and text references indicated that multiple texts were used to obtain infor-mation presented in the lesson. Some texts were read in previous lessons when the test was being taken or graded; others were present in the current lesson, the graded test that had been returned and the text being constructed during the lesson. The multiple texts that were identified provided further evidence of the linkages across lessons over time (Barr, 1987). In other words, for a student to participate appropriately in both the social and the academic tasks of the lesson, he or she had to have prior knowledge of earlier phases in the life of the test.

The existence of multiple texts, the historical aspect of lessons, and the constructed nature of the curriculum have implications for future research on both reading in classroom contexts and for in-struction in general. The findings of this study raise questions about what is the appropriate unit of observation and about what sampling procedures need to be used. Given the complexity of the lesson discussed above, no single observation tool (e.g., coding system) can be used; rather, what is needed is a set of theoretically compatible analytic procedures and tools that can be used to explore different aspects of lesson construction and classroom life (e.g., social, cognitive, textual; Green & Harker, 1988). Finally, the findings of this study raise questions about how instruction, reading, and curriculum are conceptualized. Future research, therefore, must consider the approach to be taken, the match between the theory and the method used, and ways in which the phenomena under study are conceptualized.

REFERENCES

Anderson, A.B., Teale, W.B., & Estrada, E. (1980). Low-income children's preschool literacy experience: Some naturalistic observations. *Quarterly Newsletter of the Laboratory of Comparative Human Cognition, 2*(3), 59–65.

Barr, R. (1987). Classroom interaction and curricular content. In D. Bloome (Ed.), *Literacy and schooling* (pp. 150–168). Norwood, NJ: Ablex.

Bernhardt, E.B. (1987). The text as a participant in instruction. *Theory into Practice, 26*(1), 32–37.

Bloome, D. (1981). *An ethnographic approach to the study of reading activities among black junior high school students.* Unpublished doctoral dissertation, Kent State University, Kent, OH.

Bloome, D. (1983a). Reading as a social process. In B. Hutson (Ed.), *Advances in reading-language research* (Vol. 2). Greenwood, CT: JAI.

Bloome, D. (1983b). Classroom reading instruction: A socio-communicative analysis of time on task. *32nd Yearbook of the National Reading Conference.* Rochester, NY: National Reading Conference.

Bloome, D. (1987). Reading as a social process in a middle school classroom. In D. Bloome (Ed.), *Literacy and schooling* (pp. 123–149). Norwood, NJ: Ablex.

Bloome, D., Theodorou, E., & Puro, P. (In press) Classroom lessons and procedural display. *Curriculum Inquiry.*

Bloome, D., & Green, J.L. (1982). The social contexts of reading: A multidisciplinary perspective. In B.A. Hutson (Ed.), *Advances in reading-language research* (Vol. 1). Greenwich, CT: JAI.

Bloome, D., & Green, J.L. (1984). Directions in the sociolinguistic study of reading. In M.D. Pearson, R. Barr, M. Kamil, & P. Mosenthal (Eds.), *Handbook of research in reading.* New York: Longman.

Bloome, D., & Theodorou, E. (1988). Analyzing teacher–student and student–student discourse. In J. Green & J. Harker (Eds.), *Multiple perspective analysis of classroom discourse.* Norwood, NJ: Ablex.

Cazden, C. (1983). Contexts for literacy: In the mind and in the classroom. *Journal of Reading Behavior, 14*(4), 413–428.

Cazden, C. (1986). Classroom discourse. In M.C. Wittrock (Ed.), *Handbook of research on teaching,* (3rd ed., pp. 432–436). New York: Macmillan.

Cochran–Smith, M. (1984). *The making of a reader.* Norwood, NJ: Ablex.

Collins, J. (1983). *A linguistic perspective on minority education: Discourse analysis and early literacy.* Unpublished doctoral dissertation. University of California, Berkeley.

Collins, J. (1986). Differential instruction in reading groups. In J. Cook–Gumperz (Ed.), *The social construction of literacy* (pp. 117–137). London: Cambridge University Press.

Collins, J., & Michaels, S. (1986). Speaking and writing: Discourse strategies and the acquisition of literacy. In J. Cook–Gumperz (Ed.), *The social construction of literacy* (pp. 207–222). London: Cambridge University Press.

Cook–Gumperz, J. (1977). Situated instructions: Language socialization of school-age children. In S. Ervin–Tripp & C. Mitchell–Kernan (Eds.), *Child discourse.* New York: Academic Press.

Cook–Gumperz, J., Gumperz, J., & Simons, H. (1981). *School–home ethnography project.* Final report to the National Institute of Education. Washington, DC: U. S. Department of Education.

Corsaro, W. (1985). *Friendship and peer culture in the early years.* Norwood, NJ: Ablex.

Doyle, W. (1986). Classroom organization and management. In M.C. Wittrock (Ed.), *Handbook of research on teaching* (3rd ed., pp. 392–431). New York: Macmillan.

Edwards, A.D., & Furlong, V.J. (1978). The language of teaching: Meaning in classroom interaction. London: Heinemann.

Erickson, F. (1979). On standards of descriptive validity in studies of classroom validity. (Technical Report.) Institute for Research on Teaching, Michigan State University, East Lansing, MI: IRT.

Erickson, F. (1982). Classroom discourse as improvisation: Relationships between adademic task structure and social participation structure in lessons. In L. Cherry Wilkinson (Ed.), *Communicating in the classroom* (pp. 153–182). New York: Academic Press.

Erickson, F. (1986). Qualitative methods in research on teaching. In M.C. Wittrock (Ed.), *Handbook of research on teaching* (3rd ed., pp. 119–161). New York: Macmillan.

Erickson, F., & Shultz, J. (1981). When is a context? Some issues and methods in the analysis of social competence. In J. Green & C. Wallat (Eds.), *Ethnography and language in educational settings* (pp. 147–160). Norwood, NJ: Ablex.

Evertson, C. (1985). Training teachers in classroom management: An experiment in secondary school classrooms. *Journal of Educational Research, 79*(1), 51–58.

Evertson, C., Weade, R., Green, J.L., & Crawford, J. (1985). *Effective classroom management and instruction: An exploration of models, Final report.* (NIE-G-83-0063). Washington, DC: National Institute of Education. (ERIC Reproduction Service No. ED 271 422)

Fenstermacher, G. (1986). In M.C. Wittrock (Ed.), *Handbook of research on teaching,* (3rd ed., pp. 37–49). New York: Macmillan.

Fenstermacher, G. (1987). On understanding the connections between classroom research and teacher change. *Theory into Practice, 26*(1), 3–7.

Florio, S., & Shultz, J. (1979). Social competence at home and at school. *Theory into Practice, 18*(4), 234–243.

Frederiksen, C. (1975). Representing logical and semantic structure of knowledge acquired from discourse. *Cognitive Psychology, 7,* 371–458.

Frederiksen, C. (1981). Inference in preschool children's conversations: A cognitive perspective. In J. Green & C. Wallat (Eds.), *Ethnography and language in educational settings* (pp. 303–334). Norwood, NJ: Ablex.

Gilmore, P. (1981). Shortridge school and community: Attitudes and admission to literacy. In D. Hymes (project director), *Ethnographic monitoring of children's reading/language arts skills in and out of the classroom.* Final report to the National Institute of Education. Washington, DC: U. S. Department of Education.

Golden, J. (1984). In B. Hutson (Ed.), *Advances in reading-language research* (Vol. 2). Greenwood, CT: JAI.

Golden, J. (1986). Reader–text interaction. *Theory into Practice, 25*(2), 91–96.

Golden, J. (1987). An exploration of reader–text interaction in a small group discussion. In D. Bloome (Ed.), *Literacy and schooling* (pp. 169–192). Norwood, NJ: Ablex.

Golden, J. (1988). The construction of a literary text in a story reading lesson. In J.L. Green & J. Harker (Ed.), *Multiple perspective analyses of classroom discourse.* Norwood, NJ: Ablex.

Graham, K. (1986). *The nature of the lessons and instruction in a middle school physical education class: A social interaction perspective.* Unpublished doctoral dissertation, Ohio State University, Columbus.

Green, J.L. (1977). *Pedagogical style differences as related to comprehension performance: Grades one through three.* Unpublished doctoral dissertation. University of California, Berkeley.

Green, J.L. (1983). Research on teaching as a linguistic process: A state of the art. In E. Gordon (Ed.), *Review of research in education* (Vol. 10, pp. 151–252). Washington, DC: American Educational Research Association.

Green, J.L., & Bloome, D. (1983). Ethnography and reading: Issues, directions and findings. In J. Niles (Ed.), *32nd yearbook of the National Reading Conference.* Rochester, NY: National Reading Conference.

Green, J.L., & Harker, J.O. (1982). Gaining access to learning: Conversational, social, and cognitive demands of group participation. In L. Cherry Wilkinson (Ed.), *Communicating in the classroom* (pp. 183–222). New York: Academic Press.

Green, J.L., Harker, J.O., Golden, J. (1986). Lesson Construction: Differing views. In G. Noblitt & W. Pink (Eds.), *Schooling in social context: Qualitative studies.* Norwood, NJ: Ablex.

Green, J.L. & Razinski, T. (1985). *Teacher style and classroom management: Stability and variation across instructional events.* Paper presented at the annual meeting of the American Educational Research Association, Chicago.

Green, J.L., & Wallat, C. (1981). Mapping instructional conversations: A sociolinguistic ethnography. In J. Green & C. Wallat (Eds.), *Ethnography and language in educational settings* (pp. 161-195). Norwood, NJ: Ablex.

Green, J.L., & Weade, R. (1987). In search of meaning: A sociolinguistic perspective on lesson construction and reading. In D. Bloome (Ed.), *Literacy and schooling.* Norwood, NJ: Ablex.

Green, J.L., Weade, R., & Graham, K. (1988). Lesson construction and student participation: A sociolinguistic analysis. In J.L. Green & J. Harker (Ed.), *Multiple perspective analyses of classroom discourse.* Norwood, NJ: Ablex.

Griffin, P. (1977). How and when does reading occur in the classroom. *Theory into Practice, 16*(5), 376-383.

Gumperz, J.J. (1982a). *Discourse strategies.* Cambridge, England: Cambridge University Press.

Gumperz, J.J. (1982b). *Language and social identity.* Cambridge, England: Cambridge University Press.

Gumperz, J.J. (1986). Interactional sociolinguistics in the study of schooling. In J. Cook-Gumperz (Ed.), *The social construction of literacy* (pp. 45-68). London: Cambridge University Press.

Hammersley, M., & Atkinson, P. (1985). *Ethnography: Principles in practice.* London: Tavistock.

Harker, J. (1988). Relationship between the evolving oral discourse and the discourse of the story. In J.L. Green & J. Harker (Ed.), *Multiple perspective analyses of classroom discourse.* Norwood, NJ: Ablex.

Heap, J. (1980). What counts as reading? Limits to certainty in assessment. *Curriculum Inquiry, 10*(3), 265-292.

Heap, J. (1983a). Frames and knowledge in a science lesson: A dialogue with Professor Heyman. *Curriculum Inquiry, 13*(4), 397-417.

Heap, J. (1983b). *On task in discourse: Getting the right pronunciation.* Paper presented at the annual meeting of the American Educational Research Association, Montreal.

Heap, J. (1985). Discourse in the production of classroom knowledge: Reading lessons. *Curriculum Inquiry, 15*(3), 245-279.

Heath, S.B. (1982). Questioning at home and at school: A comparative study. In G. Spindler (Ed.), *Doing the ethnography of schooling: Educational anthropology in action.* New York: Holt, Rinehart, & Winston.

Heath, S.B. (1983). *Ways with words.* London: Cambridge University Press.

Hymes, D. (1981). *Ethnographic monitoring of children's acquisition of reading/language arts skills in and out of the classroom.* Final report to the

National Institute of Education. Washington, DC: U. S. Department of Education.

Hymes, D. (1982). *Essays in the History of Linguistic Anthropology.* Philadelphia: J. Benjamins.

Iser, W. (1980). Interaction between text and reader. In S.R. Suleiman & I. Crosman (Eds.), *The reader in the text: Essays on audience and interpretation* (pp. 106–119). Princeton, NJ: Princeton University Press.

Marshall, H.H., & Weinstein, R.S. (1988). Beyond quantitative analysis: Recontextualization of classroom factors contributing to the communication of teacher expectations. In J. Green & J. Harker (Eds.), *Multiple perspective analyses of classroom discourse.* Norwood, NJ: Ablex.

McDermott, R. (1976). *Kids make sense: An ethnographic account of the interactional management of success and failure in one first-grade classroom.* Unpublished doctoral dissertation. Stanford University, Stanford, CA.

McDermott, R. (1978). Relating and learning: An analysis of two classroom reading groups. In R. Shuy (Ed.), *Linguistics and reading.* Rawley, MA: Newbury House.

Mead, M. (1972). *Blackberry winter: My earlier years.* New York: Morrow.

Mehan, H. (1979). *Learning lessons.* Cambridge, MA: Harvard University Press.

Michaels, S. (1981). Sharing time: Children's narrative styles and differential access to literacy. *Language & society, 10*(3), 423–442.

Michaels, S. (1984). Listening and responding: Hearing the logic in children's narratives. *Theory Into Practice, 23*(3), 218–224.

Michaels, S., & Cook–Gumperz, J. (1979). A study of sharing time with first grade students: Discourse narratives in the classroom. In C. Chiarello et al. (Eds.), *Proceedings of the fifth annual meeting of the Berkeley Linguistics Society* (pp. 647–660). Berkeley, CA: Berkeley Linguistics Society.

Mishler, E. (1984). *The discourse of medicine: Dialectics of medical interviews.* Norwood, NJ: Ablex.

Morine–Dershimer, G. (1985). *Talking, listening and learning in elementary classrooms.* New York: Longman.

Ochs, E. (1979). Transcription as theory. In E. Ochs & B.B. Schieffelin (Eds.), *Developmental pragmatics.* New York: Academic Press.

Philips, S. (1972). Participant structures and communicative competence: Warm Springs children in community and classroom. In C. Cazden, V. John, & D. Hymes (Eds.), *Functions of language in the classroom.* New York: Teachers College Press.

Philips, S. (1982). *The invisible culture: Communication in classroom and community on the Warm Springs Indian Reservation.* New York: Longman.

Puro, P., & Bloome, D. (1987). Understanding classroom communication. *Theory into Practice, 26*(1), 26–31.

Shulman, L. (1986). Paradigms and research programs in the study of teaching. In M.C. Wittrock (Ed.), *Handbook of research on teaching* (3rd ed., pp. 3–36). New York: Macmillan.

Spindler, D. (1982). *The ethnography of schooling: Educational anthropology in action.* New York: Holt, Rinehart, & Winston.

Spradley, J.P. (1980). *Participant observation.* New York: Holt, Rinehart, & Winston.

Stubbs, M. (1983). *Discourse analysis: The sociolinguistic analysis of natural language.* Chicago: University of Chicago Press.

Szwed, J. (1981). The ethnography of literacy. In M. Whiteman (Ed.), *Variations in writing: Functional and linguistic-cultural difference.* Hillsdale, NJ: Erlbaum.

Tannen, D. (1982). *Spoken and written language.* Norwood, NJ: Ablex.

Tannen, D. (1984). *Coherence in spoken and written discourse.* Norwood, NJ: Ablex.

Taylor, D. (1984). *Family literacy: A forum for the exchange of ideas on critical issues arising from current research on the social, cultural and political contexts in which young children learn to read and write.* Symposium presented at the National Reading Conference, Austin, TX.

Weade, R. (1987). Curriculum'n'Instruction: The construction of meaning. *Theory Into Practice, 26*(1), 15–25.

Weade, R., & Green, J.L. (1986). Talking to learn: Social and academic requirements for classroom participation. *Peabody Journal of Education, 62*(3), 6–19.

CHAPTER TWO

Social Organization of Reading Instruction

REBECCA BARR
National College of Education

Naturalistic research reveals how classroom instruction works, as well as how it fails to work well for some children. Students are members of a changing set of social arrangements as they learn during the typical schoolday. They work in small groups, with the class as a whole, and independently. In a study of first grade learning, Gumperz (1981) found that some lower-class Black children avoided first grade academic tasks by claiming that they "didn't know how to do it." Further examination of taped comments and their intonation contours suggested another explanation: The children really meant to say, "Help me; I don't like to work alone." (p. 19). That is, they were requesting company rather than indicating lack of ability.

This vignette illustrates the importance of the social context of instruction. How teachers organize their students for instruction has implications for whether children work alone or with the teacher, with a few or many other children. Organizing students for instruction would not be problematic if there were enough teachers for each child to work with a teaching adult. The typical ratio of one teacher for many students means that the teacher's attention is a scarce commodity. Further, the roles of students and teachers are asymmetrical; teachers possess both power and knowledge that students do not. These realities pose problems in the design and management of instruction.

Teachers typically respond to this situation by determining the organizational arrangements for instruction early in the year. They decide when they will instruct the total class and in what subjects; they decide whether to subdivide the class into smaller groups for other subjects and instruct each group in turn; less commonly, some decide to teach individual students. These decisions establish the social settings within which students must learn to work.

Decisions about the social organization for one instructional area have implications for the other social settings in which students work. A decision to form small groups and/or to instruct students individually, for example, has direct consequence for the amount of time that individuals work under relatively unsupervised conditions while the teacher works with other students.

How do the organizational settings that teachers establish for students influence their work during instruction? In particular, how do the goals and characteristics of groups influence the interactional patterns and learning of participants? Do teacher-led groups interact in different ways than groups composed of peers? Does evidence indicate that some organizational patterns are more effective in achieving instructional goals for some students than others? This set of questions guides my review of naturalistic studies of classroom reading instruction.

The chapter is organized into four sections. The first provides an overview of the organizational forms that characterize instruction in reading, writing, and other language arts areas. The second examines evidence concerning the interactional work of participants in teacher-led groups and raises questions for further study. The third focuses on findings about the instruction of students grouped by ability and suggests problems for future investigation. The final section examines the naturalistic evidence concerning the nature of student work in peer groups and during seatwork and identifies areas of needed research.

CLASSROOM SOCIAL ORGANIZATION

Definitions

The term "social organization" has been used in educational research to mean several different things. In the educational literature, it typically refers to grouping arrangements for instructional purposes. The meaning coincides with the formal definition of organization as "a body of persons organized for some specific purpose" (Webster). In contrast, a broader meaning has been applied to the term in the ethnographic literature. For example, Mehan (1979) writes:

> A goal of constitutive ethnography is to describe the social organization of events in such a way that is acceptable to participants. That means

starting with members' explicit formulation, then analyzing the materials until the interactional "work" of participants that accomplishes the social organization of the event that they originally formulated is located. (pp. 27–28)

A similar meaning is conveyed by Erickson and Shultz (1981) in their discussion of procedures for studying the social organization of interaction. Through detailed study of records, changes in the specific function and forms of communication behavior are used to delineate segments that are internally consistent and distinguishable from other periods of interaction in achieving a goal.

My use of the term in this chapter is more limited than the meaning in the ethnographic literature and more in line with its traditional usage in the educational literature. *Social organization* is defined broadly to include the characteristics of a group and its agenda. Groups may be characterized in terms of their size, age of participants, participant roles, and the readiness of participants for the activities undertaken. The agenda of instructional groups is usually determined by the teacher in the form of assignments that pertain to the use of curricular materials.

Ways of Thinking about Social Organization

Most studies of grouping focus on the group as the unit of analysis. That is, researchers tend to think about the consequence of small group instruction versus total class instruction or to compare individualized forms of instruction with group instruction. Alternative forms of social organization are distinguished in several different ways: For example, whether the teacher is an active participant (teacher-led groups) or not (peer groups), or whether groups are composed by ability (homogeneous ability groups) or not (heterogeneous groups). Peer groups are distinguished by such characteristics as the extent to which tasks are cooperative, the degree of task specialization, and the nature of incentives (see, e.g., Slavin, 1983; Stodolsky, 1984).

In most prior research on grouping, students placed in groups or classes on the basis of achievement are compared with comparable students in heterogeneous groups or classes. Achievement outcomes are examined to determine which grouping arrangement is better and for which students (see Findley & Bryan, 1970; Good & Marshall, 1984; Rosenbaum, 1976, for general reviews of this literature; see Hiebert, 1983, for a review pertaining to reading instruction). The intervening link of instruction has not, however, been described in most investigations. This omission represents a serious flaw since such process descriptions are necessary before it can be concluded that a form of grouping, rather than differential instruction, is responsible for achievement gain. Naturalistic studies of classroom instruction provide much needed evidence on how instruction is influenced by the characteristics of instructional arrangements.

Although viewing the group as the unit of analysis represents the dominant way of thinking about social organization, alternatives focus on the class as the unit of analysis. A grouping scheme in this sense is one that accounts for all members of a class, including the teacher. Four main forms of social organization are common in primary grades: (1) total class instruction; (2) a combined form involving a subset of the class working with the teacher while the remainder work independently on seatwork; (3) supervised seatwork with the teacher monitoring and interacting briefly with a single student, and (4) unsupervised seatwork with students working independently and the teacher otherwise involved. Consistent with this way of thinking about social organization, peer work groups would be described as a number of groups working simultaneously, with the teacher either monitoring them or otherwise occupied.

A third way of thinking about the social organization of classes considers patterns of social structure related over time. One such pattern is described on a detailed case study of a high school reading and writing course (Barr, 1987). In this case, the teacher used a series of social arrangements to achieve instructional objectives; for example, strategies for collecting evidence in order to draw conclusions about a story character were first modeled by the teacher in a total class, teacher-led form of social organization. Following this, peer groups (with the teacher available but not directly monitoring) were formed to use this strategy. For this case, the total class social organization represented a prerequisite influencing the effectiveness of peer work, which in turn influenced the effectiveness of individual interaction with text.

Alternative formulations of social organization may be more useful for some purposes than others. Class-based schemes are particularly useful for instructional planning because they describe the co-occurrence of groups in relation to teacher role. Likewise, information on the successive use of organizational forms provides a basis for teacher planning over time. A group-based perspective is most useful for the purpose of this chapter: to explore the relation between group characteristics and instructional interaction.

Organizational Structures for Literacy Instruction

Small group instruction. A variety of organizational structures are used for reading and related areas of language instruction. The most common way is to organize children into small groups for reading on the basis of readiness or achievement. Smith (1965) reports that this approach was first recommended around 1924, and recent studies indicate that such practices are common today (Fisher et al., 1978). Survey evidence indicates that this practice dominates reading instruction in the primary grades and continues into the intermediate grades (Austin & Morrison, 1963; Wilson & Schmits, 1978).

Once children are assigned to groups, there is relatively little movement from group to group. Rist (1970), in an ethnographic study of an inner-city class, describes how kindergarten children were placed by their teacher into groups which reflected the social class composition of the class. The groups, once established, persisted through several years of elementary school. Dreeben (1984) describes two ways in which teachers adjust their instructional grouping during the course of first grade instruction. The first was through individual change; the most common approach was to move students up to a higher group on the basis of skill mastery. The second was through the creation of an additional group; in classes with many low readiness children, this group usually appeared between the low and middle group; while in classes with fewer low readiness students, it appeared between the middle and high group. In general, however, group change was not common; fewer than 30% of the children in the 15 classes studied changed groups during the year. Rupley, Blair, and Wise (1982) report in their study of third- and sixth-grade teachers that more effective teachers tended to move students up to a higher achieving group while less effective teachers tended to move students down given a lack of progress. Goodlad (1984) reports that while there is some movement from group to group, in general, membership in high and low groups are quite stable during the primary grades and differences grow greater with each successive year.

While basal reading and skill activities tend to be developed in small group instruction (see, e.g., Borko, Eisenhart, Kello, & Vandett, 1984; Buike, 1980), all reading instruction does not necessarily occur in small groups. For example, story reading may occur in small groups, while skillwork based on workbook exercises may be developed as a total class activity or as seatwork in first grades (Barr & Dreeben, 1983), and many informal reading activities occur throughout the schoolday (Griffin, 1977). Nevertheless, most direct reading instruction does occur in teacher-led small groups.

Total class instruction. In middle and high school classes, as well as in some intermediate grade classes, reading instruction is often organized as a total class activity. Students are often grouped into classes or tracks on the basis of achievement. As with ability grouping within classes, studies of tracking indicate limited mobility between tracks (Oakes, 1985; Rehberg & Rosenthal, 1978; Rosenbaum, 1976).

Most reading activities are introduced to the whole class and worked on individually. For example, Bloome (1983) reports a number of reading activities in the middle school classes he studied, such as journal writing and reading, recreational reading, and covert note reading. However, direct reading instruction with a common assignment for all class members dominated. His description of recurring lesson formats in a seventh grade class exemplifies the manner in which total class forms are preceded or followed by independent seatwork forms of structural organization to constitute lessons: "(a) reading a selection from the text (orally or silently), (b) a teacher-led question–answer discussion, (c) study time for a test, (d) a test, and (e) providing feedback about the test" (p. 278).

In classes at all levels, total class instruction is used for language arts activities, other than reading, such as story discussion, writing and spelling. At the nursery school level, for example, Cochran-Smith (1984) describes total class reading and discussion of stories. At the primary and intermediate grade levels, total class language arts assignments often have the purpose of keeping children involved as teachers lead reading groups (Anderson, Brubaker, Alleman-Brooks, & Duffy, 1985; Barr & Dreeben, 1983). Individual work is consequently not closely monitored by teachers.

By contrast, in departmentalized elementary school classes and in middle and high school classes, total class reading instruction is associated with supervised seatwork. This form of social arrangement permits the integration of reading with writing and other language arts activities. Kantor, Kirby, & Goetz (1981), for example, describe a high school English class in which reading assignments facilitated the development of writing skill.

Individual instruction. Most individual work of students tends to be an extension from total class or small group instruction in that concepts, developed through teacher-led discussion, are practiced as seatwork. Seatwork arrangements represent an important organizational form because of the amount of time that students spend in them. Students in second and fifth grades spend about two-thirds of each day on academic work, the majority of which is accounted for by reading and language arts and mathematics. Of this time, 63% of the reading-language arts time is spent in seatwork in second grade and 70% in fifth grade. During this time, students are engaged in work about 70% of the time (Fisher et al., 1978; see also Rosenshine & Stevens, 1984). The results are similar in British junior classes (ages 8 to 11 years) where the typical pupil works independently for 66% of lesson time and interacts with peers about 19% of the time. While some of the latter time is task-related, most (72%) is not (Galton, Simon, & Croll, 1980).

Whether or not individual instruction occurs during seatwork depends on whether the teacher is part of the social arrangement. When the teacher is involved in another setting, such as instructing a small group, there is little opportunity for students to receive help on their work. Studies in primary grade classes reveal the difficulties children encounter when they attempt to get help while the teacher is engaged with a small group (Anderson et al., 1985; Merritt, 1982).

By contrast, when teachers supervise individual work, the opportunity for individual instruction exists. For example, Cochran-Smith (1984) describes a variety of literacy events undertaken usually spontaneously with nursery children for such varied purposes as sending messages, expressing feelings, remembering, and defining play group members. The purpose or topic of the interaction was situationally based rather than imposed by the teacher.

More formally organized, teachers may plan individual conferences to facilitate reading and writing activities. For example, Barr (1987) describes how a high school English teacher used individual conferences to help students focus and organize their plans for written themes.

Peer group instruction. Almost no naturalistic documentation is available on the use of peer groups for reading and language arts. Generally, work in peer groups is rare. Sirotnik (1983) in a survey of 129 elementary school classes in California found that fewer than 7% of the students were observed in small groups, and only 2% were in cooperative peer groups. They may be more frequently used in Great Britain than in the United States (Galton et al., 1980); however, peer interaction in group seating arrangements during independent work time may be counted as peer group work in British investigations (see, e.g., Bennett, Desforges, Cockburn, & Wilkinson, 1984) while it is typically not in U. S. studies.

In sum, certain forms of social organization are more frequently used for classroom literacy instruction than others. In particular, teacher-led groups and individual seatwork occur frequently. Teacher-led groups are often constituted on the basis of readiness or achievement and tend to be smaller than the size of the total class in the primary grades, but larger and often consisting of the total class in

the higher grades. Other language arts activities are typically introduced to the total class, but worked on individually. Seatwork arrangements differ in how much they are monitored. Individual forms
of instruction and peer groups are used infrequently for reading and
language arts instruction.

TEACHER-LED GROUPS

The focus of this section is on the *relation* between the characteristics
of groups and instructional interaction. It is logically possible that
group characteristics could bear no systematic relation to the interactional processes of instruction. Alternatively, it is possible that social
arrangements so constrain interaction among participants that one is
highly predictable from the other. With respect to this question,
evidence from naturalistic studies permits us to consider whether
teacher-led groups show similar interactional patterns or whether
they vary in response to such conditions as instructional goals or
group composition.

Studies of teacher-led total class instruction are considered first,
followed by studies of small group reading instruction. While research
on instruction in total class contexts sometimes focuses on language
areas other than reading, in small groups it almost exclusively concerns
reading development. Only small group studies that explore the
influence of curricular conditions on interaction are considered in
this section. Those that focus on the influence of the ability composition of groups on interaction are considered in the following
section.

Investigators commonly examine the interactional processes of
instructional participants in a single organizational context, either
small group or total class instruction. In the following sections, studies
occurring in total class or small group settings are examined for their
characteristics of instruction. Teacher and student engagement during
lessons can be seen to draw simultaneously from knowledge about
social participation and *academic tasks* (see Erickson, 1982, for elaboration of this distinction). Investigations of classroom discourse have
emphasized one or the other. For example, most sociolinguistic and
microethnographic studies examine the regularities of discourse and
explicate the rules for participation. Alternatively, some researchers
focus almost exclusively in the academic task dimensions of instructional interaction, including the topics and concepts introduced (see,
e.g., Barr & Dreeben, 1983) and the relationship between discourse
and textual content (see, e.g., Bloome, 1984; Cochran-Smith, 1984).

Total Class Instruction

Total class instruction usually consists of interactional sequences in which the teacher dominates in the role of information provider, question asker, and response evaluator (Bellack, Kliebard, Hyman, & Smith, 1966; Sinclair & Coulthard, 1975). As the following examples show, these patterns in total class literacy instruction are observed in classes from nursery school through high school.

Cochran-Smith (1984) studied the interaction that occurred during story reading in a nursery school class. Based on 100 story readings, three broad types of interaction were identified:

(a) Type I "Readiness" interaction sequences helped to establish or maintain norms of appropriate reading and reading-related behavior; (b) Type II "Life-to-Text" interaction sequences helped listeners make sense of events, characters, action, and information in the books being shared; and (c) Type III "Text-to-Life" interaction sequences guided listeners in their application, extension, or use of information, themes, or messages in the books. (p. 169)

The analyses from which these types emerged included detailed consideration of the relation of story content to discourse content. Of the three forms, the readiness sequences communicated teacher expectations for student behavior during story reading. The second two were both representational in format but differed in the relation of individual background knowledge to textual information. The first occurred during textual reading while the second followed it. In the "life-to-text" sequences, the teacher introduced the extratextual knowledge of word meanings, literary conventions, narrative structure, and cultural traditions that children needed to make "inner textual sense." By contrast, the "text-to-life" sequences involved the application of textual knowledge to the events of nursery school life.

In his study of a first grade class, Mehan (1979) focused mainly on the social participatory dimensions of interaction during total class instruction. His analyses indicate that the teacher has certain rights regarding the initiation of topics during lessons. The common pattern consisted of teacher initiation, student response, and teacher evaluation. Student-initiated sequences were infrequent. Lessons were composed of topically related sets; new topics could be successfully initiated only at certain junctures. Mehan noted that as the schoolyear progressed, students became better at identifying junctures between the topically related sets of lessons where new topics could be introduced.

Morine-Dershimer (1985) examined total class language arts instruction in six elementary classes (one second grade, three third,
and two fourth) over six lessons, as well as teacher and student
perception of discourse. She noted language patterns similar to those
observed in prior studies. Perhaps of most interest to this review are
variations between teachers in their use of the basic recitational
format. For example, teachers varied in their emphasis of statements
describing the purpose of activities, management comments, informational statements, and praise. They also differed in the function
of their questions, some asking more questions that provided new
information, as opposed to "testing" known information. Moreover,
students were sensitive to whether or not teachers wanted to know
what they thought. Generally, however, "what is" and yes-no questions predominated over the more open-ended ones.

The discourse of some teachers was more influenced by textbook
content than others. For example, the majority of one teacher's
lessons involved directions and explanations read aloud by children,
followed by questions read by the teacher from the teacher's guide.
The sequence of question cycles was examined in relation to the
content and purpose of the language arts lessons. Lessons based on
textbook exercises (i.e., word order and sentence meaning) were
primarily "vertical" in structure; that is, they involved a series of
structurally independent but topically related questions cycles. Lessons on poetry showed "conjunctive" development with many students responding to the same basic question. Review lessons were
characterized by vertical development in the initial cycles when
definitions were reviewed and examples of concepts considered, and
by conjunctive development in the cycles when students applied
concepts to their experience.

Bloome (1983, 1984) describes the patterns of lessons in middle
school classes composed mainly of low-achieving students. He shows
that the basic patterns of total class instruction—teacher initiation,
student response, teacher evaluation—is used for different substantive
purposes. For example, in a sixth-grade class, teacher initiative served
three different purposes: giving task directions or focusing on printed
exercises, raising questions about written exercises, and requesting
descriptions of procedures. Similarly, student responses addressed
corresponding concerns: oral rendition of directions or written exercises, text reproduction in response to questions, and description
of procedures. In an eighth-grade literature lesson, this pattern was
used to achieve somewhat different goals. While teacher initiatives
pertained to personal interpretation of text and/or elaboration, stu-

dent responses included either appropriate personal interpretations or silence.

Barr (1987) characterized the interaction occurring during total class instruction in a high school English class for the development of higher level interpretive skills. Two main patterns were observed: Both began with a teacher question and sometimes ended with a teacher comment; however, in one, the teacher question was followed by a series of student comments while the other, by a single student comment (the former is similar to Morine-Dershimer's conjunctive patterns and the latter to the vertical pattern). Quite often, the first format was used when the teacher gathered evidence about a character or his or her beliefs, and the second when students were encouraged to draw conclusions from evidence. By contrast, later in the year when difficult textual materials were read, the interactional sequences were similar to the life-to-text sequences described by Cochran-Smith (1984).

Descriptions of total class instruction from nursery school to high school level are remarkably similar in form: The teacher controls the topic and dominates the recitational format. What differs is the treatment of textual content in relation to background knowledge to achieve alternative goals: comprehension and review of text meaning; interpretation beyond text meaning; and personal application of textual knowledge.

Small Group Instruction

With few exceptions the patterns observed for teacher-led class instruction apply to discussions during teacher-led small group instruction. Although in some analyses of discourse, references to text are omitted, the typical pattern involves oral or silent reading followed by one or more cycles of teacher question, student comment, teacher comment (see, e.g., Bloome & Green, 1984; Collins, 1986; Golden, 1987; Heap, 1980). Nevertheless, the extent to which story-related concerns as opposed to other considerations dominate the topical focus depends mainly on the characteristics and goals of the teacher. For example, Au (1980; Au & Mason, 1981) found that the cultural background of the teacher influenced the content of instruction and the degree to which the small group lesson was effective in achieving instructional goals. Similarly, Green (1977) found that the objectives of the teacher influenced the content of discourse, toward the development of general knowledge or toward awareness of story content and structure.

Some evidence shows that the character of reading materials influences interaction during lessons. As part of an intensive longitudinal study of three first grade students, DeStefano, Pepinsky, and Sanders (1982) describe the character of discourse in the low and middle reading groups instructed with a systematic phonics approach. As with previous descriptions of teacher-led groups, the teacher controlled the discourse and influenced its character:

> Mostly, the talk centered on states or actions, with a relatively heavy, accompanying reference to objects. There was rarely talk about processes—things happening to people or things, the experiences people have or the benefits they might gain from these experiences. None of the respondents, including the teacher, was stylistically complicated in his or her utterances. The teacher, for the most part, demanded, commanded, questioned, and exhorted, eliciting largely single words in response from the students. (DeStefano et al., 1982, p. 124)

Whether these qualities characterize the discourse in most first grade teacher-led reading groups or only those instructed with a systematic phonics approach cannot be determined.

Some differences in discourse observed by DeStefano and her colleagues seemed to reflect the nature of the curricular activities. During the second period of observation, low-group students worked with worksheets and flashcards and did not read from a text. During instruction, the teacher produced more directives than elicitations. This pattern contrasts to that observed for the middle group during the second and third periods and for the low group observed during the third period when they read from text. Students who read from texts initiated interaction by posing questions; such initiatives were not made by the low-target-group student until the third period. These results suggest that contextual passages stimulate more diverse and extended forms of interaction than do words and sentences.

MacKinnon (1959) describes the interaction of early readers taught with two different reading programs. One was a traditional basal program that controlled the introduction of words; the other was an innovative program that controlled letter introduction, word recognition, and sentence structure (Gibson & Richards, 1957). As shown in Figure 1, because the innovative program provided information that permitted students to help each other, their reliance on other group members for help increased, while their reliance on the teacher declined during the 10 sessions of the study in comparison with students learning to read from the traditional materials. Interestingly enough, this was the only small group study in which groups were heterogeneous in ability composition. Such diversity did not preclude students helping each other; with supportive materials, it may have facilitated it.

The previous studies suggest that the agenda of groups as embodied in curricular programs influences the interaction of small groups, as well as total class groups. However, the number of studies on this issue is small, and further research is needed to document the extent to which materials influence the content and form of instruction.

Discussion

The major question of this review concerns the relation between group structure and interactional patterns. The evidence suggests that social arrangements bias group interaction toward certain patterns and away from others. The studies reviewed show that discussion in teacher-led groups conforms with a pattern in which the teacher develops questions and students respond to them. This pattern holds for small group as well as total class instruction. While this pattern

Figure 1. Mean number requests for teacher assistance and percentage of children offering suggestions in the groups reading from the Gibson-Richards materials and the traditional materials.

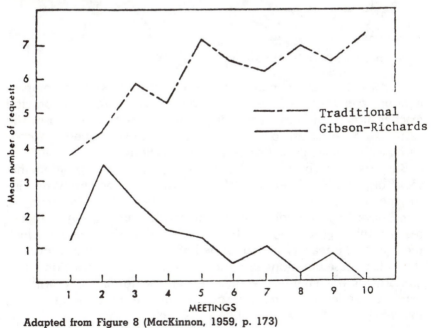

Adapted from Figure 8 (MacKinnon, 1959, p. 173)

(continued)

Figure 1 (Continued)

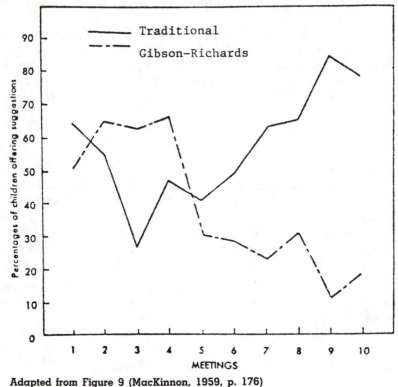

Adapted from Figure 9 (MacKinnon, 1959, p. 176)

is used to achieve a number of different objectives—text comprehension, application of textual knowledge, and interpretation, the
teacher directs the student thinking about the text in each case. The
patterns do not seem to lead to student generated questions concerning the meaning of text and its implications.

But does this consistency in evidence support the position that
social organization determines the pattern of interaction? While instructional cases that refute this conclusion are not fully documented,
some have been described more informally. The DR–TA (directed
reading–thinking activity; Stauffer, 1975) establishes a routine in which
the role of the teacher in teacher-led groups is redefined to prompt
students to raise questions about text. Yet, even this interaction might
conform, if documented, with a recitational format, one with an
extended series of student responses (in the form of questions)
following an initial teacher request.

Perhaps more persuasive evidence is provided by models for instruction in teacher-led small groups. The MacKinnon research sug-

gests that the nature of instructional materials may support a shift in teacher role. In particular, materials that provide sufficient information for children to help each other will do so if the teacher sanctions this activity. Similar to the DR–TA case, a redefinition of the teacher's role may also influence interactional patterns. In the experimental work of Palinscar and Brown (1983), following a period when teachers model question asking and summarization procedures, students assume the "teacher" role to pose questions about text to be answered by other group members. The cases considered suggest that while a redefinition of teacher role is possible, it does not occur without special training and/or modification in instructional materials. Further research is needed to document the nature of interaction among group participants when teachers relinquish their traditional role. Such evidence will let us judge the extent to which teacher-led groups can be used to develop reading strategies that involve student-generated questioning.

By suggesting that there may be benefits to instructional approaches that permit students to ask questions about text is not to argue that the recitational format is without value. On the contrary, its continued use in face of considerable criticism attests to its effectiveness. But what is the nature of its effectiveness? It seems to be a way for teachers to emphasize information that is important for students to learn and remember. The case studies indicate that the same interactional pattern permits achievement of a range of instructional goals. Cochran-Smith (1984) identified three purposes which recitational interaction supported during story reading: developing appropriate reading behavior, making sense of text, and applying information from text. Similarly, Morine-Dershimer (1985) described the use of recitation to achieve different curricular goals: a vertically structured question cycle for textbook exercises and conjunctive cycle for poetry lessons. Further research is needed to document the range of objectives for which recitational forms of interaction are used in teacher-led reading groups.

Most studies of interaction have tended to focus on the extent to which students learn rules for social participation in groups. However, research on the extent to which students master task demands, as well as social participatory demands of group instruction, is increasing. Evidence suggests that children do change their behavior during the course of a schoolyear in ways that suggest knowledge of participatory rules (Mehan, 1979; Morine-Dershimer, 1985). Yet, they continue to show problems in mastering knowledge necessary for performance in relation to academic tasks (DeStefano et al., 1982). Future research must focus to a greater extent on the interconnections between teacher explanation and questions, textual content, the nature of student knowledge required for group participation, and learning.

READING ABILITY GROUPS

Small groups are usually composed on the basis of readiness or achievement, and considerable research has been conducted to compare the social participation and academic task characteristics of high- and low-achieving groups (see Allington, 1983, for a general review of this literature). While groups are composed in such a way as to facilitate differential instruction, the question of interest is whether different instruction constitutes effective instruction.

Rist (1970) conducted one of the earliest ethnographic studies of ability groups. He observed a class of students during their kindergarten, first-, and second-grade years and noted that they were differentially treated by the teacher, depending on group characteristics. In particular, children in the low-status groups communicated less with the teacher, were less involved in class activities, and received infrequent instruction in comparison with high status children.

Other research has also documented the differential treatment of low and high reading groups. McDermott (1976), studying first grade instruction, found that low groups spent less time on reading instruction than high groups, partly because their turn-taking procedures diverted attention away from the instructional task and because of frequent interruptions by other class members. McDermott suggests that the agendas for the two groups may in fact differ, with that of the low group being the avoidance of frustration and embarrassment associated with getting through the reading lesson, a finding echoed by Eder (1982) and Gambrell (1984; Gambrell, Wilson, & Gantt, 1981) concerning time use and intrusions. Other investigators report greater time allocation to low than high groups (Hunter, 1978).

In contrast to these findings, Weinstein (1976) failed to find differential treatment of reading groups in the three first-grade classes she studied. Groups were similar in terms of their interaction with the teacher, teacher response to errors, teacher praise, and total amount of reading group time. Collins (1986) reports similar findings with respect to instructional time. Indeed, the low first-grade group received more instructional time on the average than did the high-ranked group. However, time was used differently by the two groups: High-group instruction focused on passage reading and comprehension; that of the low group emphasized passage reading and sound-word identification. Further, the two groups differed in pattern of instruction: While the typical reading cycle for the high group consisted of an oral reading turn followed by comprehension questions directed to the group, that for the low group involved an oral reading turn, followed by oral reading of the same material by the group in unison. The passages read by the low group members were shorter than those for the high groups. When children encountered difficulty, teacher prompts also differed: letter- and word-based cues for low group members and cues involving larger language units for those in the high group (see also Allington, 1980). Other research also suggests that instruction for low-group readers is more structured through the provision of advanced organizers for lessons and motivational exercises than is that of high groups (Russo, 1978; Stern & Shavelson, 1981).

At a more global level, Hart (1982) demonstrates similar differences. In her ethnography of the reading instruction in a single elementary school, she observed that the reading goals, atmosphere, and tasks changed in relation to the character of groups. Students in lower-ability levels and those in earlier grades worked in smaller, more homogeneous groups and confronted simpler assignments, more business-like atmospheres, and smaller language units than those in higher-ability levels and those in later grades. These findings are not unlike those reported by Duffy and associates (Duffy & Anderson, 1981) in their description of elementary school reading instruction.

While most naturalistic studies of reading instruction focus on a selection of lessons to describe the nature of participant interaction, Barr and Dreeben (1983) examined the accomplishments of first grade groups during the course of a schoolyear. Their findings show that high groups proceeded through the basal reader at a faster pace than low groups; accordingly, they learned more words and read more stories of increasing complexity. In the most extreme cases, high-group members read about five times the number of stories than are read by low-group members (Barr, 1975). These results are like those reported by Clay (1967) for New Zealand beginning readers; she estimates that high-group members read more than four times the number of words as low-group members. In a second study (Barr, 1985), the amount of reading differed somewhat less among first-grade groups; even so, low groups who were allocated more instructional time and read more stories were equivalent in achievement to higher ability groups from other classes.

Discussion

From the evidence summarized in the preceding section, it appears that the composition of reading groups directly influences the participants' instructional interaction. Low-group members often receive less effective time for instruction, read less material, focus on smaller units of print, and are asked more questions that require recall of information rather than reasoning than are students in higher achieving groups. That instruction of high and low groups should differ is not unexpected; indeed, one reason for forming more homogeneous reading groups within a class is to make instruction more appropriate. What is questionable is whether reading fewer stories, more isolated letters and words, and responding to informational questions constitutes "more appropriate" instruction, not to mention the social consequences of placing children who have learning difficulties in the same group. Moreover, the tendency exists for more intrusions to erode the time the group does spend on reading.

The assumption that ability grouping leads to more appropriate tasks and instruction for lower-achieving children needs to be tested directly. Using methods similar to those used in the Bennett research (described in the next section) to evaluate task appropriateness would help to clarify the extent to which small-group vs. total class assignments are appropriate for children.

Unfortunately, few test cases exist where low achieving groups are treated more like high achieving groups. Barr and Dreeben (1983) suggest that when low groups receive extra instructional time to accomplish more contextual reading, they demonstrate higher achievement. Yet, almost no studies document in detail how this may be accomplished. More research is clearly needed in this area, as well as studies of lower achieving children who receive instruction in heterogeneous small groups or total class groups. Although the wisdom in the reading field has long been that children learn best in small, homogeneous groups, little systematic evidence exists to support this practice. Just as recent data counter traditional wisdom by suggesting that children in primary grades learn better in small groups and those in intermediate grades learn better in larger groups than when taught individually (Rosenshine & Stevens, 1984), it may also be true that low-achieving children learn better from appropriate instruction in heterogeneous than in homogeneous groups.

INDIVIDUAL AND PEER GROUP ARRANGEMENTS

As described in the previous section, unsupervised seatwork is a consequence of small-group instruction, and researchers are now beginning to examine the nature of this organizational structure and its demands on students and teachers. Teacher-supervised seatwork is a somewhat less complex form of organization. This arrangement most often occurs with total class reading instruction. While there are few studies of peer group work, when it does occur it may be considered an alternative to supervised seatwork in that the teacher monitors the group's activities.

Seatwork

Seatwork must not be conceptualized simply as independent work on tasks because it almost always occurs in a broader social setting including a teacher and other students. Two major issues have been pursued. The first pertains to social participation and inquires about the rules for interacting during seatwork, which often translates into the question of how children gain the teacher or peers' attention to obtain help, stimulation, or support. The second issue, pertaining to the nature of academic tasks, inquires about task appropriateness and child awareness of task objectives.

Merritt (1982) pursued the question of how a child solicits help and attention from a teacher who works with another student or small group. She examined examples of requests, mainly during individualized time, in nursery through third grade classes. The concept of dual processing is useful in understanding independent work of students as well as the management of teachers. Children can never become so engrossed in their work that they fail to respond to the teacher's request to shift activities. In Merritt's terms, they must learn "to process more than one vector of activity even though each independently working child is involved in only one." (1982, p. 22). Independent work does not mean great absorption in activities, but rather coordinating involvement in personal work with other ongoing activities of the classroom.

Teachers are also involved in several activities. At the time they are engaged in one, they must monitor other activities that occur simultaneously. Further, teachers sometimes participate in two activities simultaneously, verbally in one and nonverbally in the other; for example, correcting one child's work while listening to another read aloud. Nevertheless, Merritt notes the commitment of teachers toward preserving ongoing activities: once engaged in an activity, they seem to "feel obliged" to remain involved until some degree of closure is achieved. Thus, although teacher availability is important to support student engagement during independent work, it is difficult to achieve when teachers are responsible for other major instructional activities.

Other research examines student work during seatwork time. Anderson et al. (1985) studied the involvement and performance of pupils from low and high reading groups in six first grade classes. From observations of work involvement and task accuracy, they identified three groups of responders: adequate, poor, and mixed. They found that all the children identified as poor responders were low-achieving readers (seven from low groups and one from a low middle group after initial placement in the high group); the main reason for their poor response was their lack of necessary reading skill to complete the assignment independently. Interestingly enough, however, only one of the eight was involved in seatwork less than 60% of the time and only two had less than 60% of their assignments correct on the average.

They argue that seatwork fulfills both managerial and instructional goals. The managerial goal is to occupy students so that they do not disturb the teacher during small group instruction. Whether or not the task was appropriate, this goal seemed to be accomplished since even students who "got stuck" on assignments were not reported to have requested help from the teacher. The instructional goal, however, was not accomplished by the students most in need of reading instruction:

> The seatwork was difficult because the gaps between the students' knowledge and the knowledge required for the task were too great for them to bridge independently. . . . Some of their assignments did provide practice at a reasonable level of difficulty, but at least 15% (and often more) of their seatwork time contributed little to their learning about reading skills. (Anderson et al., 1985, p. 133)

Anderson and colleagues also found no systematic relation between the nature of the assignment (total class or reading group) and performance ratings. In contrast, Filby and Barnett (1981) report little difference between reading group members in their success rate on written work.

In British infant school classes, there is less small group reading instruction and more monitored individual work. Bennett et al. (1984)

studied the language experiences provided to selected six- and seven-year-olds by 16 able teachers. Of a total of 205 language tasks assigned as individual work during the two terms of the study, about half involved writing and most of these were compositional in focus (54 topic writing, 39 creative writing, 10 news writing) rather than transcriptional (8 copy writing). Thirty involved comprehension, and 34 phonics and spelling. Three-quarters of the language tasks were given as class lessons. The majority of tasks did not come from a structured curriculum; most were generated by the teachers to have students practice their skills. The researchers judged the appropriateness of the tasks by observing the process through which a child completed a task, evaluating the product, and interviewing the child. A substantial proportion (55%) of tasks was insufficiently challenging for high achieving children and a similar proportion was too difficult for low achievers. Children in the middle fared better. While one might suspect that the degree of mismatch arose from the predominance of total class assignments, a similar level and pattern of mismatch obtains in math for which most tasks were individualized. Of particular interest, interview evidence indicated that teachers were not aware of instances of underestimation.

In a similar study conducted in two junior high school classes in New Zealand, Nicholson (1984) gathered evidence on the kinds of reading tasks assigned, the knowledge of the tasks required, and student strategies for coping with the tasks, especially those of low progress readers. He concludes that "the surface structure of the classroom can suggest to the teacher that content is being learned, while in the minds of pupils, there is only a maze of confusion." (pp. 449–450). In other words, while the recitational format may indicate comprehension, interview techniques such as the ones he used constitute a different way of talking to students that more accurately reveals student comprehension.

With respect to the role of teachers during supervised seatwork, Stallings (1980) concluded from observational evidence that teacher monitoring during independent seatwork increases the work involvement and reading development of low-achieving high school students, with the teacher an important participant in the social arrangement. However, teachers who interact with individual students for extended periods of time are less effective than those who limit the length of interactions.

These recent investigations of individual work structures and tasks clarify the problems faced by children doing seatwork, as well as the problems of teachers in managing and supervising it. The problem continues to be to define work that is productive, for practice if nothing else, and work that may be accomplished individually. Once children become stuck on a task, the problems of getting help, particularly from a teacher involved with a small group or an individual, are often difficult to solve. Even when support from peers is available, as described in the following section, special skill is required to obtain help, and peer group work periods are not always productive.

Peer Groups

Relatively few studies document the use of peer groups for literacy instruction, probably because of its infrequent classroom use. Because such organizational forms are rarely used, I consider the results from experimental studies that use peer groups for instruction in reading, as well as those from naturalistic studies.

Wilkinson and Calculator (1982) describe how peer groups facilitate the development of reading skill in a first-grade class. They examined student requests and responses in peer groups during the fall and spring. The reading tasks introduced by the teacher, either in total class or small group arrangements, consisted of such activities as completing worksheets or workbook pages, printing sequences from a story, or drawing a picture in response to a story. All members of a group worked on the same individual tasks for about 40 minutes each morning. The composition of reading abilities in groups differed although no formal assessment was used for group assignments. The results show that pupil requests to peers who are on-task, sincere, and to a designated listener are more likely to elicit appropriate responses than are requests without such characteristics. A decrease in pupil requests for action (and a corresponding stability in requests for information) was shown from fall to spring; this was interpreted as evidence of increasing sophistication in understanding the implicit rules of the situation. Pupil knowledge of language as assessed by two separate tests did not correlate with measured aspects of requests and appropriateness of responses. The extent to which reading proficiency influenced the occurrence and nature of requests and responses was not reported.

As noted earlier, peer collaboration appears to be more common in British than in American schools. Bennett and his associates (1984), studying math and language tasks in infant and junior classes, examined the setting in which students complete their assigned tasks. Although this might be treated as individual work, because children were seated in work groups and were permitted to discuss their work with peers, the social arrangements approximate those of peer work groups. In language area, most assigned tasks were the same for all students, although each student was responsible for an individual product. Peer collaboration was not unlike the form described by Wilkinson and Calculator (1982); however, the typical task in the British classes involved writing rather than completing worksheet tasks. Analysis of pupil to pupil talk revealed that only half of the task was task related, and of that only 16% was classified as instructionally informative. Within the language tasks, 90% involved lower order demands and most of these were spelling. While it would not appear that these peer interactions could be characterized as highly productive in terms of content, they may have enabled children to complete work without teacher assistance. (Also studied was teacher–pupil talk during language tasks; this was dominated by teacher correction or provision of spelling.)

In addition to these studies of seatwork involving individually completed tasks with peer support, several researchers have examined the feasibility of using peer support in the development of active reading strategies, as in the study reported by Barr (1987) where peer group work was used as part of the instruction in a high school English class.

Some experimental studies of cooperative work groups have involved literacy tasks. The focus has not been on examining the nature of the interaction, but on the consequences of peer interaction vs. independent work for learning. Darch, Carnine, and Kameenui (1986) found that sixth-grade students learned more from peer group practice using a graphic organizer following total class instruction than from individual practice. None of the studies reviewed by Slavin (1983) found that learning was depressed by peer group work; in sharp contrast, more than half of the 11 studies that involved language arts tasks reported significantly greater learning by peer group members. Three involved reading tasks (DeVries, Mescon, & Shackman, 1975; Hamblin, Hathaway, & Wodarski, 1971; Slavin & Karweit, 1981) and they all showed higher achievement for students working in peer groups than individually.

Discussion

The preceding review of the research is suggestive rather than conclusive. It provides some understanding of the complexities of individual work in the collective setting of classrooms. Individual seatwork is not only demanding because of the total amount of time that students spend working independently, it is also demanding because they are not really alone. Not only are there numerous opportunities for involvement in activities other than work (the British evidence suggests that nontask diversions account for a significant proportion of student time); in addition, the teacher expects children to be responsive on a moment's notice. Students must become involved but not too involved in work.

Independent work tends to be too easy for high achievers and too difficult for low achievers. While failing to challenge talented students represents a problem, more serious difficulties arise when children working without teacher support are asked to accomplish tasks beyond their capabilities. While more study time is needed, some evidence suggests that total class assignments are no less appropriate than small group assignments. Just as some evidence shows that the quality of discourse and the opportunity to learn reading is diminished in low-reading groups, members of low-reading groups do not seem to fare as well as their more fortunate higher-achieving peers during unmonitored seatwork.

Two solutions to the problems of low-achieving readers should be studied. First, more suitable seatwork assignments are needed. Further investigation of the problems that selected tasks pose for low-achieving children is needed. The methods developed by Anderson et al. (1985) and Bennett et al. (1984) provide useful starting points. From the teacher's perspective, does a mismatch occur because tasks are selected from existing curricular materials or because group (or class) rather than individual assignments are made?

Second, low-achieving readers need more support during individual work. Here the realities of the typical classroom, a single teacher and many students, come dramatically into play. The research with cooperative groups suggests a resource that is rarely used. The Wilkinson research shows that children as young as first graders can profitably help each other with seatwork tasks, although this work was accomplished under the teacher's supervision. Whether young children can develop the participatory skills to work successfully and unobtrusively in peer groups when teachers are involved with small group instruction is a question which requires further descriptive research.

In general, do cooperative peer groups offer a viable structural alternative for reading instruction? While most research on cooperative peer groups has been conducted in content areas other than reading, studies concerned with language arts tend to show learning outcomes similar to other content areas (Slavin, 1983). One major finding is that all children, regardless of ability, tend to learn better in peer groups than in teacher-led groups. An important point to note is that the pattern of interaction is not unlike that of teacher-led recitations. Instead of questions posed by the teacher, they come from cards or worksheets; students, in turn, read the questions and respond to them. New interactional patterns are not necessarily involved in the process of cooperative learning; the main difference seems to be that with the easily accessible support of peers, especially with incentives based on group learning gain, students are more motivated to help each other learn.

What is not true, however, is that the interactional patterns in peer groups must necessarily conform with a recitational format around teacher-designed or worksheet questions. Rather, as described by Barr (1987), active reading strategies introduced through total class instruction may be applied within the context of peer interaction. Some of the approaches described by Slavin (1983) and Johnson and Johnson (1975) involve group planning, critical reading, organization of information, and communication of conclusions. More research, however, is needed on how such peer group experiences are organized in reading instruction over time to be effective.

Unlike instruction in most other content areas of learning, teachers practice ability grouping in reading from the early primary grades onward; and initial placement is highly predictive of later group placement. While further research is needed to determine if such procedures are justified in terms of appropriate instruction, the costs of such a system are well known. Placement in lower achieving groups represents a caste system from which few children escape; motivation to learn is eroded and children begin to think of themselves as unable to read and learn. Cooperative groups, as well as teacher-led groups that are heterogeneous in composition, offer an opportunity for children who rarely work together on reading related tasks to interact. The evidence, though limited, suggests that such learning enhances the learning of all students (Johnson & Johnson, 1975; MacKinnon, 1959; Slavin, 1983).

CONCLUDING STATEMENT

In many respects this review of the relation between social organization and instructional interaction is premature. Sufficient naturalistic study has not been undertaken on which to base firm conclusions. The research concerning teacher-led groups does, however, reveal a consistency in interactional patterns. Reading educators should consider the purposes that this pattern serves well, as well as its limits in developing readers with active strategies. The evidence on ability groups and their instruction merits our continued attention. Further research is needed to examine alternatives to the current instruction of low groups. Finally, peer group structures represent an organizational arrangement that may facilitate communication and support across ability groupings in classes and ease some of the problems that attend seatwork. More research is needed to determine whether children can use peer support effectively during unsupervised seatwork.

REFERENCES

Allington, R. (1978). Teacher interruption behaviors during primary grade oral reading. *Journal of Educational Psychology, 72,* 371–377.

Allington, R. (1983). The reading instruction provided readers of differing reading ability. *Elementary School Journal, 83,* 548–559.

Anderson, L., Brubaker, N., Alleman-Brooks, J., & Duffy, G. (1985). A qualitative study of seatwork in first grade classrooms. *Elementary School Journal, 86*(2), 123–140.

Au, K. (1980). Participation structures in a reading lesson with Hawaiian children. *Anthropology & Education Quarterly, 11,* 91–115.

Au, K., & Mason, J. (1981). Social organization factors in learning to read: The balance of rights hypothesis. *Reading Research Quarterly, 17,* 115–151.

Austin, M., & Morrison, C. (1963). *The first R: The Harvard report on reading in the elementary school.* New York: Macmillan.

Barr, R. (1975). How children are taught to read: Grouping and pacing. *School Review, 83,* 479–498.

Barr, R. (1985). Observing first grade reading instruction: Instruction viewed with a model of school organization. In J. Niles & R. Lalik (Eds.), *Thirty-fourth yearbook of the National Reading Conference, issues in literacy: A research perspective.* Rochester, NY.

Barr, R. (1987). Classroom interaction and curricular content. In D. Bloome (Ed.), *Literacy and schooling.* Norwood, NJ: Ablex.

Barr, R., & Dreeben, R. (1983). *How schools work.* Chicago: University of Chicago Press.

Bellack, A., Kliebard, H., Hyman, R., & Smith, F. (1966). *The language of the classroom.* New York: Teachers College Press.

Bennett, N., Desforges, C., Cockburn, A., & Wilkinson, B. (1984). *The quality of pupil learning experiences.* London: Erlbaum.

Bloome, D. (1983). Classroom reading instruction: A socio-communicative analysis of time on task. In J. Niles & L. Harris (Eds.), *Thirty-second yearbook of the National Reading Conference, Searches for meaning in reading/language processing and instruction.* Rochester, NY.

Bloome, D. (1984). A socio-communicative perspective of formal and informal classroom reading events. In J. Niles & L. Harris (Eds.), *Thirty-second yearbook of the National Reading Conference, Changing perspectives on research in reading/language processing and instruction.* Rochester, NY.

Bloome, D., & Green, J. (1984). Directions in the sociolinguistic study of reading. In P.D. Pearson, R. Barr, M. Kamil, & P. Mosenthal (Eds.), *Handbook of research in reading.* New York: Longman.

Borko, H., Eisenhart, M., Kello, M., & Vandett, N. (1984). Teachers as decision makers versus technicians. In J. Niles & L. Harris (Eds.), *Thirty-second yearbook of the National Reading Conference, Changing perspectives on research in reading/language processing and instruction.* Rochester, NY.

Buike, S. (1980). *Teacher decision making in reading instruction.* Institute for Research on Teaching, Michigan State University, Research Series No. 79, East Lansing, MI.

Clay, M. (1967). The reading behaviour of five year old children: A research report. *New Zealand Journal of Educational Studies, 2,* 11–31.

Cochran-Smith, M. (1984). *The making of a reader.* Norwood, NJ: Ablex.

Collins, J. (1986). Differential treatment in reading instruction. In J. Cook-Gumperz (Ed.). *The social construction of literacy.* Cambridge, England: Cambridge University Press.

Darch, C., Carnine, D., & Kameenui, E. (1986). The role of graphic organizers and social structure in content area instruction. *Journal of Reading Behavior, 28*(4), 275–295.

DeStefano, J., Pepinsky, J., & Sanders, T. (1982). Discourse rules for literacy learning in a first grade classroom. In L.C. Wilkinson (Ed.), *Communicating in the classroom.* New York: Academic Press.

DeVries, D.L., Mescon, I.T., & Shackman, S.L. (1975). *Teams-Games-Tournament (TGT) effects on reading skills in the elementary grades.* Center for Social Organization of Schools, Johns Hopkins University (Rept. No. 200).

Dreeben, R. (1984). First-grade reading groups: Their formation and change. In P. Peterson, L.C. Wilkinson, & M. Hallihan (Eds.), *The social context of instruction.* Orlando, FL: Academic Press.

Duffy, G., & Anderson, L. (1981). *Final report: Conceptions of a reading project.* Unpublished report, Institute for Research on Teaching, Michigan State University, East Lansing, MI.

Eder, D. (1982). Differences in communicative styles across ability groups. In L.C. Wilkinson (Ed.), *Communicating in the classroom.* New York: Academic Press.

Erickson, F. (1982). Classroom discourse as improvisation: Relationships between academic task structure and social participation structure in lessons. In L.C. Wilkinson (Ed.), *Communicating in the classroom.* New York: Academic Press.

Erickson, F., & Shultz, J. (1981). When is a context? Some issues and methods in the analysis of social competence. In J. Green & C. Wallat (Eds.), *Ethnography and language in educational settings.* Norwood, NJ: Ablex.

Filby, N., & Barnett, B. (1981). *Report of a field study of reading organization.* San Francisco: Far West Regional Laboratory for Educational Research and Development.

Findley, W., & Bryan, M. (1970). *Ability grouping: 1970.* University of Georgia, Center for Educational Improvement, Athens.

Fisher, C.W., Filby, N.N., Marliave, R.S., Cahen, L.S., Dishaw, M.M., Moore, J.E., & Berliner, D.C. (1978). *Teaching behaviors, academic learning time and student achievement: Beginning teacher evaluation study* (Final Rept. Phase III-B). San Francisco: Far West Regional Laboratory for Educational Research and Development.

Galton, M., Simon, B., & Croll, P. (1980). *Inside the primary classroom.* London: Routledge & Kegan Paul.

Gambrell, L. (1984). How much time do children spend reading during teacher-directed reading instruction? In J. Niles & L. Harris (Eds.), *Thirty-second yearbook of the National Reading Conference, Changing perspectives on research in reading/language processing and instruction.* Rochester, NY.

Gambrell, L., Wilson, R., & Gantt, W. (1981). Classroom observations of task-attending behaviors of good and poor readers. *Journal of Educational Research, 74,* 400–404.

Gibson, C.M., & Richards, I.A. (1957). *First steps in reading English.* New York: Pocket Books.

Golden, J. (1987). An exploration of reader-text interaction in a small group discussion. In D. Bloome (Ed.), *Literacy and schooling.* Norwood, NJ: Ablex.

Good, T., & Marshall, S. (1984). Do students learn more in heterogeneous or homogeneous groups? In P. Peterson, L.C. Wilkinson, & M. Hallihan (Eds.), *The social context of instruction.* Orlando, FL: Academic Press.

Goodlad, J. (1984). *A place called school.* New York: McGraw-Hill.

Green, J. (1977). *Pedagogical style differences as related to comprehension performances: Grades one through three.* Unpublished doctoral dissertation, University of California, Berkeley.

Griffin, P. (1977). How and when does reading occur in the classroom? *Theory into Practice, 16,* 376–383.

Gumperz, J. (1981). Conversational inference and classroom learning. In J. Green & C. Wallat (Eds.), *Ethnography and language in educational settings.* Norwood, NJ: Ablex.

Hamblin, R.L., Hathaway, C., & Wodarski, J.S. (1971). Group contingencies, peer tutoring, and accelerating academic achievement. In E. Ramp & W. Hopkins (Eds.), *A new direction for education: Behavior analysis.* Lawrence, The University of Kansas, Department of Human Development.

Hart, S. (1982). Analyzing the social organization for reading in one elementary school. In G. Spindler (Ed.), *Doing the ethnography of schooling: Educational anthropology in action.* New York: Holt, Rinehart, & Winston.

Heap, J. (1980). What counts as reading? Limits to certainty in assessment. *Curriculum Inquiry, 10,* 265–292.

Hiebart, E. (1983). An examination of ability grouping for reading instruction. *Reading Research Quarterly, 18*(2), 231–255.

Hunter, D. (1978). *Student on task behavior during reading group meeting.* Unpublished doctoral dissertation, University of Missouri, Columbia.

Johnson, D., & Johnson, R. (1975). *Learning together and alone.* Englewood Cliffs, NJ: Prentice Hall.

Kantor, K., Kirby, D., & Goetz, J. (1981). Research in context: Ethnographic studies in English education. *Research in the Teaching of English, 15*(4), 293–309.

MacKinnon, A. (1959). *How do children learn to read?* Toronto: Copp Clarke.

McDermott, R. (1976). *Kids make sense: An ethnographic account of the interactional management of success and failure in one first grade classroom.* Unpublished doctoral dissertation, Stanford University, Stanford, CA.

Mehan, H. (1979). *Learning lessons: Social organization in the classroom.* Cambridge, MA: Harvard University Press.

Merritt, M. (1982). Distributing and directing attention in primary classrooms. In L.C. Wilkinson (Ed.), *Communicating in the classroom.* New York: Academic Press.

Morine-Dershimer, G. (1985). *Talking, listening, and learning in elementary classrooms.* White Plains, NY: Longman.

Nicholson, T. (1984). Experts and novices: A study of reading in the high school classroom. *Reading Research Quarterly, 19*(4), 436–451.

Oakes, J. (1985). *Keeping track: How schools structure inequality.* New Haven, CT: Yale University Press.

Palinscar, A.S., & Brown, A.L. (1983). *Reciprocal teaching of comprehension monitoring activities* (Tech. Rept. No. 269). Urbana, IL: University of Illinois, Center for the Study of Reading.

Rehberg, R., & Rosenthal, E. (1978). *Class and merit in the American high school.* New York: Longman.

Rist, R. (1970). Student social class and teacher expectations: The self-fulfilling prophecy in ghetto education. *Harvard Educational Review, 40*(3), 411–451.

Rosenbaum, J. (1976). *Making inequality: The hidden curriculum of high school tracking.* New York: Wiley.

Rosenshine, B., & Stevens, R. (1984). Classroom instruction in reading. In P.D. Pearson, R. Barr, M. Kamil, & P. Mosenthal (Eds.), *Handbook of reading research.* New York: Longman.

Rupley, W., Blair, T., & Wise, B. (1982). Specification of promising teacher effectiveness variables for reading instruction. In J. Niles & L. Harris

(Eds.), *Thirty-first yearbook of the National Reading Conference, New inquiries in reading research and instruction.* Rochester, NY.

Russo, N. (1978). *The effects of student characteristics, educational beliefs, and instructional task on teachers' preinstructional decisions in reading and math.* Unpublished doctoral dissertation, University of California, Los Angeles.

Sinclair, J.M., & Coulthard, R.M. (1975). *Toward an analysis of discourse.* New York: Oxford University Press.

Sirotnik, K.A. (1983). What you see is what you get: Consistency, persistency, and mediocracy in classrooms. *Harvard Education Review, 53,* 16–31.

Slavin, R.E. (1983). *Cooperative learning.* New York: Longman.

Slavin, R.E., & Karweit, N. (1981). Cognitive and affective outcomes of intensive student team learning experience. *Journal of Experimental Education, 50,* 29–35.

Smith, N.B. (1965). *American reading instruction.* Newark, DE: International Reading Association.

Stallings, J. (1980). Allocated academic learning time revisited, or beyond time on task. *Educational Researcher, 8*(1), 11–16.

Stauffer, R. (1975). *Directing the reading-thinking process.* New York: Harper & Row.

Stern, P., & Shavelson, R. (1981, April). *The relation between teacher's grouping decisions and instructional behaviors: An ethnographic study of reading instruction.* Paper presented at the annual meeting of the American Educational Research Association, Los Angeles.

Stodolsky, S. (1984). Frameworks for studying instructional processes in peer-work groups. In P. Peterson, L.C. Wilkinson, & M. Hallihan (Eds.), *The social context of instruction.* Orlando, FL: Academic Press.

Weinstein, R.S. (1976). Reading group membership in first grade: Teacher behaviors and pupil experience over time. *Journal of Educational Psychology, 68*(1), 103–116.

Wilkinson, L.C., & Calculator, S. (1982). Requests and responses in peer-directed reading groups. *American Educational Research Journal, 19,* 107–120.

Wilson, B., & Schmits, D. (1978). What's new in ability grouping? *Phi Delta Kappan, 59,* 535–536.

CHAPTER THREE

Locating the Learning of Reading and Writing in Classrooms: Beyond Deficit, Difference, and Effectiveness Models

DAVID BLOOME
University of Massachusetts at Amherst

Ethnographic research is more than a way of collecting data; it is also a way of seeing which involves the application of a theoretical frame or paradigm derived from cultural anthropology to the study of human behavior. From an ethnographic perspective, researchers attempt to describe the cultural aspects of a particular set of social events or situations. Of specific concern are issues such as how a group of people organize and give meaning to their social doings (including their everyday and life-cycle events), their ways of using language and assigning meaning, their institutions (e.g., families), and broad economic and social events.

The study of reading and writing from an ethnographic perspective begins with a redefinition of terms. Reading and writing have primarily been viewed in educational research as cognitive or literary processes. From an ethnographic perspective, reading and writing are redefined as social and cultural processes (Bloome, 1983; Heath, 1983; Szwed, 1981). Among the ways in which ethnographic researchers have redefined reading are: (a) viewing reading and writing as social events where people construct shared norms for using written language to assign meaning, and for social interaction (Bloome, 1983; Heath, 1983); (b) viewing reading and writing as a variable set of cognitive processes tied to specific social and cultural contexts (e.g., Scribner & Cole, 1979); (c) viewing reading and writing in specified ways as social attributes that identify people as belonging to specific social groups (e.g., Gilmore, 1987; Smith, 1987; Szwed, 1981); and, (d) viewing reading and writing as ways to socialize and enculturate children and others to a social or cultural group (e.g., Heath, 1982, 1983).[1]

One of the contributions that ethnographic perspectives can provide is an alternative to deficit, difference, and effectiveness models of learning to read and write. These three models idealize the process of learning by viewing it as essentially context-free. Environmental factors may increase or decrease the extent of learning, but the process of learning is substantially the same, regardless of situation or context. Deficit and difference models locate in children's homes and community settings factors that negatively influence academic achievement, while effectiveness models locate in teacher behavior potentially negative or positive influences on learning.

In the discussion of reading and writing that follows, I begin by briefly discussing deficit and difference models of school failure and effectiveness models. After that, I discuss the nature of an ethnographic perspective on reading and writing, with specific attention paid to three key constructs: the nature of culture, of events, and of language. The discussion of each construct is followed by a series of key questions that educators can ask about their classrooms and reading and writing activities within those classrooms. Finally, I will discuss how an ethnographic perspective provides a way for educators to move beyond deficit, difference, and effectiveness models.

DEFICIT, DIFFERENCE, AND EFFECTIVENESS MODELS

Deficit Models

Until recently, the relationship among home and school, and learning to read and write, was viewed in terms of a deficit–advantage model. The home and community environment for children was viewed as either deficit or advantaged in one or more areas which resulted in lower or higher academic achievement in reading and writing. In general, children from low-income families, especially low-income Black and Latino children, were considered to have either a deficit in ability (Jensen, 1969), or to come from a deficit environment (Bernstein, 1972; Bereiter & Engelmann, 1966; Moynihan, 1965; Tough, 1982). Among the factors enumerated to produce a deficit were: race and ethnicity, inherited intelligence, number of parents in the

---

[1] See Green and Bloome (1983), Bloome and Green (1984), and Guthrie and Hall (1984) for extended discussions of ethnographic research on reading.

household, income, parents' level of education, amount and quality of parental talk to children, child-rearing practices, nutritional habits, available literacy resources such as books in the home, the language spoken at home, and the value of schooling held by parents (Ellis, 1976).

Research studies supporting a deficit model were flawed in many ways. The studies on inherited intelligence were flawed by the apparent fabrication of data (Kamin, 1974). Studies on language deficits, child-rearing deficits, and so forth, were flawed by either the failure of researchers actually to look inside the homes of the population being studied or to design studies that were ecologically valid, and by contradictory findings (see Baratz & Shuy, 1969).

Difference models have tended to replace deficit models in the literature. Difference models state that because the language, intelligence, culture, and so forth, or a family or community is different from that used in schools, children from such families are disadvantaged. For example, although the language used by Black families within their communities does not lack the ability to express emotions or thoughts, because it is different from Standard English, Black children may come to school with a relative disadvantage compared with middle-class Anglo children (Fasold & Wolfram, 1970; Labov, 1982; Smitherman, 1977).

Many researchers have found this model problematic. Ogbu (1979), for example, points out that there are minority groups whose language and culture are very different from that found in school yet their children do very well in school. This fact suggests that it is not the difference per se which makes a difference in academic achievement. Ogbu (1979) further claimed that a difference model is actually a deficit model, given the political and economic content of American education and society. Simons (1979), Piestrup (1973), and Collins (1987) have found that differences in children's language were not inherently related to difficulties in learning to read but rather were occasionally (and sometimes frequently) used by educators as an arbitrary rationale for low achievement or taken as indicators of low competence and inability to learn to read.

Effectiveness Models

School effectiveness and teacher effectiveness models can be viewed as one response to deficit and difference models. Deficit and difference models generally overlooked both the school and classroom as potential factors in creating low achievement. Except for the gatekeeping function of schools and classrooms (e.g., separating "different" students and placing them into low-track classes and low reading groups), the role of schooling in achievement was not emphasized.

Effectiveness models focused on the school and classroom as key variables in producing low or high achievement in reading and writing. Both schools and teachers who produced high achievers were studied, especially those schools with teachers whose students had high achievement in reading and writing but who were from populations statistically identified as likely to have low achievement (Borg, 1980; Cotton & Savard, 1981; Edmonds & Frederiksen, 1979; Fisher et al., 1980; Rosenshine, 1980).

Many of the effectiveness studies were atheoretical. Researchers attempted to determine what was common among high-achieving schools and classes without applying an explicit theoretical frame; in general, effectiveness studies had no explanatory power (the exceptions are studies based on Carroll's, 1963, model of school learning, which is primarily concerned with time as a variable). Nonetheless, effectiveness studies led to a series of prescriptions for teaching and administering a school (Edmonds & Frederiksen, 1979; Rosenshine, 1976).

Many researchers have difficulties with effectiveness models as well. First, researchers have found that the assumptions underlying effectiveness studies are invalid. Effectiveness studies of time on task, for example, assume that students who look like they are working on the appropriate classroom task are engaged in the academic task. Peterson and Swing (1982), Bloome and Argumedo (1983) and Davidson (1985) found that although students may have looked as if they were engaged in the task, they may be thinking about something else (while students who looked as if they were not engaged actually may be), or they were engaged in mock participation or procedural display, or they were thinking about how to get through the lesson, rather than actually acquiring the academic substance of the lesson.

Problems with underlying theoretical frameworks of the deficit, difference and effectiveness models. In part, the problem with deficit, difference, and effectiveness models lies in the application of a theoretical framework derived from educational psychology to a set of educational problems which are, in large part, social and cultural problems (McDermott & Hood, 1982). Application of a theoretical framework from educational psychology is problematic because it is used inappropriately and in isolation from other theoretical frameworks that should also be employed.

The inappropriateness of any particular framework lies in the mismatch between what is being studied and the focus of attention of that particular framework. With an educational psychology framework, the focus of attention is on the psychological qualities of individuals: cognitive states, emotions, perceptions, and attributions of cause and effect.

Undoubtedly, important questions can and should be addressed by the study of psychological qualities of individuals. However, a problem arises not from using a theoretical framework derived from educational psychology, but rather from applying it to phenomena which do not directly involve the psychological qualities of individuals. Given the large number of minority and low-income students who do poorly in school and on tests of reading and writing, prima facie evidence exists of a social and cultural issue.[2] Given that this is the issue, information is needed on what happens in school, home, and other settings where students are involved in reading- and writing-related events that structure the distribution of failure and low achievement along economic and ethnic dimensions. Information is needed on what events are important to look at, the nature of the social structure of those events, and how written language is embedded in the social doings of those events.

The issue here can be compared with a chess game. From a psychological perspective, one might study the cognitive strategies and emotional states of individual players, noting their individual and developmental differences. However, such studies would not inform us about the rules of the game (e.g., the moves one can make), norms for playing the game to which players are held accountable (e.g., no talking, white always moves first), the distribution of resources for playing and practicing the game, or the role and value of the game to the social and economic structure of the community. Indeed, in order to understand the psychologiccal qualities of players, it is first necessary to understand what happens when the game is played.

Similarly, with the study of learning to read and write, it is important to understand the nature of the events in which reading and writing occur. However, studying events is not the same as studying the psychological qualities of a group of individuals. For the former, a different theoretical framework is needed.

---

[2] It may be argued that distributions of school failure by social groups reflects underlying genetic intellectual deficits (e.g., Jensen, 1969). However, given the lack of evidence of major genetic influence in the intellectual level of racial and cultural groups (cf. Kamin, 1974), arguments for a racial or genetic determinant need to be viewed as unsubstantiated personal opinions.

Consider a reading group. The teacher is communicating to students information about the process of reading and group procedures. Students are communicating with the teacher, giving communicative feedback that they understand or don't understand the communication. Thus, what happens in the reading group can be viewed as a communicative event. But, the reading group is also a social event. Children react to each other and the teacher as they establish social relationships. In the reading group, both teacher and students are held accountable for adhering to norms for interacting with each other, for interacting with printed text, for using language, and so forth. These norms are shared by everyone in the reading group, although occasionally someone may decide to break a norm (e.g., calling out an answer or reading out of turn). When that happens, one or more group members are liable to sanction the errant member negatively. In studying the reading group, one could examine the psychological qualities of the individuals in the group—for example, the self-image each student had as a reader—however, doing so would not describe the reading group itself. That description requires another theoretical framework where the focus of attention is on the social, communicative, and cultural processes involved in the situation.

An ethnographic framework is appropriate for looking at events and situations, including reading and writing events. In the next section, I discuss an ethnographic perspective of reading and writing across school and nonschool settings. There are, of course, variations among researchers in what constitutes an ethnographic perspective. The discussion below should be viewed as the presentation of one ethnographic perspective rather than either a presentation of the ethnographic perspective or as a review of ethnographic perspectives.

SOME CONSTRUCTS UNDERLYING AN ETHNOGRAPHIC VIEW OF READING AND WRITING

In this section, I discuss three theoretical issues underlying an ethnographic view of reading and writing: the nature of culture, the nature of events, and the nature of language. These theoretical foundations lead to a redefinition of reading and writing as social and cultural processes. Given the limited space in this chapter, discussion of these three issues does not fully represent the diverse ways that anthropologists and sociolinguists define culture, events, and language.

Culture

Culture is often confused with nationality, ethnicity, or civilization. In such cases, culture gets defined as the customs, holidays, dress, and traditions of a national or ethnic group. Occasionally, culture is defined as a level of development such as in statements like "they have no culture, they eat with their fingers" or "I'm taking a course at the art museum so I can get cultured." Anthropologists have generally rejected definitions of culture as nationality or as development because they are superficial and ethnocentric.

Two definitions of culture recently offered by anthropologists seem especially helpful in reconceptualizing reading and writing as social and cultural processes. The first one (Goodenough, 1971) emphasizes culture as a shared set of ways of perceiving, believing, evaluating, communicating, and acting. The second one (Geertz, 1973) emphasizes the shared interpretation of behavior, events institutions, and other processes.

Culture as Ways of Perceiving, Believing, Evaluating, Communicating and Acting. Goodenough (1971) noted that:

> People who deal recurringly and frequently with one another develop expectations regarding the manner of conducting these dealings. They make some of their expectations explicit and formulate some of them as rules of conduct. They do not consciously formulate others but react to a person's failure to abide by them as a breach of appropriate behavior, saying that he behaves or talks oddly or in a mixed-up fashion. These expectations relate not only to social conduct but to how a person does his work, how he goes about accomplishing his purposes, and the beliefs and values he cites in justifying his own acts and others' acts. The people who deal with one another and who have these expectations of one another do not necessarily agree on all details of what they expect in their mutual dealings. But the variance in their individual expectations must be small enough so that they are able to accomplish their purposes with and through one another reasonably well most of the time. . . . The expectations one has of one's fellow may be regarded as a set of standards for perceiving, believing, evaluating, communicating, and acting. These standards constitute the culture that one attributes to one's fellows; and it is in this sense of standards that I use the term culture. (1971, p. 99)

Given Goodenough's definition, one can apply the construct of culture to a broad range of social groups: national groups, regional groups, communities, classrooms, families, and so forth. For Goodenough (1971), the standards that constitute culture are shared expectations about a wide range of behavior built up through interaction over time. What one studies when one studies culture are the shared standards and expectations within a group for behavior across situations.

Of course, individuals may choose to act in ways contrary to shared expectations. However, from an ethnographic perspective, individual differences in behavior are not the focus of attention and are considered important only in what they reveal about the shared standards and expectations held by the group. For example, in classrooms there are shared expectations about what topics are appropriate for compositions. A student who chooses to write an X-rated composition violates shared expectations about writing in school. What is relevant here is not the psychological motivation or personality of the student, but rather what happens as a result of that student's behavior (what the other students and teacher do), and what all of that interactional behavior reveals about the culture of the classroom and about the nature of writing within that cultural context.

With regard to reading and writing, Goodenough's (1971) definition raises questions such as the following:

1. What are the shared standards or expectations among a group for how people are to engage in reading and writing?
2. What are the shared standards or expectations among a group for how meaning is to be assigned to written language?
3. What are the shared standards or expectations among a group for how reading and writing get defined? And, for what counts as reading and writing?
4. How do the shared standards and expectations related to written language and to reading and writing events in general get established and communicated to members, new members, and children entering the group?
5. How do the shared standards and expectations among a group vary across written language events?
6. What is the similarity and difference among groups in the set or sets of standards and expectations held for reading and writing events?

The questions above shift the focus of attention from individuals, individual differences, motivation, and learning (topics which are the focus of attention in educational psychology) to the ways that a social group has for engaging in, giving meaning to, and defining written language events.

CULTURE AS SHARED INTERPRETATION OF BEHAVIOR, EVENTS, INSTITUTIONS, AND OTHER PROCESSES

Although Geertz (1973) disagrees with Goodenough's (1971) definition of culture, viewing it as too mentalistic and too mechanistic, both of their definitions can be usefully compared to determine what alternatives they provide for reconceptualizing reading and writing. For Geertz (1973), culture is a heuristic for looking at how people assign meaning, significance and importance to behavior, events, objects, and institutions:

> The concept of culture I [Clifford Geertz] espouse . . . is essentially an semiotic one. Believing with Max Weber that man is an animal suspended in webs of significance he himself has spun, I take culture to be those webs, and the analysis of it to be therefore not an experimental science in search of law but an interpretive one in search of meaning. (p. 5)

Geertz's definition of culture (1973) is important in at least two ways. First, he focuses attention on the meaning, significance or importance of human behavior. For Geertz, culture is not behavior itself nor patterns of behavior, but rather the shared interpretation and importance given to that behavior. Second, while acknowledging that people create culture, he locates culture outside of individuals. As people interact with each other, they construct shared meanings and shared interpretive frameworks for their interactional behavior. The shared nature of those frameworks locates culture outside of individuals and in the interactions among people. From Geertz's perspective, what one studies when one studies culture is the shared meanings and importance given to behavior, and how that meaning is constructed.

For Geertz, culture is also a heuristic for describing human behavior, institutions, social events, and other processes:

> Culture is not a power, something to which social events, behaviors, institutions or processes can be causally attributed; it is a context, something within which they [social events, behaviors, institutions, and processes] can be intelligibly—that is thickly-described. (1973, p. 14)

The importance for educators of viewing culture as a heuristic is that culture cannot be used as a causal explanation for why an individual or a group behaves in a particular manner or assigns a particular meaning to some phenomenon. For example, occasionally educators will causally attribute a student's behavior or achievement level to his or her home culture. If culture is viewed as a heuristic (as a means to a description), then such causal explanations are inappropriate and invalid.

With regard to reading and writing, Geertz's (1973) definition of culture requires what are called "thick" descriptions of reading and writing activities. A thick description is more than a detailed description; it identifies what happens in detail, the meanings socially assigned, and the system of meanings in which the activity is embedded. Among the questions raised by Geertz's (1973) definition are:

1. What are the socially constituted ways that people assign meaning and significance to written language?
2. What are the socially constituted meanings assigned to various uses of written language?
3. What is the social significance of meaning of engaging in reading and writing?
4. What is (are) the system(s) of meanings for reading and writing in the social setting in which these activities occur?

The Nature of Events

By events, I am referring to face-to-face interaction. From an ethnographic perspective, face-to-face events are essentially social and cultural. They include forming groups, distributing status, enacting cultural forms, routines and rituals, and constructing a shared meaning of interpretation for a common phenomenon and the event itself. In a classroom reading group, for example, an ethnographic perspective would be concerned with the social relationships among the students and teacher, how those social relationships are established and played out, who gets counted as a member of the group and who is viewed as an "outsider," how the social group is formed, the rituals and routines performed by the group (such as designating captains), and the meaning or interpretation held by the group for what they are doing, and the use made of their reading books and other written language.

With regard to events and reading and writing, the questions asked from an ethnographic perspective concern the roles (or functions) of reading and writing in the social structuring of the event, and how the event structures the doing of reading and writing. For example, the way a student orally renders a written passage can be used as a way to distribute social status within a reading group. When one student gives an incorrect answer to a question about a story read, other students may vigorously raise their hands to answer the question in order to acquire social status among peers and the teacher.

For educators concerned about students' reading and writing development, viewing face-to-face events as social and cultural is important because face-to-face events influence how students define reading and writing within specific situations (e.g., reading group or seatwork), how they interpret written language, and the importance they assign to reading and writing.

Sociolinguists and ethnomethodologists have provided a series of important constructs about face-to-face events. In the rest of this section, I briefly discuss four constructs. First, the social context of a face-to-face event is continuously constructed, not given nor static. Second, the structure of conversation within face-to-face events adheres to a series of systematic principles. Third, meaning is situation-specific. Fourth, instructional events consist of multiple levels of face-to-face interaction.

The social context of a face-to-face event is continuously constructed. When people come together and interact with each other, if they are to accomplish successfully their social goals (such as forming groups, communicating information, forming social relationships, acquiring help to complete a task, performing a ritual), they need to establish a shared interpretive framework. That shared interpretive framework includes a notion of how each other's interactional behavior is to be interpreted. For example, in the case of two people reading a story together, one person asks a question about the story. There are many ways that question can be interpreted: It may be a general inquiry not requiring the other party to respond, or, it may be a demand for a response. The people in that event need a shared interpretive framework that will give them a shared understanding of what the question requires and what it means. In addition to a shared interpretation of the interactional demands of the question, participants also need a shared interpretation of the social consequences or significance of question. To ask a question may imply an inferior social status, a superior status, or equal status. Asking a question may designate roles such as teacher and student. When participants to an event do not share an interpretive framework, they misinterpret each other's intentions and messages and the event breaks down.

An interpretive framework is built through ongoing interaction. If a student is asked to read a story and begins to read it aloud, a teacher may respond that he or she should read it silently and then report on what happened in the story. In such a case, teacher and student have constructed much of a shared communicative framework; they have defined reading and comprehension, they have negotiated how the story is to be understood, they have constructed roles for each other with rights and obligations (e.g., the student is to offer a report of the story and the teacher is to validate and correct the report).

As the teacher and student continue to interact they will continue to build a shared interpretive framework and they may modify their interpretive framework. For example, after the student has begun a report on the story, the teacher may interrupt to ask the student how he felt about a particular event. The student responds and the teacher then comments on his or her feelings about the event. The shared interpretive framework changed; reading was redefined as a combination report and emotional response, the story was to be understood not only as a series of events but also as an aesthetic experience; the social relationship between the teacher and student changed as did the roles they played. They each provided a response to the story which did not need to be corrected or validated. Simply put, who did what, with whom, when, and how changed.

Continuing changes in shared interpretive frameworks require participants to monitor constantly what is happening and how that is to be interpreted. The ability to monitor what is happening and to respond appropriately is often referred to as communicative competence. Studies by educational sociolinguists and ethnographers have suggested that, with few exceptions, students are able to monitor and respond appropriately to instructional conversations (Wallat & Green, 1979).

But having the communicative competence to participate in classroom lessons does not necessarily mean that children will be academically successful. In some cases, appropriate participation in classroom lessons may mean appropriate responding to the teacher but not necessarily learning to read extended written discourse (e.g., DeStefano, Pepinsky, & Sanders, 1982). In other cases, *appropriate* participation for some children may mean *failing* to get the correct answer (Bloome & Golden, 1982) or assuming the social role of the classroom failure (e.g., McDermott, 1977). In such cases, *failure* can be viewed as an interactional *accomplishment.* Understanding and revealing how failure happens is a major contribution that an ethnographic perspective can offer educators.

With regard to reading and writing, there are several questions that can be asked based on events as continuously constructed:

1. In what face-to-face events in the classroom is written language used? Which are officially labeled reading or writing? which do not get labeled as reading or writing?
2. What are the shared interpretive frameworks for how written language is to be used? How do the shared interpretive frameworks vary across events?
3. What are the shared interpretive frameworks for how meaning is assigned to written language? How does that change across events?
4. How do students and teachers signal and build shared interpretive frameworks for understanding each other? for understanding written language and how it is used? for participating in classroom activities? for designating roles, including the social roles of classroom success and failure?
5. In what ways do the interpretive frameworks employed in classroom activities differ from the frameworks designated for activities? (What's the difference between what is done and what was planned?)

The structure of conversation within face-to-face events adheres to a series of systematic principles. In face-to-face events, people must be "other-oriented" (e.g., Weber, 1968). What one does must be done in a way so that other participants can follow what is happening. For example, it is not very useful to ask a question that no one recognizes as a question. Therefore, part of what one needs to do in asking a question is to make sure that others know a question has been asked and an answer requested.

Ethnomethodologists and sociolinguists have described a series of systematic principles about conversation and face-to-face interaction (see Garfinkel, 1967, 1972; Gumperz, 1982; Mehan, 1979; Sacks, 1972; Sacks, Shegloff, & Jefferson, 1974). In this section, I discuss a few and illustrate the constraints they place on face-to-face events and the implications that such constraints have for looking at reading and writing.

When people engage each other in face-to-face interaction, they establish turn-taking procedures for talk (e.g., Sacks, Shegloff, & Jefferson, 1974). Turns at talk can be distributed by a single individual (e.g., a teacher), by the person who already holds the floor, or turns can be self-selected. When there is competition for turns, there are a series of ways that turns are distributed which include combinations of speaker status, who bids for a turn first, who controls the floor, etc. The taking of a turn may occur one speaker at a time or overlap among speakers. Each of the options involved in turn-taking procedures is governed by a series of principles that participants negotiate and follow. That is, turn-taking is not random and its organization reflects the social organization of participants to each other. A good example is turn-taking in a reading group. If it is organized in strict round-robin fashion, the social relationship of students to each other is based on the equitable distribution of turns; no status hierarchy can be inferred or acquired through round-robin turn-taking procedures. In addition, round-robin turn-taking helps structure an interpretive framework for defining and relating to written language, other students and the teacher during reading group (class-wise students can figure out the portion they have to read, practice it before their turn comes, pretend to be interested but only mark time while other students are reading). The point here is not that round-robin turn-taking is either good or bad but rather that whatever turn-taking procedures are employed, they help structure social relationships among teachers and students and between students and written language.

The nature of face-to-face events can be very diverse; questions and answers, lecturing, give and take, and so forth. Changing from one genre to another (e.g., from question–answer to story telling) requires that participants signal and prepare for the change and that they ratify the change (Jefferson, 1978). Similarly with the closing of a conversation, the change has to be signaled and prepared. For example, consider a reading lesson where the teacher is asking questions and the students are responding. Suppose a student gives an unusual response, one not expected. In order for the student to explain the response, the student must signal a change in the genre (from question–response to explanation), which may also include a change in turn-taking procedures. The student and the class must prepare for the change (e.g., by providing transition statements which tie the change in genre to what has previously occurred), and the change must be ratified (the teacher and other students must give permission for the change to occur). Depending on the situation (e.g., the willingness of others to ratify the change), it may be easy or hard to change the genre of conversation. The implication for educators concerned about reading and writing is that the opportunities available to students and teachers to make themselves fully understood are structured by the face-to-face event.

That events involve a series of systematic principles which structure their occurrence raises a series of questions about reading and writing.

1. What are the turn-taking procedures (what Erickson & Shultz, 1977, call participation structures) of reading and writing events?

2. What opportunities and constraints do the turn-taking procedures of reading and writing events provide for student use of written language? and, for interpretation of written language?
3. In what ways does the use of written language influence turn-taking procedures?
4. What social, interactive work do teachers and students need to do to shift genres in using written language, in discussing written language, or in interpreting written language?
5. What social constraints are placed on variations in the structure of conversations about written language (e.g., constraints on student storytelling)?

Meaning is situation-specific. Traditionally, a written text has been viewed as having one meaning, the meaning the author intended. However, if the meaning of a written text is viewed as a function of the face-to-face event in which it occurs (e.g., the interpretive context constructed through face-to-face interaction), then the meaning of the text lies not so much in the text or even in the individuals engaged in reading but rather in the event, itself.

For example, consider the meaning of a story read in a classroom reading group. Each student in the group may read that story and understand it differently. Perhaps because of differences in background knowledge or other individual qualities, each student may arrive at a different sense of what the story was about. However, individual interpretations of the story are not pertinent to the face-to-face event. What's important is displaying an understanding of the story that the teacher views as valid. That is, since part of the interaction between teacher and students involves the teacher's assessment of student comprehension and teacher validation of student interpretation, students need to display a comprehension of the story that matches the teacher's sense of the story. Part of what must occur in the reading group is for the teacher and the students to construct a shared interpretive framework for understanding the story. Both students and the teacher must work to create that shared interpretive framework, monitor changes in it, and use it appropriately. Simply put, the meaning of the story is located in the event (in the shared interpretive framework).

The meaning of a story consists not only of its literary qualities (e.g., plot, theme, character, etc.) but also of its meaning within the social doings of the face-to-face event in which the story is used. Reconsider the reading group. Although teacher and students may discuss what happens in the story, the issue for teacher and students is the display of comprehension. Simply put, it may not matter what happens in the story; the meaning of the story is that it is a tool to display membership in the reading group and to gain social status. Students may volunteer to explain the plot or theme not because they are interested in it but rather because they can advance their social position in the group. From this perspective, what's important about a story is not its literary meaning nor the aesthetic responses students might have to it but rather the social opportunities provided by interacting with the story, teacher, and other students.

The situation-specific nature of meaning raises a series of questions about reading and writing for educators.

1. How is the meaning of a story or other written text negotiated during instruction? How is the meaning of a story influenced by what occurs in the classroom? How does the meaning and meaning-making process vary across situations?
2. What are the interactional consequences of students' different interpretations of written texts? How do the interactional consequences vary across situations?
3. What is the social meaning of students' use of written language?

Instructional events consist of multiple levels. Models of instruction have primarily stressed teacher–student interaction. The teacher does something and the student responds. However, students react to more than just the teacher, they also react to other students. Further, how students react to the teacher depends on whether they are being directly addressed by the teacher.

Several classroom researchers have described various levels of face-to-face interaction during instruction (e.g., Bloome & Theodorou, 1988; Merritt, 1982). While the levels vary, depending on the instructional activity, the number of teachers and students, and so forth, as a heuristic it is useful to consider three levels: teacher–student interaction, teacher–class interaction, and student–student interaction.

Each level of interaction has a set of standards for social and communicative behavior. Students are required to participate appropriately in all three levels. That is, they must coordinate the demands of all three levels. One example is a classroom where students sit in groups and the teacher is conducting a question–answer discussion. The teacher asks a question of Tom. Tom must not only respond to the teacher, he must respond appropriately, following standards for answering a question given by a teacher (e.g., respond quickly, use an appropriate register and tone of voice, stay on the topic, make eye contact with the teacher, use school language such as complete sentences, etc.). Bill, who is also sitting next to Tom, must also respond. However, Bill's response, like that of the rest of the class, is very different from Tom. Bill needs to show that he is listening to the interaction between Tom and the teacher and that he is following the lesson. While the teacher directly addressed Tom, the teacher was also addressing Bill and the rest of the class. Presumably, the teacher asked the question to make public knowledge that the whole class should have. When Tom gives the correct answer, the teacher can validate the answer and indirectly inform the whole class that they are expected to know that information and be able to display it in an appropriate manner.

At the same time that the teacher is interacting with Tom and indirectly with the rest of the class, students are interacting with each other. They may be sharing books or other materials, quietly discussing homework assignments or romantic affairs, and monitoring what each other is doing.

Each peer group formulates a set of standards for their interaction. Those standards may include sharing resources and responding to requests for help. To violate a peer group standard may cause other students to invoke sanctions against the errant student (e.g., give the student a dirty look). Occasionally, the norms of the peer group may contradict the norms of the teacher–class or teacher–student level. For example, the teacher may explicitly tell students to do their own work. However, the norm of the peer group may be to respond to any request for help. In such cases, the doings of the peer group must remain covert or the peer group norms may have to change.

In addition to a conflict of norms, there may also be a conflict of interpretation. The same behavior or phenomenon may be interpreted in different ways from each level of face-to-face interaction. For example, consider the possible interpretation or significance of the covert passing of a love note. Within the peer group, there may be very strong expectations that other students will pass the note to its intended receiver. Within the teacher–class context, note passing may violate norms to lesson participation but may also be viewed as indicative of adolescent behavior. Within the teacher–student context, passing a note while being addressed by the teacher may be interpreted as an insult.

Acknowledgment of multiple levels of face-to-face interaction during instruction raises a series of questions about reading and writing.

1. What are the reading and writing activities that occur within each level of interaction? What role do these reading and writing

activities have in maintaining group? In designating social position? In fostering social relationships?

2. What interpretations or significances are assigned to reading and
   writing activities and to written text within each level of interaction?
3. What ways of accomplishing reading and writing activities are
   supported by the norms of each level of interaction? What
   variation and similarity occurs across levels of interaction as well
   as across peer groups and across instructional situations?
4. What social goals are held for reading and writing within each
   level of interaction?

Language

From an ethnographic perspective, language is a tool for accomplishing social and cultural doings: These include designating social relationships, performing cultural rituals, and representing the world
in a culturally specific manner. A pertinent example is a request for
help with a writing task. Embedded in that request is a designation
of a social relationship between the two people. A student seeking
help from a friend might say something like, "How do you do this
stuff?" When requesting help from the teacher, he or she might say,
"I need some help with this assignment?" And, if the student should
ask for help from the principal, he or she might say, "I was wondering
whether you might be able to help me with this writing task I have
to do for my social studies class? It's real important." The differences
among how the student asks for help across friend, teacher and
principal are ways of signaling social relationships. The point is simply
this: Language is always about social relationships.

In this section, I discuss two aspects of language important to an
ethnographic perspective of reading and writing in classrooms: cultural variation in language use and the nature of classroom language.

Cultural Variation in Language Use. There is a great deal of
variation in how people socially organize themselves in language
events, including classroom language events (e.g., Erickson & Mohatt,
1982; Heath, 1982, 1983; Schiefflen & Cochran–Smith, 1984). For
example, there is a great deal of variation in the turn-taking protocols
of story-telling events (Au, 1980; Boggs, 1972; Heath, 1983). In some
cultural groups, one person tells the story while others listen. In
other cultural groups, one person leads the telling of a story while
others add to and embellish the story. In still other cultural groups,
there is no teller or audience, but rather everyone participates in

the telling of a story. In addition, there may be variation in the degree to which a story or narrative may be embellished. In some social groups, embellishment is expected and highly valued. While in other social groups, tellers are expected to keep to the literal narrative, embellishments are not allowed.

Variation occurs not only in story telling but in other language events as well: greetings, closings, display of factual information, telephone conversations, prayers, and so on.

The ways in which a social group organizes a language event may reflect broader cultural themes. For example, in a recent study we conducted or immigrant Chinese families in Detroit, we found families where children sat quietly and alone for many hours every day, writing long lists of words from memory or copying from newspapers or other books (Bloome, Wong, & Wampah, 1985).[3] While such activities may seem strange and oppressive to middle-class Americans, the activities were consistent with values, philosophies, and the historical experiences held by the families about learning, achievement, and family. Learning was achieved through hard work and memorization. If one did not learn it was because one did not work hard enough. Working hard was also a way that children showed loyalty, respect, and love to their family. Further, it was the family's obligation to make sure the children worked hard and learned what needed to be learned. The significance and meaning of the hard work, memorization, and copying to both the children and the family was different than what it would be for middle-class American families because of the cultural and historical context in which the activities were embedded.

How people use language in a particular situation depends on many factors, most importantly the nature and demands of the situation itself. Social groups have a broad range of ways in which they can respond to a situation. The choice they make in how to respond (and in how to use language as part of that response) is not predetermined by their ethnic identity or history but rather depends on how they, as a group, define the situation and on what they view as the most beneficial way to accomplish their goals.

---

[3] The children also engaged in many other literacy activities. What was of interest in the study were differences in literacy activities derived from comparison of the families we studied across cultural groups. However, it should also be pointed out that within cultural groups there were also variations. Our findings speak more to the economic and historical circumstances in which these families found themselves, how they interpreted those circumstances, and how they viewed the best means for dealing with those circumstances.

Given the discussion of cultural variation in language use above, a series of questions for educators are raised about classrooms, reading and writing.

1. What are the cultural variations in how children use reading and writing across classroom situations? Across nonclassroom situations? across classroom and nonclassroom situations?
2. In what social configurations (e.g., isolated and alone vs. in conjunction and cooperatively with others) do children use reading and writing in various classroom situations? Nonclassroom situations?
3. What historical experiences, previous experiences, and situational factors influence how children use of reading and writing in various classroom settings? Home settings?
4. Given cultural variations in the ways that children use language in various situations, how do those variations make sense given historical, experiential, and situational factors?

The Nature of Classroom Language. The language used by teachers and students varies across classrooms and across classroom events. Yet, there are a number of features that either reoccur with frequency or are of sufficient interest to warrant attention. From an ethnographic perspective, what is interesting about various features of classroom language is what they reveal about classrooms as social and cultural settings and about how written language is used in constructing social relationships among teachers and students. Four features of classroom language are discussed below: initiation–response evaluation sequences, text reproduction, procedural display, and subrosa literacy.

An example of an initiation–response–evaluation sequence of teacher–student interaction (hereafter I–R–E) is a teacher asking a question, a student responding, and the teacher evaluating the answer. I–R–E sequences accomplish many functions in the classroom (Farrar, 1983; French & MacLure, 1983; Hargie, 1983; Heap, 1984; Mehan, 1979). I–R–E sequences provide information. By listening to student answers other students can gain needed information. I–R–E sequences inform students about how to answer a question. If a student gives the correct information to a question but uses the wrong form, the teacher is likely to have the student (or another) correct the form of the answer. In addition, I–R–E sequences make students aware of what questions and answers the teacher thinks are important. Occasionally in an I–R–E sequence, the student may not at first provide the correct answer. Frequently, the teacher will provide additional information or hints that can help the student provide the correct answer. In such cases, I-R-E sequences may help students understand how to arrive at the correct answer. Besides academic functions, I-R-E sequences also serve social and interactional functions. In I-R-E sequences, the teacher determines what responses are correct. As such, the teacher is the authority on what counts as pertinent knowledge and the form in which that knowledge should be put. Because the teacher is the authority, student responses may be oriented to the teacher's authority and completion of the I-R-E sequence rather than the subject they are studying.

Another characteristic of classroom language involves text reproduction. In many classrooms, students are engaged in reading and writing activities that involve or require the reproduction of a text (Bloome, 1984, 1987). Students copy questions from the blackboard, copy what the teacher had dictated, copy a report from the encyclopedia, give an answer during discussion that was almost word for word what the teacher had said the previous day, and so forth. While there may be complex and sophisticated cognitive processes involved in choosing which text to reproduce, when, and how to reproduce it, the social relationship of student to text could be frequently characterized as text reproduction. Authority in form and substance was placed in previously produced and validated texts (validated either by the teacher or by their association with the schools as official textbooks or library books).

Procedural display is the display by teachers and students to each other of those interactional procedures that count as getting through the lesson (Bloome, 1987; Bloome & Argumedo, 1983). However, getting through the lesson may or may not be related to engaging the academic substance of the lesson. Procedural display can be compared with a group of actors who put on a play rendering their lines appropriately but who have little understanding of what their lines mean or about the meaning the play. In classrooms, teachers and students act and react to each other so that they can complete the lesson. But what counts as accomplishment of the lesson may be getting through it, asking the questions that need to be asked, working through a series of I-R-E sequences, and assigning related tasks. However, getting through a lesson is not necessarily the same thing as learning the substance of the lesson. For example, if a student gives a wrong answer, the teacher may help the student get the right answer. Once the right answer is given, the class may move onto the next questions, and so on, until all of the questions have been presented. Completing the questions may be taken by both teacher and students as accomplishing the lesson, but what they have actually accomplished is performing the lesson not necessarily learning the substance of the lesson.

The category of sub rosa literacy events covers those unofficial uses of reading and writing (or related behaviors) (see Gilmore, 1987), for example, passing notes, playing paper and pencil games. Ethnographic studies of sub rosa literacy activities have shown that students may engage in a great deal of literate behavior that is unrecognized and disapproved by school officials. For example, Gilmore (1987) describes how groups of Black female students at one school engaged in chants and line dances that required sophisticated metalinguistic behavior. However, school officials disapproved of the chants and did not recognize the literacy skills displayed by students who, in their classrooms, were viewed as lacking literacy skills. In my studies of adolescent reading and writing behavior, I found students writing group notes requiring cooperation among students, the display of personal information, production of original text, and audience awareness. Yet, these same students often did little more than text reproduction of a few sentences in their official classwork (Bloome, 1987).

The four characteristics of classroom language discussed above— I-R-E sequences, text reproduction, procedural display, and the difference between sub rosa and official school reading and writing— raise a series of questions for educators.

1. To what degree do I-R-E sequences characterize teacher-student interaction during reading and writing instruction?
2. What is being accomplished through the use of I-R-E sequences? how do I-R-E sequences structure the relationship of students to teacher and students to written language?
3. What definitions of reading and writing are being validated by I-R-E sequences?
4. What forms of engaging in reading and writing are being validated by I-R-E sequences?
5. To what degree does text reproduction characterize student reading and writing activity in the classroom? Across classroom activities? Across grades?
6. To what degree does procedural display characterize classroom reading and writing lessons? Across classroom events? Across grades?
7. What sub rosa literacy activities occur within the classroom? Outside the classroom?
8. What is the nature of the social context of students' sub rosa reading and writing activities?

9. What competencies with written language do students display in their sub rosa reading and writing activities?
10. How do the social contexts of sub rosa and official classroom reading and writing activities differ?

CONCLUSION

Deficit and difference models locate learning to read and write in the individual child; effectiveness (success) models locate learning in teacher behaviors. Locating learning to read and write in the child has had profound effects on educational practice, including curriculum development and evaluation, pedagogy, student evaluation, and teacher evaluation. For example, many school districts with large numbers of minority students have implemented remedial language programs or purchased language instruction programs such as Distar for students who do not speak like middle-class Anglos (e.g., Standard English). Often, underlying language education programs is an assumption that minority children speak a restricted or limited code and therefore need instruction to speak an elaborated code (that is, like middle-class Anglo students). More recently, effectiveness models have been used by some school districts and even some states to mandate a specific set of instructional practices. An underlying assumption of such mandates is that instructional practices are both context-free and content-free. That is, the specified set of instructional practices hold, regardless of how teachers and students act and react to each other or what the subject of study may be.

From an ethnographic perspective, the location of learning to read and write is in the social context constructed in the classroom; or, in other words, in the classroom culture. Within the classroom, standards or interactional expectations are established for how teacher and students are to use written language in various situations. Further, a shared interpretive framework is established for assigning meaning to written language and for understanding the significance or importance of written language events.

Because the social context of classroom events is built through how people act and react to each other, students become participants in classroom events. That is, as the teacher engages students in classroom activities, they act and react to each other creating a social context for their ongoing event. As participants, students develop a shared interpretive framework for understanding others' behavior, for assigning meaning and significance to phenomena such as written language, and for guiding their own behavior as students seek to accomplish both their own personal social goals (e.g., gaining status within the group) and group goals (e.g., performing a ritual such as attendance, saluting the flag, or just getting through a lesson). Part of the shared interpretive framework involves *in situ* definitions of reading and writing, *in situ* ways of assigning meaning to written language, and *in situ* ways for appropriately using written language.

In brief, from an ethnographic perspective, what students learn is how to participate in the various social events that make up classroom life. They learn reading and writing not as isolated, context-free cognitive skills, but rather as social processes, as part of the social context of classroom events. Reading and writing are socially defined, assigning meaning to written language is socially constrained, and how one can appropriately use written language is also socially constrained. Thus, from an ethnographic perspective, the location of reading and writing is not in individuals, but rather in the social context of events involving or related to written language. Similarly, learning to read and write is also located in the social context, in how it changes and develops over time and across events.

One implication of locating the learning of reading and writing in the social context of classroom events is that reading and writing "failure" is an achievement (McDermott, 1977). It is a social achievement by either a group within the classroom or by the classroom community as a whole. If the social structure of classroom reading and writing events is based on hierarchical relationships, perhaps involving competition among students for social status, then failures are structurally required. If a student fails to adhere to the norms for using written language or for interpreting written language within a classroom group, the student can be viewed as a nonmember and stigmatized as a failure. Further, the criteria employed for differentiating success from failure are socially constituted. In brief, reading and writing failure can be seen as a social achievement by a classroom community in defining and structuring itself.

In closing, ethnographic perspectives of learning to read and write provide alternatives to deficit, difference, and effectiveness models. Reading and writing are redefined as social processes, as ways to structure social relationships among people, as ways to formulate a group and accomplish group social goals. Learning to read and write is located in the social context of classroom events, in the ways of using written language which is socially constructed, and in the shared interpretive frameworks established.

While researchers have been able to provide a series of findings about the nature of classroom culture and classroom language, these findings are descriptive in nature. While they explain what happens within the events described, they do not provide causal explanations. Further, ethnographic findings do not provide sweeping generalizations applicable to all classrooms. Rather, they provide theoretical insights which raise questions that are applicable to all classrooms. A series of these questions have been listed throughout this chapter. The importance of these questions is that they require educators to see their classrooms and students in new ways; and consequently, lead to new or alternative actions.

REFERENCES

Au, K. (1980). Participation structures in a reading lesson with Hawaiian children. *Anthropology & Education Quarterly, 11,* 91–115.

Baratz, J., & Shuy, R. (1969). *Teaching Black children to read.* Washington, DC: Center for Applied Linguistics.

Bereiter, C., & Engelmann, S. (1966). *Teaching disadvantaged children in the preschool.* Englewood Cliffs, NJ: Prentice–Hall.

Bernstein, B. (1972). A sociolinguistic approach to socialization; with some reference to educability. In J. Gumperz & D. Hymes (Eds.), *Directions in sociolingusitics.* New York: Holt, Rinehart, & Winston.

Bloome, D. (1984). A socio-communicative perspective of formal and informal classroom reading events. In J. Niles (Ed.), *Thirty-third yearbook of the National Reading Conference.* Rochester, NY.

Bloome, D. (1987). Reading as a social process in a middle school classroom. In D. Bloome (Ed.) *Literacy and schooling.* Norwood, NJ: Ablex.

Bloome, D. (1983). Reading as a social process. In B. Hutson (Ed.), *Advances in reading/language research.* Greenwich, CT: JAI Press.

Bloome, D., & Argumedo, B. (1983). Procedural display and classroom interaction: Another look at academic engaged time. In T. Erb (Ed.), *Middle school research: Selected studies 1983.* Columbus, OH: National Middle School Association.

Bloome, D., & Golden, C. (1982). Literacy learning, classroom processes, and race: A microanalytic study of two desegregated classrooms. *Journal of Black Studies, 13*(2), 207–226.

Bloome, D., & Green, J. (1984). Directions in the sociolinguistic study of reading. In P. Pearson, R. Barr, M. Kamil, & P. Mosenthal (Eds.), *Handbook of reading research.* New York: Longman.

Bloome, D., & Theodorou, E. (1988). Analyzing teacher–student and student–student discourse. In J. Green, J. Harker, & C. Wallat (Eds.), *Multiple analysis of classroom discourse processes.* Norwood, NJ: Ablex.

Bloome, D., Wong, L., & Wampah, K. (1985). *Locating learning during classroom reading and writing activity.* Paper presented at AERA, Chicago.

Boggs, S. (1972). The meaning of questions and narratives to Hawaiian children. In C. Cazden, V. John, & D. Hymes (Eds.), *Functions of language in the classroom*. New York: Teachers College Press.

Borg, W. (1980). Time and school learning. In C. Denham & A. Lieberman (Eds.), *Time to learn*. Washington, DC: U. S. Department of Education.

Carroll, J. (1963). A model for school learning. *Teachers College Record, 64,* 722–733.

Collins, J. (1987). Using cohesion analysis to understand access to knowledge. In D. Bloome (Ed.), *Literacy and schooling*. Norwood, NJ: Ablex.

Cotton, K., & Savard, W. (1981). *Time factors in learning. Research on school effectiveness project: Topic summary report*. Portland, OR: Northwest Regional Educational Laboratory.

Davidson, J. (1985). What you think is going on, isn't: Eighth grade students' introspections of discussions in science and social studies lessons. *Thirty-fourth yearbook of the National Reading Conference*. Rochester, NY.

DeStefano, J., Pepinsky, H., & Sanders, T. (1982). Discourse rules for literacy learning in a first grade classroom. In L. C. Wilkinson (Ed.), *Communicating in the classroom*. New York: Academic Press.

Edmonds, R., & Frederiksen, J. (1979). *Search for effective schools: The identification and analysis of city schools that are instructionally effective for poor children*. (ERIC Document Reproduction No. ED 173 744).

Ellis, H. (1976). Theories of academic and social failure of opporessed Black students: Source, motives, and influences. In C. Calhoun & F. Ianni (Eds.), *The anthropological study of education*. The Hague, Netherlands: Mouton.

Erickson, F., & Mohatt, G. (1982). Cultural organization of participation structures in two classrooms of Indian students. In G. Spindler (Ed.), *Doing the ethnography of schooling: Educational anthropology in action*. New York: Holt, Rinehart & Winston.

Erickson, F., & Shultz, J. (1977). When is a context? Some issues and methods in the analysis of social competence. *Quarterly Newsletter of the Institute for Comparative Human Development, 1*(2), 5–12.

Farrar, M. (1983). Another look at oral questions for comprehension. *Reading Teacher,* 370–374.

Fasold, R., & Wolfram, W. (1970). Some linguistic features of negro dialect. In R. Fasold & R. Shuy (Eds.), *Teaching Standard English in the inner city*. Washington, DC: Center for Applied Linguistics.

Fisher, C., Berliner, D., Filby, N., Marliave, R., Cahen, L., & Dishaw, M. (1980). Teaching behaviors, academic learning time, and student achievement: An overview. In C. Denham & A. Lieberman (Eds.), *Time to learn*. Washington, DC: U. S. Department of Education.

French, P., & MacLure, M. (1983). Teachers' questions, pupils answers: An investigation of questions and answers in the infant classroom. In M. Stubbs & H. Hillier (Eds.), *Readings on language, schools and classrooms*. London: Methuen.

Garfinkel, H. (1967). *Studies in ethnomethodology.* Englewood Cliffs, NJ: Prentice-Hall.

Garfinkel, H. (1972). Remarks on ethnomethodology. In J. Gumperz & D. Hymes (Eds.), *Directions in sociolingustics.* New York: Holt, Rinehart, & Winston.

Geertz, C. (1973). *The interpretation of cultures.* New York: Random House.

Gilmore, P. (1987). Sulking, stepping and tracking: The effects of attitude assessment on access to literacy. In D. Bloome (Ed.), *Literacy and schooling.* Norwood, N.J.: Ablex.

Goodenough, W. (1971). *Culture, language, and society.* Reading, MA: Addison-Wesley.

Green, J., & Bloome, D. (1983). Ethnography and reading: Issues, approaches, criteria and findings. *Thirty-second yearbook of the National Reading Conference.* Rochester, NY.

Gumperz, J. (1982). *Discourse strategies.* New York: Cambridge University Press.

Guthrie, L., & Hall, W. (1984). Ethnographic approaches to reading research. In P. Pearson, R. Barr, M. Kamil, & P. Mosenthal (Eds.), *Handbook of reading research.* New York: Longman.

Hargie, O. (1983). The importance of teacher questions in the classroom. In M. Stubbs & H. Hillier (Eds.), *Readings on language, schools and classrooms.* London: Methuen.

Heap, J. (1984). *Understanding "interruptions" in oral reading.* Paper presented at meeting of the American Educational Research Association, New Orleans.

Heath, S. (1982). Questioning at home and at school: A comparative study. In G. Spindler (Ed.), *Doing the ethnography of schooling.* New York: Holt, Rinehart, & Winston.

Heath, S. (1983). *Ways with words: Language, life and work in communities and classrooms.* New York: Cambridge University Press.

Jefferson, G. (1978). Sequential aspects of storytelling in conversation. In J. Schenkein, (Ed.), *Studies in the organization of conversational interaction.* New York: Academic Press.

Jensen, A. (1969). How much can we boost I.Q.? *Harvard Educational Review, 39*(1), 1–123.

Kamin, L. (1974). *The science and politics of IQ.* New York: Wiley.

Labov, W. (1982). Objectivity and commitment in linguistic science: The case of the Black English trial in Ann Arbor. *Language in Society,* 11(2), 165–202.

McDermott, R. (1977). Achieving school failure. In H. Singer & R. Ruddell (Eds.), *Theoretical models and processes of reading.* Newark, DE: International Reading Association.

McDermott, R., & Hood, L. (1982). Institutionalized psychology and the ethnography of schooling. In P. Gilmore & A. Glatthorn (Eds.), *Children in and out of school.* Washington, DC: Center for Applied Linguistics.

Mehan, H. (1979). *Learning lessons.* Cambridge, MA: Harvard University Press.

Merritt, M. (1982). Distributing and directing attention in primary classrooms. In L. Wilkinson (Ed.), *Communicating in classrooms.* New York: Academic Press.

Moynihan, D. (1965). *The Negro family: The case for national action.* Washington, DC: U. S. Department of Labor.

Ogbu, J. (1979). *Minority education and caste.* New York: Academic.

Peterson, P., & Swing, S. (1982). Beyond time on task: Students' reports of their thought processes during classroom instruction. In W. Doyle & T. Good (Eds.), *Focus on teaching.* Chicago: University of Chicago Press.

Piestrup, A. (1973). *Black dialect interference and accommodation of reading instruction in first grade.* Monographs of the language-behavior research laboratory. Berkeley: University of California.

Rosenshine, B. (1976). Classroom instruction. In N. Gage (Ed.), *Psychology of teaching methods.* Chicago: University of Chicago Press.

Rosenshine, B. (1980). How time is spent in elementary classrooms. In C. Denham & A. Lieberman (Eds.), *Time to learn.* Washington, DC: U. S. Department of Education.

Sacks, H. (1972). An initial investigation of the usability of conversational data for doing sociology. In D. Sudnow (Ed.), *Studies in social interaction.* New York: Free Press.

Sacks, H., Schegloff, E., & Jefferson, G. (1974). A simplest systematics for the organization of turn-taking for conversation. *Language, 50,* 696–735.

Schiefflen, B., & Cochran–Smith, M. (1984). Learning to read culturally. In H. Goelmann, A. Oberg, & F. Smith (Eds.), *Awakening to literacy.* Exeter, NH: Heinemann.

Scribner, S., & Cole, M. (1979). *The psychology of literacy.* Cambridge, MA: Harvard University Press.

Simons, H. (1979). Black dialect, reading interference and classroom interaction. In L. Resnick & P. Weaver (Eds.), *Theory and practice of early reading* (Vol. 3). Hillsdale, NJ: Erlbaum.

Smith, D. (1987). Literacy as a social fact. In D. Bloome (Ed.), *Literacy and schooling.* Norwood, NJ: Ablex.

Smitherman, G. (1977). *Talkin and testifying: The language of Black America.* Boston: Houghton–Mifflin.

Szwed, J. (1981). The ethnography of literacy. In M. Whiteman (Ed.), *Variation in writing: Functional and linguistic-cultural differences.* Hillsdale, NJ: Erlbaum.

Tough, J. (1982). Language, poverty and disadvantage in school. In L. Feagans & D. Farran (Eds.), *The language of children reared in poverty.* New York: Academic Press.

Wallat, C., & Green, J. (1979). Social rules and communicative contexts in kindergarten. *Theory into Practice, 18*(4), 275–284.

Weber, M. (1968). *Economy and society.* New York: Budminster Press.

SECTION II
Perspectives on Social Studies

FOUR

Empowering Students: Beyond Defensive Teaching in Social Studies

LINDA M. MCNEIL
Rice University

Locating knowledge across the curriculum must include an analysis of the role of the teacher in making knowledge accessible to students. The teacher's role in mediating the content of the culture for students is complex. At the point where the students' learning, the broader cultural content defined as subject disciplines, and the organization of the school converge, school knowledge (or curriculum) is "located" within the dynamic interaction of which teachers are the center. Where the purposes and values represented by these converging forces are congruent, the teacher's personal contribution to the character of school knowledge may not be visible, or may not be easily discernible from other factors shaping the content of what is being taught. However, when any of those factors are in conflict, or represent differing cultural or organizational or policy values, the teacher's role can be crucial in determining how the values in conflict will be played out in determining what is taught and what is learned.

Because of the organization of American public schools, teachers often find themselves at the center of conflicting structures and policies. American schools tend to be organized so as to process aggregates of students through age-graded courses toward standard certificates or diplomas. The goal of equitable access to public education for all students has led to the establishment of schools which tend to be organized to serve these aggregates of students. The wisdom of teaching, however, is that teaching and learning are highly individual experiences which cannot be mass-produced. As described in McNeil's (1986) book, these twin goals of serving the masses while trying to educate individuals have become institutionalized in the goals and organization of the 20th-century American high school. The administrative structures and policies are too often organized in support of the aggregate goals: the purposes of mass education. As such, they embody the constraints characteristic of large-scale, bureaucratic institutions, including standard rules of behavior, accountability, and uniformity. Originating with the social control goals of the early high school, including Americanization of large numbers of immigrants and credentialing workers for industrial production, these constraints often take the form of controls rather than supports and often subordinate individual initiative to predictability and regularity. The ideal which draws many individuals into teaching, however, is the belief that the ability or desire to teach is more like a gift or calling than a job in a bureaucracy, is more related to nurturing children and enhancing their cultural heritage than to regulating student behavior. Quite often the institution itself provides no opportunity for this tension in goals to be addressed or resolved. The institutional silence regarding such a conflict is left to the teacher to address when it becomes inevitable in making choices of what to teach, how to provide learning experiences, how to value students' studying and learning.

One response teachers have made to administrators' inordinate attention to behavior controls and credentialing, as reported in previous ethnographic studies of classrooms (McNeil, 1984), has been to teach defensively.[1] Apologizing for assignments and watering down content, teachers in several midwestern schools separated their personal, complex knowledge of course topics from the oversimplified content of course lectures in order to meet student resistance to demanding assignments. Teachers used specific instructional techniques to transform historical, political and economic content into "school knowledge," reducible to efficient and easy-to-grade fragments of fact. The school knowledge was not indicative of teachers' store of knowledge (as shown in extensive teacher interviews) about the subjects they were teaching. The ironic effects on the students was that even though they did comply cooperatively with assignments, not resisting lectures or written work, they did keep believing the simplified course content. Like their teachers, they came to view "school knowledge" as instrumental to schooling (learned for tests,

---

[1] This research, "The Institutional Context Controlling Classroom Knowledge," was funded by a grant from the National Institute of Education, U. S. Department of Education, and conducted under the auspices of the Wisconsin Center for Public Policy, with Linda McNeil, principal investigator and project director. Details of this research methodology and analysis are reported in *Contradictions of Control*, a report to NIE (1983) and *Contradictions of Control: School Structure and School Knowledge* (New York and London: Methuen/Routledge & Kegan Paul, 1986).

for example) but not credible to appropriate into their own personal knowledge. The tendency to trivialize and "manage" complex social studies curricula in an attempt to achieve classroom control built walls between official social studies knowledge and students' personal knowledge and conceptions about how to learn.

Curriculum theory has tended to interpret such teaching as the almost inevitable product of schools which primarily serve the socialization and economic production goals of a capitalistic society (Apple, 1982; Bourdieu & Passeron, 1977; Bowles & Gintis, 1976). From the viewpoint of a societal purpose for schooling, the economic mandates for credentialing and sorting of workers built an artificial stratification of knowledge within schools and artifical fragmentation of knowledge between schooling and the common-sense culture, especially when that culture was different from the elite cultural values held by those who determined public educational policies. That school knowledge should seem alien to personal knowledge, then, was not a new idea to this ethnographic research. What was new was that the teachers were not unaware that their treatment of knowledge content in the classroom seemed divorced from their own personal store of knowledge; they were not the unconscious tools of bureaucratic schooling.

In fact, when interviewed, these teachers provided explanations for their tendencies to make course content fit school processes rather than their personal enthusiasms. They gave as their rationale their need to work within the controlling bureaucratic structures. Because so much of their rationale for their instructional strategies derived from their perceptions of the administrative structure, a second major ethnographic research project was designed to examine course content, and social studies teachers' mediation of it, in schools where the administrative context emphasized academic, educational purposes rather than merely school goals of keeping students processed through graduation requirements, of keeping the school "smooth running" (McNeil, 1984). Magnet, or specialized desegregation, high schools were set up so that teachers were hired and programs designed for academic quality which would draw students of all races from their home schools in a large urban district to the integrated education provided by the magnet schools.[2] A desegregation plan developed under force of court order buttressed local

[2] Funded by a grant from the National Institute of Education, "Structuring Excellence: The Potential for Constructive District-Level Intervention," is a two-and-a-half year study of students' access to knowledge in magnet high schools in a large urban district: Linda M. McNeil, project director.

administrative initiatives to support the building of programs around educational purposes rather than the ordinary processing of students through standard requirements for graduation. With administrative backing in the hiring of teachers, oversight of program development, provision for resources and involvement in recruiting of students, these teachers would be working under conditions which affirmed their educational goals. Such teachers, it was expected, were more likely to teach in ways that involved the students and brought their personal and professional knowledge of their subject into the classroom. Extensive ethnographic research, including classroom observation, participant interviews, and analysis of administrative policy, was designed to determine whether in fact these teachers felt administrative goals to be in conflict with their educational purposes, and if not, whether the supportive administrative structure helped overcome teachers' tendencies to create their own authority and efficiencies by controlling students through the control of classroom knowledge.

DEFENSIVE TEACHING: CASE STUDY OF MIDWESTERN HIGH SCHOOLS

Before analyzing the teaching strategies of the magnet teachers to determine how they engaged students through their mediation of course content, a review of the techniques of defensive teaching by which previously studied teachers controlled the content of their courses, is in order. The teachers observed were mostly middle-aged, white teachers (all but one were male) in midwestern high schools where communities support education with high taxes, discipline problems are few, teachers belong to unions, buildings are safe, and most students go on to 2- and 4-year colleges (see McNeil, 1986, for more details on the communities and individual teachers). Many of the teachers had master's degrees in their fields; several were very active in professional organizations or community boards. None of the schools had serious problems, and three of the four had reputations as good schools.

There was nothing in the characteristics of the schools that gave a hint of the way the social studies teachers observed would teach their classes. After a decade of inquiry-based social studies curricula and teaching methods available in methods journals and teacher education programs, the expectation of wide variation in instructional methods and purposes seemed justified as assumptions underlying the classroom research. Instead, just as documented in national studies such as *A Place Called School* (Goodlad, 1983), the instruction across the different schools and classrooms conveyed a sense of sameness of teacher-centered lessons, bored students, and often simplified content. Contributing to the appearance of general sameness were very specific teaching techniques by which teachers, aware that they were doing so, kept course content and interaction on a controlled level that maintained their authority over content and minimized "inefficient" student exchanges.

Fragmentation

The teachers reflected that the information they provided to their students had to fulfill two goals: to convey information about American history and economics to their students (and they almost all saw this as the teacher's role rather than as a process that involved student inquiry or participation in gathering information) and to impose firm limits on the complexity and topicality of class discussions and on the efficacy of presentation (McNeil, 1986, p. 166).

The simplest and most prevalent teaching technique which filled this dual purpose was *fragmentation.* When teachers considered the content of the lesson to be essential to students' learning and when information was likely to be included in tests, it was most likely to be presented in the form of fragments of information: lists of dates, place names, laws, events, vocabulary, and other brief pieces of information. Such presentation gave the teacher the benefit of covering a great amount of material in a short amount of time and prevented the necessity of explaining complicated relationships, controversies, or values. A primary example is labor history. This conflict-laden area of the nation's history was, in several classrooms, reduced to lists of early labor unions and their leaders, the "weapons" of labor against management (strike, boycott, etc.), or of management against labor (e.g., lockout, injunction, etc.). Without going into the working conditions, economic trends, or such issues as displacements by technology or immigrants, teachers could feel they had covered labor history in their chronology of American history. Rarely were the components of the lists capsulations of extended narrative descriptions, discussion of issues, or summaries of out-of-class readings. They stood alone as the sole treatment of the topic.

The fragmentation of content gave students the benefit of certainty; they knew what they would be tested on and what was considered important for them to know. Teachers explained that one purpose for using lists and other abbreviated forms of content was to close off controversial discussion which, as in the 1960s protest era, might lead to student cynicism and rejection of consensus ("official") interpretations. Ironically, their resulting lack of in-depth consideration generated in itself student cynicism. Many students were curious about the topics and occasionally had information which differed from that of the teachers. Without a chance to discuss these differences, the students felt great distance from the course content and saw it only as valuable to learn for the test. In interviews, students across all ability levels voiced concern that this content was not credible, was not becoming a part of their personal knowledge. It remained "school knowledge," and they would wait until later to learn "what you really need to know." Out of school, they might learn; in school, they were consumers of teacher-supplied knowledge.

Mystification

When teachers mystified a topic, they underscored its importance but presented it in a way that made it unknowable. Topics which could not be readily reduced to items in a list but which were on course outlines or otherwise necessary to be "covered" included major institutions (e.g., Federal Reserve, Supreme Court), complicated processes (e.g., foreign exchange, capitalism), and abstract concepts (e.g., free enterprise and progress). These were typically mentioned with a kind of reverence but left on the level of slogans. Students were to internalize the importance, or in some cases, the inherent values, behind the terms, were to write them into their notes, but were to understand that they did not have to attempt to understand in any detail what the term implied. Often the implication was that only experts could know. In some cases, it was clear that the teacher did not fully understand the topic. Other topics would be explained by the teacher rather clearly in an interview, but treated much more simply and vaguely in class, showing a wall between the teacher's personal knowledge and what he or she might feel appropriate for classroom treatment.

Students did often internalize the emotional content of the term (as with free enterprise and capitalism, especially), but would feel themselves powerless to know about the topic themselves. They were learning that on some issues they should remain dependent on other's information rather than attempt to find out for themselves. This dependence puts them in the role of clients, dependent on the bureaucratic rewards for compliance but not participants (in this case, engaged learners) in the process of production.

Omission

Whereas mystification gave the benefit of seeming to cover important topics while avoiding the burden of preparing adequate lessons on them (or losing face when students realized teachers did not understand them either), and avoiding the unexpected in student discussion, some topics which called for equally inefficient treatment could be avoided all together. By omitting complicated and especially current material, teachers retained their role as knowledge authority in the classroom, a role several of these teachers had found threatened by student dissent in the Vietnam era. By holding to a consensus view of history, teachers could avoid recent events by saying that "historians do not all agree on that yet." Anything not held by consensus was not appropriate for class treatment. Controversy, which challenged both authority and efficiency, could be avoided if the topics themselves were left out of the curriculum.

Not all teachers omitted controversial topics. At the school where teachers felt most supported by the administration to pursue academic goals, teachers had fewer walls between their personal/professional stores of knowledge and their classroom knowledge. They often showed tapes of news analysis from television, invited speakers to school, and discussed current events. Yet even these teachers bracketed certain topics as "emotional," not "factual," and not admissible to class discussion (e.g., opposition to nuclear energy). The benefits of omission accrued mainly to the teachers in helping produce efficiencies; they did not help teachers avoid student cynicism and independent thought. Omission was one teaching strategy of which students were aware enough to voice unhappiness with it in interviews. Their curiosity about current happenings made them wish that their social studies courses, especially those labeled Contemporary U. S. History, would help them understand current, controversial events.

Some of these events included those in which controversial individuals played a key role. For example, students had heard their parents and other adults debating the merits of the Nixon presidency, the (mostly negative) political and moral issues of Watergate, and the much more nebulous but equally debatable foreign policy decisions made by Nixon and Henry Kissinger. Many students were genuinely open to information on these topics, even those who felt fairly opinionated after years of hearing family or newscast discussions. However, they were not open to the silence to which their teachers treated the Nixon administrations. And several students expressed a combination of sadness and anger that the teachers' own chronological course outline, which brought the class to the topic of the Nixon presidency, somehow permitted the teacher to condense the treatment of the topic to a few key phrases on the outline (e.g., the names of Nixon's vice-presidents, and the opening of diplomatic relations with the People's Republic of China), dismissing the rest of the issues with "Nixon was our president so recently that historians don't yet agree on. . . ."

Other omissions students expressly noticed and resented were those most closely related to them (inflation), to the standing of the U. S. relative to other countries ("they always say the U. S. is the best but we never really hear much about the other countries and what they are like; how can we know?"), and to ongoing controversy (such as the merits of the U. S. involvement in Southeast Asia during the years these students had been young children).

Defensive Simplification

While fragmentation, mystification, and omission are all teaching techniques which simplify content, defensive simplification is distinguished by the openness with which teachers back off complicated, in-depth instruction in order to gain at least minimal compliance from the students. Although teacher-training literature is full of theories and strategies about motivating students, the teachers observed had other ways of dealing with the student apathy and resistance that they knew to be likely when a demanding topic or assignment would be announced. They would announce the topic, then apologize for its difficulty and promise that it would not demand too much work. Real treatment of topics such as political parties, early industrialization, and immigration laws would demand a great deal of teacher preparation, informative resources (available in the school or developed by the teacher), perhaps multiple teaching strategies to assure that students of many ability levels comprehended the issues involved, and would provide opportunities for students to become engaged in the consideration of the topic.

Rather than make this effort, especially in the face of students who were apathetic, working at minimal levels just to meet graduation or passing requirements, teachers would often give a very brief sketch of the topic, give students a one-page handout to read in class, show a filmstrip, or choose some other presentation which seemed to deal with the topic but which did not demand effort form students appropriate to their really learning the subject. The need to teach and at the same time to avoid student resistance made teachers achieve balance between the two by the ritual of seeming to teach the topic:

> The teacher makes a few remarks, the students groan, the activity (lecture, filmstrip, or whatever) proceeds and is briefly concluded; the teacher asks if there are any questions and there are none. (McNeil, 1986, p. 176)

Teachers and students meet in a path of least resistance; the students have few demands made on them in exchange for their cooperation with class procedures and teacher-supplied course content.

IRONIES OF DEFENSIVE TEACHING

Not all teachers teach defensively. The case studies which brought to light this model of instruction have shown that when teachers do not feel supported in their academic efforts by administrative priorities or student response, they often use teaching techniques which subordinate their own personal and professional knowledge of their subject to defensive, apologetic presentations which trivialize course content and cause students to disengage from significant interaction with the content of the course. In trying to strengthen their authority over course content and control students, teachers ironically weaken their authority by appearing to possess only surface subject knowledge, or by limiting treatment of the topic to its simplest, least interesting forms. These teaching techniques cut across expected differences of teachers' educational level, political philosophy, age, or expressed teaching philosophy. In addition to undermining their authority as subject matter experts, such teachers threaten the credibility of their course content. More serious, they teach students that their proper role is as client, trading bits of knowledge for such institutional rewards as required credits, or as consumer, recipients of teacher-supplied or institution-supplied knowledge, rather than as producer of knowledge or citizen-user of the ideas and information they learn in school.

Over time, the cycle of lowering expectations set up by defensive teaching produces minimal teaching which ritualizes teaching instruction, waters down content, disengages students, and makes administrators think that they need to focus even more attention on controlling apathetic or uninvolved students. The teachers react to these administrative priorities and attention to procedure with increased controls, decreases in significant instruction and even more distance between the students and the instructional process.

Such reform reports as *A Nation at Risk* (National Commission on Education, 1983), "Recommendations" (Select Committee on Education, 1984), and *A Place Called School* (Goodlad, 1983) suggest that many of our teachers are not competent. They suggest that teachers are not well trained or educated, that they do not know their subjects, and that they do not demand enough from their students. Most of these reports suggest that we need more professional teaching staffs, but they offer few remedies beyond more external controls, such as testing present and prospective teachers, or tying teacher paychecks to student performance on standardized tests.

But the first wave reports, such as *A Nation at Risk,* and many of the state-legislated reforms, and the second wave, with reports such as the one by the Carnegie Forum (1986) and others, aimed at teacher professionalism, miss the dynamics which produce much of our dull, watered-down instruction. They miss the institutional context within which teachers work, and they miss those effects on students which are not captured by standardized tests and which in fact may be contradicted in students' test scores. When we consider first the instructional context, we note that these teachers observed as teaching defensively were not untrained; they would have had high scores on any teacher-competency test or subject matter or pedagogy. Their teaching strategies, which arose from their accommodation to institutional pressures, were to keep the school smooth running, build curricula around procedures (instead of the reverse), avoid disruptions, and meet minimum standards academically while using teacher free time for paperwork duties or patrols. These defensive patterns of instruction were not often substitutes for lack of subject matter knowledge. They represent not a lack of skills brought to the teaching situation, but a kind of de-skilling of the teacher, a splitting of the professional knowledge and skills from the immediate tasks of teaching because the institutional demands pressure teachers to bracket their professional expertise and give priority to keeping things efficient.[3] De-skilling of teachers is often thought of as imposed, as with

---

[3] This mode of teaching has its roots in the social efficiency era of American public schooling in the 1910s and 1920s, and in the organization forms inherited from that period. Its reinforcement has been linked to the growing role of schools as credentialing agents. The accountability models being proposed as new in the 1980s are new only to those who have not studied their earlier attempt to rationalize curriculum along the input-output models borrowed from economics. See Raymond Callahan's *Education and the Cult of Efficiency* (Chicago: University of Chicago Press, 1967).

the so-called teacher-proof curricula designed to overcome expected inadequacies in elementary teachers' backgrounds. The de-skilling of these secondary teachers is more participatory, as they subordinate their expertise in course content to meeting minimal standards of efficiency in their schools.

The students, whose inexperience makes them too unskilled to be accurately described as deskilled, still experience a de-skilling of the *role* of the student as that role encompasses becoming equipped with skills and knowledge requisite to active, significant learning. Under defensive teaching, students meet minimum expectations with minimum effort. The watered-down content is so divorced from the real world that it becomes suspect to them. They say they learn it for tests but do not learn it to make it their own. This has serious implications for evaluation; many of these students scored well on teacher-made and standardized tests; their rejection of course content did not necessarily translate into low grades. Nor did low-scoring students always fail to understand the lesson; sometimes they failed to see the worth in learning it. Or they remembered tested facts but could not join them into a set of coherent ideas. Just as defensive teaching cut across expected differences among teachers, disengagement among students cut across differences in student ability, gender, and attitude.

By transforming the potentially rich content of economic, biographical, political, and social history to "school knowledge," the teachers transformed in turn the role of teacher and student. The teacher role did not take full advantage of the teachers' personal knowledge, and the students distanced themselves from the official school knowledge in return, placing a wall between what you really need to know" and "what you learn in school." By seeing the processing of school knowledge as fitting institutional requirements rather than as making knowledge and ways of knowing accessible to students, teachers inadvertently fostered not only their own alienation but that of the students. They abdicated their own power as valued sources of knowledge and failed to empower their students within the context of school learning.

EMPOWERING STUDENTS: CASE STUDY DATA FROM MAGNET SCHOOLS

For the role of the teacher in mediating school knowledge to overcome the tendency to place institional efficiencies above authentic engagement with course content, that teaching must engage the teachers' and students' personal knowledge without artificial separation from school knowledge. The goal must be to make school knowledge somehow consonant with what Dewey (1958) termed "significant learning experiences," learning that leads to more learning. This can be done by an individual teacher who makes the effort against the expectations of minimal effort, but it is more likely to be done, as the two sets of case studies show, when the tension between the goals of controlling and credentialing students and that of educating them is resolved at the institutional level in favor of education.

What would engaging, nondefensive teaching be like? While there are many successful teachers who engage students in active learning, their methods cannot all be catalogued here. To develop a picture of engaged, skilled teaching strategies, it is useful to compare them with defensive teaching strategies (see Table 1). The purpose is not to create a taxonomy of engaged teaching, but to illustrate the fact that defensive teaching strategies are reversible, not inevitable. A critical aspect of engaged teaching strategies is that they are found in magnet high schools. These teachers have been hired to work in programs where the content areas (e.g., medical professions, engineering, the arts, etc.) are sufficiently attractive to warrant students' long, voluntary bus rides to integrate the schools. Advertised as "the best education money can't buy," the purposes of these schools is not only to fulfill racial quotas but also to provide Black, Anglo, and Hispanic students with academic backgrounds which will enable them to attend college, and often, receive scholarships to major in these specialized areas.

Administrative support for the magnets includes the pressure of a court order approving the establishment of these schools, and considerable use of central office staff to recruit and place teachers and students, to gather resources and arrange student transportation. Many of these programs, whether existing as separate campuses or housed as "schools within schools," benefit from personnel, equipment, or funds donated by private sector industries and individuals; some have advisory boards of professionals in related fields. At best, they represent serious efforts to combine district- and building-level administrative support for academic quality.

Within this context, where the goal of educating students was viewed as primary, teachers were less likely to teach defensively. As well trained as their counterparts cited in the earlier study (McNeil, 1984), they were all more willing to bring their personal store of knowledge into the classroom and to teach in ways that engaged students. Such teaching rarely carried the immediate efficiencies typical of defensive teaching and avoided the alienating effects which caused students to hold school-supplied knowledge suspect.

Integrating Knowledge

Presentations of knowledge in fragments and lists gives students a sense of what is important to study for tests, but provides little sense of how the fragments of fact are related. The lack of coherence means not only that students are often unable to understand the relationship among the isolated facts of a lesson, but that the fragmented information has less credibility for students than information supplied in more integrated (but not necessarily more accurate) form by their peers, parents, television, or employers. When historical information is encountered by students in context, and when they are involved in integrating the separate pieces of information, they are more likely to learn the facts, understand the overall issue and feel competent in raising questions about those parts they do not understand.

Table 1.   Models of Teaching as Locating Knowledge

	Defensive Teaching	**Empowering Teaching**
Teacher	De-skilled, personal knowledge separated from classroom knowledge	Professionalized, personal knowledge evident in course content and ways of knowing
Student	Passive role as client or consumer	Active role as participant, learner
Course Content	*Fragmented,* reductive information, often shaped by evaluation methods and "outcomes"	*Integrated,* coherent contextualized information
	Mystification of complex topics; reliance on experts to "know"	*De-mystification* through exploration of multiple explanations, active participation in interpreting, solving
	Omission of controversy and complexity; distancing of students from topics	*Inclusion* of issues, conflicts, ambiguities, current topics, personal curiosities
Teaching Style	*Defensive simplification,* apologetic, undemanding presentations	*Teaching* with authority, teacher as model of learning

A case in point is labor history. As presented defensively in fragments and lists, labor history was not a topic which the students interviewed could explain or comment on. More importantly, when asked about other economic that bore on labor directly, students rarely recognized that their lessons on labor history were interrelated (e.g., questions about whether they had ever studied about an industry, about the way work is performed, about corporations). Labor history, a contested and colorful part of our cultural heritage, had been reduced to social studies, facts to learn for a multiple-choice test.

In contrast, in the magnet school for gifted and talented students, the teacher of American history taught labor history as issues rather than facts. She gave a lecture on the background of the times, then made assignments that brought students into the search for facts, for significant persons and laws, and pivotal events, and for the values involved in the conflicts between labor and management in 19th-century American industrialism. Library research was not an academic exercise but a prelude to a trial for selected robber barons. Several students served as judge and counsels as workers, industrial accident victims, creditors, and other plaintiffs brought suit against the robber barons for their labor policies (low wages, "goons" that attacked labor organizers, lack of disability compensation, unsafe working conditions, etc.). The industrialists brought character witnesses (corrupt politicians, among others), bankers, and economic analysts as well as their own testimony to verify the creation of jobs, products, productivity, and economic growth in the development of the young nation. More than a role-playing exercise in costume, the trial was a culmination of the extensive individual and group research into the characters and issues. Each person taking the witness stand had to convey by his or her testimony the facts of that person's relation to the overall picture of growing industrialism, the values represented by that person's presence in the trial, and the spirit of that individual's role in this segment of history.

The trial, which lasted several days, involved noise (much audience response to clever costumes and inventive testimony), inefficiency (clumsy bags of costumes stashed around the room, bags of notes and library books, delays in starting the trial as witnesses and defendants dressed), and unpredictable information. A teacher concerned about right answers easily translatable into objective tests might have preferred to supply the important information, and then let student discuss or role play. This teacher took the risk of letting students not only research their character but work as teams of plaintiffs or defendants to clarify and build their cases. Within their teams, and between the opposing sides, students became very dependent on information supplied by other students. The teacher did clarify or add information after each day's trial, but she also noted that witnesses corrected information from other witnesses; the audience reacted when facts were misstated. Students were very aware that they were responsible for conveying significant knowledge on this topic to each other. It is clear that as the trial progressed, students grasped many complexities about the interdependence of economic factors, about the centrality of conflict to our labor history, and to the reason our society has no clear and easy consensus on this period of history.

In the lectures and discussions which followed (on regulatory law, re-organization of labor unions and later New Deal policies), students would refer in class discussions in questions to this trial and to the issues raised in it. Clearly, this enactment was a serious learning experience. It might be explained away by the fact that the students in this magnet program were very bright, some gifted, an easy group to whom the teacher could give significant responsibilities. However, even though her assignment was clearly in the spirit of the pedagogy of this school (to involve students in learning), it ran counter to her resources, the students' time pressures, and the school district's press for teachers to cover extensive chronology in U. S. history. This school's library was so inadequate that, except for news magazines, most of the students said they never went into the library. The teacher's classroom resources included a few of her own copies of reference books but nothing adequate for a project of this size. With the students' 30–90-minute bus rides each way and lack of in-school resources, such a project is not lightly assigned. This teacher felt that such teaching should be for all students, not just the gifted; she chose, as did many magnet teachers, to teach in a magnet school because such teaching was more valued in the magnets than in regular schools.

Demystification

Mystification of course content involved presenting a topic as important to know about but unknowable. The complexity of mystified topics either demanded additional teacher explanations or required multiple presentation forms to make them intelligible to students of varying abilities and backgrounds. Their very complexity led to the implication that students should trust experts ("the system works") rather than attempt to learn about the topic themselves. Avoiding mystification involved more than clarifying complexity by presenting a set of facts in a list, which still kept the topic removed from the students' own knowledge. What teachers needed to do was find ways to deal with complex topics that engaged students in unlocking the complexity. When a "right" answer does not exist, at least teachers can lead exercises in raising the right questions and in exploring perspectives and lines of inquiry that motivate students to seek further information. A history teacher who was successful in involving many students in the complex topic of amnesty and work permits for immigrants succeeded because she provided both a supportive environment for an immigrant student to discuss his views of the pending federal immigration law and the resources necessary for the class to read the terms of the law and opinions held on its legality and ethics by a number of elected and appointed public figures. A critical moment occurred in class after an immigrant student made an impassioned explanation opposing his carrying an identification card, while others in the class (of Black and Anglo background rather than Hispanic and Asian) would not. A student called out, "But you are legal." The reply stunned the class: "But my parents are not." An academic issue, usually considered as a "vocabulary word" on a current events test, or in a simple pro-and-con debate, became anything but academic. Suddenly, giving real consideration to the converging issues in this one piece of legislation seemed urgent. This teacher not only recognized this as a "teaching moment" and allowed the class to continue to explore the topic, but she also provided the intellectual and personal atmosphere in which her students were not content to leave potentially mystified topics to the experts.

The stock market is another candidate for mystification. Students need to know that our economy relies heavily on privately and publicly owned corporations for production. Yet few high school students can be expected to discern the complex workings of the stock market, much less the internal workings of a corporation. So, many teachers reduce the characteristics of a corporation to a list (which usually compares corporation elements with those of a single proprietorship, partnership, and conglomerate), and mystify the stock market with a few vague comments and little detail. Students need to know that they should trust the stock market to function, and they know they can learn about it later but not at school.

Two magnet teachers approached the topic with the goals of making the stock market a part of students' personal knowledge of the economy. They wanted to link macro (or systemic) economic processes with the micro (or personal) economic issues such as investments, labor, price, cost, and management. The first teacher concentrated on an individual corporation. His lesson included research (on a corporation, its history and its present status), record keeping (of the 15 days' stock prices), calculations (charting price fluctuations and averages, calculating profits and losses), and interpretation (writing a report on the wisdom of having chosen this stock to follow, supported by documentation in charts and related figures). Roughly following a schema that would move students from factual information to interpretative and analytical treatment, and then to application of information and interpretations, the teacher required students to know facts, to analyze them in light of factors contributing to their being facts, and then to use their information to make decisions. By comparing their hypothetical investment with those of classmates, students also served as genuine sources of information rather than as gatherers of their own information or passive recipients of teacher-supplied content. This activity occurred in a magnet school which has a skeletal social studies library; many students did not subscribe to newspapers at home.

There was another imperative at work in addition to the teachers' own view of students as active learners. In this particular magnet, for health professions, there is little distance between the scientific/medical knowledge presented in classrooms and the application of that knowledge as students move into clinical and laboratory rotations in area hospitals. For these students, who readily see the school-supplied science and lab curricula as credible, social studies knowledge must have equally narrow distance from the students' real worlds if it is to be credible. Students are less accustomed, after a year or two at this school, to acquiring school knowledge primarily for preparing for school tests.

Another magnet teacher took an even more active view of teaching students to understand stock markets. His school did not have a career focus, but did draw very bright students who were able to handle complex information. His approach to the economy of stock investment was to have students create a corporation, develop a real product (such as first aid kits for use in autos), sell shares of stock, elect officers and run the corporation to produce and market the product. Their grade depended on their profits and losses. The most recent class made over a 300% return on their investment by their careful study of market analysis, product quality, and effective sales. Because the magnets tended to have fewer extracurricular activities (prevented in part by time taken up by bussing), the project was significant in giving students responsibilities in decision making and in working cooperatively.

Neither of these activities taught students everything an educated person should know about corporations and stock markets. Each could have been trivialized into a cute exercise without the research and analytical components. As the projects were developed, each helped students toward greater confidence in acquiring and evaluating information, in taking responsibility to raise critical questions, and in unpacking a complex topic. The teacher was not the sole authority and the projects were not easily evaluated by simple factual tests. Their cost in teacher efficiency and knowledge control was offset for these teachers in their benefits to the students as they learned to bring many resources to the understanding of complex questions.

Omission/Inclusion

Teachers who feel pressured to retain tight control over their students tend to omit controversial, current, or complicated material. Controversial topics can lead to unanticipated discussions, unresolved issues (thus, no "right" answer), or to challenges to the teachers' information. The magnet social studies teachers have a much broader definition of admissible topics than do the teachers mentioned in the earlier study. The magnet teachers saw themselves as still learning; they did not see current events as topics to be avoided for lack of consensus either within the class or among experts.

Elections are a good example of the difference between defensive and engaged presentation. In previously observed schools, teachers who taught defensively expected students to learn the names of major candidates in national elections for the time periods studied. Candidates' platforms or issues were presented in list form; elections in progress were usually avoided to omit controversy. A typical class period might follow this pattern: The teacher would ask, "Who ran for president in 1932? Who was his running mate? Who was the Democratic candidate? Who was the Republican candidate?" Silence would greet these questions. The teacher would provide some clues to the time period: "What year did the stock market crash?" Then, usually, the teacher would fill in the names and the issues on each party's platform. If the election was noted for some special landmark ("first Catholic president"), then that was added to the list of names and phrases on the board. One teacher followed the ritual of every election recitation with the question: "What did this president want from Congress?" then, "What did he get?" The dynamics of elective politics and the three branches of government, much less the societal context of that government, were lost to the students.

During the semester of observation at the magnet school for gifted and talented students, a national election was made a primary vehicle for teaching several major concepts in history and government. These included the study of interest group politics (and the accompanying issues of racism, integration, immigration, social class, and gender stratification, and geographic differences), the role of the electorate, analysis of media, analysis of specific issues, and practice in public opinion polling. The election was so central to the course that I asked the teacher how he taught the course in off years. He answered that "there is always an election," and that the class would study local and state elections in years that had no national elections because the course topics were much less remote when they were related to a real contest. In addition to background lectures by the teacher, the students had to do a great deal of research on their own, alone and in teams, depending upon the topic. They worked in groups to develop position papers, then held debates, simulating the League of Women Voters' presidential debates. More politically partisan than students in any other school, these students brought their own political preferences into the classroom but were assigned to research and present counter positions as well. In one set of issues debates, the "candidate" was backed by a team that helped prepare his or her positions; the team had to field a Republican candidate in the presidential debate and a Democratic one in the vice-presidential one, and vice versa. In this case research as well as natural preference guided their preparation.

For the final class activity, students were sent out in teams to do exit polling. Their results were called into the school where other students fed the results into their class computer program; their goal was to project the winners before they were correctly predicted by a local television newscast. The project involved complicated design of the computer program, study of the city's neighborhoods and sampling techniques, and willingness to meet and talk with all kinds of people. The racially integrated classes were very open in dealing with the racial component of voting; their education in racial politics was definitely not a matter of school knowledge. They went into all kinds of neighborhoods; quite by accident two Black girls were assigned to a precinct in a neighborhood known as the center of John Birch Society and Ku Klux Klan activity. Their presence as exit pollers turned out to be an education for voters in that area, as it was for the girls themselves and for their teachers and classmates as they discussed their experience in class the following day. These students learned about elections in a way that they remember and can explain in terms of voting age, franchise, historical barriers to voting, interest groups, platforms, and media coverage because they have encountered them directly. They viewed the teacher and class-room and, more importantly, each other as credible sources of significant learning.

OVERCOMING DEFENSIVENESS

The magnet teachers felt that they have the subject matter and classroom authority to make demanding assignments of their students. They occasionally simplified a topic to gain student compliance, but only rarely. Because their students have chosen the magnet program, the teachers experience fewer problems with student apathy or possible resistance. When they simplify content, or rush through lists of facts, it is often on material that is in their view less important (but included in the official curriculum guide) than content they wish to treat in greater detail and with greater student involvement. There is little apology that accompanies the simplification; the broader goal is to treat some topics in depth and in ways that integrate varied approaches and interpretations in order *to give students models of learning.*

This kind of teaching cannot hide behind the caveat, "there's not much we can do here." It acknowledges to students that the teacher has some responsibilities, whatever the school setting, to educate. One English teacher in a magnet school whose students do not have to take competitive entrance exams to gain admission, nevertheless expects those students to learn significant literature in her class and to learn to interpret literature, just as in their science and magnet specialty classes they are required to make judgments on the basis of complicated material. Her seniors were divided into groups to read such classics as *Portrait of an Artist as a Young Man* by James Joyce and Dostoyevski's *Crime and Punishment.* Each group has written and discussion assignments built on their reading. However, the culminating activity makes each group the teaching resource for the entire class. Each group must research and enact a scene from the play which reveals not only the major characters and theme (and conflicts and setting) of the novel, but something of the author's biography and the novel's significance to literature in general. In a school with few extracurricular activities, the enactments provide an opportunity not only for public speaking and staging, but also for organizing and linking intellectual activity to practical situations. The teacher provides the requirements and the collegial atmosphere; he or she lays the groundwork through months of literary analysis, writing and discussion. Then, acting only as a resource consultant, the teacher takes the risk of having the groups "teach" each other. Her hope is that identifying their friends' efforts with the titles will ultimately lead them to read all the these works on their own.

Such magnet teachers do not teach in ideal schools; in fact, two of these teachers joked about their faculty "happy hour": meeting at 7:30 a.m. at the photocopy store on their way to work to prepare materials for a school that provides neither a copy machine nor reimbursements for copies teachers make outside. What differentiates the magnet teachers from those in the defensive teaching study is that these magnet teachers are not resisting administrative restrictions on their teaching by tightening controls on their students. Such controls are actually increasing at the administrative level in their schools as state-legislated reforms and district-level policies are requiring greater and greater conformity with outcome measures and proficiency-based content which threaten to trivialize content selections and methods of evaluations. These teachers, even in the face of such "reforms," hold a model of teaching that assumes that students must participate, that teachers' personal knowledge is a part of their professional store of knowledge and that both are integrally related to the knowledge they bring to the classroom. They are not threatened by students who go beyond the textbook, who bring up facts not previously known to the teacher (no negative "class participation" grade for this behavior as was the case in some previously observed classes), and who ask other students as well as the teacher their questions.

It has been heartening to spend 2 years in classrooms watching teachers affirm students' ability to participate in learning, watching students see school knowledge as credible and worth their effort. These teachers, working in schools with inadequate libraries and uneven classroom resources and students of all races have resisted the tendency to participate in their own de-skilling by trivializing course content, bracketing their personal knowledge and distancing their students from school knowledge. In a day when teachers are being criticized as incompetent, lazy, and uneducated, these individuals demonstrate that engaging student learning is still possible. Their teaching, and indeed the system of magnet schools, is based in part on a set of assumptions about the role of learners, the possibilities within students, and the relevance of school learning— the equipping of students with active, participatory learning skills, rather than with passive habits that make them clients and consumers of school practice.

BACK TO DEFENSIVE TEACHING?

While these assumptions sound like boring, familiar truisms common to our curriculum guides, they are in fact being seriously challenged by a wave of school reforms. The dull instruction of our mediocre schools is grounds for reform. But the reforms such mediocrity is generating unfortunately tend to be aimed at making the rituals of teaching and learning more measurable, more "scientific," a more rational and accountable version of their duller aspects. They do not seriously challenge the assumptions and dynamics that made the mediocre teaching so prevalent. What is wrong with teaching is that it so often transforms rich cultural content into school knowledge or pieces of information that can be easily assessed through worksheets, multiple-choice tests, and fill-in-the-blanks exercises. The accompanying skills have become the skills needed to do well in school, to make good scores in processing these fragmented pieces of information.

The new component of the 1980s reforms is the force of state policy behind them, and in some districts, the linkage between teacher pay and student performance on standardized tests. Defensive teaching, as documented in my earlier research (McNeil, 1984), was an individual accommodation to institutional reward structures that fostered minimum standards. It had the chance of being overcome by the removal of one of the inciting factors: administrative preoccupation with controls to the de-emphasis of educational purposes, or student disengagement or resistance.

The magnet schools demonstrated the potential for engaged instruction when in fact those two factors cited above are not only absent but replaced with strong administrative policy actions, such as hiring teachers committed to the academic program, giving teachers a chance to develop the curricula, and student commitment to the magnet specialty of their choice.

There are many teachers who engage students in significant learning; in this district, many of them tended to be in magnet schools, the schools where they could legitmately place their students' needs and their professional knowledge ahead of state-adopted texts. Some of these teachers say that their personal philosophy is that all students should be taught this way; however, in the district and in the state, engaging students goes against the expectations of standard results. Engaging teaching looks beyond the schools' transformation of knowledge to the needs of assessment instruments and toward the students' needs to make connections with a complex world. For this to occur, teachers need to resist being deskilled and need to restructure learning experiences which will empower students to learn along with the teacher.

As state-mandated, centralized reforms move teachers in this district beyond their personal philosophies for engaged teaching, and threaten the culture of the magnet faculty which supports such teaching, the observed magnet teachers face very difficult choices. They can teach to standardized, proficiency based outcomes, following required chapters in sequence and losing their students (and their own motivation), or they can resist these patterns of de-skilling, fearful that their students may learn well but not test well on district- and state-mandated test. Or they can leave the profession (McNeil, 1987). As controls tighten, always in the name of reform, these teachers are seriously considering exiting teaching rather than being deskilled. They have said of their magnet schools, "if you can't teach here, you can't teach." As their paychecks become tied to student performance on tests of trivial content, content with little coherence and little relation to teachers' or students' thought, the best of these teachers find less and less flexibility for teaching in ways that empower students beyond short-term outcomes. If such de-skilling reforms do not seriously damage our schools, it may be because such teachers sustain a vision and resist the dilution of their profession with the same imagination they have used so far in the magnets to make school knowledge credible and authentically educational.

REFERENCES

Apple, M.W. (1982). *Education and power.* Boston: Routledge & Kegan Paul.

Bourdieu, P., & Passeron, J.C. (1977). *Reproduction: In education, society and culture.* London: Sage.

Bowles, S., & Gintis, H. (1976). *Schooling in capitalist America.* New York: Basic Books.

Callahan, R. (1967). *Education and the cult of efficiency.* Chicago: University of Chicago Press.

Carnegie Task Force on Teaching as a Profession. (1986). *A nation prepared: Teachers for the 21st century.* Washington, DC: Carnegie Forum on Education and the Economy.

Dewey, J. (1958). The child and the curriculum. In R. Archambault (Ed.), *Selected works of John Dewey.* New York: Holt, Rinehart & Winston.

Goodlad, J. (1983). *A place called school.* New York: McGraw Hill.

McNeil, L.M. (1984). Defensive teaching and classroom control. In M.W. Apple & L. Weis (Eds.), *Ideology and practice in education.* Philadelphia: Temple University Press.

McNeil, L.M. (1986). *Contradictions of control: School structure and school knowledge.* New York and London: Routledge & Kegan Paul.

McNeil, L.M. (1987). Exit, voice and community: Magnet teachers' responses to standardized reform. *Educational Policy, 1*(1).

National Commission on Excellence in Education. (1983). *A nation at risk.* Washington, DC: Government Printing Office.

Select Committee on Education. (1984). *Recommendations,* Austin, TX.

CHAPTER FIVE

The Social Nature of Social Studies

CATHERINE CORNBLETH
State University of New York at Buffalo

Schooling and social studies education are primarily social activities. They are socially constructed, transacted, and sustained. To emphasize their social nature is to highlight interrelated historical, cultural, political, and economic dimensions of schooling and social studies education in contrast to technical, rational, or psychological ones. Most people, educators and laypersons alike, tend to view social studies education and school learning from a technical perspective. Our conceptions and practice of curriculum and teaching are most often technical. So too are conventional modes of education research. The pervasiveness of technical rationality[1] in modern consciousness generally (Berger, Berger, & Kellner, 1973) and U. S. society in particular, increases the need for explicit attention to the social dimensions of schooling, including and perhaps especially of social studies education.

The problem with technical rationality in this context is not only its limits and resulting distortions but, more importantly, its taken-for-grantedness, that is, the rarely questioned assumption that "that's the way things are." Yet, the way things are depends to a considerable extent on one's perspective or paradigm. By paradigm, I mean a world-view or framework of knowledge and belief through which

---

[1] By technical rationality, I refer to a mode of thinking or approaching tasks that places a premium on efficiency and is characterized by analytic reduction, linearity, and preoccupation with procedure. Phenomena are assumed to be composed of discrete elements that can be identified, separated, treated one at a time, and reassembled without damage to the whole. Further, it is assumed that there is an order to things that is sequential and often hierarchical. That sequence is usually taken to be linear and one-dimensional. Thus, reasoning, curriculum construction, and learning to teach are assumed to be processes composed of separable parts arranged in sequential order as steps to follow. Following predetermined correct procedures is given priority over the substance of the task or the character of the outcome.

we "see" and investigate the world. Paradigms refer to working assumptions about the world and how it is to be studied, understood, and acted upon, that is, interrelated concepts and values, questions, procedures, and actions. Commitment to a particular paradigm involves affiliation with a community whose members mutually share, sustain, and shape the paradigm. How we see, think about, study, and act on matters of social studies education profoundly affects the learning made available to students (see Cornbleth, 1985a).

A paradigm is like a window to the world. It enables us to see what is "out there." But, just as windows have frames that limit one's view, so too do paradigms. Their conceptual, normative, and procedural frames limit what can be seen and how it is to be interpreted. While a technical or empirical-analytic paradigm fosters pursuit of "what" questions or questions of efficiency, it does not encourage pursuit of "how" questions of explanation or understanding. Nor does it encourage questioning the language, assumptions, or purposes of schooling and social studies education or exploring structural alternatives. The latter are concerns of paradigms variously characterized as symbolic, interpretive, or social, and as critical (see, e.g., Popkewitz, 1986).

My interest is in the social formation and functions of school knowledge and knowledge about schooling. The more specific purpose here is to explore the meanings and implications of the social nature of social studies education, particularly for curriculum design and studies, for classroom research, and for critique. In so doing, I draw on recent conceptual and empirical literature in the fields of curriculum and social theory as well as classroom research. After sketching a conception of curriculum as socially constructed curriculum-in-use, providing illustrations, and showing its construction from classroom studies, I consider implications for studying and understanding what happens in social studies classrooms. Finally, I suggest the need for a critical social perspective that extends beyond the particulars of a given situation.

CURRICULUM-IN-USE[2]

To propose that schooling and social studies education, including curriculum and its construction, are social activities is to view people in schools as jointly creating and acting on shared meanings or

---

[2] This section draws freely on a earlier paper, "Reconsidering Social Studies Curriculum," (Cornbleth, 1985b).

definitions of their situations as they interact over time in a particular setting (see, e.g., Waller, 1932; Woods, 1978). Such a social perspective rejects deterministic (structural and naturalistic) notions of human thought and action, instead viewing teachers, students, and others as creators as well as consumers, transmitters, and, perhaps, victims of their environments. Further, it gives attention to the mutual influences not only among school phenomena but also among schools, encompassing social structures, and history.

From this perspective, curriculum construction is an ongoing social activity, shaped by various contextual influences within and beyond the classroom and accomplished interactively by teachers and students. Curriculum thus consists of the actual, day-to-day classroom interactions of students, teacher, ideas, and materials. *The curriculum is the curriculum-in-use.*

In contrast is the technical rationality underlying the prevailing conception of curriculum as document or plan and of curriculum construction as an objective, technical project separate from both policy making and implementation. Here, curriculum is a tangible product such as a syllabus or a package of materials accompanied by directions for classroom use. Curriculum construction is largely a technical development task consisting of a set of procedures to be followed: specify objectives to be obtained by students; select or create content, activities, and materials; devise means of assessing student attainment of objectives; provide directions for intended use. Development is typically undertaken by specialists outside the schools or by teacher committees guided by specialists. The curriculum product thus produced is then disseminated for implementation by teachers. Change is seen as a function of the curriculum product; to change the nature and effects of social studies education, one changes the curriculum product.

Within the dominant perspective where curriculum is viewed as a product and curriculum construction as a technical project, the focus is on what students are to learn (e.g., information, skills, attitudes, values) and how well (i.e., easily, rapidly, accurately) they learn it. While substantial questions have been raised about the viability of the technical curriculum perspective (Cornbleth, 1985b), the more serious concern is that a procedural approach to curriculum tends to obscure critical questions including the nature of knowledge and how it can and should be made available to students, how the social structure and relations of schooling affect attempts to educate, and how a particular selection, organization, and distribution of knowledge benefits some groups and not others (see Cornbleth, 1984; Goodman, 1984; Popkewitz, 1982b).

In effect, technical rationality offers a curious form of problem solving wherein problems and solutions are predetermined. The problem is usually taken to be that too few students are learning whatever is considered desirable for them to learn (e.g., map reading skills, economic principles). The solution is to change the curriculum by including or emphasizing whatever it is that students are to learn. Technical rationality simply specifies the procedures by which this solution is to be obtained. Major curriculum decisions have been abdicated to others (Kliebard, 1979; Reid, 1978).

Particularly when the public intention and justification of social studies education is to foster democratic belief and equitable social practice, consideration of questions such as those raised above ought not to be ignored. By neglecting questions of interest and value as well as the conservative values implicit in a technical project view of curriculum and its construction, technical rationality tends to perpetuate illusions of neutrality and benevolence.

In the alternative, social process view, the focus is on what learning opportunities are actually made available to students, how those opportunities are created, and what values they reflect and sustain. Curriculum as product is seen as one aspect of the context that shapes curriculum-in-use.

A social process view does not separate curriculum policy making, construction, and implementation as a linear sequence of discrete events. Instead, it assumes dynamic interaction among policy, planning, enactment, and their structural sociocultural context. In other words, curriculum is constructed and reconstructed in practice. Whereas a technical perspective views curriculum as instrumental to practice, a social perspective sees curriculum as existing in practice, not independent of it. Further, a technical project view tends to be prescriptive of classroom practice while the social process view is descriptive and interpretive. Curriculum as product is intended to guide and thereby change and improve practice; curriculum as process is intended to explain and thereby enhance awareness and understanding of practice. To the extent that studies of curriculum-in-use increase awareness of conditions that appear to impede or facilitate curriculum reconstruction to foster desired values, they may support reform efforts. From a social perspective, curriculum causality and change are complex and problematic. Causality and change (or stability) are seen to involve the interplay of biographical (personal and professional), sociocultural, and institutional elements as well as curriculum products. Curriculum construction and reconstruction both reflect and respond to the larger contexts of school environment, community milieu, prevailing ideologies, and history (see Popkewitz, 1981; Popkewitz, Tabachnick, & Wehlage, 1982). These features of a social perspective are well illustrated in recent social studies classroom research.

SOCIAL STUDIES CURRICULUM-IN-USE

Studies of curriculum-in-use focus on classroom practice and how it is created and sustained. Curriculum-in-use encompasses both subject matter and social organization, the latter including teacher and student roles (and attendant rights and obligations) and patterns of interaction. Social organization provides a setting for academic activities that can extend or constrain students' learning opportunities. Recitation activities, for example, reflect the super- and subordinate roles of teachers and students, respectively, and the limited communication patterns found in many classrooms. Learning opportunities are constrained by the recitation format insofar as students are discouraged from offering comments, raising questions, or pursuing ideas. Not only does social organization have academic effects and academic activity have social consequences, but the ongoing construction of curriculum-in-use communicates normative messages including meanings of authority, responsibility, knowledge, work, and success (Cornbleth & Korth, 1984).

In a study of English, science, and social studies teachers and their classes in a suburban middle school, Cornbleth, Korth, and Dorow (1983) sought to understand how teachers and students created the curriculum at the beginning of the school year. During the previous school year, we had observed classes and talked with teachers at the school in an effort to understand what learning opportunities and instruction were made available to students (Korth & Cornbleth, 1982). Interested in how the curriculum we observed came into being, we returned on the first day of school the following year to investigate how teachers and students created their curriculum-in-use.

Typically, classroom curriculum research is initiated during the school year. Such research provides access to curriculum-in-progress but does not reveal what occurred previously that likely influenced and might explain what is subsequently found. We assumed that how students, teachers, and other school personnel begin the school year establishes a framework for what follows, including what students have an opportunity to learn and how they are enabled to learn it. While there are continuities from year to year—in facilities, policies and procedures, course requirements, staff and students, and community expectations—and what has been described as a "recurring rhythm" (Smith & Geoffrey, 1968, p. 21), schools do not simply reopen in early autumn and carry on from the previous spring. In a sense, schools and curriculum are re-created at the beginning of each school year.

We found that the teachers' major goal during the first days of school seemed to be to create a personal image and classroom atmosphere, as if setting the stage for a play that they would be starring in and directing. Although the means they employed and the images they created varied considerably, there were significant commonalities in the messages communicated, for example: teachers should be obeyed, and students would benefit from accepting and meeting teacher standards. The teachers appeared to us to be acting in what they saw as their students' best interests. They presented themselves as knowledgeable helpers and expected their students to trust them.

The roles and patterns of interaction that emerged were clearly teacher-dominated. Students seemed to anticipate and accept that establishment of classroom social organizational ground rules would be initiated and controlled by teachers. Most students did not appear either surprised or resentful; from their facial expressions in class, some seemed a bit amused at times. Students accepted their teachers' claim to set the rules and wanted to know the ground rules (cf. Edelsky, Draper, & Smith, 1983). While not denying teacher authority, students did engage in minor rule violations (e.g., talking without permission, not turning in homework on time) as if to test the limits of teacher tolerance, and they took advantage of breaks such as transitions between activities to move around and talk quietly with one another. For the most part, students appeared content to find some "wiggle room" and did not directly challenge teacher-defined boundaries of appropriate behavior. Instances of student noncompliance provided temporary diversions that served to ameliorate but not to alter their classroom situation.

While the teachers were assertive in creating a classroom social organization, they seemed to be easing students into academic activities. For the most part, teachers' academic demands during the first weeks of school were minimal. The implication was that if students made an effort, they would get passing grades; school was to be taken seriously, but not everyone was expected to do well academically. Overall, efforts to create classroom social organizational ground rules, usually in the form of behavioral or procedural regulations, were quite explicit during the first weeks as were the rules themselves. In contrast, academic expectations remained less clear, at least less clearly academic in any conventional sense.

Consistent with the nondemanding nature of the academic tasks, the pace of activities in the science and social studies classes was slow, particularly during the first week. Seatwork-worksheet activities, for example, were often teacher-directed in a step-by-step manner with comments such as "don't write in the answer until I tell you," "one part at a time," and "just hold up for a second." The English classes, in contrast, moved at a brisker pace, perhaps because many of the activities involved review of previously studied subject matter (e.g., grammar, dictionary use).

None of the teachers relied on or even followed a single textbook. Multiple materials, including teacher-made materials, were frequently used. The curriculum-in-use in these classrooms appeared to be shaped less by courses of study or textbooks than by institutionally sanctioned teacher beliefs and teacher–student interactions.

"Basic" skills and information were emphasized in all the classes (e.g., vocabulary in science and social studies, spelling and grammar in English). Study skills such as outlining and map and graph reading also had high priority. Skills, however, were often addressed in isolation from subject matter. For example, students in a seventh-grade social studies (geography) class read and constructed bar, line, circle, and pictographs. On set of graphs in their workbook showed the average annual income of Black and white families in the U.S., 1964–76, clearly illustrating the increasing gap between them. In a review activity, workbook questions about the graphs were asked and answered without any mention of the substance and meaning of the information presented. Also, while comprehension (as distinguished from information acquisition and reproduction) tasks were not uncommon in these classes, only one instance of student involvement in reasoning or problem solving was observed. Here too, skills were separated from subject matter, with students working on puzzles unrelated to the physical science that they had been studying.

The separation of skills and subject matter trivialized and reified both. Typically, subject matter was treated as an archive of bits of predetermined information to be acquired while skills were to be applied mechanistically to obtain right answers. The possibility that skills might be used to question information presented by authorities such as textbooks or to create knowledge was not entertained.

The teachers' emphasis on order and personal control, on students following rules and directions, resulted in clearly differentiated super- and subordinate teacher and student roles. Emerging patterns of activities were highly structured by the teachers. Much of the time was spent in a form of recitation (teacher questions, student answers, and teacher elaborations) and teacher-directed individual seatwork, both intended to foster the acquisition, recall, and application of factual information. While an orderly flow of teacher-directed activities seems to have had several benefits (e.g., a high proportion of class time was spent in academic activity, teachers could and did assist individual students while other were "working"), learning opportunities were constrained, and student initiative was usually tolerated but not encouraged. The priority teachers gave to establishing an orderly flow of activities and maintaining their authority in the classroom social order appears to have precluded open-ended activities involving divergent thinking and reasoning about academic matters and the expression of student ideas and beliefs except during assigned creative writing periods in English.

Congruence between academic expectations and social organization in these classes was high. The social ground rules provided an environment conducive to "doing the work." Classroom academic and social rules were supported and encouraged by the school administration and documents such as staff and student handbooks. In describing what they expected students to learn, the principals used the phrase "academic responsibility," by which they meant following the rules and doing the work. Apparent consensus regarding school goals and practices served to realize and maintain them.

Among the normative messages that might be communicated by the observed curriculum-in-use are that students' thoughts and feelings are unimportant, that patience and passive compliance are rewarded while initiative and originality are not, and that learning (or work) occurs primarily in situations structured and directed by others. Meanings given to authority, work, and success further illustrate the nature of the curriculum created in these classrooms. Authority was claimed by the teachers largely on the basis of personal expertise and assertion. It was implicitly and broadly defined as the right to decide, supervise, and evaluate classroom activity. Teacher demands, moderated by humor, justification, and expression of concern for students, appeared to be accepted as reasonable by most students. Authority was a characteristic or right of those teachers who had worked hard and earned it, which was inaccessible to students. Here, as in Dreeben's (1970) analysis of school experience and authority, students had ample opportunity to learn how to cope with and make the best of subordinate positions in authority relationships, but they had little opportunity to assume authority and responsibility for themselves.

Regarding work, it was not uncommon for teachers to compare students with employees. "I'll treat you as if this were your job and I'm your employer," one teacher told his students on the first day of school. Much of the work that students were to accomplish was mechanistic in form and substance—more like that of factory or clerical personnel than of managers, professionals, or artists. Students were expected to do the work but not to participate in its planning or evaluation; they had little voice in deciding what they would do, how they would do it, or the basis on which it would be evaluated. Also, while schoolwork was to be taken seriously, it was not presented as enjoyable or satisfying in itself, but as a means to future, usually material rewards. Generally, it was presented as instrumental to survival in a routinized and sometimes hostile adult world. Norms of orderliness, timeliness, and effort also were justified in terms of preparation for adult work (cf. LeCompte, 1978). It seems that the activities, interactions, and sentiments that constitute schoolwork and, by implication, foreshadow adult work, come to be taken for granted and accepted not only as the way things are but also as how they should be (cf. Popkewitz & Wehlage, 1977). Like the meaning given to authority, the teachers' interpretation of work appeared unnecessarily and undesirably narrow. Rather than expanding students' options, teachers seemed to be circumscribing them.

The operative definition of success at the middle school reflected the meanings given to authority and work. School success was defined primarily in terms of points earned for grades and promotion to the next grade level. School success, in turn, would lead to adult success on the job and material comfort. The prevailing message was that quality of school life and life after school depends on the quantity of things possessed (e.g., points, automobiles) and that survival and success defined in these terms are achieved by fitting in and making the best of one's situation, not by trying to change it. Although not necessarily contrary to students' present and future interests, the messages about authority, work, and success are clearly conservative. In a sense, we were witness to the middle class schooling itself.

Other studies of elementary and secondary social studies classrooms (e.g., McCutcheon, 1981; McNeil 1981; Stake & Easley, 1978; White, 1980, 1986) also reveal the interrelation of classroom social organization, academic activity, and treatment of subject matter. These studies vividly illustrate how teachers' management and socialization concerns play a major role in shaping the curriculum-in-use. For example, in the social studies classes at Willow Elementary School studied by White (1980), the selection and treatment of subject matter were subordinate to teacher concerns with establishing and maintaining the classroom social order and with modeling and rewarding good habits and politeness. Consistent with the value placed on courteous behavior, Willow teachers presented other peoples and cultures positively and minimized cultural differences. Consequently, subject matter was often superficial and occasionally grossly distorted, as when a kindergarten teacher exhorted students to look at the "lovely, nice tomahawk" (p. 23) and a second-grade teacher accepted nonauthentic souvenirs that students brought to class as accurate representations of Indian culture. Most of the conflicts between social order and subject matter were resolved at the expense of the latter.

In 11th-grade contemporary U.S. history classes, McNeil (1981) found less concern with politeness than with control. She observed that course content was "tightly controlled" by teachers and treated as "lists of facts, brief descriptions, chronologies" (p. 317). Teachers avoided recent events and controversy, further limiting the scope and depth of the subject matter and its treatment in these classes. The teachers felt a strong need to maintain classroom control and were concerned that the introduction of diverse historical interpretations or the examination of current issues would provoke classroom disruptions as had occurred a decade earlier in the school. Despite privately expressed personal reservations regarding the efficacy and equity of U. S. political and economic institutions, the teachers wanted students to come to appreciate these institutions, not to question them or become cynical. Interestingly, conversations with students revealed that their apparent acquiescence to the emasculated history they were offered was often little more than strategic public compliance to obtain good grades accompanied by private rejection of most of what they were taught.

These studies of curriculum-in-use illustrate (a) the interrelation of subject matter and social organization, (b) social organization as a setting for academic activities that often constrains students' learning opportunities, and (c) the predominance of teacher concerns with classroom management and student socialization. They also indicate the key role of the classroom teacher in the process of curriculum construction and suggest how teachers create and mediate curriculum. Teachers seem to be more powerful determinants of students' actual classroom experiences than are curriculum documents and materials. Yet, while teachers tend to reject the passive-compliant role accorded them by a technical view of curriculum construction, they are not autonomous actors. It seems clear that curriculum-in-use is shaped by its milieu as well as by its participants and that changing the curriculum-in-use would be a complex undertaking.

Changing Social Studies Curriculum-in-Use

Features of technical project and social process views of curriculum and its construction can be further illustrated with reference to a specific social studies curriculum change effort, the Pittsburgh Critical Thinking Project (PCTP). The PCTP was a three-year (1982–1985) externally funded project to foster students' critical thinking through reading, discussion, and essay writing in social studies classes in the city's public schools. Three features distinguishing the PCTP from most other school district curriculum change efforts were (a) the initial emphasis on testing for desired student outcomes, not constructing a new curriculum document or directing altering classroom practice, (b) the joint creation of all PCTP materials, including the critical-thinking tests, by the project staff (of university faculty and school district administrators) and a steering committee of 25–30 elementary, middle, and high school social studies teachers and supervisors, and (c) the support of a field study during the second and third years to examine the meanings given to critical thinking in classroom practice and to provide feedback to project staff and participating teachers.

While there is a coherent theoretical base to the conception of critical thinking and the kind of essay testing that evolved (see Cornbleth, 1985c; Moss & Petrosky, 1983), the PCTP as a whole is best described as theoretically eclectic. The school district superintendent's belief in testing as the primary tool for changing teaching and learning framed the project. Testing was seen as providing feedback and impetus to changing curriculum-in-use, the assumption being that classroom practice will change (and teachers will be more receptive to change) as "need" is seen in relation to student performance. Thus, in order to alter classroom practice and enhance students' critical thinking and writing, objectives were stated, and tests were created, administered, and scored. Only later were instructional support materials created and in-service workshops provided. No explicit conception of curriculum was offered or followed as a basis for project decisions or actions.

In the PCTP orientation booklet for teachers new to the project, critical thinking is described as a dynamic process of questioning and reasoning, of raising and pursuing questions about our own and others' claims and conclusions, definitions and evidence, beliefs and actions. The sample critical-thinking essay test in another PCTP booklet for teachers presents an excerpt from Thomas Paine's *Common Sense* and asks students to:

Imagine you are a colonist reading the following article by Thomas Paine. Think about whether or not his arguments have convinced you to support the fight for independence from Britain. Be prepared to explain and support your decision.

Students are further directed that their compositions should include:

A topic statement telling whether or not you would support the fight for independence;

Evidence from the passage to support your topic statement;

Explanations of why these points would or would not convince you; and

A concluding statement that sums up your position.

To date, there is no social studies/critical-thinking curriculum document. The social studies courses of study for each grade level remain as they were when the PCTP began although revision is anticipated in the near future to incorporate critical thinking objectives, materials, and activities. If this revision occurs, it will serve to institutionalize what has already occurred more than to initiate change. In this important respect, the PCTP did not follow a technical project approach to curriculum. Nor did it separate planning from implementation to the extent found in most curriculum projects. Yet, in some respects, the PCTP was technical in nature and execution. For example, the materials created by the project staff and steering committee are expected to be used by the more than 500 other teachers in the district who teach social studies in grades 3–11. More importantly, the creation and refinement of the critical-thinking objectives and essay tests, which have been mandated by the school district administration, reflect a technical approach to product development. There is a curious similarity here with the recent calls for school reform in the U.S. that emphasize higher standards and frequent testing but say little about the substance and process of teaching and learning.

Aspects of a social process view are evident in the PCTP field study, which involved classroom observations, teacher interviews, and document review. The focus of the field study was on the meanings given to critical thinking in classroom practice, not on implementation of a predetermined critical-thinking model (in fact, no such model was provided). The field study enabled the project staff to begin to understand how teachers were interpreting critical thinking and the conditions of schooling that seemed to facilitate or impede critical thinking and teaching (Cornbleth, 1985c).[3] To the extent that there was a PCTP conception of curriculum, at least among the project staff it seemed to be an implicit social process view of curriculum-in-use. Tensions between the technical (testing) and social process (classroom practice) aspects of the PCTP were evident throughout the second and third years, particularly in competition for attention and resources; until the end of the third year, test development took precedence. While technical concerns seem to have predominated, social process considerations were not totally neglected. The social studies curriculum in the Pittsburgh Public Schools can be seen as still in the process of reconstruction. The extent to which and how classroom practice and student learning outcomes have been changed and improved to foster critical thinking as a result of the PCTP remains an open question.

STUDYING SOCIAL STUDIES[4]

A social perspective has implications for research in social studies education as well as curriculum conceptions and practice. Here, my focus is on classroom studies that attempt to describe, understand, and perhaps explain "what's happening" in social studies classes. My interest is less with the particular procedures employed than with the underlying assumptions and with the values and purposes of classroom research.

Most classroom research in social studies and other school subjects has been asocial or technical in character. Its purpose has been to determine the efficiency, effectiveness, or effects of one or more treatments such as teaching strategies, means of classroom organization and management, and curriculum materials. Little or no attention has been paid to the nature, meanings, or influence of classroom context, process, or participant conceptions that would enhance understanding and enable explanation of observed "effects." Even asocial research, however, is a social activity, carried on within

---

[3] Space limitations preclude presenting the findings and interpretation of this field study here. It can be noted, however, that (a) the meanings teachers gave to critical thinking in their conversations and classroom practice differed considerably from the official project conception and expectations, and (b) the teachers' interpretations "made sense" in relation to their pre-existing beliefs and practices, classroom conditions, and the school district's goals and operating policies (i.e., their social context).

[4] This section builds on ideas elaborated in "On the Social Study of Social Studies" (Cornbleth, 1982b).

the interactive context of a particular community and quite sensitive to participant conceptions of what constitutes acceptable research.

It is my contention that meaningful classroom research is social study in which phenomena of interest are contextualized, treated as dynamic and interactive, and considered in relation to participant interpretations (Cornbleth, 1982b). There are numerous ways of defining and partitioning context, the appropriateness of which depend on the purpose and focus of study, that is, context of what?[5] Physical and temporal contexts are often distinguished from social context although physical settings are socially constructed, and time and history are socially interpreted. Physical context might be examined in terms of availability, arrangement, access, use, purpose, and meanings as well as characteristics such as the variety and technology of classroom space, facilities, and materials. For example, King's (1982) study not only describes the availability, arrangement, and access to play materials in kindergarten classrooms but also vividly illustrates their use, meanings, and social functions.

Temporal context refers not only to the number of minutes allocated or actually used for social studies, or whether it is morning or afternoon (or Monday or Thursday), but also to the sequence and pacing of events within and across activities. Classrooms also exist in the context of particular historical periods (e.g., Cold War, nuclear era, electronic age), which are likely to influence what is taught and learned. Social studies seems particularly susceptible to history in this respect as illustrated in McNeil's (1981) study of high school U. S. history classes. Classrooms also have their own histories; what happens at one point in times sets a precedent for and affects subsequent events as suggested by Cornbleth et al.'s (1983) study of curriculum construction at the beginning of the year in a middle school.

Social context includes nested layers: interpersonal, including dyadic, group; institutional, including school, school district, state legislature and department of education; community, including parent and local interest organizations; and societal, including national values and political movements. Interpersonal context, for example, frames individual behavior. Even at the dyadic level, behavior is not simply a function of individual attributes such as age, gender, ethnicity, I. Q., or reading level, but also of the situation in time, place, and culture. Goffman (1964) has well detailed the "neglected situation," arguing that interpersonal interactions, such as those between a teacher and one or more students, constitute social situations with distinguishing

---

[5] See, for example, Cornbleth and Adams (1987) on the contexts of teacher education policy change.

cultural characteristics and structures. They are more than sequences of observable behavior. "Cultural rules establish how individuals are to conduct themselves . . . and these rules for comingling . . . socially organize the behavior of those in the situation" (Goffman, 1964, p. 135). In other words, interpersonal interactions are social contexts that shape participants' behavior; understanding observed interpersonal behavior requires identification of the operative cultural rules. And, these rules are generated in part by the participants. At the interpersonal level, "social contexts consist of mutually shared and ratified definitions of situation" (Erickson & Shultz, 1981, p. 148) as well as the actions that participants take on the basis of their definitions (see Stebbins, 1975; Waller, 1932).

Classroom activities might be fruitfully viewed as interpersonal or social settings that provide varying opportunity for both academic and social learning (Korth & Cornbleth, 1982) as illustrated in the previously presented studies of curriculum-in-use. Another illustration is Smith's (1980) experimental study of student conceptions, on-task behavior, and achievement in different concept discussion contexts in 11th- and 12th-grade social studies classes. His findings that student commitment to discussion and attentiveness varied with the discussion context suggest that future research might give more attention to the underlying structures of classroom activities.

· Contextualization of social studies classroom research goes beyond detailing samples and settings to consider what difference context seems to make. Classroom research is decontextualized and asocial when the phenomena of interest are examined in isolation as if they were independent of time, place, and social location (see Mills, 1959). To ignore the multiple contexts of schooling and social studies education is to obscure or misrepresent their social origins and nature. Social activities, including schooling, are "context dependent and can only be understood within their contexts" (Mishler, 1979, p. 2).

The interactive and participant conceptions dimensions of social classroom research are integral to the conceptualization of context just presented. Interactive study attends to interactions among classroom participants, phenomena, and their contexts. For example, students and teachers interact with curriculum materials and with one another; together, these interactions shape the use of curriculum materials, how students and teachers relate to one another, and what students learn (see Cornbleth, 1982a). Social study minimizes the artificial fragmentation and separation of elements that distort understanding of classroom conditions, events, and impact. Interactive studies also tend to be dynamic, portraying the flow of interaction and change over time, including trends and patterns, rather than providing a snapshot at one point in time or a composite that averages observations across occasions.

Participant conceptions include their purposes and interpretations, that is, their definitions of the classroom situation and their goals in the situation. How participants "see" their situation influences their actions, which, in turn, serve to modify or sustain both the situation and their definition of it. Goldenson's (1978) study of the effects of an experimental civil liberties unit on senior high school students' attitudes provides one illustration. He found that attitude change was mediated by students' perceptions of teacher credibility; positive attitude change was greater when students perceived the teacher as fair, knowledgeable, concerned, interesting, and understandable. Another illustration is provided by Boag and Massey's (1981) study of how the perspectives of elementary teachers mediated a social studies curriculum change effort.

The importance of incorporating participant conceptions into classroom research is based on the assumption that behavior is purposeful and that outsiders cannot adequately interpret the actions of insiders without access and sensitivity to their meanings and purposes as well as to the contexts and interactive course of observed activity. Teachers and students do what they do because they see their actions as serving desired ends. Their activity might seem absurd (or worse) to the observer unacquainted with their conceptions of the situation in question. Illustrations are provided by the PCTP field study of the meanings given to critical thinking in social studies (Cornbleth, 1985c) and a study of teacher perspectives on responsibility (Cornbleth & Korth, 1984).

Attention to participant conceptions and the context of their construction would enhance understanding and explanation of classroom process and possibilities for change. Social study incorporates the contexts of meanings within which participants act and considers their conceptions and actions in their larger social contexts:

> It allow[s] one to understand how people's conceptions shape their behaviour, and how such conceptions and behaviour change over time in an evolving process of interaction . . . the dialectical process of how people create the very social structures that in turn shape them. (West, 1975, p. 36)

TOWARD A CRITICAL SOCIAL PERSPECTIVE

Although a social process view of curriculum extends the technical project approach, there are undesirable limits to construing curriculum and its construction as curriculum-in-use. A social perspective offers a fuller and more dynamic view of curriculum, but tends to accept curriculum-in-use as is; it does not necessitate confronting assumptions, implications, and possibilities of practice or considering what may yet be. Further, critical questions are likely to be neglected in both technical and social curriculum perspectives. Neither, for example, requires that philosophical, social, and political questions regarding what is taught, how, or to whom be explicitly addressed (see Cornbleth, 1985b). The same concerns arise with a social compared with an asocial, technical, or empirical-analytic perspective in classroom research (see Cornbleth, 1986). In other words, while a social perspective is preferable to a technical one for the reasons already elaborated, it is not sufficient. What is needed, I believe, is a critical dimension, that is, a critical social perspective.

Some social studies of curriculum-in-use do address questions of opportunity, equity, and social justice in ways that indicate an interest in reform that would extend the range and accessibility of these values. Both technical and social perspectives and research, however tend to be ahistorical and conservative of the status quo. In arguing the self-serving, ritualistic nature of technical curriculum reform activity, Popkewitz (1982a) observes that the acceptance of technical language "has important implications for the development of consciousness about the purposes, practices, and outcomes of schooling. This language filters out critical thought about the underlying values of school work by focusing upon the surface qualities of the procedures" (pp. 20–21). The same can be said of a social perspective, which enables us to filter out critical thought by focussing upon social interaction and celebrating practice.

If commitment to democratic social education is to be more than cosmetic, there is a need to reconceptualize relationships among curriculum product, process, and context in ways that integrate curriculum policy, planning, and enactment (Reid, 1975) and that confront rather than obscure questions of value and interest. A viable, enlightening social studies education for all students requires dynamic, multidimensional conceptions of curriculum-in-use and classroom research. Instead of separate or competing perspectives, technical and social features might be brought into a critical framework.

The fragmentation and technification of curriculum and research language and activity that I criticize can be seen as part of a broader trend toward occupational specialization and professionalization. The price of this technification has been too high in education and other fields. In curriculum, for example, it includes the arbitrary division of curriculum labor and distortion of curriculum segments considered in isolation, evasion of responsibility for curriculum experience and effects, limited understanding of curriculum past and present, and unnecessarily narrow visions for the future. In other fields, efforts to reverse the trend toward overspecialization and technification have already begun. Witness, for example, the modification of assembly line production procedures and the emergence of "holistic medicine." If we began to reject fragmentation and technification by reconstructing our conceptions and practice of social studies curriculum and classroom research to integrate technical, social, and critical dimensions: (a) curriculum and research, informed by practice and attention to questions of value and interest, could become more responsible and responsive to democratic ideals; (b) curriculum construction, seen as extending into the classroom and involving the interplay of product, process, and context, could better contribute to fostering desired student learning; and (c) greater awareness of crucial curriculum questions and how they have been answered, sometimes by default, could prompt substantive reform of curriculum-in-use.

REFERENCES

Berger, P., Berger, B., & Kellner, H. (1973). *The homeless mind: Modernization and consciousness.* New York: Vintage.

Boag, N., & Massey, D. (1981). Teacher perspectives on program change. *Theory & Research in Social Education, 9*(3), 37–59.

Cornbleth, C. (1982a). Old versus new curriculum materials use in science and social studies. *Curriculum Perspectives, 2*(2), 25–33.

Cornbleth, C. (1982b). On the social study of social studies. *Theory & Research in Social Education, 10*(4), 1–16.

Cornbleth, C. (1984). Beyond hidden curriculum? *Journal of Curriculum Studies, 16*(1), 29–36.

Cornbleth, C. (1985a). Social studies curriculum construction and reconstruction. *Social Education, 49*(6), 554–560.

Cornbleth, C. (1985b). Reconsidering social studies curriculum. *Theory & Research In Social Education, 13*(2), 31–45.

Cornbleth, C. 1985c). *Socioecology of critical thinking.* Paper presented at the annual meeting of the American Educational Research Association, Chicago.

Cornbleth, C. (1986). Social studies research reconsidered. In C. Cornbleth (Ed.), *Invitation to research in social education.* Washington, DC: National Council for the Social Studies.

Cornbleth, C., & Adams, D. (1987). The drunkard's streetlamp: Contexts of policy change in teacher education. In Higher Education Group (Ed.),

Government and higher education: The legitimacy of intervention (pp. 314–344). Toronto: Ontario Institute for Studies in Education.

Cornbleth, C., & Korth, W. (1984). Doing the work: Teacher perspectives and meanings of responsibility. Educational Forum, 48(4), 413–422.

Cornbleth, C., Korth, W., & Dorow, E.B. (1983). Creating the curriculum: Beginning the year at a middle school. Paper presented at the annual meeting of the American Educational Research Association, Montreal.

Dreeben, R. (1970). Schooling and authority: Comments on the unstudied curriculum. In N.V. Overly (Ed.), The unstudied curriculum: Its impact on children. Washington, DC: Association for Supervision and Curriculum Development.

Edelsky, C., Draper, K., & Smith, K. (1983). Hookin' 'em in at the start of school in a "whole language" classroom. Anthropology & Education Quarterly, 14(4), 257–281.

Erickson, F., & Shultz, J. (1981). When is a context? Some issues and methods in the analysis of social competence. In J.L. Green & C. Wallat (Eds.), Ethnography and language in school settings. Norwood, NJ: Ablex.

Goffman, E. (1964). The neglected situation. American Anthropologist, 66, 133–136.

Goldenson, D.R. (1978). An alternative view about the role of the secondary school in political socialization: A field-experimental study of the development of civil liberties attitudes. Theory & Research in Social Education, 6(1), 44–72.

Goodman, J. (1984). Social studies curriculum design: A critical approach. Paper presented at the annual meeting of the College and University Faculty Assembly, National Council for the Social Studies, Washington, DC.

King, N.R. (1982). School uses of materials traditionally associated with children's play. Theory & Research in Social Education, 10(3), 17–27.

Kliebard, H.M. (1979). Systematic curriculum development, 1890–1959. In J. Schaffarzick & G. Sykes (Eds.), Value conflicts and curriculum issues. Berkeley, CA: McCutchan.

Korth, W., & Cornbleth, C. (1982). Classroom activities as settings for cognitive learning opportunities and instruction. Paper presented at the annual meeting of the American Educational Research Association, New York City.

LeCompte, M. (1978). Learning to work: The hidden curriculum of the classroom. Anthropology & Education Quarterly, 9(1), 22–37.

McCutcheon, G. (1981). Elementary school teachers' planning for social studies and other subjects. Theory & Research in Social Education, 9(1), 45–66.

McNeil, L.M. (1981). Negotiating classroom knowledge: Beyond achievement and socialization. Journal of Curriculum Studies, 13(4), 313–328.

Mills, C.W. (1959). The sociological imagination. New York: Oxford University Press.

Mishler, E.G. (1979). Meaning in context: Is there any other kind? Harvard Educational Review, 49, 1–19.

Moss, P.A., & Petrosky, A.R. (1983). *A proposal for measuring critical thinking.* Pittsburgh: MAP Critical Thinking Project, Pittsburgh Public Schools.

Popkewitz, T.S. (1981). The social contexts of schooling, change, and educational research. *Journal of Curriculum Studies, 13,* 189–206.

Popkewitz, T.S. (1982a). Educational reform as the organization of ritual: Stability as change. *Journal of Education, 164,* 5–29.

Popkewitz, T.S. (1982b). Whither/wither the curriculum field? *Contemporary Education Review, 7*(1), 15–21.

Popkewitz, T.S. (1986). Paradigm and purpose. In C. Cornbleth (Ed.), *Invitation to research in social education.* Washington, DC: National Council for the Social Studies.

Popkewitz, T.S., Tabachnick, B.R., & Wehlage, G. (1982). *The myth of educational reform.* Madison: University of Wisconsin Press.

Popkewitz, T.S., & Wehlage, G. (1977). Schooling as work: An approach to research and evaluation. *Teachers College Record, 79*(1), 69–85.

Reid, W.A. (1975). The changing curriculum: Theory and practice. In W.A. Reid & D.F. Walker (Eds.), *Case studies in curriculum change: Great Britain and the United States.* London: Routledge and Kegan Paul.

Reid, W.A. (1978). *Thinking about the curriculum.* London: Routledge and Kegan Paul.

Smith, B.D. (1980). Influence of solicitation pattern, type of practice example, and student response on pupil behavior, commitment to discussion, and concept attainment. *Theory & Research in Social Education, 7*(4), 1–17.

Smith, L.M., & Geoffrey, W. (1968). *The complexities of an urban classroom.* New York: Holt, Rinehart & Winston.

Stake, R.E., & Easley, J.A. (1978). *Case studies in science education. Vol. 1: The case reports. Vol. 2: Design, overview, and general findings.* Urbana, IL: Center for Instructional Research and Curriculum Evaluation, University of Illinois. (Also available from U.S. Government Printing Office, Washington, DC.)

Stebbins, R.A. (1975). *Teachers and meaning: Definitions of classroom situations.* Leiden: Brill.

Waller, W. (1932). *The sociology of teaching.* New York: Wiley.

West, W.G. (1975). Participant observation research on the social construction of everyday classroom order. *Interchange, 6*(4), 35–43.

White, J.J. (1980). *Social constraints in the construction of knowledge about different cultures.* Paper presented at the annual meeting of the College and University Faculty Assembly, National Council for the Social Studies, New Orleans.

White, J.J. (1986). Ethnographic research. In C. Cornbleth (Ed.), *Invitation to research in social education.* Washington, DC: National Council for the Social Studies.

Woods, P. (1978). Negotiating the demands of schoolwork. *Journal of Curriculum Studies, 10*(4), 309–327.

CHAPTER SIX
Research Trends in Social Studies Education

KATHRYN M. BORMAN
University of Cincinnati

INTRODUCTION

Research in social studies education has recently begun to view teaching and learning as a mutually constructive process (Armento, 1986), shifting from process-product research which ignores interaction in favor of input and output factors framed by behaviorist assumptions. The research focus in the process-product mode is typically upon "measurable, observable and discrete items of behavior as learning outcomes and . . . on identifiable elements of instruction that reinforce student behavior" (Armento, 1986, p. 965). Although much current research in social studies education shows considerable promise in its capacity to allow a holistic understanding of teaching and learning, nonetheless, concepts and models drawn from a behaviorist educational psychology still dominate the field.

As Armento and others have observed, there are apparent signs of an increased willingness on the part of researchers in social studies education to adopt alternative paradigms. In the recent National Council for the Social Studies publication, *Review of Research in Social Studies Education: 1976–1983,* two chapters surveyed studies using ethnographic methods (White, 1984) and other nontraditional approaches (Stanley, 1985). However, ethnographic studies are still less frequently undertaken in dissertation research by doctoral students in social studies education than any other type of research including descriptive, experimental, analytical, developmental and historical designs (Hepburn & Dahler, 1985). According to the survey conducted by Hepburn and Dahler, ethnographic studies accounted for barely 1% of the 394 dissertations completed during the period 1977–1982 as compared with the 177 (more than 45%) identified as descriptive studies. Nonetheless, Hepburn and Dahler conclude that along with analytical and developmental designs, ethnographic research is in ascendancy and will likely increase in importance in the field.

Despite the optimism of Hepburn and Dahler, quantification in a narrow and descriptive sense continues to dominate the research literature reported in the field's leading journal, *Theory and Research in Social Education*. As a result, much of the discussion in this journal is in the form of disputes about both researchers' theoretical assumptions and their methodological errors. For example, in a recent article, Romanish is taken to task by Watts (1984) for Romanish's earlier (1983) study of bias in high school economics texts. In his descriptive account of the biased orientations of major texts in secondary economics education, Romanish claimed both that the field lacked a consensual view of what constitutes economics education and that a broad-based literacy in economics as opposed to a narrow focus on free enterprise economics should inform the textbook curriculum. Because Romanish did not either employ a theoretical orientation from which to derive his views or utilize a panel of individuals to review the texts in question, Watts found his colleague's research an easy target for his critique.

Although Watts's review of the Romanish study highlights the theoretical and methodological flaws in its design and execution, Watts neglects to make the more important point, namely that the enumeration of biasing statements in textbooks has little informational value for either teachers or researchers. Instead, Watts rather piously concludes, "To charge academic authors of bias . . . [as Romanish does] is a serious matter, deserving near-legal proof and at least a solid and well-explained framework for evaluating whether bias does exist. . . . We must do better . . . when we examine textbooks and other educational materials for ideological bias" (Watts, 1984, p. 35). While there may be utility in explication of concepts presented in social studies texts, there are likely other more productive avenues for research. For example, it is probably the case that teachers elaborate, critique, or otherwise expand (or delimit or ignore) the text in their classroom instruction. In my view, social studies education should abandon the entire enterprise of concept counting and enter the classroom community to determine how the curriculum is processed.

THE ETHNOGRAPHIC ADVANTAGE

In fact, the shift to more thorough-going process-oriented research designs has begun to occur as suggested previously. In her study of economics instruction in secondary school classrooms, McNeil's (1985) orientation to the curriculum goes beyond the explication of texts used in classroom instruction. Her theoretical views in this research derived from sociological theories of social organization and assumed that instruction and learning are embedded in and modified by the organization of learning, knowledge, and achievement in schools; particularly the hierarchical relationship between classroom teachers and school administrators (Popkewitz, 1985). In other words, her research was designed to document the complexities and subtleties of classroom practices. Teachers in the McNeil study tended to process social studies content through what McNeil terms "defensive teaching." Teachers relied on lists of facts and the memorization of this information coded in the jargon of the discipline in their presentation of the curriculum. Students, though mystified, were not the passive learners they appeared to be. During interviews with students McNeil learned that they were capable of critical, observant interpretation of the classroom process. McNeil, through her use of long-term observation and detailed interviews with teachers and students, was able to formulate a set of classroom teaching processes that she includes in her rubric of what is termed "defensive teaching" in her study. Although her examples are derived from a series of case studies rather than a national survey of economics teachers, the generalizations are presented in a manner that makes them both accessible to teachers and testable by researchers in other classrooms. Obviously no gifted teacher would wish to rely upon such defensive strategies as "fragmentation" (the presentation of bits of information such as lists of dates, place names, laws, events, "vocabulary" and the like) or "mystification" (the presentation of complex and abstract concepts as slogans). However, the thick description McNeil uses to present her analyses of defensive teaching can be instructive in teacher training and supervision and serve as a cautionary to administrators and other policy makers. One of McNeil's most important conclusions is that defensive teaching does not originate in teachers' poor pedagogical skills or lack of subject matter knowledge but, rather, is a response to the lack of support for academic teaching provided by administrative priorities and student interests.

The McNeil study illustrates the value of ethnographic or in-depth case study research. There are four dimensions to her research in this connection which are particularly noteworthy and are presented in some detail here to illustrate the general usefulness of this type of research. First, the design and subsequent results and analyses provide a holistic understanding of classroom processes. What teachers and students do in the classroom is not seen in isolation from other activities, interests and processes in the school system and surrounding community. Second, specific activities and behaviors are carefully analyzed and presented. A hallmark of good ethnography is its capacity to reflect back to the reader the image of the social group under study.

Erickson has suggested that the ethnographic report include nine main elements: empirical assertions, analytic narrative vignettes, quotes from field notes, quotes from interviews, synoptic data reports (maps, frequency tables, figures), interpretive commentary framing particular description, interpretive commentary framing general description, theoretical discussion, and, finally, a report of the natural history of inquiry in the study (Erickson, 1986, p. 123). These elements contribute to the store of specific information important to the field of social studies education in constructing a usable repertoire of teaching straegies, student response, organizational linkages and community characteristics and activities that should properly be a goal of a field which, in its proponents' terms, aims to develop a comprehensive understanding of the curriculum as product, the curriculum as project, and the practice of teaching of the curriculum (Cornbleth, 1985). Because the written ethnographic report relies heavily on verbatim material from field notes and interviews, it is likely to include also the researcher's bracketed impressions, interpretations and commentary. As Erickson points out, the nine elements listed previously in addition:

> Allow the reader to survey the full range of evidence on which the author's interpretive analysis is based. They . . . [also] allow the reader to consider the theoretical and personal grounds of the author's perspective as it changed during the course of the study. (Erickson, 1986, p. 123)

It is difficult to imagine any controversy similar to the one involving Watts and Romanish over a researcher's intentions and frameworks in the wake of an adequately reported ethnographic or case study.

The third important dimension of McNeil's study is that it is embedded in social theory. Mere description of observable phenomena does not constitute research. The field of social studies education has strayed far from its roots in the social theory of Dewey,

Waller, and others by succumbing to the narrow empiricism of behaviorist psychology. Social theory derived from sociology and anthropology forms a natural context for research in a field whose traditions and subject matter are socially significant. Fourth, and finally, in McNeil's study as in other, similarly closely observational work, social actors replace the text as the object of inquiry. Social actors may be the individual members of the classroom community but may also include administrators, parents, and community members related to each other through a web of social structures and social relationships.

THEORY-BUILDING IN SOCIAL STUDIES EDUCATION: THE EMPIRICAL-ANALYTICAL, INTERPRETATIVE, AND CRITICAL SCIENCES PERSPECTIVES

Thus far, the discussion in this chapter has considered the problems of research in social studies education from the perspective of research methodology. I have suggested that highly quantitative research in the behaviorist tradition lacks informational value because of its narrowness. Put another way, such research as the Romanish study lacks reliability and validity, making its contents valueless except as a point for argumentation and debate. In contrast, qualitative research provides a highly descriptive context in which to understand significant educational issues.

In this section of the chapter my argument is centered on the contents of research in the field of social studies education. My argument is simple: The field has been dominated by a conservative, even reactionary, ideological framework, in part derived from the methodology which has predominated the field. Armento sees three major influences at work in social studies theory building: the empirical-analytical, the interpretative, and the critical sciences (Armento, 1986, p. 942). Each perspective provides a particular paradigmatic view of the major activities in social studies education: "citizenship training and a combination of reflective inquiry/social science" (Armento, 1986, p. 943). The empirical-analytic tradition is associated most obviously with a behaviorist methodological orientation and seeks to explicate "measurable, observable and discrete" variables through causal, correlational analyses. In educational research as well as other research in the social and behavioral sciences, this perspective has been taken to task for its conservative bias. For example, Bredo and Feinberg (1982) argue that positivistic research is limited by its tendency to deny the interdependence of theory and method. Instead, the positivistic tradition holds to law-like statements regarding social phenomena, seeking to find empirical proofs supporting or refuting these assertions. Thus, because of its restricted focus on the "development of logical, integrated theoretical systems" (Bredo & Feinberg, 1982, p. 25) the positivistic tradition is by its very nature a conservative and restrictive approach.

Feminist scholars have made even harsher judgments about the perspective, asserting that research in the positivistic tradition is embedded in the logic and discourse of Western thought which is thoroughly drenched by the assumption that "male experience is human experience" (Harding & Hintikka, 1983, p. 4). Thus, in the words of Stiehm, social and behavioral scientists still suffer an "Aristotelian hangover" in the manner in which classification systems, terminology, and the logic of research itself denies full stature to women. Whereas men are "heads of household," women in social science research are often construed as family members—appendages, not citizens (Stiehm, 1983). In addition to having implications for political and social theory, these formulations have clear implications for public policy as evidenced in federal job-training programs focussing on the head of the household who may be a woman's husband or father. Even when women are the targets of such programs, issues such as child care, transportation, and housing are ignored, making these programs inaccessible to many eligible women (Gideonse, 1984). Feminist scholars are among those most vocal in their rejection of the designs and conceptions inherent in positivistic research. No matter what their theoretical or ideological persuasion, all critics of the empirical-analytic orientation agree that this perspective is explicitly conservative politically. With respect to schools and schooling, it assumes that schools serve basically useful and desirable ends, that strong and effective administrative leadership is the key to a smooth operation of schools, that teachers and students occupy the lowest positions in the school hierarchy, that school knowledge is manifest in the text, that schools are fully embedded in their surrounding societies, and that change is evolutionary.

The interpretative perspective, grounded in social interactional theory in sociology, allows the researcher to frame the inquiry around questions related to the establishment and maintenance of the formal and informal rules that govern social life. This perspective is particularly useful in constructing investigations of classroom interaction through studies that examine the culture of a social group under investigation, or more finely focused research that considers either the hidden or the explicit curriculum (Weis, 1986). In analyzing the culture of the social group, the researcher must adopt the position of the participant observer in order to gain the insider's perspective.

The goal of the student of classroom culture is to leave the field with enough knowledge and understanding of the group to be able to formulate the rules underlying comembership. To a certain extent, the researcher, while not necessarily enjoying the status of full membership, is capable of articulating norms, values, and beliefs which underlie the group's behaviors and activities; the investigator leaves the field knowing the culture. The same understanding is developed ideally in investigations of the hidden and explicit curriculum, although it is more limited. There are numerous examples of research in the interpretative tradition investigating the entire cultural landscape or the more restricted terrain of the curriculum.

One of the most comprehensive studies in this tradition is Shirley Brice Heath's (1982; 1983) study of a community in the Piedmont region dominated by the textile industry, which employed many parents of the children who were participants in the study. Not only did Heath spend considerable time in the classroom during the course of her 10-year residency in this community, but she also made frequent observations in the homes of both the children and their teachers. Because her focus is on the language of socialization and the ethnography of communication, she provides a highly detailed account of how verbal strategies in community and home settings varied and differed from those employed in the classroom. Question-asking protocols used by parents, family members, and friends in the homes of Black community residents, for example, were frequently designed to elicit playful responses from children, especially if the questioner occupied a low status in the community or were another child. Thus, when a child almost 4 years old was asked by his exasperated parent, "Whadya do with that shoe?", the child responded appropriately with a rhymed chant that amused his audience (and had the desired effect of calming his frustrated mother).

In summarizing her discussion of the language environment experienced by these children in their homes, Heath concludes that far from being excluded from participation in conversationally rich environment, children were bathed in wide variety of styles, speakers and topics. However, in contrast to their classroom environments, children in their homes "were not engaged as conversationalists through special types of question addressed to them" (Heath, 1982, p. 119). Children experienced few interactions at home which explicitly prepared them for the kinds of specific information-seeking questions of the type regularly used by their middle-class teachers at school.

Heath's analysis of school–community language socialization differences did not stop with her presentation of the differences which she uncovered in children's language environments in both places. Rather, she used her ethnographic field work as a springboard for allowing teachers as "change agents" (in Heath's terms) to begin to ask questions of their own practices based on the insights gained from comparisons they were able to draw after having analyzed Heath's findings.

A set of smaller-scale studies using the interpretive framework is being conducted by Catherine Cornbleth and her associates. Her work is notable because her principal research orientation is social studies education. In a recent study of a middle school, however, she and her colleagues investigated the establishment of social and academic ground rules in several different subject area classrooms, including the English, science, and social studies classes of teachers who impressed the researcher's as "careerists," teachers who "believe their work is important, enjoy it most of the time and intend to remain in teaching" (Cornbleth, Korth, & Dorow, 1986, p. 6). The investigation centered on three guiding question:

1. How were classroom academic and social rules and patterns of interaction established?
2. What seemed to be the purposes and effects of the emerging academic and social organizational ground rules and routines?
3. What meanings were given to authority, responsibility, work, and success?

The research was undertaken to clarify an earlier finding uncovered during the previous year's research in the same setting. Specifically, the investigators had noticed that although 90% of class time was devoted to academic work, a smaller amount (21%) of that time was spent in "comprehension or reasoning tasks." In short, the researchers focused attention on the creation by teachers and students of what they term the "curriculum in use."

While the interpretative position allows the researcher to develop a holistic view of the social group in question, it takes the emergent values orientations of the group for granted, not questioning the political ideology that surrounds and informs *both* observed activities and interactions and the researcher's own position vis-à-vis the observed social scene. The most radical and politically informed analysis is undertaken from the perspective of the critical sciences whose objective is "liberation from dominating forms of social control" (Van Maanen, 1975, as quoted in Armento, 1986, p. 942).

In social studies education there are clear signs of theoretical developments that can fruitfully lead to investigations informed by radical thought. The theorists who are developing these frameworks have in common the predisposition to make gender, race, and social class problematic. The research literature in the critical science mode that I will summarize and review next has for the most part not been considered under the rubric of social education research studies principally because with the exception of Anyon (1978) and Giroux the individuals engaged in constructing radical social theory have not been regarded as members of the social education fraternity. Nonetheless, the scope and focus of the research is powerfully suggestive of concepts that may fruitfully guide other investigations more directly related to the domain of social studies education. Aronowitz and Giroux (1985) have formulated a set of the essential questions to form the basis for what they term a new model for educational theory and research. These questions include:

> What is school knowledge?
> How is school knowledge organized?
> What are the underlying codes that structure such knowledge?
> How is what counts as school knowledge transmitted?
> How is access to such knowledge determined?
> What kind of cultural system does school knowledge legitimate?
> Whose interests are served by the production and legitimization of school knowledge? (Aronowitz & Giroux, 1985, p. 145).

In posing these questions, certain dimensions of the process of schooling already embedded in the social studies education research literature are highlighted. For example, the final question on the list might be reframed to ask: What particular concepts from the literature are invoked in courses aimed at citizenship training?

There are a number of traditionally ignored issues raised by a focus on the production of classroom knowledge. These primarily center upon the ways in which knowledge is mediated in the classroom by teachers and students. Classroom processes and outcomes are "placed in a framework that considers social, political and economic outcomes in addition to the curriculum and student learning" (Borman & Spring, 1984, p. 213). This focus goes well beyond the concept counting research perspective. As in the example presented earlier in this chapter, the text as it is elaborated, delimited, or ignored by the teacher and classroom knowledge as it is created, discarded or sustained by teacher and students becomes of central concern. Aronowitz and Giroux (1985) argue that modes of inquiry associated with critical sciences models of schooling must take into account "theories of knowledge forms; theories of knowledge content; and theories of classroom social relations and knowledge appropriation" (p. 149).

By knowledge forms is meant the manifest (as opposed to the hidden) curriculum and specifically textbooks, teacher manuals to accompany such texts, and other related course materials such as "handouts," "workbooks," and the like designed by textbook manufacturers to accompany the text. It is important to emphasize that studies of knowledge forms from a critical sciences perspective do not isolate written material from classroom interaction during the course of instruction. While researchers may vary in emphasis on, for example, cognitive processing components (Cornbleth, 1985) as opposed to the relationship between curriculum design and the deskilling of teachers (Apple, 1982), they share a common concern with the questions mentioned earlier, all of which focus on the social and cultural determinants and outcomes of the school process itself.

In a sense, theories of knowledge content are more limited than theories of knowledge forms in that the analysis is restricted to the materials themselves. However, these studies do not employ mere concept counting but rather depend upon the critical sciences' objectives, summarized by the intent to examine, analyze, and portray the underlying political ideology of the materials in question. For example, Aronowitz and Giroux point to the series of questions addressed in the research of Brenkman whose research questions "link formal analysis of the material with a sustained interrogation of its content" (1985, p. 151). These include: Who are the authors' sponsors? What are their interests in the issues? Who is the intended audience? What alternative viewpoints or arguments exist that are not mentioned or acknowledged? These questions can, as Aronowitz and Giroux assert, be used in a critical analysis of course materials. They wisely suggest that this form of analysis be undertaken by teachers in evaluating course materials they are considering for classroom use. As we have seen, left in the hands of researchers, these procedures are likely to generate more heat than light; however, these same questions can empower teachers to become their own sources of information about the curricular materials they utilize on a daily basis.

Finally, theories of classroom social relations and knowledge appropriation allow for perhaps the most comprehensive and radical approaches to educational change. Notions of educational empowerment are not new. Critics of the "banking concept" of active teaching accompanied by passive acquisition of cultural capital have included Paulo Freire, John Ogbu, Henry Giroux, and others. Most recently, the ethnographic research of Kathleen Wilcox (1982), Peter

McClaren (1985), and Lois Weis (1985) have placed the educational institution in the context of the community and demonstrated the importance of home influences and peer culture upon the acquisition of school knowledge in the elementary school (Wilcox), middle school (McClaren), and community college (Weis). These studies all demonstrate the importance of understanding the process of school learning as a highly complex, culturally informed activity. School learning, as these studies show, is actively mediated and influenced by teachers and students in highly intricate ways. But perhaps the most informative research in its capacity to alter radically educational practice is that which has been developed over the past 11 years by the Kamehameha Elementary Education Program (KEEP) for Polynesian–Hawaiian children, among the most disenfranchised U. S. ethnic minority students (Jordan, 1985). These children are among those whom John Ogbu has termed caste-like minorities, a group which also includes Blacks, native Americans, Chicanos, Puerto Rican Americans and urban Appalachians, all of whom have been incorporated into U. S. society in the face of enormous social injustice and political and economic constraints.

The KEEP program serves as a model for educational change of a truly radical sort. Its programmatic shifts over more than a decade of work have moved the staff's efforts from an initial focus upon culture theory and ethnographic information to the construction of an academically successful program in literacy learning for ethnic minority students that has most recently been exported with major modifications to the Rough Rock Navajo community in Arizona (Vogt, 1985). According to Jordan, the KEEP research effort is unique in several ways:

> KEEP's research and development efforts are centrally focused on devising curriculum that will raise school achievement of Hawaiian children from families of low socioeconomic status to meet and surpass national norms.
>
> KEEP is not affiliated with a university or any government institution but derives its revenues from a trust established by the Bishop estate for the educational benefit of Hawaiian children.
>
> KEEP is non-hierarchically and multi-disciplinarily organized to involve both research specialists in linguistics, psychology and anthropology and classroom teachers working collaboratively together. (Jordan, 1985, pp. 106–107)

The most important lessons learned from the KEEP project from the time of its inception in the early 1970s to its dissemination in 1985 to Rough Rock include several watchwords to others concerned with similar issues. First, the team, through traditional anthropological and psychological perspectives and methodologies, achieved "a fairly good understanding of what was going wrong in classrooms in terms of mismatches between the expectations and demands of school and the culture of the children" (Jordan, 1985, p. 107). However, although this fieldwork provided teachers with an intellectual analysis of the cultural incompatibilities (*and* compatibilities) between home and school, this information was of no help in changing classroom practices. In Jordan's words:

> The issues involved in such an applied task were too complex, the knowledge base needed was too broad to be either the sphere of any one discipline or to be dealt with in simple interaction between social scientist and educator. (1985, p. 107)

In other words, ethnographic research did not provide a quick fix for educational practice, even though it was driven by sophisticated techniques and democratic, collaborative processes. The outcome of this intensive research followed by equally intensive soul searching was the creation of the KEEP lab school program, which allowed for ongoing collaboration, classroom experimentation, and curricular modification. The result has been the development of a number of "translation teaching strategies" harmonious with the child's natal culture and behavior and linked with successful classroom outcomes. These strategies were not only generated in accordance with culturally compatible (and academically success-oriented) features but also were designed to violate teacher norms as little as possible. Jordan describes this latter "constraint" on classroom curricular and teaching alterations with references to the principle of least overall change and its related point, the corollary of change least foreign to educational practices. These last features assisted the program innovators in making classroom innovations stick.

The important features of the KEEP research agenda outcomes for radically changing the process of classroom teaching and learning are suggested in Table 1, which lists a number of the translation strategies developed in connection with culturally compatible classroom practices. The translation strategies are derived from the observation of children's interactions in home and school settings, acknowledgment of classroom practices, and continuous back-and-forth discussion between researchers and teachers in at least one of four ways. On the basis of ethnographic evidence documenting sociocultural factors in common across school, home and peer group, specific "school effective" features, such as the creation of learning centers staffed by the child's peers are created.

A second strategy is to eliminate or avoid a particular cultural component in classroom practice in order to foster children's academic success. Because Hawaiian children tend to react to adult authority by "ceasing to respond in a one to one confrontation with a teacher . . . KEEP teachers try to avoid direct, insistent questioning of individual children who have not volunteered a response" (Jordan, 1985, p. 114). Rather, teachers address questions to the group at large and particularly praise volunteered responses. Similarly, teachers

Table 1.   Types of Translation Strategies and Examples of Culturally Compatible Classroom Practices*

Translation Strategy	Example of Natal Culture Element/Child Behavior	Example of Culturally Compatible Classroom Feature	Classroom Outcomes
Encourage: Elicit: Build on	Group setting of learning events; cooperative nature of teaching and learning group context of work	Centers organized for routine practice of academic skills; peers as legitimate source of help in centers	Task engagement; task completion; teacher has culturally appropriate "supervisory" role
Avoid:	Stop verbalizing reaction to adult confrontation	Participation in reading lesson discussion and other verbal performance events is voluntary; little intensive individual questioning	Children stay engaged in lesson event; interaction with teacher is maintained
Ignore:	High levels of peer interaction	Nonacademic interaction in centers; concurrent with of interspersed with on-task behavior is allowed	On-task behavior continues; congenial atmosphere; teacher–student interaction is maintained; children's time is not wastd trying to establish illegal peer contacts
Shape; extend	Selective attending to adults	Contingent social reward attending to teacher instructions	Children attend to teacher in limited but academically sufficient contexts

* Adapted from Jordan (1981, 1983).
   (Source: C. Jordan (1985), "Translating culture: From ethnographic information to educational program," *Anthropology & Education Quarterly, 16*(1), p. 113.

also turn their backs on behaviors which they traditionally are inclined to monitor. A KEEP teacher, Lynn Vogt, describes the process by which she learned to modify her organization of the classroom:

> During my first year at KEEP, independent work was done in individual "homeroom seats," and one of the hardest teacher rules to enforce was "do your own work." Hawaiian children are accustomed to helping one another, being helped more often by peers or siblings than by adults. . . . In school this manifests itself in high rates of peer interaction, frequent scanning for errors, and soliciting peer help. Teachers tended not to think of this as assistance, or teaching by modeling, but as *cheating!* . . . [T]he students got pretty sophisticated at techniques to avoid trouble with the teacher and still behave like Hawaiian helpers. They were especially good at timing how long it took the teacher to write a single word on the board. They'd be out of their seats, helping someone with an answer, and back into their seats before the teacher could turn back around. (Vogt, 1985, pp. 5–6)

Allowing for nonacademic, interpersonal interaction in learning centers provided the organizational change that led to the maintenance of teacher–student rapport, provision of a congenial atmosphere, and other favorable classroom outcomes.

The fourth type of strategy discussed by Jordan in Table 1 "involves shaping or extending natal culture elements in some way" (Jordan, 1985, p. 114). In this case, teachers build upon adult behaviors familiar to children from their home environments. Some situations and modes of interaction are foreign to students and, much as roles and styles of classroom questioning observed by Heath, may serve to shut down children's participation in the very classroom processes that strengthen their literacy skills.

Although these strategies were developed over a long period of time with a particular group of children, it appears that with careful monitoring, the approach can be transferred to other settings. In 1983, members of the KEEP staff, including researchers and teachers, worked with a similar team in Arizona to establish classroom practices at the Rough Rock School that were more harmonious with natal Navajo culture than had previously been the case. Lynn Vogt's fascinating account of Rough Rock suggests that culture is as important in classroom process and outcomes as is "plain basic good education."

Going into the Rough Rock program, the participants had formulated two guiding hypotheses. They reasoned that given similar sibling child care and other home-based responsibilities present in the early experience of both Hawaiian and Navajo children, centers would work well in the native American classroom. As a second hypothesis, participants determined that patterns of teacher–student interaction similar to those in place at KEEP in specific learning contexts would be cognitively effective, but that changes would likely be required to adapt to Navajo sociolinguistic patterns. A third area, behavior management techniques, was left open-ended, the difference that cultural differences make became apparent almost immediately:

> On the second day of school one boy came into the room shouting and elicited in me a "no nonsense" warning followed by an "I mean business" desist statement. In Hawaii, this is a common routine, and quick handling of the first challenge is important to signal the nice-but-tough nature of the teacher. However, from the moment of my warning, my intuition told me that this wasn't going to work in the same way in Rough Rock. And it didn't. The resulting stand-off and confrontation was recorded on videotape for posterity (endearingly referred to as "Lynn Meets the Navajo War Chief"), and on day two we were on the drawing board with respect to cultural adaptations to program. After consulting with Navajo staff members, and careful observation in the school and community, we learned that both extremes of the "tough-nice" repertoire were ineffective with Navajo children. Praise was effective when handled more subtly than with Hawaiian children, but it was seldom very effective for cuing desired behavior, as it is in Hawaii. And misbehavior was more easily controlled by ignoring or looking down and giving a short, stern lecture to the whole group of students. (Vogt, 1985, p. 8)

From the experience of the KEEP and Rough Rock research team, it may be concluded that strategies in social control or behavior management may be more closely linked to and affected by natal culture than are teaching strategies. It is certainly the case that it was relatively more difficult to transport the former approaches wholesale from one cultural setting to another in the KEEP/Rough Rock experiment.

The important lesson to be learned overall from the record of research and applications during the decade of the KEEP effort is that changes in classroom practice can be made in congruence with natal cultural features. However, they require radical assumptions about such basic issues as who shares in the research/implementation of a project, what is the focus of the research effort, and how long does the process of implementation last. It may be that programs of the breadth of KEEP are simply too expensive to serve as models in any general sense. However, there are numerous invaluable principles to be learned from the KEEP project, and many of them derive from the importance of designing a truly collaborative program of research and application, of implementing an interdisciplinary and multidisciplinary approach, and most significantly, of recognizing the reality of culture.

REFERENCES

Anyon, J. (1979). Ideology and United State history textbooks. *Harvard Educational Review, 49*(3), 361–386.

Apple, M.W. (1982). Curricular form and the logic of control: Building the possessive individual. In M.W. Apple (Ed.), *Cultural and economic reproduction in education*. London: Routledge & Kegan Paul.

Armento, B.J. (1986). Research on teaching social studies. In M.C. Wittrock (Ed.), *Handbook of research on teaching* (3rd ed.). New York: MacMillan.

Aronowitz, S., & Giroux, H. (1985). *Education under siege*. South Hadley, MA: Bergin & Garvey.

Borman, K.M., & Spring, J.H. (1984). *Schools in central cities*. New York: Longman.

Bredo, E., & Feinberg, W. (Eds.). (1982). *Knowledge and values in social and educational research*. Philadelphia: Temple University Press.

Cornbleth, C. (1985). Critical thinking and cognitive processes. In W.B. Stanley (Ed.), *Review of research in social studies education*. Washington, DC: National Council for Social Studies.

Cornbleth, C., Korth, W., & Dorow, E.B. (1984). Creating the curriculum: Beginning the year in a middle school. Pittsburgh, PA: University of Pittsburgh Press.

Erickson, F. (1986). Qualitative methods in research on teaching. In M.C. Wittrock (Ed.), *Handbook of research on teaching* (3rd ed.). New York: MacMillan.

Gideonse, S. (1984). Introduction. In K.M. Borman, D. Quarm, & S. Gideonse (Eds.), *Women in the workplace: Effects on families*. Norwood, NJ: Ablex.

Harding, S., & Hintikka, M.B. (Eds.). (1983). *Discovering reality*. Boston: Ridel.

Heath, S.B. (1982). Questioning at home and at school: A comparative study. In G. Spindler (Ed.), *Doing the ethnography of schooling*. New York: Holt, Rinehart, & Winston.

Heath, S.B. (1983). *Ways with words*. Cambridge, England: Cambridge University Press.

Hepburn, M.A., & Dahler, A. (1985). An overview of social studies dissertations, 1977–1982. *Theory & Research in Social Education, 13*(2), 73–82.

Jordan, C. (1981). *Educationally effective ethnology: A study of the contributions of cultural knowledge to effective education for minority children*. Unpublished dissertation, University of California at Los Angeles.

Jordan, C. (1983). Cultural differences in communication patterns: Classroom translation strategies. In M. Clarke, & J. Handscombe (Eds.), *TESOL 82:*

Pacific perspectives on language learning and teaching. Washington, DC: Teachers of English.

Jordan, C. (1985). Translating culture: From ethnographic information to educational program. *Anthropology & Education Quarterly, 16*(2), 105–123.

McClaren, P. (1985). *Schooling as a ritual performance.* Boston: Routledge & Kegan Paul.

McNeil, L. (1985, April). *Client and consumer roles: The message of social studies methods and content.* Paper presented at the annual meeting of the American Educational Research Association, Chicago.

Popkewitz, T.S. (1985, April). *Curriculum studies in teacher education: Problems and paradoxes of knowledge.* Paper presented at the annual meeting of the American Educational Research Association, Chicago.

Romanish, B. (1983). Modern secondary economics textbooks and ideological bias. *Theory & Research in Social Education, 11*(2), 73–82.

Stanley, W.B. (1985). Research in social education: Issues and approaches. In W.B. Stanley (Ed.), *Review of Research in Social Studies Education.* Washington, DC: National Council for Social Studies.

Stiehm, J.H. (1983). The unit of political analysis: Our Aristotelian hangover. In S. Harding, & M.B. Hintikka (Eds.), *Discovering reality.* Boston: Ridel.

Vogt, L. (December, 1985). *Rectifying the school performance of Hawaiian and Navajo students.* Paper presented at the annual meeting of the American Anthropology Association, Washington, DC.

Watts, M.W. (1984). A response to Romanish: Ideological bias in secondary economics textbooks. *Theory & Research in Social Education, 11*(4), 25–35.

Weis, L. (1985). *Between two worlds.* New York: Routledge & Kegan Paul.

Weis, L. (1986). Sociology of education: Its usefulness in a teacher education program. *Educational Foundations, 1*(1).

White, J.J. (1984). What works for teachers: A view of ethnographic research studies as they inform issues on social studies curriculum and instruction. In W.B. Stanley (Ed.), *Review of Research in Social Studies Education: 1976–1983.* Washington, DC.

Wilcox, K. (1982). Differential socialization in the classroom: Implications for equal opportunity. In G. Spindler (Ed.), *Doing the ethnography of schooling.* New York: Holt, Rinehart, & Winston.

SECTION III
Perspectives on Mathematics and Science

CHAPTER SEVEN

Teaching as Discourse: The Social Construction of a Mathematics Lesson*

DOUGLAS R. CAMPBELL
Michigan State University

INTRODUCTION

In this chapter I would like to argue that children's access to academic knowledge in classrooms depends on acquiring discourse patterns for talking about the manifest content of instructional activities. I will first briefly review sociolinguistic and microethnographic classroom research which has identified the social interactional knowledge children need for participating in instruction, but which until recently has neglected how the actual subject matter content of lessons affects and is affected by the social dimensions of classroom life. This will set the stage for an overview of my own research on the use of questions in teaching elementary mathematics in English in Philippine classrooms. I will then present examples from one classroom lesson that are the basis for my argument that children's access to mathematical concepts depends on being exposed to language for talking about them, where by "language" I mean more precisely the discourse frames essential for instruction about concepts.

* The research on which this chapter is based was conducted in a Tagalog-speaking community in the Philippines during 1975. I would like to express my appreciation to the Philippine-American Educational Foundation and the Institute of International Education for their financial support for this work. Among the many whose assistance and insights are reflected in this report, I am especially grateful to the teacher whose classroom is depicted here, and to Michelle Rosaldo, who before her tragic and untimely death first encouraged me to see how instruction in discourse and in mathematics might be seen as necessarily complementary, rather than as in conflict. The interpretations presented here, of course, are my responsibility alone.

Along the way I will also illustrate the importance of taking seriously both the language of instruction and the whole lesson as important contexts in discussions about how to see students' access to knowledge as contextualized. In showing how I was able to locate the discourse dimensions of teaching and learning in one lesson, I will also argue that in searching for contextual *constraints* on knowledge transmission one might also identify features of "context" that can be regarded more positively than the term "constraints" implies, and that are irremediably intertwined with and thereby constitutive of manifest subject matter content. I will conclude with some reflections about what my evidence from the bilingual, second-language case in the Philippines suggests more generally about access to academic knowledge in monolingual situations; about mathematics in particular as an otherwise relatively context-free enterprise; and about issues of equity in access to academic learning in our schools.

On the Social Interactional Dimensions of Classroom Learning

In sociolinguistic and microethnographic work on classrooms that has been accumulating over the last 15 years, there has been ample demonstration that children's learning of the official academic curriculum cannot be understood apart from the more invisible social, interactional dimensions of how classroom lessons are organized (see Cazden, John, & Hymes, 1972; Cherry-Wilkinson, 1982; Green & Wallat, 1981; Hymes, 1974; Stubbs, 1976; Trueba, Guthrie, & Au, 1981). With respect to the language of instructional exchanges (and question-answer sequences in particular), much attention has been given to the problematic relation between the *forms* and *functions* of utterances, that is, the fact that syntactic forms and semantic functions do not necessarily stand in a one-to-one relationship. While "questions" prototypically perform the function of requesting information through the interrogative form, they can also issue commands, make statements, and request actions; and information requests can be accomplished by declarative forms as well as by imperatives, depending on the context in which the utterance is produced. For children in classrooms, the problem is how to know when an interrogative form is intended to request information, versus issue a command (as in "Class, will you please be quiet?"), or when a declarative or imperative is being used to elicit answers.

As Mehan (1981) has argued, the coding category "asks a question" (which is typical of the measurement approach to classroom interaction in process-product research) takes this interpretive problem for granted. It relies on the coder's ability to hear utterances as the classroom participants do. This is especially troublesome where interrater reliabilities, which often amount to measures of culturally shared perceptions, are presumed to provide the foundation for valid codings of behavior produced by children from different cultural backgrounds.

Across the sociolinguistic and microethnographic literature on classrooms, several distinct ways have been identified by which the problematic nature of questions can interfere with learning experiences and with wider educational and social opportunities for different children. Those focusing on minority children's problems in school have argued that the difficulty resides in part in culturally organized differences between classroom and home in the situational appropriateness of asking questions in the first place (Boggs, 1972; Erickson & Mohatt, 1982; Goody, 1978; Heath, 1982; Levin, 1978; Phillips, 1972). One result of this can be lowered teacher expectations for student performance, as well as student rejection of academic achievement as an unviable source of personal esteem, both of which in turn feed into cycles of self-fulfilling prophecy adversely affecting subsequent success in educational and occupational arenas (Erickson, 1976; Labov & Robins, 1969; McDermott, 1974; McDermott & Aron, 1978; Mehan, 1978; Rist, 1970; Rosenthal & Jacobson, 1968).

Those who have addressed the issue of what *any* child needs to learn about social interactional rules for participating in instructional activities have shown that children must learn to associate different classroom rules for questioning and answering with the different events and subevents that constitute the unfolding contexts for subject matter learning in school. Failure to learn the rules and the different times when they are in effect can put a child in jeopardy of having performance mistakes misevaluated as lack of ability (Bremme & Erickson, 1977; Erickson, 1982a; Erickson & Shultz, 1981; Florio, 1978).

A third line of research has focused on the particular channels and features of verbal and nonverbal behavior which define form/function relationships, as intended by speakers on the one hand, and as understood by listeners on the other hand. Work in this area has concentrated on cross-cultural and interethnic differences that might lead to misunderstandings of the functions of classroom interrogatives, though it is also claimed that such misinterpretations are potentially entailed in any face-to-face interaction, even when shared communicative backgrounds can otherwise be presumed (Cook-Gumperz & Gumperz, 1982; Gumperz, 1982a, 1982b; Gumperz & Herasimchuk,

1975; Gumperz & Tannen, 1979). Failure to share interpretations of classroom question–answer exchanges can interfere with the transmission of the overt academic content of those utterances.

Important as these and related lines of work have been in deepening our understanding of how the transmission of academic knowledge is influenced by continuities and discontinuities in social knowledge about language use, there has been increasing recognition among sociolinguistic and microethnographic analysts that the pendulum of corrective concern for the neglected social dimensions of classroom life has perhaps swung too far, at the expense of examining how the manifest content of different subject areas can itself be a kind of discontinuity faced by children in school, and can have reciprocal impact on the social rules for appropriate interaction in the classroom (see Erickson, 1982a, 1982b; Griffin & Mehan, 1981).

Furthermore, whereas much of the work in sociolinguistics more generally has been concerned with going beyond conventional views of linguistic competence as consisting only of formal grammatical rules at the sentence level and referential definitions of lexical items (Gumperz, 1982a; Hymes, 1974), there are classroom situations in many parts of the world in which even those basic aspects of language use cannot be presumed—for example, wherever the medium of instruction is not the children's native language in the first place. As in the Philippine situation I will describe, using English as medium of instruction makes English itself inextricably part of the mathematical subject matter being taught, which in turn has consequences for how the mathematical content as such is transmitted to children. What will initially appear to be a case of how the language of instruction is an especially severe constraint on access to academic knowledge in the classroom, I hope to show instead as revealing how the transmission of subject matter content is irremediably tied to discourse patterns necessary for its communication, and is therefore not so much constrained by the forms and functions of language use as it is *constituted* by them.

LOOKING AT ELEMENTARY MATHEMATICS LESSONS IN THE PHILIPPINES

During the 1960s, a "modern mathematics" curriculum was introduced to Philippine elementary schools. A major goal of this innovation was to replace traditional rote methods with "guided discovery." It was thought that better classroom questioning by both teachers and children would improve problem-solving skills and attitudes assumed to be crucial for modernizing Philippine society. In my participation in this effort as a Peace Corps Volunteer, I observed that although many teachers nominally adopted a question-centered approach, they continued to dominate their classrooms by asking virtually all the questions and by seeking only "facts" for answers. They would also give away answers by how they phrased their questions and evaluated student responses. Since it had been formulated in a Western "scientific" milieu, the innovation was seen by some (including me) as failing because of irreconcilable conflicts with traditional Philippine cultural values and patterns of interaction concerning appropriate adult–child relationships.

The purpose of my study of classrooms in a Philippine school was to explicate what else might be going on with the use of questions in instructional exchanges, beyond what was immediately apparent. (This followed from my increasing dissatisfaction with "cultural obstacle" explanations for difficulties in cross-national curriculum innovation; see Campbell, 1981, 1986). By taking a close look *through* the surface of questioning patterns, I discovered a dynamic realm of interactional work by which questions were used to construct answers, and on the basis of which Filipino children can be seen as active partners in instruction, rather than as passive recipients of knowledge.

The study was conducted in a small town in a Tagalog-speaking area. Tape recordings were made of 78 lessons in a public elementary school, involving eight classes across grades 1 through 6, and topics in mathematics, science, and social studies. Mathematics and science were taught in English, social studies in Tagalog. In the analysis phase, the question "What are they doing here?" was addressed to the 21 grades 4–6 mathematics lessons. The answer "They are 'searching' for answers" was proposed as a way of indicating that the participants' key problem was in locating and articulating *answers* rather than in interpreting *questions*. This metaphor gave way upon further analysis to the answer "They are 'going for' the answers," as a better depiction of how questions assemble answers.

As I have elaborated elsewhere (Campbell, 1981, 1986), this formulation is consistent with the ethnomethodological view that "answers" and "lessons" are the mutually accomplished productions of teachers and students (Mehan, 1978), and with the Vygotskian view of learning as a socially mediated process involving teachers locating and accommodating children's current "zone(s) of proximal development" (McNamee, 1979; Vygotsky, 1978; Wertsch, 1978; Wertsch & Stone, 1978). As I shifted my focus from questions to answers, I also found myself taking the manifest content of the lessons more and more explicitly into account.

TEACHING MATHEMATICS AND ENGLISH IN A PHILIPPINE
GRADE 6 CLASSROOM

Let me now present a grade 6 mathematics lesson from my data set, as illustration of how I came to see that access to mathematical concepts requires instruction in the discourse patterns necessary to talk about them. The lesson was the first in a sequence of three on the topic of "mathematical sentences"; the purpose of this lesson was to establish definitions for "number sentence," "set sentence," and "number phrase." During the lesson the teacher recorded on the board her target "generalization" (as she called it), thus providing a record of the answers she was "going for":

> Mathematical sentences express complete ideas about numbers and sets. Kinds of mathematical sentences:
> 1. Number sentences express complete ideas about numbers.
> 2. Set sentences express complete ideas about sets.
> Number phrases are parts of number sentences that have no complete ideas.

A summary chart of the lesson's main phases and subphases is presented in Appendix 2; this chart is organized in terms of the main concepts that were the focus of the teacher's instructional strategy.

In reviewing the tape and transcript of the lesson in order to accomplish this segmentation of the lesson's mathematical content, I became increasingly aware of the children's difficulties in producing the English required for answering the teacher's questions. I had originally decided to focus my analysis on the intermediate grade mathematics lessons, on the assumption that the use of English as medium of instruction would be much less an intrusive factor than it would be with the younger children in the lower grades—as it was, by and large. Nevertheless, the more closely I examined this lesson, the more I realized that not only could the use of English not be ignored, it could be more profitably incorporated into the analysis with respect to the question of how the teacher and students managed to confront and surmount such an obvious obstacle to their teaching and learning about mathematics. As we shall soon see, I eventually concluded that teaching English during the lesson was less an obstacle to the mathematics and more an essential feature of what access to mathematical concepts necessarily entails.

The children's troubles with English in this lesson occurred at several different levels. In the realm of listening comprehension, there were numerous instances throughout the lesson in which the children's answers suggest they did not understand the teacher's questions. However, from the taped evidence alone it is not clear whether they did not understand the English per se or whether instead they had difficulty with either the cognitive complexity of the mathematical content or the ambiguities of the tasks required of them.

In the realm of production, though here too it is impossible to disentangle completely the extent to which the "problem" was due to the language, content, or context of the instruction, there is nonetheless clearer indication that English was indeed a major source of difficulty. Seeing these difficulties was facilitated by the teacher's own attentiveness to them, which in and of itself further strengthened my initial impression that English was a serious obstacle to the transmission of mathematical ideas in this lesson. Before addressing this latter issue, let us first examine examples of the kinds of production problems the children had, and how the teacher dealt with them.

Assuming that the children understood a question well enough to have an answer, their first production task was "getting started." Throughout the lesson it often happened that the teacher received no response to her question. This could have meant that no one knew the answer, but it could also have been due to their need for a little prompting. The teacher did not necessarily know the reason for an absent response, though she did provide a retrospective definition of the trouble by the amount of time she waited, and by the nature of what she did next to help get them started. Sometimes her repetitions, reformulations, and elaborations of the original request were major sources of help for students who were not prepared to answer the question as given. But these moves were also occasionally all that was necessary for eliciting an answer that in some sense was already there, as in lines 62–65 of Exhibit 1, where Ro only had to repeat an earlier answer. (See Appendix 1). Among the various simplification moves the teacher made when she formulated follow-up questions, most were occasioned by her judgment that the students needed more help than just a push to get started. Nevertheless, all such moves also performed the starting function, and some were more clearly oriented to that task, as in lines 197–207 of Exhibit 1, where she used a "sentence completion" prompt.

On other occasions, the teacher determined that the nominated child needed the first word or two to get started on an answer that otherwise should have been available. For example, the exchange in lines 547–555 (Exhibit 1) occurred after they had finally established (again) that number sentences express ideas about numbers. The teacher now wanted the student to formulate the answer as a com-

EXHIBIT 1. HELPING THE CHILDREN "GET STARTED"

62	T:	Will you say it, Ro _____ ?
63		((pause))
64	T:	Say it again. =
65	Ro:	= Mathematical -- sentence.

- -

197	T:	Alright,
198		look at the sentences in group B.
199		What ideas -- or complete ideas --
200		do they express?
201-203	Ss:	((three Ss overlap answers; all are unintelligible))
204	T:	What ideas: -- do they express?
205		((pause))
206	T:	Ideas about: __⊥__ ?
207	S:	Ideas about set.

- -

547	T:	Alright, what do you say now?
548		((pause))
549	T:	Is _____ .
550		((pause))
551	T:	The number: ⊥ ?
552	Is:	The number -- ssse:ntences --
553	T:	express
554	Is:	ek-express
555		complete ideas -- about -- numbers.

- -

338	T:	No:w let's go ba:ck to our sentences,
339		and let us compare
340		the sentences in group A -- and --
341		group B. ((pause))
342		How do you compare -- the sentences in
343		group A -- and in group B?
344		((pause))
345	S:	Mam.
346		((pause))
347	T:	Ro _____ .
348	Ro:	The group- the group A
349	T:	The sentences: ⊥ ?

EXHIBIT 1. HELPING THE CHILDREN "GET STARTED" (Continued)

350	Ro:	The: sentences -- sentences --
351	T:	[ ] in group
352	Ro:	of group A =
353	T:	= in --
354	Ro:	in group A
355		is a number sentence =
356	T:	= (a:re)
357	Ro:	are -- number sentence =
358	T:	= ses
359	Ro:	sentences -- while the -- set B --
360		is -- set -- set -- sentences.
361	T:	((chuckles)) Who can say it again?

plete sentence. He needed two assists before he was truly on his own (lines 551 and 553). There were also cases in which a child began to answer, but in the teacher's view needed to be reoriented right away. It is difficult to know for sure whether the child was heading for a wrong answer, or was simply off to a bad start because of trouble with the language. In lines 338–361 of Exhibit 1, the latter seems to have been the case. Throughout the sequence, Ro did appear to be on the right track, once the teacher had restarted him (line 349), and in spite of further production problems.

Once a child was under way with an answer, the problem was to "keep going." The children sometimes had difficulty handling this on their own. Throughout the lesson, their answers had a halting, hesitant sound, as they paused to decide what came next, caught themselves in the middle of the wrong word, or doubled back to sentence or phrase beginnings to be sure they were on the right track. Some of these difficulties are illustrated in Exhibits 2 and 3.

Examples in Exhibit 3 illustrate different kinds of help students derived from the teacher, through what I call "intra-turn prompts," that is, prompts made by the teacher while the student still officially had the floor. Most commonly, the children hesitated between words, indicating uncertainty about how to proceed. At such points, the teacher usually provided the next word or phrase (lines 369, 442, 564, 566). The students also occasionally needed help completing a

EXHIBIT 2. TROUBLES WITH "KEEPING THE ANSWERS GOING"

262	T:	Why do you say no? --
263		No _____ .

264	No:	Because they- -- they are -- incomplete.

403	T:	Repeat. ((pause))
404		Pu _____ .

405		((pause))

406	Pu:	The sentences -- of group in A --
407		group A --

408	T:	The sentences in group A: $\perp$?

409	Pu:	The sentences -- in group A -- are
410		number sentences -- while --
411		( ) sentences- -- sentences
412		in: -- group B -- are -- set sentences.

466	Mu:	The sentences -- in group A --
467		are -- are-

468	T:	You just say -- the
469		number sentences: $\perp$? =

470	Mu:	= The number
471		sentences are- -- complete --
472		while -- the (setel)- -- set
473		sentences are -- incomplete.

660	T:	= Who can correct this sentence?

661		((pause))

662	S:	Mathematical sentences express complete ideas
663		about- ((pause)) about -- numbers:: -- and sets.

750	T:	= So what are number phrases?

751	S:	Number phrases -- are: -- are the par- ay
752		the parts of sentences that have no complete ideas.

word on which they had made a recognizable start (as in lines 175–176). The teacher's normal method of prompting was to provide just the segment, word, or phrase needed, and with rising intonation. But she also occasionally repeated part of what had already been said, either to bolster a shaky start (lines 171–173), or to reinforce a momentum not yet in full swing (lines 602–604). And, it also happened that a child did not require all the help which the teacher started to give. In lines 619–624, Le needed only the first part of the missing word in order to proceed on her own, even before the teacher had finished her prompt. Finally, line 716 is an example of a different mode of prompting, in which the teacher inserted a question into a break in the child's answer. Here, she took the last three words of the child's start and transformed them into a "slot-*what*" question (a variation of the "sentence-completion" format, which she then used in line 718; see Johnson, 1979, pp. 15, 25).

In addition to the work of starting an answer and keeping it going, the teacher also actively monitored and corrected the children's grammar. This work was accomplished either upon completion of a child's response, as illustrated in Exhibit 4 ("post-turn corrections"), or within the response's ongoing production, as in Exhibit 5 ("intra-turn corrections"). The latter cases are especially revealing of the teacher's close attention to the language dimension of her teaching. In general, it is *through* the teacher's correcting work that we can best see the types of grammatical mistakes the children made.

The most obvious and frequently corrected production errors were in three categories for which there are plausible sources in the structure of Tagalog, the children's native language. First, the children continually did not use plural forms of nouns (see Exhibit 4: lines 34, 36–37, 39–43, 207, 211–213, 591–593). In Tagalog, plurals are formed by placing the particle *mga* before the noun, rather than by using an affix. Second, they also had difficulty with English prepositions (Exhibit 2: lines 406–408; Exhibit 4: lines 655–663; Exhibit 5: lines 89–93, 350–355, 389–393). Tagalog relies on *sa* to indicate, given the context, the relations "in," "on," "at," "to," "for," "from," "by," "into," "with." (There are additional prepositional forms built on *sa;* the term also enters into the complex Tagalog verb-focus system; see Schachter & Otanes, 1972.)

Third, there were a number of verb-related problems. At one point, a child left out the verb (see Exhibit 3: lines 563–565); in Exhibit 5, there are several examples of trouble with the English copula "is" (lines 76–80, 89–90, 104–105). The former case was probably due to their unfamiliarity with the word "express" and to their difficulty in producing full sentence responses. The latter can be traced to the lack of a copula in Tagalog. (The particle *ay* occurs in structures resembling English copula usage, but it functions as a marker for an inversion construction having stylistic implications; see Schachter & Otanes, 1972, pp. 485ff.) There was also an occasional problem with subject/verb number agreement (Exhibit 5: lines 354–357); Tagalog verbs are only optionally marked for number.

EXHIBIT 3. "INTRA-TURN PROMPTS"

---

166 T: What ideas -- do -- the sentences in group A
167   express?

168   ((pause))

169 T: Ro _____ .

170   ((pause))

171 Ro: The: --
172 S: ex-express
173 T: They expre:ss: _↑_ ? =
174 Ro: = They
175   express i-
176 T: ideas about: _↑_ ? =
177 Ro: = ideas
178   about ((pause)) about numbers.

- -

364 T: As _____ .

365   ((pause))

366 T: The sentences: _↑_ ? --
367 As: The (sen)- --   = the sentences -- in
368   group A --   are number
369 T: are
370 As: sentences while- -- while the
371   sentences -- in group B -- are
372   letter sentence- -- are -- are
373   letter sentences -- (   ).

- -

438 T: = What is the *difference* between the two?

439   ((pause))

440 T: Es _____ .

441 Es: The:: --
442 T: The number sentence =
443 Es: = The
444   number sentence like group- --
445   in group A -- (   ) uses a
446   number while -- while the
447   examples -- in group B uses a set.

- -

EXHIBIT 3. "INTRA-TURN PROMPTS" (Continued)

561	S:	The numbers -
562		((pause))
563		the number sentences -- complete =
564	T:	= express: ⊥ ? =
565	S:	= express --
566	T:	ideas: ⊥ ? --
567	S:	ideas -- about -- numbers.

- -

602	S:	Set sentences- -- set sentences express
603	T:	express
604	S:	express complete ideas about sets.

- -

615	T:	= Now what is the difference? ((pause))
616		((pause))
617	T:	Le _____ .
618		((pause))
619	Le:	Number sentences --
620	T:	expre-
621	Le:	express
622		complete ideas about numbers,
623		((pause)) and set sentences ex-express
624		complete ideas about sets.

- -

713	T:	What is a number phrase?
714		((pause))
715	S:	Number phrase is- ((pause)) did not have- ((pause))
716	T:	Did not have what?
717	S:	Complete ideas.
718	T:	It has no complete: ⊥ ? --
719	S:	ideas.
720	T:	ideas. =

There were other production problems which are not so obviously associated with Tagalog, but which nevertheless contribute to my sense that the children had only a tenuous grasp on the medium of instruction. There are two examples of the children's difficulty in matching the structure and content of their answers to what was required by the teacher's question. Early in the lesson, GI got a right

EXHIBIT 4. "POST-TURN CORRECTIONS"

33	T:	What are they?
34	S:	Sentence.
35	S:	Ss:-
		[
36	Ss:	Sentence. =
37	T:	= ses:: =
38		Again.
39	Ss:	Sentence. =
40	T:	= ses::
		⌐
41	S:	ses:.
		[
42	Ss:	ses:.
		[
43	Ss:	ses:. =

- -

126	G1:	No.
127	T:	No they: ⊥ ?--
128	G1:	No they (are).
129		((pause))
130	T:	Repeat.
131		((pause))
132	G1:	No- -- no they: --
133	( ):	(Here).
134	T:	No they don't.
		[ ]
135	G1:	No they don't.

- -

158	T:	Given ( ), that was given already.
159	S:	Set sentence.
160- 163	T:	Sets: = alright. = Other mathematical sentences -- express -- ideas -- about -- sets:.

- -

204	T:	What ideas: -- do they express?
205		((pause))
206	T:	Ideas about: ⊥ ?
207	S:	Ideas about set.
208	T:	Yes:. =
209		= Will you repeat- -- the answer,

EXHIBIT 4. "POST-TURN CORRECTIONS" (Continued)

210		As _____ ?
211	As:	Ideas about set.
212	T:	Sets:.
213	As:	Sets. =

- -

589	T:	Repeat.
590		((pause))
591	Ad:	The: -- set sentences express -- complete
592		ideas about -- set.
593	T:	Sets:.

- -

648	S:	Mathematical sentences -- express complete
649		ideas.
650		((pause)) ((T writes on board))
651	T:	Make it complete.
652		((pause))
653	T:	Add something to make it clear.
654		((pause))
655	S:	Mathematical sentences express
656		complete ideas with
657		numbers and sets.
658	T:	Complete ideas: $\perp$?-- with: $\perp$? -- numbers -- and sets.
659	Ss:	[numbers -- and sets. =
660	T:	= Who can correct this sentence?
661		((pause))
662	S:	Mathematical sentences express complete ideas
663		about- ((pause)) about -- numbers: -- and sets.

- -

731	Pu:	Numbers phrases -- have no -- complete --
732		answer.
733		((pause))
734	T:	It's already there.
735		Have no complete ideas.
736		When they have no complete ideas
737		they have no answers. =
738		= Ano? *[Isn't it?]*

EXHIBIT 5. "INTRA-TURN CORRECTIONS"

75	T:	Proceed.
76	S:	((reading from board)) Two hundred plus one hundred --
77		great- --
78	T:	is greater than =
79	S:	= great- greater
80		than -- fifty plus twenty.

- -

85	T:	Group B.
86		((pause))
87	T:	Im _____ .
88		((pause))
89	Im:	((reading from board)) Set -- set Y -- eqi- -- is
90	T:	is
91	Im:	equivalent set N.
92	T:	to
93	Im:	to set N.
94	T:	Again. =
95		= Set Y is equivalent to set N.
96	Im:	Set Y is e- -- is e- -- quivalent
97	T:	quivalent
98	Im:	to se-
99	T:	is equivalent
100	Im:	is equivalent -- to set N.

- -

104	S:	((reading from board)) Set N -- not equivel- not e- is not
105	T:	is
106	S:	equivalent ((pause)) (we)- --
107	T:	Proceed.
108	S:	((reading from board)) Set N -- is -- not equib- --
109		equal -- to set N.

- -

350	Ro:	The: sentences -- sentences --
351	T:	in group

EXHIBIT 5. "INTRA-TURN CORRECTIONS" (Continued)

352	Ro:	of group A =
353	T:	= in --
354	Ro:	in group A
355		is a number sentence =
356	T:	= (a:re)
357	Ro:	are -- number sentence =
358	T:	= ses
359	Ro:	sentences -- while the -- set B --
360		is -- set -- set -- sentences.
361	T:	((chuckles)) Who can say it again?

- -

382	T:	Repeat. =
383		= Very good. --
384		Ju _____ .
385	Ju:	The group of: --
386	T:	( )
387	Ju:	The: -- set of: --
388	T:	The sentences: ? =
389	Ju:	= The sentences of group A -- in: --
390	T:	in
391	Ju:	set A --
392	T:	in group A =
393	Ju:	= in group A: --
394	T:	are
395	Ju:	[
		are number sentences -- while
396		the- while set- -- while set B =
397	T:	= the sentences: ? =
398	Ju:	= while the sentences in
399		the set B --
400	T:	in group B =
401	Ju:	= in group B are --
402		set sentences.

- -

EXHIBIT 5. "INTRA-TURN CORRECTIONS" (Continued)

595	T:	Al _____ .
596	Al:	Set se- -- set sentences ((pause)) is a
597		complete ide-
598	T:	[express =
599	Al:	= express --
600		complete ideas about nu- -- sets.

answer, but she was unable to expand it into a complete sentence with the proper verb form without the teacher's help (Exhibit 4: lines 126–135). Another child offered what the teacher transformed into the answer she wanted, but the key word ("set") was part of what was really a different answer, and in a different construction, than what the original question required (Exhibit 4: lines 158–163). Throughout the lesson, the children often did not have the proper lexical item available where they otherwise seem to have grasped the intent of the question. For example, one boy repeatedly wanted to use "set" for "group" (Exhibit 5: lines 385–393, 398–402) and "sentence" (lines 395–398), and "group" for "sentence" (line 385–389). The term "equivalent" posed a problem, as did "differentiate" (as we will soon see). Late in the lesson, Pu remembered that "answer" was used to talk about "number phrases" earlier, but he had apparently not absorbed that it was but a synonym for what the teacher was really after, "ideas" (Exhibit 4: lines 731–737). Finally, the children did not always come up with complete definitions for terms already so covered—though these difficulties are also dependent on the extent to which the academic content of the lesson had been understood.

Elsewhere I have addressed the issue of whether the children's troubles in producing this lesson's target answers were a result of the teacher's *orientation* to their English, rather than of their actual difficulties with the English required for this lesson (Campbell, 1981). I demonstrated there that although the children could in fact answer questions without problems with English and without the teacher's help with their language, their problems with the medium of instruction are further apparent in the difficulty they often had with repeating answers which they had just heard. Furthermore, there were numerous problems with English that the teacher either did not notice, or "let pass"; these I take as evidence of the difficulties and of their not merely being an artifact of the teacher's attention. And, throughout the lesson, even with the teacher's help on specific

English problems, the children still stumbled and hesitated with their answers, in ways not themselves amenable to correction, but possibly influencing how frequently she requested repetitions.

Although my cumulative impression from this lesson is that the children did indeed have difficulties with English and that the teacher's language orientation in her mathematics teaching was correspondingly not unwarranted, there still remains the question of whether her efforts might have been overextended, in terms of what was required for the children to absorb lesson content. While it was obviously necessary to provide help in getting answers started and keeping them going, did she really need to inject corrections of plural forms, number agreements, and prepositions, where the essential mathematical meanings of the answers were not at stake? Did it really matter that her target definitions of concepts in this lesson be learned word for word? Might not the teacher's call for repetitions of answers have so routinized her instruction that effective problem-solving and inquiry related to these particular concepts were stifled? In short, was she not in fact too busy teaching English, at the expense of the mathematics?

We can never know for sure. I do not mean to dismiss indications that this teacher's language orientation might have been in conflict with the mathematical agenda of the lesson. But it is also important to appreciate how language and mathematics were necessarily interconnected here. Consider in particular the teacher's frequent call for answer repetitions. The fact that she continually had students repeat answers, and to do so in full sentences, does of course contribute to the appearance of a lesson on language rather than on mathematics. Yet we must not forget that repetitions can serve an important reinforcing function for the mathematical content, which is especially critical in a second-language situation such as this, where there is definite reason to believe that the children did not in fact have full access to the mathematical content *because* of the medium of instruction imposed on them.

More importantly, we must not overlook the nature of this particular lesson's content. They were dealing here with mathematical ideas *as* ideas, and with the defining of terms—in short, with the production of sentences. That the sentences they were to produce were themselves *about* sentences (of a mathematical sort) only underscores and makes more visible a point which is applicable to less "meta"-oriented content. If students are to understand mathematical concepts and operations, as well as use them in computations, they will sooner or later necessarily be involved in *talking* about them. Thus, drilling answers, especially those in full sentence form, is not merely the result of some separate, possibly conflicting goal of instruction; it is inextricably bound to what is required for the fullest presentation and use of mathematics. Although it is commonplace to acknowledge that language learning goes on all day, not just in language arts classes—and not only in second-language situations— I am arguing that the effort to teach it in this lesson was not intrusive upon but *intrinsic* to instruction in mathematics, however agonizing the process might have been to them as participants, and to us as observers sympathetic to the advantages of learning mathematics in their native language.

Up to this point, I have made my argument about the interconnectedness of mathematics and the language of its expression on the basis of sequences of classroom talk examined in isolation from each other and from a view of their place in the whole lesson as a "context." Though in the limited space available here I cannot fully remedy this situation, I will now summarize a longer exposition presented elsewhere (Campbell, 1981) of what I learned from returning to this lesson as a coherent whole in order to examine how the children's difficulties with English and the teacher's attention to them fit into the overall ebb and flow of the lesson.

Having established with the children definitions for "number sentence," "set sentence," and "number phrase," and having had them compare the definitions of "number sentence" and "set sentence," the teacher asked the children to "differentiate" the two types of mathematical sentences. As revealed in the Appendix, almost 6½ minutes were required before the teacher's target answer was elicited, compared with only 2½ minutes for the "comparison" task, and only 12 minutes for everything that had occurred up to that point. When the children failed to provide the answer the teacher sought for the "differentiate" question, she began a series of simplifications, involving first a reformulation of the original question into "What is the *difference* between the two?" and "Find the differences between the two." When these also failed, she began to review the basic definition of "number sentence" already established earlier in the lesson, first with the open-ended question "What can you say about the number sentences?", eventually leading to the question "What do *these*—number sentences—express?" (Exhibit 6: line 508). As Exhibit 6 reveals, she had to continue to reduce the complexity of her questions and the answers they required, until in effect, all else having failed, she selected the answer "numbers" from the children's offering of both "numbers" and "sets" to what had become a multiple-choice question frame, "About what? = Sets or numbers?" (line 537).

EXHIBIT 6. "WHEN ALL ELSE FAILS"

507	T:	Now,
508		what do *these* -- number sentences --
509		express?
510		((pause))
511	T:	What complete ideas -- do they express?
512		((pause))
513	T:	What are the sentences about?
514		((pause))
515	S:	The sentences about ( ).
516		((noise from the next room))
517		((pause))
518	T:	Hmm,
519		Ro _____ .
520		((pause))
521	Ro:	Complete mathematical sentences. =
522	T:	= Yes, they are complete mathematical
523		sentence.
524		The question is, what complete ideas
525		do they -- express?
526		((pause))
527-	Ss:	((four Ss overlap/"cascade" the response "five"))
530		
531	T:	Anong buong -- kaisipan -- ang kanilang --
532		ipinaghahayag? [What complete ideas do they express?]
533		What complete ideas do they express?
534		((pause))
535	T:	Complete ideas about: ⊥ ?
536		((pause))
537	T:	About what? =
538		= Sets or numbers?
539	S:	Sets.
540	Ss:	Sets.
541	Ss:	Sets.

(continued)

201

EXHIBIT 6. "WHEN ALL ELSE FAILS" (Continued)

		[
542	S:	Numbers.
		[
543	S:	Numbers.
		[
544	S:	Numbers.
545	T:	Numbers. ((T writes answer on board))

In the initial stages of my analysis, this extended sequence of trouble was especially compelling to me as evidence that the language of instruction here was exclusively a serious obstacle to the teaching of the mathematics. Upon closer scrutiny of the teacher's simplification strategies in this sequence, however, I began to recognize phrasings that I had heard in earlier phases of the lesson. I gradually realized that the teacher's attention to the English of the children's answers throughout the lesson could be seen as intricately tied to the mathematical content per se. I would now like to summarize the evidence for my claim that the teacher's orientation to language was intrinsic to the mathematical ideas she presented. This depiction of this lesson would not have been possible without having taken the whole lesson into account as a relevant context for making sense of isolated exchanges.

This account is predicated on a number of assumptions about this teacher and her students, not the least of which is that she was quite aware of their difficulties with English as the medium of instruction. Given how constantly she and her colleagues referred to the extra burden of having to teach subject matter content in English, this is not surprising. But I am further assuming that she was so aware of the language dimension of her teaching that she deliberately presented the mathematical content of the lesson in close concert with the language required to express it. She did this in order to prevent disruptions possible because of problems with the English medium, and in order to resolve any language-based troubles that might nevertheless intrude as she developed the mathematical ideas. I contend that she was engaged in various types of "work" toward these ends throughout the lesson, but especially at the outset. The upshot of this work over the course of the lesson was that she was indeed teaching English as much as mathematics—but that this is better seen as a necessary process of teaching mathematics *as* language.

Thus, by the time the teacher first posed the "differentiate" question, she had already given considerable attention to the key mathematical terms, verb phrases, and sentence structures which would eventually come together in her target generalization. In what I call "foundation work," she informally introduced these elements into the public stream of talk quite early in the lesson; for example, the critical frame "express (complete) ideas about X," which was the core of the definitions of number and set sentences, as well as essential to the answer to the "differentiate" question, was introduced with the very first utterance of the lesson: "Class, what do we say, or write, when we wish to *express—some ideas?* ((pause)) You like to say something. You want to *express an idea.* What do we say or write?" (my emphasis). These foundations formed the basis upon which the teacher eventually assembled the generalization. They were also in place for the additional work that would later be necessary as more serious troubles emerged.

As the lesson proceeded, the teacher gradually elaborated and juxtaposed the foundation elements into ever closer approximations of their eventual final forms, both by her subsequent questions and in the subtle transformations which she performed on the students' answers. This is "shaping work," which is exemplified by how the teacher took a child's answer "set sentence" (to the question "What—do the other mathematical sentences *deal with?*") and expanded it into a complete sentence which transformed "set sentence" into "sets"; reinforced the use of the phrase "express ideas about X"; and attached this phrase to the concepts "mathematical sentence" and "set": "Sets: = alright. = Other mathematical sentences—express ideas—about—sets:." From the vantage point of "shaping work," the teacher's attention to the lexical forms and syntactic structures of the answers in English was less an *intrusion* of grammatical concerns into the realm of mathematics, and more an essential part of the overall shaping of the concepts to be learned.

"Anticipation work" is a broader way of depicting what the teacher was doing with the mathematics and the English. In particular, it involved having the children repeat answers in drill fashion, which served the purpose of determining whether they had absorbed an answer, and of reinforcing their acquisition of it. But the repetitions also served as preparation for what the teacher anticipated to be production problems they might have later. Drilling, therefore, may appear to have intruded on the smooth flow of knowledge transmission in the short run, but may also have facilitated that flow in upcoming phases of greater conceptual difficulty, where insufficiently mastered phrases and sentences from earlier phases might indeed interfere with what the children could learn. Overall, the teacher's efforts anticipated the difficulties the children *might* have with the English, in such a way as either to avoid problems in the first place, or to respond to them with the accumulated experience of already accomplished foundations and shapings.

Amidst all of this, the teacher was constantly evaluating the children's progress, in terms of how well they were doing on *this* question *now*, in order to determine how well they were likely to do with what she would ask them next, and how well they were progressing toward what she was driving at for the lesson as a whole, all of which can be considered "monitoring work." Because she was dealing with children whose abilities differed, she needed to be especially careful in judgments she made about the class as a whole from answers provided by only one or a few children, and how she drew on her prior knowledge of an individual's abilities in treating a given answer as a sign of learning by the class as a whole. All of this entailed that aspect of monitoring which I see as "barometer reading": the location of indicators within children's answers of an approaching storm of trouble.

What, then, was the cumulative effect of these types of work by the time they reached the "differentiate" phase of the lesson, and how did it condition what then happened? Although the essential elements of the target answer had been laid down and shaped, the children had had various problems with both the language and the concepts required to produce answers, and they had not in fact been required so far to produce the full sentence definitions of "number sentence" and "set sentence" which would eventually be conjoined into the answer to the "differentiate" question. The teacher, therefore, through her monitoring work, likely had only modest expectations for what she was about to ask, if not more serious reservations about troubles yet to come. It was, accordingly, in her best interest to move on cautiously, and to look for further signs of trouble, in order to draw on what had already transpired for remedies as necessary.

As she moved on, there were immediate signs of trouble. No one responded when she asked the class to differentiate the number sentences and the set sentences. The first child called on was unable to answer; and the teacher was already beginning "elaboration work," by providing a reformulation and specification of the basic question: "How do you differentiate? = What is the difference? Between the two?" Gl then produced a truncated version of the answer to the earlier question about *comparing* the sentences: "In group A—number sentences while—in group B—set sentences." This was the first overt sign that perhaps they did not understand the teacher's question, and as such was possibly a barometer to the teacher of what the rest of the children might have been having difficulty with. But perhaps the teacher was not sure yet either; her next move was to highlight the core of her original question: "I said *di::*fferentiate, ha? Now look at the sentences very well. Find the differences."

Without waiting for a response to this request, she began "probing work" into the strength of the foundations she might otherwise have been taking for granted, by asking them again about what ideas the number sentences expressed: "What can you say about the number sentences? = What ideas do they express?" The first wrong answer was from Mu: "The number sentences are—complete—while—the (setel)—set sentences are—incomplete." This foreshadowed deeper troubles; Mu appeared to be grasping at an earlier contrast made between "number sentences" and "number phrases." The teacher then called on Le, at what I claim became a major barometer reading and turning point in the lesson. Le had been the only child who could produce a virtually flawless version of the answer to the "comparison" question in the previous phase; later, she would be called upon to produce the complete "differentiate" answer. Thus, the teacher might have reasoned, "If she can't answer even the review question about number sentences, which we have already covered fairly thoroughly, then the rest must be really lost!"

The question was posed: "What complete ideas do:—the number sentences express? About what? ((pause)) Le ____ ." And the result? Le hesitantly offered "The:—number phrase," thus following Mu's wrong turn. They *were* in trouble. My claim for how the teacher read Le as a barometer here is that she now realized much more was at stake than just their comprehension of the "differentiate" question; the foundations which had been laid down in the earlier phase of "Presenting Concepts and Terms" had not set well enough. After repeating one more time that she wanted them to *differentiate* the groups of sentences, she moved unequivocally to remedy the more fundamental problem of how well the target answer's foundation elements had been absorbed, beginning an extended sequence of "repair work."

At its outset, the teacher's repair work can also be construed as "recourse work," in that her main strategy was to reach back to the foundations established in earlier parts of the lesson. In lines 507–511 (Exhibit 6), she was effectively directing their attention to the specific sentences on the blackboard; this amounted to repeating a question they had been able to answer in an earlier phase. But since they could not answer it now, the teacher began a series of steps that constitute "simplification work." When the first step, however, did not produce the answer she wanted (lines 513–521), she made the more dramatic simplification moves represented in lines 531–545, in which she translated the recourse question into Tagalog (lines 531–532); repeated it in English (line 533); truncated it into "sentence completion" form (line 535); further reduced its demands by the "slot-*wh*" form (line 537); and began to give up, for all practical purposes, by providing a multiple choice, or guessing, opportunity (line 538). Finally, when even this amount of telling resulted only in their cascaded production of *both* answers (lines 539–544), she effectively concluded that all else had failed by virtue of grabbing from the stream of talk the answer "numbers" which her "grabbing work" and blackboard recording reified as correct (line 545).

This left them at a different turning point for the lesson. In effect, they had reached the pit of their troubles and could now begin the gradual climb back to the original question, through what I call "recovery work," a process which was not without its own stumbles and delays, but which nevertheless in fairly short order set the stage for Le's formulation of an answer so painfully and persistently pursued: "Number sentences—express complete ideas about numbers, ((pause)) and set sentences ex-express complete ideas about sets."

Whether the teacher might have avoided this trouble altogether by not having begun with a difficult term such as "differentiate" is less the point here, I would like to argue, than that she did a remarkable job in assessing that the children's difficulties were much more than their comprehension of this term alone. I claim that she sensed the fragility of the foundations developed for the "number sentence" and "set sentence" components of her target answer, and that for her, Le's wrong answer was especially revealing of this. I have tried to show that the various types of work conducted in the early phases of the lesson had as their purpose preventing and remedying just the types of troubles that did occur later.

Lest we be tempted to second-guess what the teacher might have done differently at various places in the lesson, I want to emphasize that in teaching there is always the element of risk, of reaching for an answer too soon, or too late. Here, she took a chance that enough about the "number sentence" and "set sentence" definitions had been established earlier to permit their taking a shot at contrasting these terms with each other. That she did misjudge their readiness should not detract from the reasonableness of taking that chance, given the careful preparatory work she had conducted, the fact that they had succeeded in the "comparing" task, and her own readiness from prior foundation, shaping, anticipation, and monitoring work to meet the "differentiate" problem head-on. In the process, she was able to give them further opportunities to practice the English frames necessary for talking about these concepts. Had she not been "going for the English" as much as the mathematics all along, the children could not have re-established the foundations for contrasting the mathematical ideas encapsulated in linguistic forms, and for eventually encapsulating the lesson's work as a "generalization" to be written down and remembered.

CONCLUSION

In support of my argument that children's access to academic knowledge in classrooms depends on acquiring discourse patterns for talking about the targeted content of lessons, I have in this chapter focussed on the details of language use in a grade 6 mathematics lesson taught in a Philippine classroom. I have tried to show that for this lesson, at least, the use of English as the required medium of instruction can be seen as more than just interfering with mathematics instruction. By providing examples of the children's troubles with English, as well as the ways in which the teacher attended to those troubles, I hope to have demonstrated that her careful work with the correctness and completeness of their English actually contributed to rather than hindered their understanding of the mathematical content of the lesson. This is a consequence, I contend, of the need for children to be able to control discourse patterns for talking about the mathematical concepts they are learning, in order that they be able to make their own use of those concepts, for further conceptual learning and for problem-solving applications in their lives.

I would like to offer some suggestions for how this argument might apply to situations beyond the one I have illustrated from the Philippine context. In particular, what does my analysis suggest about children's access to academic knowledge in both the monolingual and multilingual classroom settings that are typical in societies such as that of the United States?

With respect to those common instructional situations in the United States and in other parts of the world that are monolingual—that is, teacher and students are all native speakers of the medium of instruction—it might seem that the need to focus on discourse patterns for talking about manifest lesson content is less compelling than is obviously the case where, as in the Philippines, command of the medium of instruction cannot be assumed in the first place and so must be closely attended to while teaching the content. On the other hand, it is possible to see a second-language situation such as the Philippine case as providing relatively easy access to and visibility of a phenomenon that is also present but rather more invisible and subtle where the language of instruction per se is not an issue.

For myself, it was precisely the realization that teaching mathematics in the Philippines might require teaching English discourse patterns (as well as grammar and vocabulary) for talking about it that I began to appreciate the suggestion of Michelle Rosaldo (personal communication) that teaching any content might benefit from attending to the discourse concomitants of concepts and skills, in order for the learning to be maximally effective as it occurs, as well as applicable beyond the immediate instructional event. This would be no less the case for a monolingual situation, because the participants' unproblematic sharing of the medium of instruction does not obviate the fact that there are patterns of discourse which are necessarily involved in instructional activities in general, as well as some that are possibly unique to the particular features of the subject matter content in focus in a given lesson.

Mathematics seems to me to be an area for which this insight is especially appropriate, in that the tendency to see mathematics as a language system in its own right, with characteristics purportedly distinct from (and even superior to) everyday language, makes the discourse required for talking about mathematical concepts and problem-solving applications difficult to acknowledge and describe. Analyzing how mathematics and English are taught in tandem in a second-language situation in another cultural and linguistic setting can therefore provide a model from which, by contrast, the intertwining of subject matter and the discourse of its expression can become more visible in less obvious situations, such as the monolingual classroom, and for any kind of subject matter instruction.

As for the implications of my analysis for multilingual situations in the United States, it is of course important to acknowledge a major difference in circumstances. In the Philippine community where I did my study, all the classroom participants had in common both their own native language and the encounter with English as a second language. By contrast, in multilingual situations in the United States, where English is the medium of instruction, it is also typically the native language of at least the teacher and some if not most of the non-minority children in the class. Insofar as the situation in the United States (and in many other parts of the Philippines as well, where more than one native language is spoken in the community) is therefore complicated by greater diversity of language and cultural backgrounds than existed among the teachers and students with whom I worked, the importance of my argument about the intertwining of subject matter and discourse might seem to pale before the face-to-face struggles and political debates that revolve around issues of personal identity, ethnolinguistic loyalty, and psychosocial well-being in the formation of bilingual education policies.

Nonetheless, I would like to conclude with the suggestion that, whatever one's position is on the issues of assimilation, transition, and maintenance of language use and cultural identity in discussions about bilingual education in the United States and elsewhere, it remains crucial to examine closely the experience of teachers and children in classrooms as they confront whatever mix of language goals and languages in use with which they are presented. I offer my analysis as a model of what might be learned when one attempts to move beyond the obvious (e.g., English as the medium makes teaching mathematics very difficult where it is not a learner's native language) to show in detail what classroom participants are able to do to cope with, confront, finesse, even triumph over whatever may stand in the way of effective teaching and learning. I can only hope that such analytic efforts as might be mounted in the variety of multilingual circumstances existing in the United States can result in descriptions of classroom life that will be used as resources in larger and more comprehensive efforts to assure equality of access to quality educational experiences for all children, regardless of language and cultural background, and irrespective of one's position in debates about the advantages and disadvantages of pluralism in education and society.

REFERENCES

Boggs, S.T. (1972). The meaning of questions and narratives to Hawaiian children. In C. Cazden, V. John, & D. Hymes (Eds.), *Functions of language in the classroom* (pp. 299–327). New York: Teachers College Press.

Bremme, D.W., & Erickson, F. (1977). Relationships among verbal and non-verbal classroom behaviors. *Theory Into Practice, 16*(3), 153–161.

Campbell, D.R. (1981). *"Going for the answers" with questions in a Philippine elementary mathematics classroom.* Unpublished doctoral dissertation, Stanford University, Stanford, CA.

Campbell, D.R. (1986). Developing mathematical literacy in a bilingual classroom. In J. Cook-Gumperz (Ed.), *The social construction of literacy* (pp. 156–184). Cambridge, England: Cambridge University Press.

Cazden, C., John, V., & Hymes, D. (Eds.). (1972). *Functions of language in the classroom.* New York: Teachers College Press.

Cherry-Wilkinson, L.C. (Ed.). (1982). *Communicating in the classroom.* New York: Academic Press.

Cook-Gumperz, J., & Gumperz, J. (1982). Communicative competence in educational perspective. In L.C. Wilkinson (Ed.), *Communicating in the classroom* (pp. 13–24). New York: Academic Press.

Erickson, F. (1976). Gatekeeping encounters: A social selection process. In P. Sanday (Ed.), *Anthropology and the public interest* (pp. 111–145). New York: Academic Press.

Erickson, F. (1982a). Classroom discourse as improvisation: Relationships between academic task structure and social participation structure in lessons. In L.C. Wilkinson (Ed.), *Communicating in the classroom* (pp. 153–181). New York: Academic Press.

Erickson, F. (1982b). Taught cognitive learning in its immediate environment: A neglected topic in the anthropology of education. *Anthropology & Education Quarterly, 13*(2), 149–180.

Erickson, F., & Mohatt, G. (1982). Cultural organization of participation structures in two classrooms of Indian students. In G. Spindler (Ed.), *Doing the ethnography of schooling* (pp. 132–174). New York: Holt, Rinehart, & Winston.

Erickson, F., & Shultz, J. (1981). When is a context?: Some issues and methods in the analysis of social competence. In J. Green & C. Wallat (Eds.), *Ethnography and language in educational settings* (pp. 147–160). Norwood, NJ: Ablex.

Florio, S. (1978). *Learning how to go to school: An ethnography of interaction in a kindergarten/first grade classroom.* Unpublished doctoral dissertation, Harvard University, Cambridge, MA.

Goody, E.N. (1978). Towards a theory of questions. In E.N. Goody (Ed.), *Questions and politeness: Strategies in social interaction* (pp. 17–43). New York: Cambridge University Press.

Green, J.L., & Wallat, C. (Eds.). (1981). *Ethnography and language in educational settings.* Norwood, NJ: Ablex.

Griffin, P., & Mehan, H. (1981). Sense and ritual in classroom discourse. In F. Coulmas (Ed.), *Conversational routine: Explorations in standardized communication situations and prepatterned speech.* The Hague, Netherlands: Mouton.

Gumperz, J.J. (1982a). *Discourse strategies.* Cambridge, England: Cambridge University Press.

Gumperz, J.J. (Ed.). (1982b). *Language and social identity.* Cambridge: Cambridge University Press.

Gumperz, J.J., & Herasimchuk, E. (1975). The conversational analysis of social meaning: A study of classroom interaction. In M. Sanches & B. Blount (Eds.), *Sociocultural dimensions of language use* (pp. 81–115). New York: Academic Press.

Gumperz, J.J., & Tannen, D. (1979). Individual and social differences in language use. In C. Fillmore, D. Kempler, & W. Wang (Eds.), *Ability and language behavior* (pp. 305–325). New York: Academic Press.

Heath, S. (1982). Questioning at home and at school: A comparative study. In G. Spindler (Ed.), *Doing the ethnography of schooling* (pp. 102–131). New York: Holt, Rinehart, & Winston.

Hymes, D. (1974). *Foundations of sociolinguistics: An ethnographic approach.* Philadelphia: University of Pennsylvania Press.

Johnson, M.C. (1979). *Discussion dynamics: An analysis of classroom teaching.* Rowley, MA: Newbury House.

Labov, W., & Robins, C. (1969). A note on the relation of reading failure to peer group status in urban ghettos. *Florida Reporter, 7*(1), 54–57.

Levin, P. (1978, November). *Questioning and answering: A cultural analysis of classroom interrogative encounters.* Paper presented at the annual meeting of the American Anthropological Association, Los Angeles.

McDermott, R.P. (1974). Achieving school failure: An anthropological approach to illiteracy and social stratification. In G. Spindler (Ed.), *Education and cultural process: Toward an anthropology of education* (pp. 82–118). New York: Holt, Rinehart, & Winston.

McDermott, R.P., & Aron, J. (1978). Pirandello in the classroom: On the possibility of equal educational opportunity in American culture. In M. Reynolds (Ed.), *Futures of Education* (pp. 41–64). Reston, VA: Council of Exceptional Children.

McNamee, G.D. (1979). The social interaction origins of narrative skills. *Quarterly Newsletter of the Laboratory of Comparative Human Cognition, 1*(4), 63–68.

Mehan, H. (1978). Structuring school structure. *Harvard Educational Review, 48*(1), 32–64.

Mehan, H. (1981). Ethnography of bilingual education. In H. Trueba, G. Guthrie, & K. Au (Eds.), *Culture and the bilingual classroom* (pp. 36–55). Rowley, MA: Newbury House Publishers.

Philips, S. (1972). Participant structures and communicative competence: Warm Springs children in community and classroom. In C. Cazden, V. John, & D. Hymes (Eds.), *Functions of language in the classroom* (pp. 370–394). New York: Teachers College Press.

Rist, R.C. (1970). Student social class and teacher expectations: The self-fulfilling prophecy in ghetto education. *Harvard Educational Review, 40*(3), 411–451.

Rosenthal, R., & Jacobson, L. (1968). *Pygmalion in the classroom: Teacher expectation and pupils' intellectual development.* New York: Holt, Rinehart, & Winston.

Schachter, P., & Otanes, F. (1972). *Tagalog reference grammar.* Berkeley, CA: University of California Press.

Schenkein, J. (Ed.). (1978). *Studies in the organization of conversational interaction.* New York: Academic Press.

Stubbs, M. (1976). *Language, schools, and classrooms.* London: Methuen.

Trueba, H., Gutherie, G., & Au, K. (Eds.). (1981). *Culture and the bilingual classroom: Studies in classroom ethnography.* Rowley, MA: Newbury House.

Vygotsky, L.S. (1978). *Mind in society: The development of higher psychological processes.* Cambridge, MA: Harvard University Press.

Wertsch, J.V. (1978). Adult-child interaction and the roots of metacognition. *Quarterly Newsletter of the Laboratory of Comparative Human Cognition, 1*(1), 15–18.

Wertsch, J.V., & Stone, C.A. (1978). Microgenesis as a tool for developmental analysis. *Quarterly Newsletter of the Laboratory of Comparative Human Cognition, 1*(1), 8–10.

APPENDIX 1. TRANSCRIPTION CONVENTIONS

The following are the transcription conventions used in this chapter. These conventions were adapted from the system worked out by Gail Jefferson and her colleagues (see Schenkein, 1978, pp. xi–xvi).

Symbol	Example	Explanation
	Le ___ , Ro ___ , etc. Le, Ro, etc.	Wherever the teacher names a child, the first two letters of the name, followed by underscoring, are used in the body of the transcript and in utterances quoted in the text. Only the first two letters are used in referring to identified children in the text, and in designating speaking turns in the transcript.
	S, Ss	These are used in the transcript to designate children who speak but who cannot be identified; "S" refers to one child, "Ss" to two or more.

[ ]	T: Set sentence.
	     [ ]
	S: Set sentence.
	          [
	S: Set-
		Brackets are used to indicate overlapping talk across two or more speakers. They and the utterances they link are aligned as closely as possible to the actual points at which overlapping begins. Occasionally, the end points of overlap are also marked.

=	S: Set. = S: = Number. = T: = Number.	The *equal sign* is placed between utterances which are so precisely timed with respect to each other that there seems to be no pause between them. This is called "latching": it can occur both within and between speaker turns. Wherever possible, the latched lines are lined up according to the equal signs; the spacing on the page does not always permit this, however.
⌐_	T: It is: ⌐_ ? -- S: ⌐_ not.	This symbol is used to link up talk which neither overlaps nor latches, but which seems more closely connected across speaker turns than is normal. It often designates a succeeding speaker's talk which seems to overlap into a pause created by the previous speaker, as in the use of the "sentence completion" format for asking a question.
-	S: The:- [T: The set.	A *single hyphen* indicates an abrupt halt or break in the stream of talk, as when someone is uncertain or is interrupted.

(continued)

APPENDIX 1. TRANSCRIPTION CONVENTIONS (Continued)

--	S: The -- phrase?	*Long dashes* are used to indicate brief pauses, too short to time, but noticeable as hesitation on the speaker's part.
,	T: Set, or sets.	The *comma* also designates a brief pause, but is used instead of the long dash when the pause occurs at the end of a syntactic phrase or clause, as in normal written discourse.
	((pause))	Longer pauses are shown in this fashion, both within and between speaker turns.
: :	T: Sets: : . Al:right.	*Colons* are used to indicate prolongations of syllables. More are used to indicate longer stretching.
___	T: D̲ifferentiate.	Syllables or words which are <u>underlined</u> are spoken with noticeable emphasis.
: ⊥ ?	T: It is: ⊥ ? -- S: not.	This combination of symbols marks the "sentence completion" question, in which the teacher starts a declarative sentence but indicates with rising intonation and final word lengthening that the children are to provide the words which will complete it (or, "fill in the blank").
↓	S: They [S: They do not.	An *arrow* between speaker designations indicates that the first speaker's utterance becomes indistinguishable from those that follow it, as when one child begins and the rest of the class join in.
( )	T: It is (there). S: The ( ).	*Parentheses* are placed around transcribed material about which there is some doubt, concerning either what was said or who said it. Empty parentheses mark sounds which could be heard but not deciphered.
(( ))	T: ((chuckles))	*Double parentheses* mark comments, contextual information, non-verbal activity, etc.
[ ]	T: Ano ito? [What is it?]	*Slanted brackets* enclose English translations of Tagalog utterances.

APPENDIX 2. THE LESSON'S CONTENT/ACTIVITY PHASE STRUCTURE

Grade 6-A Mathematics: "Mathematical Sentences" August 27, 1975 Time: 52:50 minutes	tran- script line no.	elapsed time	total time for phase
Preliminaries			2:02
OPENING GREETINGS	1	0:00	0:09
INTRODUCING THE SCOPE OF THE LESSON			1.53
Recognizing Sentences	5	0.09	1:10
Types of Sentences	50	1.19	0:37
Purpose of Lesson: "Mathematical Sentences"	67	1:56	0:06
Lesson Proper			21:24
PRESENTING BASIC CONCEPTS AND TERMS			7:32
Reading Examples of Mathematical Sentences	70	2:02	1:35
Types of Mathematical Sentences	120	3:37	3:32
Content: Numbers versus Sets	120	3:37	1:05
"Number Sentence"	164	4:42	1:03
"Set Sentence"	197	5:45	1:24
Number Phrases	251	7:09	2:25
COMPARING SELECTED TERMS			8:44
Comparing "Number Sentence" and "Set Sentence"	338	9:34	2:17
Differentiating "Number Sentence" and "Set Sentence"	415	11:51	6:27
Posing and Paraphrasing the Task	415	11:51	1:11
Reviewing "Number Sentence"	450	13:02	4:03
Reviewing "Set Sentence"	577	17:05	0:23
Summary: "Number Sentence" vs. "Set Sentence"	606	17:28	0:17
Formulating the Difference between Sentences	615	17:45	0:33
RECAPITULATING AND REVIEWING THE CORE TERMS			5:08
Defining "Mathematical Sentences"	634	18:18	1:26
Naming Two Kinds of Mathematical Sentences	671	19:44	0:31
Defining "Number Sentence"	684	20:15	0:16
Defining "Set Sentence"	690	20:31	0:29
Reading the Generalization in Unison	699	21:00	0:23
Defining "Number Phrase"	709	21:23	2:03
Evaluation Activities			29:07
DOING SEATWORK EXERCISES	766	23:26	20:52
COPYING HOMEWORK ASSIGNMENT	1090	44:18	8:15
Closings			1:12
CLOSING THE LESSON	1213	52:33	0:17
End of Lesson End of Tape Recording	1221 1230	52:50 53:45	0:55 —

CHAPTER EIGHT
The Language of Science Teaching

J.L. LEMKE
City University of New York/Brooklyn College

PERSPECTIVES FOR A STUDY OF SCIENCE CLASSROOMS

Science teaching is a profession whose use of language blends scientific discourse with the more familiar talk of classrooms and the common parlance of everyday speech. In this chapter we will look closely at the use of language in the science classroom to see how a community's specialized uses of language, by enabling us to make just those kinds of meanings appropriate to particular kinds of situations, enlists us all in perpetuating social patterns we are too busily caught up in to examine critically, or seek to change.

People *do* things with language, mainly with other people. Language in use is a tool for social action: giving orders or enlisting cooperation, negotiating relationships, obtaining and sharing information, seducing, insulting, impressing, soothing, praying, deceiving, praising and damning, buying and selling, persuading and dissuading, beguiling, demanding, and offering—everything we can do with one another, for one another, and to one another with speech.

The kind of language heard on a particular occasion will be a function of the uses to which speech is being put there and then. It will vary systematically with the kind of situation that people are bringing into being through their speech and other actions. The language specific to a particular *type* of situation has been called its linguistic *register* (Halliday & Hasan, 1985). In describing the register, we pay attention to the activity in which language is playing a part (e.g., teaching a science lesson), the personal or professional relationships of the people speaking and listening (e.g., student–teacher relationships), and the way in which language is being used as part of the activity (e.g., to control face-to-face behavior by giving spoken instructions). When the language use situation changes in any one of these respects, we usually have a different register. This means

216

there will be differences in the vocabulary, grammar, and organization of the language used. So, the register of classroom mathematics teaching will differ from science teaching to the same class, by the same methods, at least in its use of those portions of the English language with which we convey the meanings specific to mathematics (as opposed to science). If a teacher faced an evening class of adult business executives, but used the same methods of instruction for the same science topic, we would still expect the language used to reflect the differences in social relationships and social status. And if the lesson were being prepared as a written script to be performed in a studio in front of only a video camera, for later viewing by students, we would find still other kinds of differences in the way language was used, even if the topic and student audience were the same as for the regular lesson.

The register of classroom science teaching is best understood as a kind of *hybrid* among other registers. First, it has obvious relations to the other registers that use *scientific language,* though it will differ in the uses to which that language is being put. The science teacher speaking to a student and the working scientist speaking to a colleague or assistant may both ask questions about electrical voltage, but the phrasing and sequence of questions and answers tend to reflect the very different activities of the speakers. A scientist's or science teacher's *spoken* words will not read exactly like a scientific article or textbook, but they still reflect the influence of the more formal written science registers. Science classroom register also has close relationships to the other registers of *classroom teaching,* regardless of subject area. Whether mathematics or history or science, talk about going over homework, and teachers' ways of evaluating and praising answers, are shared by these registers because the activities they are used in share common teaching methods. Finally, part of the language used in the register of science teaching does not seem particularly specialized, either as a form of scientific language or language peculiar to classrooms. The function of building up shared meanings between teachers and students often requires use of common, colloquial ways of saying things, which I will simply call the language of *everyday speech.*

Here are some examples of actual science classroom language that show the features of these three kinds of talk and their combinations, all taken from the same lesson:

Scientific:	This is a representation of the one-S orbital.
	When an atom is in its ground state its electrons hold the lowest possible energy.
Classroom:	Please take out your homework, homework ten.
	That's from the other class, we might as well use it for review.
Everyday:	Uh, look how fancy I got. It's, uh, fat and skinny.
Combined:	Where was I? Chemical periodicity, number two.
	Electron comes to town, wants to go into the cheapest hotel.

Teachers learn to speak a socially defined and rather uniform linguistic register of classroom science teaching that combines, either in pure or mixed forms, elements of the language of science, the language of schools and classrooms, and everyday speech. It would be wrong, however, to assume that the science classroom register is an entirely *harmonious* synthesis of these elements. We will see that there is an almost explicit tension in the register between scientific and everyday ways of saying things, and this tension is often exploited in the continual contest between teachers and students that lies beneath the surface of even the most cooperative lesson. There is also a less easily noticed, but still very important tension between the science content talk of the classroom and the classroom rules and procedures part of what is said, as if the two belonged to separate realities. In addition to both of these, there is the implicit tension between the language of working science and the language of classroom science, reflecting important differences in what people are up to and what society's stake is in these different social activities. We will return to these issues very soon, but now, having briefly characterized this register, let's consider what sense we can make of language use in actual science classrooms.

OBSERVING SCIENCE LESSONS

By the time I came to do the research described in this chapter, I had spent many hundreds of hours as teacher educator and consultant, observing lessons by new and experienced teachers, teaching classes, discussing lessons I'd observed with teachers, and talking with students about their reactions to lessons. I had already noticed the tension between "scientific" ways of saying things, or at least the ways teachers and students took to be normal for a science lesson, and more colloquial, everyday ways of talking that were often laughed at or corrected, but which always seemed to draw an unusual amount of attention from students, particularly when they were said by a teacher. I had often noted that students who had been looking around the room, or out the window, or talking to their neighbor, very quickly became attentive when a teacher stopped speaking in the more usual language of classroom science and became more playful or more personal.

Together with a linguist experienced in studying school language (Shirley Heath), I observed and recorded several dozen junior and senior high school and university science classes in physics, chemistry, biology, and earth sciences. I will not use the university data here, but concentrate on that from the schools. These were large urban schools filled with students from a wonderful diversity of ethnic groups and social and economic class backgrounds. They were schools with good reputations in their communities for academic standards, and most of the classes I observed were like those I had seen in many schools in different parts of the country, urban and suburban.

The records of our observations consist of field notes and audio (also some video) tape recordings. The field notes were made on the spot in the classroom as things happened. They supplement the recordings and give the context of what is said: background information on the teacher, curriculum, and class; relation of the lesson observed to other lessons; description of what was on the board and the demonstration table; who sat where, and who talked to whom, and when.

The observations were selective and focused in two ways. First, we made note of information useful in interpreting what would be heard on the tape. When a teacher said, "Now, look at this," we noted what "this" seemed to be. But we also noted where the students were actually looking at that point. At a given moment, some students will be looking at or writing in their notebooks, some will be whispering to a neighbor, others will be looking out the window, copying from the board, reading a hidden magazine, or even looking at the teacher (or where the teacher wants them to be looking then).

From these observations, we tried to estimate what percentage of students were at various moments during the lesson *communicatively engaged* with the principal activity of the lesson and how many seemed disengaged, not paying attention, restless, distracted, bored, and so forth. This turned out to be easier to do than expected, since human social group behavior is patterned, and many students would become engaged or disengaged at about the same moments. We double checked our estimates against each other, and later against the videotapes. Rarely would there be a discrepancy of more than

10%; any changes in engagement were usually much bigger than this small margin of error. What we found was that *students are three to four times as likely to show signs of close engagement with the lesson when the teacher is breaking the usual rules of formal, impersonal ways of talking classroom science as when the rules are being followed.*

I have already used Halliday's notion of *register* to describe how the resources of a language may be used in ways specific to a particular activity. A burgeoning literature of studies of classroom interaction has evolved which describes specifically the registers of the classroom and how language and other actions are used to accomplish lessons. Heath (1978) describes teachers' language and some of its uses. Sinclair and Coulthard give a detailed analysis of some regular patterns of language use in classroom dialogue (1975), and Mehan (1979), Griffin and Humphrey (1978), and Griffin and Mehan (1979) have extended this work and placed it in the context of studies of how students learn classroom routines. A full account of my own research is also available (Lemke, 1982) as are recent collections of related studies edited by Green and Wallat (1980), Wilkinson (1982), and the more recent chapter by Cazden (1986). What practical help can we derive from all these perspectives when we come to analyze field notes and transcripts of real lessons?

At the risk of oversimplifying for a moment, I can point to two basic principles that will take us a long way:

1. Look for relations between the ways students and teachers co-operate or compete, and the ways in which the content of the lesson is developed;
2. Look at the relation between both of these aspects of the immediate situation and the larger scale, longer term social patterns that are being maintained or perhaps changed by what's happening in the moment.

I want to expand briefly on these two key points and illustrate them by analyzing some episodes from the science classes I have observed and recorded.

If a teacher asks, "What element has two electrons?" and a student answers, after raising his or her hand and being acknowledged by the teacher, "Helium?," and the teacher then says just "Helium," and moves on to another question, typically two different sorts of things are occurring. First, something is being said, overall, about the atom helium having two electrons. A system of *thematic relations* is being developed in the dialogue, relations among the themes of chemical elements, atoms, electrons, nuclei, and so forth. By looking at what was said before and after we can construct larger patterns of themes; for example, that the atoms of different elements have different numbers of electrons, whether or not this is ever said explicitly. Students are often expected to do the same, to pick up a way of talking chemistry that is not so much a body of knowledge or concepts as a shared way of making sense by using the language of chemistry that bridges between the academic-scientific community that the teacher represents and the way students and teacher are talking at the moment.

But this thematic use of language is not the only thing happening in that little dialogue. Part of a little behavioral ritual, a recognizable classroom *activity type,* is being enacted here, with a special twist. The typical pattern of question and answer in the classroom is that teachers ask, students answer, and teachers evaluate the answer before going on. So that last "Helium" said by the teacher will be taken by everyone as a confirmation that the answer was acceptable. But the total game of question and answer has many possible options and strategies with which it can be played by both sides. There are degrees of positive evaluation, there are negotiations over who will have the right to answer and whose answer will count, there are many options that follow a wrong answer, and there are many strategies to avoid answering or to cajole an answer.

As an illustration of different ways to answer, a student who answers with a *questioning* intonation, "Helium?", expresses uncertainty, hedging against committing oneself to this answer, and implicitly exposes the pretense of this classroom ritual: The teacher *knows* the answer. So it makes as much or more sense for students to ask *the teacher* as for the teacher to have asked them. By simply confirming the student's questioning answer and ignoring it as a question, the teacher is maintaining the *usual* pattern of the game. And the usual pattern of the game strongly favors teacher control of the dialogue. The language of the classroom always reflects the unequal power relation among the participants and not just their unequal mastery of the thematics of science.

These two aspects, the dynamics of the social interaction *and* the development of the thematic content of the subject, are, in principle, separable, but in practice they are interdependent aspects of the same flow of behavior. Our first basic principle tells us to separate these aspects only so that we can then look more carefully at their relations to each other.

Our second principle guides us to look for the reflections of the larger social system in what is happening all the time. Really, we need to look to many moments to draw conclusions about wider social implications of what we may be seeing. What sort of social power is it that lets some people get away with asking questions to which they already know the answers? Try it with a friend, or your supervisor, and see what happens. Who has the right, or power, to *test* someone else, to set criteria, or say what is the best answer? The note of uncertainty in the student's answer can be heard as a small challenge to the pretense of the game, as a hedging that signals the danger of a failure for which one may be punished by someone with the power to do so. But it is also in part an expression of the common uncertainty, not to say fear, that people in our community have when dealing with technical and scientific matters. Surely that is part of an important wider social pattern that is partly created by what happens everyday in science classrooms.

ANALYZING EPISODES

Real lessons do not have a unified overall structure; they consist of a greater or smaller number of distinct episodes. The initial episode begins with the task of getting the lesson started. Teachers say such things as:

> C'mon people, let's go
> OK. As we can all see, we have three Do Now questions on the board.
> Now on Friday we were talking about . . .

Teachers also make a bid to start the lesson by closing the door, erasing the board, or just coming to the front of the room and looking at the class. They don't need to ask the class directly to get started; they can refer to the activities that typically occur early in the lesson, such as going over questions on the board, handing in homework papers, and so forth. Or they can refer to past time and picking up where work had left off in a previous lesson.

EPISODE 1

The first episode we will analyze (see transcript A) begins with the teacher saying, "Before we get started . . . before I erase the board . . .", which alludes to the typical starting signal of erasing the board.

TRANSCRIPT A

1.   T: Before we get started . . . before I erase the board . . .
2.   S: Shhh!
3.   T: Uh . . . look how I fancy I got (points to board)
4.   S: (makes a funny noise)
5.   S: Shh!
6.   T: This is a representation of the 1S orbital.
7.   S'pozed to be of course – three dimensional.
8.   What two elements could be represented by such a diagram.
9.   Jennifer?
10. J: Hydrogen and helium?
11. T: Hydrogen and helium. Hydrogen would have <u>one</u> electron —
12.   somewhere in there — and helium would have?
13. S: <u>Two</u> electrons
14. T: Two (pause) This is 1S, and the white would be?
15.   Mark?
16. M: 2S
17. T: Two S. And the green would be?   uh . . .   Janice.
18.   J: 2P   2P
19. J: 2P
20. T: 2P. Yeah, the green would be 2P<u>x</u> and 2P<u>y</u>. If I
21.   have one electron is the 2Px, one electron in the 2Py,
22.   two electrons in the 2S, two electrons in the 1S, what
23.   element is being represented by this configuration?
24.   (screeching noise) Oo! That sound annoys, doesn't
25.   It's Ron?
26. R: Boron?
27. T: That would be – that'd have uh– <u>seven</u> electrons, so
28.   you'd have to have one here, one here, one here, one
29.   here, one here. Who said it-you?   What's—
30. S: Carbon
31. S: Carbon   Carbon
32. T: Carbon, Carbon. Here. Six electrons.
33.   And they can be anywhere within those— confining
34.   orbitals. This is also from the notes from before.
35.   The term orbital refers to the average <u>region</u> transversed
36.   by an electron. Electrons occupy orbitals that may
37.   differ in size, shape, or space orientation. That's—
38.   that's from the other class, we might as well use it
39.   for review.

<u>Note</u>: Underlined words signify vocal stress or emphasis. "S" refers to "student(s)" responding, with no specific person named.

But by saying *"before* we get started," the teacher also indicates a desire to begin a *preliminary* activity that will later be followed by the *real* work of the main lesson, the new work for the day. Any beginning is a joint accomplishment of the teacher, who usually takes responsibility for the first bid to get started (just as students often make the first bid to *end* a lesson), *and* the students, who must ratify the bid to start, cooperating with it as they do in the first episode by quieting down and even "shushing" other students.

This episode is a *brief review.* Reviewing thematic content taught before is its function, but that function can be accomplished not only by question and answer, as here, but also by a teacher monologue or in other ways, that is, using other *interaction patterns* (also called *participation structures*). The question-and-answer pattern, of course, can also be used for other functions than review, such as development of new thematic content, diagnostic quizzing, and so forth. Specifying both *function* and *interaction pattern* goes a long way toward identifying the particular activity type going on at any point during a lesson.

Once this episode does get under way, the teacher asks a question and calls on Jennifer to answer. Her response is made with questioning intonation, but is evaluated by the teacher with a firm declarative repetition of the word that she had said. This exchange is the prototype for the simplified example presented in the last section. You can now see that this teacher regularly confirms answers by repeating them. Sometimes he prefaces a question with a brief preparatory remark (as in lines 11–12), and he sometimes follows his evaluation with a brief supplementary comment (as in line 20). These are regular options of this question and answer interaction pattern. It would be possible to rewrite this whole dialogue as a teacher monologue with the same science content being presented; it is the social interaction pattern that would then be different.

Two interesting examples emerge in this episode of the tension between the use of language to develop the thematic content of the science lesson and its use to produce a smooth cooperative pattern of behavior which the teacher can dominate. In lines 17–20, the teacher has asked a fairly easy and predictable question in the complete-my-sentence format he favors here. Janice immediately answers, "Two P." A few lines before, a similar question was answered without the student being formally called on; the answer was accepted and things moved on normally (lines 12–14). Here the teacher first says "uh . . ." and Janice then repeats her answer loudly and clearly, taking the "uh" as a request for a clearer repeat. But now the teacher, instead of saying "Two P" himself as we expect, says "Janice" as if calling her to answer. He is trying here to enforce the rule that students should wait to be called on before answering, even though he does not enforce it all the time. When Janice does repeat her answer yet again, it is less loud and clear than the last time, and the teacher doesn't even let her quite finish it before he overlaps her speech with his own confirming repeat of "Two P." Both these features suggest that Janice and the teacher both know that her last repeat was purely pro forma, since her earlier answer has been clearly heard by everyone. The teacher has sacrificed the efficient development of the science themes here to an enforcement of order in the interaction pattern, a particular order which gives him the power to control who will speak when.

A little later in the episode something quite different happens. In lines 21–32, we find a difficult question asked; a bright student, Ron, is called on to answer it; his answer is not acceptable to the teacher, and the thematic development is in danger of ending up in confusion, when another student calls out the answer the teacher wanted "Carbon," interrupting him. The teacher tries to ascertain who said it, perhaps with an eye to acknowledging him by name and getting a repeat, as with Janice, but many students now call out this same answer, and the teacher proceeds simply to confirm it and go on. He could well have persisted in finding out who said it first, could have admonished the class not to call out, but here sacrifices the orderliness of the interaction pattern and his own position of control, briefly, in order to get the thematic development back on track, to complete the exposition through dialogue of the science content that he had begun with his question.

In this episode the exposition of thematic content is itself just as subtle as the social interaction. If you compare the exact phrasing of the teacher's questions in line 8 and lines 20–23, you can see that they help develop an entirely *implicit* contrast, important to the whole lesson, between *orbital diagrams* that *can* represent *several* elements, and *electron configurations* which *do* represent only a *particular* element. This contrast in turn is just a small part of the system of thematic relations among the terms *element, orbital, electron, atom* (which is never explicit here) and so forth. These relations can only be learned by experience of their usage in relation to one another in the language of the classroom or the textbook. The system of relations cannot be deduced from definitions alone, and in any case these are seldom repeated, usually a little vague, and hardly ever memorized. To a much greater degree than we may realize, science as a thematic system is learned the same way we learn the semantic system of our native language: *implicitly,* by hearing, speaking, being corrected, but mostly by actively shaping our speech to conform with what we hear around us. We infer patterns of meaning relations between terms and longer expressions from their repeated usage in a variety of different contexts. We will return later to some of the implications of this discourse model of classroom learning. But first another example of how subtle and implicit it can often be.

If you are not familiar with the symbol names for orbitals used in this episode (1S, 2P, etc.), you will probably not have noticed that the systematic relations between the orbitals are being implicitly reviewed all through lines 6–20: first 1S *vs.* 2S, then 2S *vs.* 2P, then 2Px *vs.* 2Py. These contrasts are then precisely and explicitly stated only in the teacher's final summary at the end of the episode in exactly the same order in lines 36–37, for these pairs of orbitals differ precisely in size, in shape, and in space orientation within the atom, respectively. The discourse of the science classroom constantly and pervasively shows this kind of subtle implicit structure of building thematic relations. This occurs to a degree that is almost certainly outside the conscious recognition of the teacher and students as it happens. It is rather a feature of the organization of information in spoken discourse.

By contrast, explicit formulation of definitions and relationships is a brief and occasional part of lessons. This inevitably means that those students who are accustomed, outside school, to hearing and using indirect strategies of thematic development similar to those favored by the register of science classroom discourse, will learn faster and better than those whose experience has not accustomed them to deciphering information that is coded in language in just this way. Speakers of nonstandard dialects of English, those whose first language is not English, and those from social groups that use different strategies for organizing thematic information in spoken discourse will be particularly at a disadvantage. All students, however, find it difficult to *use* actively the science register elements of classroom discourse. The importance of this fact can be more fully appreciated in a different classroom episode.

EPISODE 2

This second episode does not follow the common question-and-answer pattern; it presents us with an example of a very interesting, though certainly less common, recurrent pattern of classroom discourse: the teacher–student debate. Typically, an episode of this kind will begin with a student challenge to the teacher on *content* in the lesson: doubting, questioning, or contradicting it. On minor matters, teachers may accept correction, but in debates they defend the position that they have stated through a series of exchanges with one or sometimes a few students. Debates usually end when the teacher closes off the discussion, very often by appealing to some authority or law of science. The teacher is very much on the defensive in the debate, responding to student initiatives rather than directing the dialogue through questions.

Let's look first at the social interaction, and then at the thematic development in a typical debate (see Transcript B) from a lesson on the role of light and heat from the sun in weather. The transcript begins as the teacher has just finished writing on the board a summary of the preceding discussion, which was conducted according to the usual question and answer pattern. He now states out loud the main conclusion of that discussion (lines 1–3). As he does so, Eric starts to say something, but says it mainly aside, to his neighbor. The teacher asks him if he has a question. Because of the rule that students should not speak unless called on, especially to another student while the teacher is talking, his question functions in part to admonish Eric (a common technique). But in this case Eric *does* have a question. It is not unusual, and it turns out to be quite significant that serious student questions are often asked after an initial (officially illegal) conversational aside with a neighbor. The rules of good behavior (in Episode 1, raising your hand; here, not talking to your neighbor) are not always compatible with productive dialogue about the ideas of the lesson.

In this case, Eric's question functions as a challenge because it questions what the teacher has just said, presenting it as inconsistent with something that the teacher has said earlier. The teacher replies by conceding part of Eric's point, but defends himself by invoking a distinction (light vs. heat) that has already been important in the lesson. Eric now denies the applicability of the distinction (line 10), and the teacher defends it with an example (that fluorescent lights aren't hot), but another student helps Eric by contradicting the example, and Eric actually forestalls the teacher's attempt to cut him off (lines 14–15). This attempt incorporates the word "essentially" which the teacher frequently uses to mark important statements and often simultaneously to end little episodes of discussion. But not this time.

Eric initiates a logical argument with "so . . ." and then deprives the teacher of a turn in the exchange by continuing with "because . . ." and making a rather complex sounding argument (lines 18–21). So far the teacher has not used the verbal forms for explicit reasoning

TRANSCRIPT B

1. T: The <u>ground</u> is now creating <u>heat</u> energy <u>from</u> the light
2. E: Well– (aside)
3. T: energy. Eric, you have a question?
4. E: Yeah, how can it be the ground creates the heat energy,
5.   if the <u>sun</u> creates the heat energy?
6. T: <u>Well</u>, on the <u>sun</u>, and <u>in</u> the sun, the sun <u>is</u> creating
7.   a tremendous amount of heat energy. But it's sending
8.   most of its energy here as <u>light</u>. Traveling through
9.   space.
10. E: But light is <u>hot</u>, light is heat.
11. T: No! Some light is not hot at all. When I turned on
12.   these fluorescent lights today, I haven't roasted yet.
13. A: The bulb has heat.
14. E: Yeah, but when the bulb is on you get –the bulb gets hot.
15. T: And essentially–
16.   most energy from the sun comes here in the form of light,
17.   and <u>not</u> heat.
18. E: So the ground can't be <u>creating</u> heat because if the
19. T: Well–
20. E: ground wasn't dark, then it wouldn't absorb the light,
21.   and the light is heat, so it's not <u>creating</u> it.
22. T: No, light is <u>not</u> heat. The light is light energy.
23. E: Yeah, and <u>heat</u> is heat energy! (students laugh)
24. T: And if you remember back, to the eighth grade — and you
25.   should have learned a <u>rule</u>, and if you didn't it's O.K.,
26.   we'll learn it now. You can change energy from
27. E: What was it?
28. T: one form to another, but you can't create it or destroy it.
29.   Well I don't know if that's true anymore either. But —
30.   you can <u>change</u> it, from one form to another. And,
31.   that actually happens. The ground creates heat energy,
32.   from the light, which causes something very interesting.
33.   (pause) Oy! Attacked! Attacked by erasers in my
34.   old age! Oy.

<u>Note</u>: Underlined words signify vocal stress or emphasis.

(*if, so, because, then,* etc.). It is Eric who has done so. The teacher's forms have simply been those of assertion. The teacher responds to Eric by contradicting part of his last argument, and in doing so states an apparent tautology: "light is light energy." Eric then shifts the social significance of the debate by mocking the teacher's statement with a tautology of his own (line 23). Other students laugh at this, enforcing on the teacher an implicit rule against such empty sounding statements. The students feel they are being talked down to here by a tautology that doesn't sound logical. They are misinterpreting the force of the teacher's statement, but they are still using against him an accepted norm of science classroom discourse that tautologies or circular arguments are unacceptable. This is a fairly sophisticated class, but other classes also insist that their science teachers talk "scientifically" or what they believe to be scientifically. What is at stake now (and typically is in these debates) is not just thematic content, but the competence of the teacher.

The teacher's last resort is to the common strategy of invoking authority, particularly the outside authority of science. Given what has just happened (Eric's mockery), there is a double meaning to what the teacher actually says now (lines 24–26). Implicitly he reminds them that he is the one who has the authority to say what they 'should have learned,' but he will be generous ("it's OK") and let them learn it now. But Eric is not cowed yet, and quickly interjects a pro forma question ("what is it?"). That question is in effect a bid to redefine what the teacher will say next, making it seem to be another response to a student initiative rather than the teacher's way of regaining control of the discussion. The teacher does not quite let Eric finish the question; he has already begun to state the rule (lines 26 to 28). At this point, an ironic twist occurs; since the teacher knows that the observer (myself) is a physicist, he looks at me when he admits he may not have the rule quite right himself. The chain of authority from scientist to teacher to student, at least as seen by the teacher, becomes briefly visible.

The teacher uses his authoritative "rule" to reassert his *original* statement and quickly bids to move the topical development onto the next point ("which cause something very interesting"). He begins to write on the board. This typically is his most definite signal that an episode is at an end. His joking comment when the eraser he is using slips from his grasp, ricochets off the chalk rail and hits him, functions in this context as a plea for sympathy for a teacher who has come under attack. But in fact this teacher and his class have, on the whole, a very friendly and cooperative relationship, and he and Eric get along well together. We need to remember that in analyzing the microscopic details of any social interaction, we necessarily magnify the significance of what passes very quickly for the participants and may hardly be noticed at the time. Even so, when subtle patterns of conflict repeat regularly in lesson after lesson, across many teachers and classes, they can point to deeper contradictions and implicate wider social issues in what we observe in microcosm. I return to these questions in the next section.

Thus far, the science content of the lesson has scarcely been mentioned. But our judgments, and those of the participants, about the social functions of what was being said have necessarily relied on the relations of meaning among the terms and expressions used. Whether the teacher's saying "light is light energy" counts as a tautology or not, and how we take Eric's reply (as a counterargument or mockery), depends upon how we view the meaning relations of the terms used. So also does our judgment of whether a student, or the teacher, is really making a logical argument or just putting on a show of words. As with the other episode we analyzed, the full argument that the teacher is developing is never *explicitly* stated at any point. We do not finally hear, even at the end, what the relation between the sun's creation of heat energy and the earth's creation of heat energy (at issue between Eric and the teacher throughout) is, in the teacher's view. As typically in all these science lessons, the system of thematic relations that is needed to make sense of what is said must be gleaned from context, that is, from specific ways that expressions are used in relation to one another, differently at different points in the discourse. It is difficult to isolate one episode like this and discuss thematic developments in it apart from what has been said earlier in the lesson (or yesterday, or even "in the eighth grade"). I have given a more complete analysis elsewhere (Lemke, 1982), but we can still usefully note a few important strategies used in this episode.

Classroom talk frequently sets up contrasts or oppositions between pairs, or several, terms. These relations are very important for the meanings being developed. At the start of this episode there is a contrast between *heat* and *light* in the expressions "heat energy" and "light energy." Not only do the two words appear in the same frame (i.e., with *energy* following), but one is vocally emphasized, "*heat.*" This continues a pattern of contrasting these terms begun in previous episodes. Eric, in his challenge, introduces a new contrast, again with similar frames and vocal emphasis, between *sun* and *ground.* In the teacher's initial reply, there is a contrast between *in* and *on* (i.e., the sun) that is not further developed, another between *creating* energy and *sending* energy, and the *heat* vs. *light* contrast is used again and reinforced. Note, however, that the teacher's statement is still very *implicit:* There is no *on the earth* or *earth* (or *ground*) *is creating* to balance the concession made at the beginning of the statement, though this is precisely the contrast needed to answer Eric's objection. The teacher is speaking in terms of a system of thematic relations in which what he says makes perfect sense, *if* you are already familiar with this way of talking about light and heat, or *if* you are experienced enough with the particular forms of discourse organization that teachers favor to pick up on its cues to implicit thematic relations.

When students speak, they may be using a different and unfamiliar system of thematic relations, and they may use different forms of discourse organization, from which the teacher may not be as readily able to deduce the meaning relations that their statements imply. *Which* students get the benefit of the doubt, *whose* words a teacher searches more carefully to construct familiar meanings from unfamiliar expressions for them may depend on a teacher's prejudices or simply on how far apart the thematic and discourse organization patterns and expression of a teacher and various social groups of students may be. Consider Eric's long argument (lines 18–21).

At first reading, many teachers don't find much sense in what Eric says. And it unfortunately seems to be true that those who have read the transcript with the student's real name, Erin, are even more likely to find it flighty, jumbled, and illogical. The more familiar you may be with the teacher's viewpoint, with the typical science register's way of speaking of these matters, the harder it may to reconstruct the sense in what Erin[1] has said. In fact, she has picked up a theme from earlier in the lesson, that *darker surfaces absorb more.* From this she produces her contrast between *creating* energy and *absorbing* it, which, given the assumption that light and heat are pretty much the same thing, at least where sunlight is concerned, makes it quite logical for her that since the ground is dark, and the light-heat energy is coming from the sun, the ground must be *absorbing* it rather than *creating* it as the teacher has said. With even this partial reconstruction of the nonstandard thematic relations that Erin is working with, her verbal argument sounds much more logical than when viewed against the background of the more usual thematic system.

Whether something sounds logical to us depends *both* on differences between the thematic relations it assumes and those we use to interpret it *and* on differences between the *forms* it uses to express logical relations and those we are used to. Erin's sequence of clauses does amount to a logical argument, but they come one after the other in a rather unfamiliar way, as well as expressing a different view of the topic. Of course it is not easy for teachers,

---

[1] The male name, Eric, was deliberately used earlier to illustrate how a student's gender may be relevant to how we interpret her arguments, and how much benefit of the doubt we give her.

especially in the press of debate or under the pressure of time, to hear and translate into more familiar terms what students are striving to express in a register they're just beginning to master. But misjudgments as to whether what is said is logical or not, and so whether it is often even serious or not, may lead us to conclude that the other person is stupid, or trying to obfuscate or even insulting us (e.g., Erin's reaction to line 22). Judgments which color our views of students, or their views of us, are easily influenced in cases such as the ones we are discussing by our expectations and our prejudices. The sex, the race, the dress, the speech, the behavior of a student may be clues to better understanding the unfamiliar things they say, or they may mislead us or blind us in the effort to find *their* meanings, instead of only noting the absence of *ours*.

LANGUAGE AND SOCIAL RESPONSIBILITY

Careful study of the details of interaction patterns and thematic development in the language of science teaching can give us a feel for the living activities they help create. Those activities are themselves part of a wider social life that the study of language should illuminate. How does science classroom talk reflect and contribute to our attitudes to science and education? What larger social patterns does it help to perpetuate? How can its study help us to see those patterns more clearly so that we can reflect upon their implications and, if we choose, act more effectively to change them? The talk we have examined here takes place between teachers and students in science classrooms, but the patterns of our social life that it helps delineate may well extend beyond in other guises into the talk of scientists and nonscientists, experts, and novices, specialists and nonspecialists in business, government, or any other way of life. Anywhere, in fact, that a specialized way of using language, like that of science, is associated with power over others.

Let's consider two kinds of patterns in science classroom talk. The first has to do with maintaining the distance between scientific language and everyday speech; the second, with rationalizing success and failure in learning science.

Here are some examples of the first pattern. In one lesson, teacher and students are trying to describe a shape that has no everyday name. When the teacher seems content with descriptions such as: "kind of a skinny eight" or "the infinity symbol" (∞), a student says in surprise, "you don't have a name for it?" The student recognizes that these descriptions do not count as part of the technical language of science. When the teacher emphasizes that the shape is three-dimensional by saying, "It's fat. It's uh . . . fat and skinny" another student says, "That's nice and scientific," and the teacher acknowledges the irony in her comment. Later in the same lesson the teacher says, ". . . if it was put together by *nature*," contrasting *nature* with *printer* and *chemist*. A student chimes in, "Mother Nature, huh?" and other students laugh. Still later in that lesson the teacher says that electrons come in pairs "because they like to have these opposite spins." The swift reaction form another student is: "They *like* to?," underlining a verb more normally used to speak of people than electrons. In all these cases, and many more in other lessons, students comment on or laugh at things that teachers say which mix together our colloquial ways of speaking about matters in human terms with science topics that are "supposed to be" spoken of in a different way. In one lesson, when the teacher introduces the theme of how large a cell might grow to be by referring to a science fiction movie about a giant cell, a classroom leader and frequent rebel calls out in apparent exasperation to his friend down the aisle, "Why can't he explain *science* in a scientific way!" His emphasis on the word *science* even suggests a contrast to nonscience domains where this complaint need not be made.

Many examples from many lessons allow us to piece together the participants' picture of how science ought to sound in classroom language (Lemke, 1982, pp. 253–262). It should be as *explicit* as possible, without reliance on gestures, all-purpose words, and meanings left to be understood from context, all of which features are common in colloquial speech. It should be more like *written* English in its choice of words and grammar, with a formal sounding style that eliminates pronouns such as *we* or *you* and colloquial forms like *gotta*. Of course, it's supposed to use *technical terms,* but also common terms in specialized ways. It must avoid ambiguity, mystery, fantasy, humor, and colorful language. Most basically, I think it is expected to avoid the *humanness* of everyday language: no personification, no mention of specifically human attributes, actors, or types of action; no metaphors that call up human, emotionally loaded images. The result is familiar to all of us: the cold, impersonal world of science that seems so alien to the more personal, human world in which we are familiarly comfortable. The world of scientific language is a world where things simply are as they are; it is not a world of human action. No matter that this image is contrary to the real life of working science, which is as personal as any other part of social life. Even when it deviates from this "ideal" of scientific language, as it often does, classroom language still works to maintain

the separation from everyday speech. This has at least two consequence we should ponder.

First, it perpetuates not only the myth of a pure, disinterested
scientific objectivity—a myth that may serve the narrow interests of
scientists or those who profit from their work—but also a second
myth of objectivity, that nature simply is *as it is,* a fixed and given
reality so presented in scientific language as to encourage only an
attitude of acceptance. This strengthens the patterns many people
acquire of simply accepting everything that can cloak itself in scientific
language, separating itself from the everyday world, where we *do*
know that *people make things seem* as they do, and we do look
deeper. A *disjunctive* scientific language, one that defines itself over
against the wisdom of everyday speaking, is a particular way of talking
science that is alienating and supportive of dogmatism, if not deceit.
It represents a contradiction in the ethic of science, and its per-
petuation in schools ought to be challenged.

A further consequence of the alienating experience of classroom
science, which for most students is mainly an experience of its
language, is that it leaves students with little inclination to pursue
science further. How many students will regret, much less resent,
being deprived of access to the formidable power that science offers
those who can use scientific and technical information for their own
purposes, if they are first persuaded that such a cold, impersonal
subject can have little interest for them? How many people are
turned off to science in this way? How willingly they disenfranchise
themselves because of the subtle alienation of a false view of science.
The emotional tastes and preferences society inculcates in women,
and in many poorer and lower-middle-class groups, neatly ensures
that they will be the least likely to pursue an interest in a subject
presented as a cold, impersonal one. We glimpse here one of the
many important processes by which social relations of predominance
are reproduced.

In following up the wider social implications of language use in
the science classroom, we should consider not just the features of
its scientific language, but the rules of its common patterns of social
interaction through language. In the second episode we analyzed,
we noticed that Erin (alias Eric) asked her question challenging the
teacher and initiating the debate only after conferring with her
neighbor in an "illegal" aside. Students as well as teachers will tell
you that in the classroom students should not carry on such side
conversations during the lesson, especially when the teacher is talking.
In fact, if a teacher admonishes a student only by name (e.g., "Robert,

c'mon"), it is usually understood that what Robert has been doing, among all possible infractions of common rules, is talking out of turn.

The general rule against such talk is part of an elaborate code that governs who may talk when—and even about what—during the lesson. It is a code that gives the teacher, in principle, total dominance of the lesson. In practice, of course, students frequently call out answers without being called on, and even more frequently talk to their neighbors when they shouldn't. And, as in Erin's case, it is just as well for the progress of classroom education that they do. While some asides are wholly unrelated to the themes of the lesson, and some are joking comments in the students' battle to maintain some sense of self-esteem in what an adult would consider to be a rather degrading social situation, in many cases one student will ask another about something the teacher said that he or she missed, or ask what the current task is, or even ask for an explanation of something heard but not understood.

These asides often check for confirmation or support for an idea or question which the student will later publicly contribute to the discussion, creating what most experienced teachers know are among the best moments in any lesson: those when a student shows interest, makes connections, voices confusions. Because the teacher always seems busy talking, because most students have had bad experiences of being humiliated when asking questions in class, many students are reluctant to speak up at all and are more likely to do so when they have checked out their point with even one other student before making it publicly. Classes in which there is very little or no side talk among students, or classes in which there is little student initiative, tend to be too quiet and produce only an intellectually stifling one-way, teacher-dominated communication pattern. Those classes which have a lively and interesting dialogue usually have quite a bit of side conversation as well. Most teachers do not in fact admonish students every time they talk to a neighbor, and it's a good thing they don't.

This code of student silence, except when called on to *respond,* lives on its own contradictions. It is both highly functional in the classroom, and in principle forbidden, for students to carry on side conversations during the lesson. Side talk is necessary for the smooth functioning of the classroom as a social system, and so it occurs. It is also *not* strictly suppressed; the rules against it are only intermittently enforced. The net result is twofold: By occasional enforcement the principle is maintained that such talk is wrong, but at the same time the rule is consistently broken to keep things running smoothly. It is not hard to think of other situations in social life in which a law or rule of conduct is maintained *as* the law, as a matter of principle, despite the fact that it is broken all time, and despite our knowing that we wouldn't get along very well if it couldn't be broken. We can call these phenomena "social hypocrisies," but it remains to ask what the function may be of maintaining these pro forma rules as *the rules*?

I propose that they operate as part of an *ideology:* that is, as a system of beliefs that systematically hides its own true social functions. If the rules were strictly enforced, the ideology would be exposed as such because we would have to question the *basis* of a rule whose enforcement made our lives impossible. But by permitting a rule to be broken as often as necessary to avoid this, this maintenance continues to serve its hidden function. What might be the hidden functions of a rule against students talking to one another during the lesson? What ideology does it maintain?

Consider the educational assumptions behind a strictly enforced rule against side talk. The presumption is that classroom learning is essentially an *individual* process between separate, isolated students and the teacher. It is this assumption that justifies the rule, but observation of classes shows that what happens there is a highly *social* process: a complex, cooperative and competitive, mutually adjusting pattern of interaction among all the participants. The rule belongs rather to a picture of classroom learning that distorts its social nature to make it seem as if each student is solely responsible for what he or she learns or fails to learn in class. It is a picture in which it is easier to justify and rationalize educational failure as individual failures to learn. It makes it easier to maintain a system of social rewards based on the assumption that successes and failures in school are strictly individual, rather than interactional and social phenomena.

This assumption, and the system of awarding grades, opportunities, jobs, and radically different standards of living to people in our society that is based on it, seem to call for some critical reflection. At the base of this system, of course, behind the grades and before the opportunities, most often stand *test* results. According to this interpretation, it is no accident that the only classroom activity type in which the rule against talk between students is strictly enforced is *test taking,* that moment when the social process of the classroom is temporarily replaced by an artificial set of separate, isolated individuals.

This second example of wider social ramifications of a pattern of classroom language converges in at least one of its consequences with the first example. Students come away from their experience in science classes with a strong sense of having failed to really understand most of what was presented to them *and* with the belief that that failure reflects on them *as individuals.* "Science is just beyond me," they say, or, "You have to be a real brain to do science." They are led to believe in their own inadequacy, which serves, in part, to raise by contrast the prestige of those who do succeed in science, making them great believers in their own superiority and the relative unintelligence of those who "can't do science." But those who fail are consoled by the fact that, after all, this impersonal, inhuman science isn't something they'd really want to do anyway.

The patterns of language use in science classrooms contribute at one and the same time to a view of science as belonging to a world divorced from that of normal human activity and to the illusion that failure to understand scientific language reflects on us rather than on social practices that do not teach what they test nor test as they teach. Not only is testing artificially "individual" compared with a teaching that is more realistically social, but the standard we hold up of true success in learning science is the ability to use it actively, as we might fluently speak a foreign language, for the special purposes for which its thematic systems are designed. But what we teach is presented as if it were merely information about the world, rather than the complex system for making verbal and symbolic meanings about that world that we know the special language of science really is. If our teaching of foreign languages produces few fluent speakers, our teaching of science produces few scientifically literate citizens— and for much the same reasons. To learn to speak a language or use a specialized linguistic register like that of science, we need extensive practice in actively speaking and writing it in realistic social situations, for purposes that make sense to us, communicating with others, some of whom are more fluent users than we are yet.

The analysis of classroom communication locates learning in the mastery of specialized patterns of language use. Teachers and students employ linguistic, symbolic, and behavioral resources for social meaning-making to develop the thematic relationships we call the "science content" of lessons, and to enact the complex patterns of social interaction by which the life of the classroom or the laboratory is lived. Most students practice those interaction patterns in class after class, year after year, and become true masters of the games of cooperation, competition, conflict, and control that enliven classroom life. But very few in a short year or two, a few hours a week, get much practice at talking science, either in general dialogue or as part of specific tasks. A discourse model of learning makes sense of the fact that most students will not master the thematic systems to anything like the degree of skill they achieve in classroom tactics.

This state of affairs is no accident. It reflects and contributes to the maintenance of wider patterns of social power and control in our society, and is in turn the product of complex patterns woven moment by moment, by teachers and students, in what they say and do in classrooms. We are, all of us, every moment making the social order what it is, and we must accept responsibility to decide whether we shall go on doing so or begin to make it differently. Ultimately the social value of the detailed and systematic study of the patterns of language use in any social practice is to show us the wider implications of what we do unaware every day, so that we can no longer remain innocent of the harm we do, or complacent in actively supporting social inequities we do not like but never saw directly in terms of our daily work before.

As a teacher, I could not see what I taught myself to see as an observer with the help of a broader linguistic and social perspective. In my teaching now I am just beginning to apply the principles I have sketched here. One of them tells me that solely as an individual I cannot succeed in changing social patterns, in my classes or outside them. But by sharing a different way of looking at science and teaching, locating learning in regular patterns of discourse and social practice of which we must become aware, speaking differently about science and teaching, we begin already to do differently, to make our way where before it was made for us.

REFERENCES

Cazden, C. (1986). Classroom discourse. In M.C. Wittrock (Ed.), *Handbook of research on teaching* (3rd ed.). New York: Macmillan.

Green, J., & Wallat, C. (1980). *Ethnography and language in educational settings.* Norwood, NJ: Ablex.

Griffin, P., & Humphrey, F. (1978). Task and talk at lesson time. In R. Shuy & P. Griffin (Eds.), *The study of children's functional language and learning in the early years.* Arlington, VA: Center for Applied Linguistics.

Griffin, P., & Mehan, H. (1979). Sense and ritual in classroom discourse. In F. Coulmas (Ed.), *Conversational routine.* The Hague, Netherlands: Mouton.

Halliday, M.A.K., & Hasan, R. (1985). *Language, context and text.* Geelong, Victoria (Australia): Deakin University Press.

Heath, S.B. (1978). *Teacher talk: Language in the classroom.* Arlington, VA: Center for Applied Linguistics.

Lemke, J.L. (1982). *Classroom communication of science.* Final report to the National Science Foundation. ERIC *Research in Education.* (ED 222 346)

Mehan, H. (1979). *Learning lessons.* Cambridge, MA: Harvard University Press.

Sinclair, J.M., & Coulthard, M. (1975). *Toward an analysis of discourse.* London: Oxford University Press.

Wilkinson, L.C. (1982). *Communicating in the classroom.* New York: Academic Press.

CHAPTER NINE

Policy Implications Related to Teaching and Learning Mathematics and Science

CYNTHIA WALLAT
AND
CAROLYN PIAZZA
Florida State University

INTRODUCTION

One of the original purposes of this volume was to further the creation of a multidiscipline perspective for thinking about the academic and social nature of schooling. In the last two chapters, Professors Lemke and Campbell point out that the acquisition of reasoning and problem-solving skills can be explained in terms of how teachers and students organize their behavior within and across instructional settings, and how the "public school system is a 'dependent variable' of larger social and economic forces" (Kirst, 1986b, p. 341). In keeping with this perspective, the multi-discipline content of this chapter focuses on research and policy directions in mathematics and science education.

In particular, we consider two key questions:

1. What directions are needed for researchers and policy makers to work together and conceptualize instruction to reflect the social nature of the educational process?
2. How can the present need for information regarding policy implementation overcome the poor record of collaboration between scholars and decision makers?

To frame this chapter, we propose three points of departure: the Venue, the Verdict, and the Venture. Under Venue, we explore current reform efforts aimed at teacher quality and mathematics and science instruction, and discuss how research related to Lemke and Campbell's work can inform the implementation of reforms such as higher standards, time on task, and student and teacher assessment. While it is true that state education policy has become visibly active and new mathematics and science education policies are in place, the focus has changed to consider whether these policies can be implemented in ways that improve teacher quality and improve mathematics and science.

The Verdict section outlines available findings on teaching and learning that lend support to implementing strategies to foster the development of reasoning skills in mathematics and science in specific contexts. The congruence between recommended directions for implementing mathematics and science policies and past research converges on the unsolved issue of how to help decision makers conceptualize instruction to reflect the social nature of the educational process.

Finally, Venture underscores the potential for bringing policy and research together. The irony is that while the educational community and policy makers agree that research could help avert education going the way of other reform movements and falling once again into neglect, the verdict on utilization of research by policy makers is so negative (Wallat, 1987). Representatives of both the educational and political community have taken seriously the charges of scientific and technological illiteracy, and the need to shift today's definition of school mathematics and science to reflect preparation for an economy strongly based on the production and use of knowledge (Hurd, 1985). Consequently, the question, "how can educational research be done well and at the same time be more responsive to decision-makers?" has, as Strike (1979) points out, a long future.

In the following section, we begin exploring this future by considering recent policy ventures affecting mathematics and science.

THE VENUE: IMPROVING TEACHING QUALITY, IMPROVING MATHEMATICS AND SCIENCE

The fact that state education policy has become visibly active in the past few years is now a truism in the literature (Mitchell & Encarnation, 1984). In the first half of the 1980s, more than 100 national reports concluded that there was a crisis in education (Hurd, 1985). A tidal wave of legislation aimed at achieving higher academic standards, more time on task, more rigorous testing for both students and teachers, and more use of effective teaching performance passed through the states (Wallat & Piazza, 1986). Mathematics and science were singled out as subjects in serious need of state level reform (e.g., National Commission on Excellence in Education, 1983; National Council of Teachers of Mathematics, 1980; National Science Foundation, 1983; Task Force on Education for Economic Growth, 1983).

> Education policy has now passed through the "alarmed discovery" and "crisis activity" phases of the "issue attention" cycle . . . the processes of implementation and adoption, along with the elimination of unworkable reforms, have begun in earnest. (Kirst, 1986b, pp. 342–343)

In other words, included in the range of concerns now being heard regarding mathematics and science are policies which were designed to affect standards, time, testing, and performance. An overview of each of these policy categories, discussed against emerging sociolinguistic research, including Lemke and Campbell's work, demonstrates how legislative concerns may already overlap research concerns.

Higher Academic Standards

Approximately 70,000 different scientific journals report the results of research in diverse fields of science and technology. Yet, educators complain that the "movement to reform [mathematics and] science education is faltering for lack of [policies to ensure] intellectual nourishment" (Hurd, 1985, p. 357). The reason for this is simply because policy reforms were aimed at immediate action and visible results in the number of mathematics and science units students were required to take rather than address the fact that "distinction between one scientific effort and another are identified not by [discrete] disciplines, but by the problems being researched, such as cognition . . . antibodies . . . forecasting" (Hurd, 1985, p. 354). To address this, the mathematics and science curriculum would need to be reformulated not as extra test items, but "to include facts and concepts that . . . leave a great deal of room for interpretation in terms of human and social affairs" (Hurd, 1985, p. 354). As Professor Campbell's chapter points out, measuring knowledge of content by relying on test scores misses too much of what is actually accomplished in teacher–student interaction. That an observer might capture a lesson's content by considering the mutual interchange between teacher and student suggests that the recognition of teaching and learning as a social process can provide a barometer of the transmission of social and academic knowledge in subjects across the curriculum.

On a similar issue, as Professor Lemke's chapter points out, the dynamics of social interaction in the science classroom can be made visible if we interpret how teachers and students learn to articulate feeling both comfortable and uncertain when dealing with technical and scientific matters. In other words, observers of classrooms can learn to "see" the development of content of scientific subjects, and how what happens in classrooms are reflections of how society at large is sometimes comfortable and sometimes uncertain about scientific and technological change.

Time on Task

There is agreement that more time on task is needed for American students, but the public's willingness to expand the schoolday or schoolyear has not been forthcoming (National Research Council, 1985). One alternative means that has evolved to increase significantly the amount of effective learning time devoted to mathematics and science is extensive use of computers. The first wave of reports of effective computer time pointed to better test results and 10% score increases (Lesk, 1986); however, an investigation into why and where test scores went down led to some serious implications of more time on mathematics and science tasks. The first finding was that school organizational structures are not prepared to deal with the consequence of more individualized time on computers. The tradition of grade levels and sequenced curriculum stands in the way of findings which point not to the objective of everyone in the class being on par with one another, but rather students being less alike than they used to be (Lesk, 1986).

Another unexpected consequence of computer use is that students spend more time thinking about content. For example, five students and their teacher may have six different interpretations of what a mathematics operation is (Lesk, 1986). As Professor Campbell points out, the question of whether these kinds of consequences are perceived as "success" or "failure" can be answered through the use of methodologies that can identify and take into account the range of personal meanings and interpretations that encompass the transmission of knowledge. In other words, effective use of time on task to accomplish the objectives of development of reasoning skills in mathematics and science requires a systematic research program on the range of unexplored outcomes resulting from efforts to teach these skills (National Research Council, 1985, p. 53). To build toward a recognition of these unexplored social processes, researchers, including Lemke, suggest that we consider alternatives to current testing programs, which fail to explain how multiple interpretations develop during problem-solving tasks.

Rigorous Testing of Both Students and Teachers

Researchers generally agree that the theory of learning that underlies our evaluation of mathematics and scientific literacy "rests on sentence-level grammar and therefore neglects discourse-based understandings" (Cook-Gumperz, 1986, p. 9). The emphasis on state-mandated testing programs will no doubt continue to neglect unexplored consequences such as those introduced above until such time as new images of discourse, or communicative competence are generally known and understood (Wallat, 1984). As developed further in later sections, the discourse-based understandings reified in the work of Lemke and Campbell may serve the need to develop new metaphors to formulate state educational testing directions based on what successful problem-solving groups do:

> Focus discourse around a topic,
> Collaboratively create a social world verbally,
> Handle literate discourse in the oral mode (Heath, 1986)

Effective Teacher Performance

Studies of teacher planning (e.g., Shavelson & Stern, 1981) indicate that teachers think about instruction in terms of context and content. As researchers such as Stodolsky (1984) have pointed out, most teachers use very different instructional formats (i.e., recitations, seatwork, lectures, group work, tests) as they switch from subject to subject. In mathematics, for example, very little stand up teaching occurs. Use of an individualized curriculum, for example, makes "extensive use of materials and tests, and children work on their own most of the time" (Stodolsky, 1984, p. 15). What the formulators of effective teaching performance policies failed to see in calling for development and use of indicators based on the effective teaching behavior literature (cf. Wallat, 1987) was that the teacher effectiveness approach ignored a central aspect of classroom life: the interaction between subject matter, student, and teacher. "No one asked how subject matter was transformed from the knowledge of the teacher into the content of instruction" (Shulman, 1986, p. 6) and, the student's role in this process. In other words, the policy formulations regarding the use of effective teaching strategies were not based on an understanding of instruction which reflects the social nature of the educational process. Lemke and Campbell's work show how the growing sociolinguistic work on classroom language contributes to our understanding of the mutual construction of knowledge and how the production and comprehension of meaning is interpreted in light of the immediate situation. As argued in the next section, teaching and learning policies in mathematics and science may accomplish higher academic standards across colleges and public schools if they are based on understandings of how a particular reasoning skill in mathematics and science operates in a specific substantive context (National Research Council, 1985). In other words, how mathematics and science teaching and learning policy directions can be shaped to reflect the social nature of the educational process.

THE VERDICT: MORE IS KNOWN THAN IS USED

The goals of mathematics and science education as stated by planning commissions, legislative task forces, and creators of school improvement programs consistently emphasize reasoning, thinking and problem-solving skills. The test scores and literacy rates that are cited "show that such an education is possible but that it is not typically achieved in contemporary American education" (National Research Council, 1985, p. 30). The question is why do the recommendations and statutes aimed at curricular changes appear to have so little effect on the day-to-day problem-solving classroom activities?

Recently, a multidiscipline group addressed this question:

> There is irony in the circumstance that the transfer and use of knowledge from the mathematical and scientific disciplines, through the evolution of agricultural, medical, and engineering schools of industrial and governmental development centers and laboratories, has led to the economic and technological advancement of the United States and improved health for its citizens, yet the transfer of information about the teaching and learning of mathematics, science, and technology has been severely limited. More is known than is used. (National Research Council, 1985, p. 44)

Formulating an answer such as, more is known than used, might, at first, seem based on a simplistic method of inquiry and debate.

In fact, the opposite is true. In the early 1980s, the National Research Council, the research arm of the National Academy of Science, established a Committee on Research in Mathematics, Science and Technology. Eighteen scholars representing 10 disciplines (anthropology, chemistry, communications, education, engineering, mathematics, political science, psychology, psychometrics, sociology) addressed the question of what is known about mathematics and science teaching and learning as well as what broad categories of research are worth pursuing (i.e., what is known and can be built upon).

The four categories of recommended focused research (development of *reasoning;* quality learning time through better *instruction;* quality learning time through better *settings* for learning; quality learning time through *learning systems*) serve a useful purpose of identifying coherent clusters of research that policy makers and practitioners can tap as support for their objectives and proposed innovations. In other words, the categories capture relatively clear disciplinary strengths and traditions. What is equally important in terms of thinking about the implications of implementing mathematics and science policies is the multidiscipline committee's conclusion:

> We think that more is known about education than is currently being utilized effectively . . . and we think that the educational community can improve education by more effective integration of research and professional experience. (National Research Council, 1985, p. 59)

Just what is known within the four coherent clusters of research supported areas of improving schooling was addressed at the 1986 American Educational Research Association's annual meeting by six of the committee members representing political science, cognitive psychology, physics, anthropology, sociology, and education (National Academy of Sciences Committee, 1986). The committee chairperson, James March, representing political science, introduced the committee's four areas of recommendations by pointing out the "we know you don't just write an agenda, and expect it to be acted upon." Rather, the intent of such work is to build on what's going on, to give shape to building new images of educational research, and to give recognition to what is going on. Moreover, the nature of this research clearly intersects with the political concerns of legislators and undergirds the conclusion that the problem is not ignorance, but choice.

Among the areas of choice for further policy implementation, work in cognitive psychology identified by a National Academy of Science Committee member, Robert Glaser, were: How does knowledge get organized in different fields? How do students learn to recognize this organization? What kind of theory gets to go into the development of tests on problem solving?

These three questions clearly move the focus on cognitive psychology into the social realm. A succinct review of what is known about the social nature of schooling has been offered by Meighan (1981):

> One of the significant features of schools is their position as an agency of socialization. . . . School is an inescapable fact of life for all but a few in contemporary society. . . . One set of [social] functions has been described as "people processing." Schools screen, assess and grade the population for occupations and therefore significantly influence their life chances. . . . However, schools are simultaneously involved in "knowledge processing" since some knowledge is selected, deemed to be of higher status, and embodied in the curriculum. (pp. 264–265)

Clearly, these two social functions will be emphasized differently in different schools, but at least three dimensions of social life in schooling can be considered across sites. As explicated below, the processes involved in administrative organization, creation of specific situations for learning, and the use of language highlight a social perspective on schooling.

> One aspect of the social nature of educating is the institutional setting of learning. A school develops conventions, rituals, and routines to solve its administrative problems. It organizes children into groups . . . [or classes], distributes particles of time for subjects and activities and allocates . . . facilities. These have been shown to have a marked influence on those within the school. . . .

> Another aspect of the social nature of learning refers to the complex dependence on the immediate environment or situation. Pupils are not just interpreting new knowledge (itself of social origin), but the cues and attitudes accompanying it. These include the status of the new knowledge (this is mathematics, not PE, and it is deemed to be more important), the use of information (with math I can pass examinations and get a better job), the reaction of peers (our group dislikes the history teacher and his subject) and the relationship to other knowledge (my father thinks metalwork important because it is practical knowledge).

> A further consideration is the use of language as the main vehicle of learning, since this is a social, not an individual, construct. It is external

to us, created by others, and [is related to the knowledge processing aspects of schooling]. (Meighan, 1981, pp. 266–267)

The members of the National Academy of Science Committee gave recognition to social perspectives such as the above in a variety of ways. Arnold Arons, who described himself as a physicist interested in the education of teachers, reiterated the committee's conclusion that there is not a wasteland of knowledge about mathematics and science education. The problem Arons sees in choosing to use available knowledge is how colleges and universities are going to organize themselves to address the tough question of preservice training of teachers. Drawing upon his own work, he suggests that policies which simply cut down the number of education courses and add mathematics and science won't produce what is needed in public schools. The content of undergraduate courses does not address what teachers need in order to handle what ideally goes on in public school mathematics and science. In short, what Arons is directing our attention to is research that makes use of a set of social functions upon which analysis can be based and which, typically, results in formulating questions about possible interactions (<----->) among the following aspects of social behavior in schools:

1. Conceptualizations of pupil actions:
   individualistic <-----> collective.
2. Conceptualizations of knowledge:
   discipline-based <-----> general topics/themes.
3. Conceptualizations of learning:
   reproduction <-----> production.
4. Conceptualizations of assessment:
   product (scores) <-----> process (method).
   (cf. Meighan, 1981, pp. 167–168)

In order to develop further an inquiry about possible <-----> interaction among and between these aspects of social behavior, the next step is to consider what areas of research can be tapped on the basis of their relatively clear disciplinary strengths and traditions.

Areas of knowledge from applied and basic research on teaching and learning that are becoming known but seldom used were identified by an anthropologist on the National Academy of Science Committee, Frederick Erickson. Giving examples of recent work in ethnography of communication, conversational analysis, and interpretive sociolinguistics (cf. Gumperz, 1986), Erickson pointed out that the application of knowledge of what goes on in group formations and time spent in "reasoning" wouldn't look like what most people expect in classrooms. Participation structures that could be characterized as reasoning dialogue and engagement may not match the schematic expectations that many teachers and classroom observation researchers hold about what schools should look like (e.g., see Wallat, 1987 for an analysis of how the dynamics of a literary criticism type of reading lesson are not captured through the use of teacher performance observation systems based on effective teaching literature).

The committee members who represented sociology and education (Cora Marrett and David Wiley) further developed the panel's theme of the need to consider the social nature of teaching and learning. Marrett pointed out that we have some choices to make based on knowing that children are influenced by home and community as well as school conditions. Succinctly, the choice is whether to continue using a "garbage bag" approach to consider if and/or how school district differences, school group differences, peer group differences and ability differences interact with mathematics instruction in school and/or perceptions of science. The policy and professional choice that she sees is upon us is to continue to point to SES as influential without saying why, or to reach agreement on what home and school variables are critical for study. Continuing this argument, David Wiley noted that the result of emphasizing critical variables in policy directions may well be that practitioners and assessment designers have to acknowledge and act upon past findings which point out that reasoning is embedded in instruction strategies, curriculum tasks, schooling practices home and community activities, and so forth. In other words, the choice is between continuing to emphasize a cognitive view of the nature of teaching and, as such limit schooling to the first four findings listed in Table 1, or to adapt a view of teaching and learning as both a cognitive and social process and move on to address the last six findings in Table 1.

As highlighted in Table 1, implementation of ways that ensure a continued use of problem solving; a continued confrontation of already learned beliefs; a continued use of successful problem-solving steps; a continued availability of modeled comprehension skills; and a continued monitoring of within group processes, cannot be guaranteed if we ignore the social nature of educating (i.e., understandings of how particular reasoning skills in mathematics and science operate in a substantive context).

As we argue in the last section of this chapter, steps can be taken by scholars and policy makers to develop clearly articulated frameworks for conceptualizing instruction to reflect the social nature of the educational process.

Table 1. Building on Findings Identified by the National Academy of Sciences Committee on Improving Mathematics, Science, and Technology Education (National Research Council, 1985)

Strengths of A Cognitive View of Schooling

1. Can learn how to use a scientific relation from its written description, i.e., students reading scientific text practice finding different kinds of information (cf. Larkin & Reif, 1976).

2. Can learn not to be constrained to particular solution paths, i.e., tutor-teacher or computer-gives advice only when students head toward an unproductive end (cf. Anderson, 1981).

3. Can learn to categorize problems according to the relationships they involve—combine, compare, change—and, as such learn associate skills in basic mathematical operations (cf. Riley, Greeno, & Heller, 1983).

4. Can learn to interpret new information on the basis of prior knowledge, problem solving, and comprehension if instruction is aimed at helping students articulate their initial conception of facts and principles and then accept, modify, or reject them in light of their predictive power, congruence with new facts, and the like (cf. Collins & Stevens, 1982).

Limitations of a Cognitive View of Schooling

5. Cannot guarantee that when students master problem-solving techniques they will use them (cf. Schoenfeld, 1979; 1980).

6. Cannot guarantee that learners will simply discard their previously created processes and organizations of knowledge when they are instructed (cf. McCloskey & Kohl, 1982).

7. Cannot guarantee that schools will create opportunities that provide modes of instruction which demand interrogation of the learner's knowledge and thinking and modes of instruction that demand confrontation with new knowledge (cf. National Research Council, 1985).

8. Cannot guarantee that schools will create opportunities for all children to practice the problem-solving protocol that researchers have found that expert problem-solvers use:

   > Analyses of expert vs. novice problem solvers indicate that problem solving proceeds through an analysis of the historical background of the problem, the posting of a solution, its consideration in light of the subproblems or the implication of possible solutions, and testing the proposed solution through the strength of the argument presented (cf. Voss et al., 1983).

9. Cannot guarantee that schools will create opportunities for all children to practice the general reasoning skills that researchers have found increase students' skill in understanding what they read.

   Analysis of training sessions designed to focus children on internalizing skills that foster comprehension point to the importance of skills modeled by the teacher:

   > Leading dialogues involving paraphrasing main ideas;
   >
   > Leading dialogues involving questioning ambiguities;
   >
   > Leading dialogues involving predicting questions that are implicit in a given passage;

(continued)

Table 1. Building on Findings Identified by the National Academy of Sciences Committee on Improving Mathematics, Science, and Technology Education (National Research Council, 1985) (Continued)

> Leading dialogues involving hypothesizing the area of themes in a given text passage (cf. Palinscar & Brown, 1984).

10. Cannot guarantee that analysis of instruction and analysis of curriculum covered will identify levels of tasks that are appropriate and relevant to students needs, nor can analysis of teacher instruction alone take into account differential treatment that can come as readily from peers as from a teacher (National Research Council, 1985, p. 28).

THE VENTURE: BRINGING POLICY AND RESEARCH TOGETHER

As noted in the beginning of this chapter, it is an ironic circumstance that while both the education research community and policy makers agree that the omnibus reform and school improvement efforts of the 1980s may well go the way of other reform movements and fall once again into neglect, the verdict on utilization of research by policy makers is so negative (Wallat, 1984, 1987). As Kirst (1986a) argued, if education is not to fall once again into neglect we need to focus on the problems, successes, and unanswered questions of state reforms.

Insightful views of the problems, successes, and unanswered questions of state reform are available. At issue is to create ways that these views can become part of the social processes of awareness of choices, selection of choices, and implementation of choices as a means of closing the gap between the policy and research community. As a summary of the work described in this chapter, the following sections address this issue.

AWARENESS OF CHOICE: THE POLICY COMMUNITY

Recently, the National Association of State Boards of Education reported the results of a national survey of information needs of state policy makers (Cohen, 1986). Respondents were asked to identify their number one information need for improving teacher quality and improving mathematics and science. Analysis of responses provides some clear direction regarding how policy makers can find answers to the questions they "are already clamoring for" (Kirst, 1986b, p. 343).

The knowledge that policy makers find most useful is information on what other states are doing. Awareness of strategies and choices that are developing in other states serves to provide both a motivational and strategical function (Cohen, 1986). With comparative data, decision makers can make choices about what is safe to consider trying and how their state can take steps not to be left behind. Given the preference for this type of problem solving, it is not surprising to hear that decision makers are far more interested in presentations that contextualize information in such a way that it will develop meaning in their own state. In other words, decision makers are asking for help in thinking through how their constituency would make use of the information. While policy makers report that they rely on their respective state department of education for raw data, they depend upon their staff as their main source for awareness, analysis, and interpretation of educational issues.

Available case studies of research utilization by these staff members (Fuhrman, 1986) suggest that their major information needs are: (1) what is known about classroom processes, and (2) how to keep aware of what is going on in educational research and development projects in other states. The persons called upon most frequently by staff members are those who are sensitive to links between issues, and those who are aware of what is going on in research. From many years of attempting to find out how the educational research community can overcome the poor record of collaboration between scholars and decision makers, we have learned several lessons. As outlined by Kirst (1986b), the lessons and implications from studies of research utilization are:

a. Utilization varies greatly by state;

b. While states can be characterized along a continuum of dependence upon written reports to dependence upon oral presentation, the lesson for researchers is to be a broker or to find a broker (i.e., individuals who will take general findings from research and be able to say, "This is how it fits into our state history of teacher policy");

c. The key is face-to-face interaction. Even with a written report in hand, the broker needs to say, "I'll take you through this and point out how it fits into our state context.

Selection of choice(s): The Research Community

The demographic data presented in Table 2 point out that there are at least 39 states to choose from to meet the need for information on what other states are doing in mathematics and science classroom process research.

Table 2 identifies universities across the nation that were represented at a recent meeting of educational researchers (AERA program, 1986).

Table 2. Resource Guide for Projects Across the States (Research Reported at a Recent Annual Educational Research Meeting) (cf. AERA Program, 1986)

Location of Current Science Research Projects	State	Location of Current Mathematics Research Projects
Stanford U.C. Berkeley U.C. San Diego U.C. Davis	California	San Diego State U.C. Berkeley U.C. Irvine U.C. Santa Barbara
	Colorado	U. of Colorado (Boulder)
Yale	Connecticut	
U. of Delaware	Delaware	U. of Delaware
Gainesville	Florida	Fla. Int'l U. of Miami
U. of Georgia	Georgia	Georgia State U. U. of Georgia
	Hawaii	U. of Hawaii
	Illinois	Northern Ill. Northwestern Southern Ill. U. of Chicago U. of Illinois
	Indiana	Indiana U.
	Iowa	Iowa State
	Kansas	U. of Kansas
	Kentucky	U. of Kentucky
Johns Hopkins	Maryland	Johns Hopkins U. of Maryland
Radcliffe South Eastern Mass U. U. of Mass	Massachusetts	Radcliffe South Eastern Mass U. U. of Mass
Michigan State U. U. of Michigan	Michigan	Eastern Michigan Michigan State U. U. of Michigan
	Minnesota	DePaul
	Mississippi	U. of South Miss.
U. of Missouri	Missouri	U. of Missouri
	New Hampshire	U. of New Hampshire
	New Jersey	Rutgers
Colgate Cornell Pace U. U. of Rochester	New York	CUNY Columbia Cornell NYU

Table 2. Resource Guide for Projects Across the States (Research Reported at a Recent Annual Educational Research Meeting) (cf AERA Program, 1986) (Continued)

		Syracuse
		U. of Rochester
	North Carolina	U. of North Carolina
Clark U.	Ohio	Kent State U.
		Ohio State U.
		U. of Cincinnati
U. of Pittsburgh	Pennsylvania	Carnegie-Mellon
		U. of Pittsburgh
	Rhode Island	R. I. College
	Tennessee	Memphis State U.
		Peabody/Vanderbilt
		U. of Tennessee
U. of Wisconsin-Madison	Wisconsin	U. of Wisconsin-Madison
Texas Christian	Texas	
U. Texas-Austin		
U. of Houston		
	Virginia	VPI

Given the expectation that this society will continue to be concerned about its economic position in world markets (i.e., dependence upon the expertise of mathematicians and scientists), and given the expectation that education will continue to be dependent upon active state and local policy systems, and "given the prevalence of incomplete knowledge in complex systems and the need to act accordingly" (Glass, 1979, p. 14), the question—How can educational research be done well and at the same time be more responsive to decision makers?—has, as Strike (1979) argues, a long future.

A good glimpse of what that future could be has been suggested in the work of the many scholars referred to in this chapter. It is not hard to imagine the following topics included in face-to-face presentation to a legislative staff member interested in how researchers and policy makers can jointly build on what is known.

Presentation Step 1

There are coherent clusters of research supported categories that policy makers and practitioners can tap as support for their objectives and proposed innovation:

Development of reasoning
Quality instruction

Quality settings
Quality learning systems

Presentation Step 2

Research is available to give shape to each of these categories: to develop images of competent teachers and learners; and, to create metaphors that decision makers can use to create meaning with their constituency. For example, Table 3 outlines a set of metaphors that may help shift perceptions and expectations from "education" to "educating."
Presentation Step 3

Across the nation rules and procedures are being created and/or modified for ensuring accountability with a multitude of state regulations now in place to effect higher academic standards in colleges and public schools, more time on task, more rigorous testing for both students and teachers, and more use of effective teaching and effective school research. In some cases, simply including the following accountability questions in state audits, program reviews, and/or approval guidelines, will influence the use of social processes of awareness of choice, selection of choice, and implementation of choice.

Table 3.   Shift from Product to Process i.e., Shift from the Noun 'Education' to the Verb 'Educating' (cf. Meighan, 1981)

Shift from Product Metaphors ———→ to ———→ Process Metaphors	
Basics as learning subjects (e.g., mathematics and science)	Basics as learning processes (e.g., problem-solving, reasoning)
Subjects as collections of information (e.g., fixed categories)	Subjects as sets of questioning procedures (e.g., questions that focus discourse around a topic)
Learner as depository of knowledge	Learner as explorer and meaning maker
Teacher as subject instructor	Teacher as facilitator
Location of learning as special places called school	Location of learning as diverse social settings
Assessment as grades and certificates —Written performance	Assessment as profiles of achievement and performance —Conversational —Interpersonal —Organizational —Rational (i.e., can formulate new meanings to meet changes in the environment)

Category	Accountability Question
Reasoning	How does mathematics and science knowledge get organized into the curriculum? (i.e., Who participates in developing multi-discipline mathematics and science curriculum?) How are students taught to recognize this organization? (i.e., How many students are involved in curriculum discussions between public school and university faculty?)
Quality Instruction	How does the content of undergraduate mathematics and science courses match up against the results of surveys of what students want to know regarding topics in these areas? (e.g., disease control, space flight dangers)
Quality Setting, Quality Learning Systems	What participation structures are teacher evaluators and/or teacher support teams required to observe in classrooms? (i.e., How is the development of reasoning skills embedded in instructional strategies, curriculum tasks, schooling practices, and enhancement of home/school/community interaction projects?)

IMPLEMENTATION OF CHOICES: THE SOCIAL WORLD OF EDUCATION

Indeed, the potential exists for bridging the gap between research and policy in curriculum areas of mathematics and science. This potential can be realized through the efforts of scholars and policy makers to direct their actions in ways that lead to implementing concepts of schooling as both a cognitive and social process.

As has been shown, given the present need for information regarding implementation, the need to account for political and social and economic consequences to reform efforts, and, the simple, ever-present need to know, the time seems ripe for recognizing the possibility that we *can* overcome the poor record of collaboration between scholars and decision makers.

REFERENCES

AERA. (1986). *AERA Annual Meeting Program.* Washington, DC: American Educational Research Association.

Anderson, J.R. (1981). *Tuning of search of the problem space for geometry proofs.* (Tech. Rept.). Pittsburgh: Carnegie-Mellon University.

Cohen, M. (1986, April). *Information needs and sources of state education policy-makers: Report of a national survey.* Paper presented at the annual meeting of the American Educational Research Association, San Francisco.

Collins, A.M., & Stevens, A.L. (1982). Goals and strategies of inquiry teachers. In R. Glaser (Ed.), *Advances in instructional psychology* (Vol. 2). Hillsdale, NJ: Erlbaum.

Cook-Gumperz, J. (1986). Introduction: The social construction of literacy. In J. Cook-Gumperz (Ed.), *The social construction of literacy* (pp. 1–15). New York: Cambridge University Press.

Fuhrman, S. (1986, April). *Research utilization in the state policy making process: Report of case studies.* Paper presented at the annual meeting of the American Educational Research Association, San Francisco.

Glass, G.V. (1979). Policy for the unpredictable (Uncertainty research and policy). *Educational Researcher, 8*(9), 12–14.

Gumperz, J.J. (1986). Interactional sociolinguistic in the study of schooling. In J. Cook-Gumperz (Ed.), *The social construction of literacy* (pp. 45–68). New York: Cambridge University Press.

Heath, S.B. (1986, April). *Mexican origin students: The researcher's commitment to past and present.* Paper presented at the conference Research Perspectives on Language, Literacy and Schooling, School of Education, Division of Language and Literacy, University of California, Berkeley.

Hurd, P.D. (1985). Perspectives for the reform of science education. *Phi Delta Kappan, 67*(5), 353–358.

Kirst, M. (1986a, April). *Discussant: Improving research utilization by state education policy makers.* Paper presented at the annual meeting of the American Educational Research Association, San Francisco.

Kirst, M. (1986b, April). Sustaining the momentum of state education reform: The link between assessment and financial support. *Phi Delta Kappan, 67*(5), 341–345.

Larkin, J., & Reif, E. (1976). Physically important integrals with calculus. *American Journal of Physics, 44*(6), 515–518.

Lesk, R. (April, 1986). *Influence of technology on teacher preparation.* Paper presented at the Special Interest Group on Research in Mathematics Education Symposium on "Developing models for the preparation and growth of teachers of mathematics: Emerging implications from research." American Educational Research Association, San Francisco.

McCloskey, M., & Kohl, D. (1982). Naive physics: The curvilinear impetus principle and its role in interactions with moving objects. *Journal of Experimental Psychology: Learning, Memory, & Cognition, 9*(1), 146–156.

Meighan, R. (1981). *A sociology of educating.* New York: Holt, Rinehart, & Winston.

Mitchell, D.E., & Encarnation, D.J. (1984). Alternative state policy mechanisms for influencing school performance. *Educational Researcher, 13*(5), 4–11.

National Academy of Sciences Committee. (1986, April). *Improving mathematics, science and technology education: A research agenda.* Sym-

posium presented at the annual meeting of the American Educational
Research Association, San Francisco.

National Commission on Excellence in Education. (1983). *A nation at risk:
The imperative for educational reform.* Washington, DC: U.S. Government Printing Office.

National Council of Teachers of Mathematics. (1980). *An agenda for action:
Recommendations for school mathematics in the 1980's.* Reston, VA:
National Council of Teachers of Mathematics.

National Research Council. (1985). Committee on Research in Mathematics,
Science, and Technology Education. *Mathematics, science, and technology education: A research agenda.* Washington, DC: National Academy Press.

National Science Foundation. (1983). *Educating Americans for the 21st Century.* Washington, DC: National Science Foundation.

Palinscar, A.S., & Brown, A.L. (1984). Reciprocal teaching of comprehension—
fostering and comprehension-monitoring activities. *Cognition & Instruction, 1*(2), 117–175.

Riley, M.S., Greeno, J.G., & Heller, J.J. (1983). Development of children's
problem-solving ability in mathematics. In H.P. Ginsburg (Ed.), *The
development of mathematical thinking.* New York: Academic Press.

Schoenfeld, A.H. (1979). Explicit heuristic training as a variable in problem-
solving performance. *Journal for Research in Mathematics Education,
10,* 174–187.

Schoenfeld, A.H. (1980). Teaching problem solving skills. *American Mathematical Monthly, 82*(10), 794–805.

Shavelson, R.J., & Stern, P. (1981). Research on teachers' pedagogical thoughts,
judgments, decisions, and behavior. *Review of Educational Research,
51*(4), 455–498.

Shulman, L.S. (1986). Those who understand: Knowledge growth in teaching.
Educational Researcher, 15(2), 4–14.

Stodolsky, S.S. (1984). Teacher evaluation: The limits of looking. *Educational
Researcher, 13*(9), 10–16.

Strike, K.A. (1979). An epistemology of practical research. *Educational Researcher, 8*(1), 10–16.

Task Force on Education for Economic Growth. (1983). *Action for excellence:
A comprehensive plan to improve our nation's schools.* Denver: Education Commission of the States.

Voss, J.F., Greene, T.R., Post, T.A., & Penner, B.C. (1983). Problem-solving
skill in the social sciences. In G. Bower (Ed.), *The psychology of learning
and motivation: Advances in research theory.* New York: Academic
Press.

Wallat, C. (1984). An overview of communicative competence. In C. Rivera
(Ed.), *Communicative competence approaches to language proficiency
assessment* (pp. 2–33). Clevedon, Avon, England: Multilingual Matters
LTD.

Wallat, C. (1987). Literacy, language, and schooling: State policy implications. In D. Bloome (Ed.), *Literacy and schooling* (pp. 291–309). Norwood, NJ: Ablex.

Wallat, C., & Piazza, C. (1986). The nation responds: Directions for literacy, language, and teacher performance research. *Theory into Practice, 25*(2), 141–147.

SECTION IV
Perspectives on Computer Literacy

CHAPTER TEN

Collaborative Practices during Word Processing in a First Grade Classroom*

JAMES L. HEAP
Ontario Institute for Studies of Education

INTRODUCTION

In this chapter I formulate how writing was done collaboratively by novices using a personal computer for word processing. Because collaborative use of a computer requires students to use all of the language arts, I ask, "Can there be practical, pedagogical advantages in turning writing into a coordinated, collaborative effort at the early Primary Level?" During my observations, students spoke, listened, wrote, and read. This may be particularly fruitful in classrooms where the native language of students is other than the language of instruction.

This research demonstrates that investigation of computers in education cannot be concerned solely with contextually independent features such as hardware and software. Computer use in classrooms is situated, task-specific use, and is socially and culturally

* This article is a considerably shortened version of a paper originally prepared for presentation at the annual meetings of the American Educational Research Association, April, 1986, in San Francisco. Preparation was supported by the Social Sciences and Humanities Research Council of Canada, Grant No. 410-85-0607. Research reported was funded under contract No. 1206-04-777 ASN 62984 by the Ontario Ministry of Education. This article reflects the views of the author and not necessarily those of the Council or Ministry. The author appreciates the discussions with, and the comments and support of the following friends and colleagues: Christine Bennett, Clare Brett, Bryant Fillion, Peg Griffin, Angela Hildyard, E. Judy Horn, Hugh Mehan, Shawn Moore, Amelia Nanni, Sharon Purdy, David Rehorick, Margaret Riel, Adele Sanderson, Ronald Silvers, David Smith, Lucy Suchman and Jordan Titus. The author wishes to thank Christine Bennett for her extensive and thoughtful editing. Her assistance was of great value.

organized. In this chapter, I explicate the micro-organization of one type of computer use as it is articulated with the tasks of writing. This ethnomethodological account of collaborative computer writing is an example of how to focus on the situated, task-specific use of computers.

The computer as word processor has great potential for developing basic skills (Daiute, 1985), and one use which has been least explored (Dickinson, 1985) is collaborative computer writing. In this chapter, I describe the sociocultural organization of such writing in a first grade classroom, focusing on how the problems of writing together are handled by the distribution of rights and responsibilities in relation to three sets of practices: composing, inputting, and arranging.

The theoretical and methodological perspectives of the article derive from ethnomethodology. Collaborative writing is conceived as organized by students' displayed orientation to tasks, rights, responsibilities, and concerns of deference and demeanor. Cognitive processes in writing are of interest as they are brought to bear interactionally to solve problems of "Where are we?" and "What next?".

Insofar as my account tells us what writer–helper collaboration *is*, rather than only what covaries, empirically, with collaboration, my argument succeeds in developing a set of claims which, when taken together, are quasi-analytic a priori judgments about culturally possible ways of organizing some activity. This is the type of claim set I regard as the aim of ethnomethodological inquiry (Heap, 1980a).

PART I: THE RESEARCH AND THE METHODOLOGY

1. The Research

Videotaping and observations were done in a first grade classroom in a Roman Catholic school in a prosperous working class section of a major urban center. Data were collected during a 3-week period in May, 1984. Earlier observations had been done for 1 week in October, 1983 while students learned to use the computer and the word processing software. The data consist of field notes and 13½ hours of videotape of students working at a computer. The teacher was interviewed, and copies of the students' computer-written stories were collected.[1] Only one computer was used in the classroom. It was placed on a student desk, with two to three desk chairs clustered around it in an area known as the computer center.

One student was the designated writer. That student would choose a helper, and sometimes a third student collaborated. The position has arisen spontaneously each of the years the teacher has a computer center in her classroom. The students who are quickest to pick up the fundamentals of using the computer for story writing spend time near the computer, offering advice, until the position is institutionalized. The designated helper is supposed to function like a technical adviser, having primary responsibility for arranging text on the video monitor through use of the computer keyboard. In practice, every helper assisted in all aspects of writing.

At the computer center, the writer and helper interacted continuously around appropriate responses to program instructions, story titling, sentence development, inputting, arranging the text, and closing and printing a story. After printing a hard copy, and having it corrected by the teacher, typically with the writer and helper involved in the correction process, students collaborated in editing and correcting the story on the screen. Then they printed hard copies of the story for all students in the class. All of these collaborative activities were videotaped, but the analytic focus of this study was upon the interactional work through which writer and helper produce a first draft of a story.

2. The Methodology of Ethnomethodology

The approach taken in this research is one version of ethnomethodology (Heap, 1980; Heap, 1984). Ethnomethodology is the study of the practices used by members of a culture to organize their reasoning, actions, and interactions, as recognizable, intelligible, orderly, that is, rational, events in a social world (Garfinkel, 1967; Heap, 1984). The essential aim of ethnomethodology is the generation of knowledge about how human events *possibly* can be culturally organized (Heap, 1980), that is, how they can be organized by members of a culture, to be recognized and taken for granted by members of that culture.

---

[1] The teacher, Sharon Purdy, and her husband, Thomas Purdy, developed and designed the word processing program, *Write/One,* which was used in the classroom (Purdy & Purdy, 1983). This particular version ran on the Apple II series.

Ethnomethodology is a child of phenomenology and analytic philosophy. From phenomenology (Husserl, 1962; Schutz, 1962) comes a theory of consciousness as a relation between the object-as-known and the acts through which the object is known. Methodologically, this theory frames a *situated perspective:* activity organization is viewed from the perspective of its accomplishment in real time. From analytic philosophy (Austin, 1970; Wittgenstein, 1958) comes the notion that language provides both resources and limits for what can be said about events. Methodologically, this leads to the requirement that activity organization be formulated from the perspective of what speakers of some culture's language could understand, recognize and identify the activity to be. An important point is that the ethnomethodologist is also, or must become, a member of the culture under study.

In line with the ethnomethodological requirement that claims about activity structures be based on recoverable evidence, videotapes are repeatedly reviewed to locate patterns which exemplify an idealized type of structured phenomenon. Using this approach I reach the general practices of collaborative writing.

An idealized pattern is matched against strips of videotaped interaction and by imaginatively varying properties of the structure, I can begin to trace the practices of collaboration in writing. Each strip of videotaped interaction serves as a reminder and constraint in the enterprise of recollecting culturally possible ways of doing whatever it is that persons appear to be doing (Heap, 1984).

PART II: THE SITUATED PERSPECTIVE

1. A Situated Perspective on Writing

This research on collaborative writing begins by treating the presence of the other person and the use of the computer as the most important aspects of the writing task environment under study (Flower & Hayes, 1981). This new situation involves cognitive processes which differ from those usually looked at by cognitive theorists in studying writing with stylus and paper by a solo writer (Heap, 1985).

Writing involves a number of components (planning, translating, reviewing) and each of these processes is made up of subprocesses (generating, organizing, goal setting) which in turn consist of sub-subprocesses (Hayes & Flower, 1980). At any point in the writing process, the writer is expending effort at a number of levels (Scardamalia, Bereiter, & Goelman, 1982). While collaborative writing makes use of these components of composing, it alters how they are organized. The general models of writing so far developed remain useful, but "processing" during collaborative writing has to be understood as more complex, because of a differentiation of tasks (Scardamalia & Bereiter, 1985).

To examine collaborative writing one must first develop a sense of the production requirements which face all writers. I use a situated perspective on writing. This is an epistemological position concerned with how phenomena are known and interpretable from within their own settings (Heap, 1984). As this situated, epistemological perspective relates to work on writing, it is like process-oriented models which try to give an account of how writing is shaped at the point of transcription (handwriting or inputting) (Matsuhashi & Quinn, 1984).

2. Two Production Requirements in Writing

A. Location: Three Levels. The situated perspective for studying writing activities brings to the fore two production requirements facing writers. First of all, the writer needs to be able to determine where he or she[2] is in carrying out the actions which constitute the intended activity. The writer must be able to locate where he or she is in the document-transcribed-so-far. I treat the signs-appearing-on-a-surface as a document, while the meaning realized through reading those signs I call the text (Heap, 1977). The locational requirement can be handled through document formatting conventions (Morrison, 1987) which allow the writer to locate the point at which transcription stopped or can start.

A second level of the locational requirement requires that the writer be able to locate where he or she is in the text- (meaning)-transcribed-so-far. This will be the same as in the document, but while the writer can see where the signs stop on a page (document), the writer must know what the signs mean in order to know where he or she is in the intended text. Punctuation, paragraphing, headings, and pagination are helpful.

At a third level of the locational requirement, producing a text (meaning), the writer must be able to determine where he or she is

---

[2] Human sensibilities demand that exclusive use of the male pronoun be avoided. I believe that the double-barreled pronouns (he/she, him/her), when used with the masculine pronoun always in the primary position, are little better. Lacking an asexual pronoun with which I am comfortable, I have resorted to alphabetizing the position of the primacy of the pronouns: her/him, he/she. It is serendipitous that this usage seems to provide equal opportunity for primacy of position.

in executing the plans for conveying the intended meaning. The writer can manage the plan location requirement through conventions for indicating sections of the document such as headings, sequentially numbered sections, and extra spacing.

As the writer is in the midst of transcribing, problems of location are not present. When a sentence or paragraph has been transcribed, the writer will know where he or she is at the document and text levels, but a directional problem can arise.

B. Direction: Dependent upon Location. The writer is constrained by the text-(meaning)-so-far, but also is constrained by what the text should be. At any point in the writing process, the problem can arise: "What should be written next?" I call this the directional requirement: having to decide where to go from here, from these "locations." Resolution of the directional requirement depends upon resolution of the locational requirement at its three levels.

PART III: COMPUTERS

1. Computers And Writing

A theory of collaborative word processing requires a theory of computer (hardware and software) use. Software is usually defined as programs for the computer (Sippl, 1983), but users encounter software as programs for the user. I shall use the term "computer" to mean the hardware-and-software complex as encountered from the perspective of the user.

When the computer is the medium of expression in writing, a distinction must be introduced within the framework for studying writing as proposed by cognitive theorists. In using the computer to write, we still compose, but it is differentiated into two types of operations. In phenomenological terms (Husserl, 1962), the operations have three components: act, instrument, and object. They are organized as follows.

ACT	INSTRUMENT	OBJECT
1. Inputting	Display keys	Signs & symbols Letters & numerals (document)
2. Arranging	Executive keys	Organization Meaning (text)

Acts of inputting use display keys to produce signs and symbols on a display screen. Acts of arranging use executive keys to arrange the signs and symbols on the screen. Acts of transcription are defined as inputting or arranging in terms of their effect on the display screen. The keys achieve these effects in ways more complicated than the ways in which other writing instruments achieve their effects.

Computer keys are indexical (Heap, 1975); that is, their effects are program dependent. What may achieve display of a sign at one point in a program, may at some other point achieve an executive effect on the text. For example, in the word processing program WordStar, depressing the "d" key at the "No-File Menu" initiates the opening of a file, while within a file, depressing the "d" key (alone) produces a "d" on the screen.

2. Computers And Collaborative Writing

One difficulty with extant theories of writing, with rare exception (Bereiter, 1980), is that they often mistake typical features of writing (with styli) for essential features of writing. The computer medium facilitates ways of working that are difficult with the paper and pencil medium (Riel, 1983), and in collaborative computer writing, students share the task in ways that enhance the intended benefit of the writing assignment (Levin & Boruta, 1983).

3. Verbalization In Collaborative Computer Writing

In my observations, collaborative writing at the computer consisted of social interaction. Writing was talk. Composing was done aloud, and the transcribing of this talk into electronic text was done in talk. Inputting was done as physical acts of finding and depressing keys, and as verbal acts of pronouncing the letter. Only arranging of the text, by the helper, using the executive keys, was often done without verbalization. Helpers sometimes said "space" when hitting the space bar. When this occurred it sounded as if the helper were teaching or reminding the writer that a space was required (Austin, 1970) as a part of the document (signs). The return key was pressed to end a writing session. The spoken word "return" seemed to signal an end to the writing.

4. Turn Organization In Collaborative Computer Writing

Persons take turns verbalizing during collaborative writing. The question of how turns can be organized is a large one.[3] The turn ordering system captured on my videotapes was quite similar to that found in naturally occurring conversation. Either party could self-select as next speaker, and speaker turns could be designed to "select" next speaker (Sacks, Schegloff, & Jefferson, 1974). At the computer, the content of turns at talk seemed not to be directly referential. That is, talk which generated the composing of the text was rarely talk about the text. Instead, composing talk was a verbal rendering of what the text could be. Composing talk consisted of offering possible parts of the story, or what the text could be read to be. In this latter form, composing talk, or what counted as composing talk, consisted of reading aloud what the text-so-far said. This was often accompanied by movement of a finger along the line of screen text being read, an action which I call *finger reading*.

Additionally, the pronunciation of the signs being input counted as turns at talk because the speaker has the floor. The other person rarely spoke while signs were being pronounced, unless it was to repeat the sign, as when the sign was being dictated for inputting.

Talk during collaborative efforts typically was task-oriented (Heap, 1983). During collaboration self-selection to speak and the choice of what to say reflexively established and presumed a distribution of rights and responsibilities in relation to the task. These rights and responsibilities, as enacted, enforced, and negotiated by collaborators, undergirded the resolution of text production and social coordination problems.

PART IV: THE SOCIAL ORGANIZATION OF COLLABORATIVE WRITING

1. Rights And Responsibilities of Writers

The ways in which the production requirements of writing were handled was transformed in the process of collaboration by the rights and responsibilities of the participants, for example, ownership of the story flowed from the allocation of a turn to write at the computer. The helper's contribution to what appeared on the screen was allowed

---

[3] A 3-year research program on the social organization of writing with styli and computers is currently underway.

to stand only if "authorized" by the writer. A jointly authored story was not a sanctionable aim or expectation of parties to the setting.

From the videotapes it was possible to formulate the normative orders as invoked and enforced, and the following is the analyst's rendering of the social organization of apparently enforceable expectations of writers and helpers. These expectations are not seen as causing the behaviour observed.

2. The Normative Order at Three Levels of Writing

A. *Level One: Composing*. The writer had the right to compose, and was obligated to exercise that right. Whether the writer composed a part of the story or not, he or she had responsibility for what appeared on the screen, and was treated by the teacher as having responsibility for the hard copy of the text.

While the writer had the right to compose, the helper had only the incidental privilege to compose. If the helper is understood as a technical aid, participating because he or she knows better than the writer how to operate the computer, then we would not expect the helper to be involved in composition, but on my videotapes helpers were always involved at some point in composition. However, they were involved only in an incidental fashion. They rarely initiated compositional acts. The writer was the one who proposed an idea or the wording of a possible story part. Helpers' contributions consisted largely of offering words which could be used in the writer's story.

There is evidence supporting the formulation of rights and responsibilities for composing as normative orders which interactants could invoke. When helpers initiated verbal composing, their suggestions typically were rejected as being in some way odd, or if they were accepted it was only as solutions to dead ends in story development. As evidence of the writer's right and obligation to compose, we have the recurrent fact that helpers waited for writers to formulate ideas for a next sentence after the conclusion of inputting the last sentence on the screen. The claim that the writer was responsible for what ended up on the screen receives support from the way the teacher corrected the hard copy of the story, almost always addressing the writer. As well, there are places on the tapes where helpers disclaimed responsibility. For example, when one writer was trying to come up with a title, the helper said: "It's not my problem, it's your/ it's your turn."

B. Level Two: Inputting. At the second level, the configuration of rights and responsibilities was similar to, yet differed from, that of composing. On the writer's side, the one difference was that no obligation to input was displayed or enforced. On the helper's side, the right to act was stronger, and more delimited, than in composing. I say that the helper had license to input in order to convey the idea that when the helper did input, it was usually under the authority of the writer, who could be said to have issued the license. In that inputting was delegated, it seems that neither side in the relationship felt that the writer was obligated to do the actual inputting.

The helper's rights in inputting seem more closely to have flowed from an assumed technical ability. The helper presumably knew the keyboard better than the writer. This presumption seems to have held true in spite of the differentiation into display keys (letters, numerals, etc.) and executive keys (delete, space, return, etc.). The writer made primary use of the display keys while the helper had primary responsibility for the operation of the executive keys. The helper, having been at the keyboard as both writer and helper, had the opportunity to become particularly familiar with the display keys. This would be especially likely when the helper was given the license, repeatedly, to input. The more the helper was licensed to use the display keys, the more reason there would have been to let the helper input.

Evidence for the organization of rights and responsibilities at this second level is provided from consideration of practices of student dictionary use. A student dictionary is a blank, lined workbook, with a letter of the alphabet printed at the top of each of 26 pages. When students wanted to use a word which they could not spell, they took their dictionary to the teacher, who printed the word on the appropriate page. The dictionaries were not alike, as students sought their own vocabularies, but there were similarities as words became popular. All students in Mrs. Purdy's class had such a dictionary. Sometimes both the writer and the helper would have their dictionaries at the computer center, thus increasing the number of words at their disposal for use in story inputting.

I say that the helpers and writers displayed an orientation to the license of the helper because of the way in which dictionary use was organized. The following pattern emerged: If the writer owned the dictionary which had the needed word, the writer would input while consulting the dictionary, or the writer would dictate the word to the helper, thereby issuing a license for the helper to input. If the helper owned the dictionary containing the needed word, the helper would dictate to the writer, while the writer did the inputting.

Occasionally, helpers would hand over the dictionary to the writer for the writer to use while inputting.

What was least likely to happen was the helper inputting directly from her or his dictionary. In cases where this did occur, the writer was occupied with some other task. In one instance where a helper input directly from his own dictionary, the writer authorized the inputting, saying that the helper could go ahead because the helper had the word, "baseball," in his dictionary. In that the helper commenced inputting before the writer issued any authorization, the instance appears to have been a case of the writer normalizing what would otherwise have been an apparent violation of the preferred order (the helper acting on his own initiative, without license).

C. Level Three: Arranging. At the third level the allocation of responsibility shifts from writer to helper, but at this level, unlike at the other two, both interactants had full right to act. As the "expert," the helper had responsibility for seeing that arranging acts were undertaken, and that the executive keys were used correctly at the correct point in text production. On the Apple II+, using the *Write/ One* program (Purdy & Purdy, 1983), the executive keys were the left arrow key (which deleted the character to the left of the cursor), the right arrow key (which made space for insertion of text), the space bar, the shift key, and the return key.

Cursor movements were infrequently used during inputting. Each cursor movement required the use of two keys together. For instance, to move the cursor down a line, the control key had to be held down while the lower-case "b" key (b for bottom) was depressed. The cursor could be moved left, right, up a line, and down a line without deleting any character.

What is most interesting about the differentiation of responsibility for inputting and arranging acts is the way in which this distribution was serendipitously facilitated by the organization of the hardware and software. This organization in turn rendered rational the seating arrangement preferred at the computer. The writer sat in front of the computer with the helper seated to the right. On the Apple II+, the executive keys are arranged around the edges of the keyboard in a shallow U-shape. By sitting on the right side of the writer, the helper had access to all the executive keys required to run the program and arrange the text. The exception is the control key, which is at the left side of the keyboard. The writer had easy access to all the keys on the board, and thus was in position to exercise the right to input, and the right to arrange.

Given that both parties had the right to arrange, it is not surprising to find that use of the executive keys was sometimes competitive.

Writer and helper in each session of story writing had to work out who would use the executive keys. Sometimes it was done by the helper announcing what he or she was going to do next. At other times, the helper simply waited to see what the writer would do after inputting a word. If nothing was done, the helper would hit the space bar, thereby moving the cursor in preparation for inputting the next word. Typically, the helper hit the space bar after inputting a word for the writer.

PART V: PRODUCTION REQUIREMENTS AND COLLABORATIVE WRITING BY NOVICES

The locational and directional production requirements examined in Part 2 were formulated in terms of writing activities done in a solo mode. The question now is how the tasks and problems are altered by the presence of an Other who has rights and responsibilities.

However rights and responsibilities are divided on the three levels of writing, a set of social coordination requirements intersects the solution of the two text production requirements. Not only must a writer solve her or his own location and direction requirements, but two interlocking coordinational requirements must be handled. First, the designated writer has to work to make obvious or inferable (a) her or his orientation to production requirements, and (b) how he or she intends to solve them. Second, the helper in the writing activity must determine (a) when the designated writer orients to production requirements, and (b) how that Other intends to meet those requirements. The requirements can be called interlocking because the way in which the writer meets her or his coordinational requirements may provide resources for the helper to meet her or his own requirements. It is through handling this set of coordinational requirements that participants achieve a working consensus on "where we are" and "where we are going."

The consensus has an ordered character in relation to the solution of the production and coordinational requirements. The ordering comes from the distribution of rights and responsibilities, as these are enacted by collaborators. Before inputting can occur, something must be composed. Initiating composing falls to the designated writer. If collaborators solve "where we are" and "what next" in composition, they can turn to inputting, where the helper sometimes acquires license to key in the words. Inputting, as a sequential activity done collaboratively, requires close coordination on solutions to the locational and directional requirements. Before, during, and after inputting, arranging can occur. Either party can engage in arranging acts, but only the helper has responsibility for how the text is arranged.

When the writers are novices, there is one less level of production requirements to face. Novices typically do not do planning which takes them beyond the next sentence they can think to write (Bereiter & Scardamalia, in press). This means that individually they do not orient to compositional plan location or plan direction requirements. Therefore, they do not coordinate their actions at the plan level. This does not mean that they cannot initiate such planning, but if they do, then collaboration will break down unless the initiator keeps the other person informed.

The novice may find her or his work to be more difficult because of social coordination requirements. Novice writers must find ways to work together without a plan. Without a plan, all the action, attention, and coordination has to be at the "point of transcription." This is the point of attention for analyses from a situated perspective. The question is how novices, through their practices, meet the production and coordination requirements which define collaborative writing.

We shall examine three sets of practices which handle writing production requirements as they intersect the three levels of computer writing: composing, inputting, and arranging. Practices at the first two levels, where only one participant has strong rights, are collaborative. At the level of arranging, both parties have equal rights, and practices are coordinated, but not strongly collaborative.

1. Composing Practices

At the computer, writing is talk. The collaborative practices of interest are discourse practices. In composition, three practices are noteworthy: candidacy, cloze, and oral reading. Two of these practices make contributions to handling the directional production requirement, while the third can be used in ways which contribute to solving both directional and locational requirements. All three aid in social coordination of production.

A. Candidacy. The candidacy practice solves the "what next?" problem. The practice consists of the designated writer taking a turn at talk which occupies itself with generating candidate text. The practice can be initiated at the beginning of a story, or after the inputting of any sentence. It is concerned with producing a story part. A story part can be a complete sentence or the initial part of a sentence.

The following example comes from a story called "It's Spring." Vince is the designated writer (student names are masked) with Norm as his helper. After inputting the second sentence of the story Vince said:

1. V: 'We can play:::*tag*' . . No . . . 'The sun is bright.' The sun is bright in spring.'

In this turn Vince is presenting candidate story parts, marked in single quotation marks. Three candidates are presented, with an evaluation or decision being voiced after the first. Vince rejects "We can play tag" (in the transcript, colons are used to mark an elongated sound). He builds a second candidate, then follows it quickly with an extended version which connects with the title of the story.

The candidacy practice solves the two interlocking coordination requirements. By uttering words which are heard as a candidate story part, the designated writer displays an orientation to the direction production requirement of deciding "what next?". By verbally producing a possible story part, the writer makes available a tentative intention to meet the direction requirement in a particular way. It is tentative because the story part offered may not be input. The helper, in hearing the writer's talk as offering a candidate story part, solves her or his problem of determining when and how the writer intends to meet the directional requirement of composing whatever will be next in the story.

B. Cloze. The use of the candidacy practice as initiated by the writer can occasion the use of a cloze-like practice. Persons familiar with cloze devices for measuring reading comprehension will recognize this practice in collaborative writing. In tests of reading comprehension, students are given passages of text paraphrasing a passage the student has been assigned to read. The student must cloze the sentence by filling in the blank. Such a sentence might read: "Silver Cloud helped his mother make maple———."

In collaborative composition the writer produces a candidate story part which is heard as an incomplete sentence. The helper aids in solving the "what next?" requirement by filling in the blank; offering a candidate cloze part. For example:

V: The sun is:::
30 N: (/old the sun costs colda hurryup) *hot*/
V: /is::/

N: /'hot'

The oblique at the end of one line and at the beginning of the next marks "latched turns," where there is no gap, but no overlap between turns (Sacks et al., 1974). What appears on line 30 between parentheses is my rendering of what it sounds like Norm is saying. Norm seems to generate a number of candidate cloze items, until he hits on "hot," which he utters with emphasis. Vince repeats the end of his candidate story part and Norm repeats his preferred ending.

What is most interesting about the candidacy practice and the close practice is their "offered" character. The candidate story part is tentative. Tentative parts need not be voiced. When they are voiced, they are heard as candidates. Since the writer has the right to input whatever he or she desires, the voicing of a possible story part marks that part as being merely a candidate. It announces where the story might go. Since the writer does not have to voice candidates, doing so could be a display of a concern for helper approval, or acknowledgment of the writer's candidate story part. Even though the helper's right to compose is only an incidental privilege, the writer's voicing of candidate story parts both offers and validates that privilege.

The fact that the helper offers candidate cloze parts necessitates recognition of the writer's responsibility for what is composed. In that the writer is taken as the person having the final say, the helper's offered cloze parts necessarily have only a candidate status. The offering of cloze parts by the helper displays to the writer that the helper has a sense of the writer's projected direction for the story. Both the writer's and the helper's practices are important for how they simultaneously solve the directional production requirement and achieve coordination of any such solution. *Private cognitive processes are made public through collaboration.*

C. Oral Reading. The third practice is oral reading. During a writing session, the story on the screen will be read aloud by the participants. The reading is sometimes accompanied by one or more students running a finger under words as they are pronounced. The practice has uses and effects which observers cannot recover, but as mature writers will sometimes read text to see how it sounds, or to get a "running start" to break through a problem, the practice could have similar functions for novice writers.

As students use the practice it seems to work as a device for collecting attention and directing it to what has been input so far. It provides a way of solving the locational production requirement. It pulls attention over the document-(signs)-so-far, rendering it publicly as the text-(meaning)-so-far. To appreciate how it works at both the document and text levels of the locational problem, consider that it would be possible for Primary Level collaborators to run fingers under the graphemes on the screen, without publicly decoding to sound. In such circumstances, the participants would achieve a co-ordinated understanding of where they were in the document (signs), but it would be an open question as to whether each apprehended the same meaning (text). Thus, it would be unresolved as to whether each could be said to be at the "same location" when coordinated silent reading of the document stopped. Oral reading by one or both collaborators does not demonstrate that both parties understand the text in the same way. However, oral reading does provide an opportunity for both participants to "hear the document" and recall it as the words/text which they previously, verbally composed. The odds of their knowing where they are are better than if the location requirement is solved purely by silent reading, or even by silent reading with the use of a finger as a place marker.

The oral reading practice can solve the locational requirement, and also serve to resolve the directional requirement when material is incomplete.[4] When the oral reading practice was used on incomplete story parts it operated in a way similar to the candidacy practice. It occasioned the offering of candidate cloze parts. Such parts were often produced in the discourse as if they were a continuation of what appeared on the screen. For example, in one of the stories which I videotaped, the screen displayed the last line in the document as "She is printing," the writer read aloud "She is printing," and the helper chimed in, without a gap, completing the sentence with a candidate cloze part: "her story." Through this precision timing, the helper displayed an appreciation of "where we are" in the text and "what (could be) next."[5]

For my set of observations, work on any story produced with a helper involved the writer and helper as "senior" and "junior" author, respectively. Helpers exercised their incidental privilege to compose in all cases.

---

[4] While the text's sentences may be deficient in syntactical ways which render them incomplete for a mature reader, what counts as incompleteness in the setting is a sentence which does not have a period. The absence of a period occasions work to produce text which would make it appropriate, in the view of the participants, to place a period. As students were meticulous in putting in periods, the work of producing further text typically was addressed toward the last story part on the screen.

[5] When the cloze practice is used with candidate story parts, orientation is displayed to "what (could be) next," but not to "where we are in the text." This is because candidate story parts are only candidates, they are not, and do not always become, text.

2. Inputting Practices

Inputting consisted of verbalizing, searching, and checking. Inputting practices turned an oral representation of the text into an electronic representation. When inputting, collaborators had to solve the problem of what letter to input next.

A. Verbalizing. Verbalizing took two different forms. If one person verbalized the letters being input while another person did the inputting, the function was interactional, in the sense of communication. This verbalizing was like dictation: one letter of a word at a time. The dictator would say the letter, then wait for the other person to input the letter. I observed no cases of a student dictating without timing the delivery to alternate with inputting. If dictation was interrupted, the dictator reinitiated the dictation from the beginning of the word. Reinitiating the dictation from the beginning of the word solved any emergent locational problem after the interruption. By alternating dictation and inputting of letters, collaborators were assured of not losing track of where they were at the level of inputting.

Dictating was combined with a checking practice. The dictator pronounced the letter, looking at the word in a dictionary, and then watched the video screen. If the letter which appeared was not the one just dictated, the dictator would engage in repair practices (Schegloff, Jefferson, & Sacks, 1977), such as gasping or saying something like "No," which brought a quick response from the inputter, who typically corrected the error.

In the second form of the verbalizing practice, the person inputting verbalized what was input. Verbalizing usually preceded or coincided with depressing a key. The function may be interpreted as interactional in two ways. It let the other person know where the inputter was in the inputting process. The other interactional function of verbalizing was more subtle and consequential. To appreciate the function, it is important to note that while the inputting was occurring, the other person did not speak to the person inputting. I conjecture that the silence occurred because the inputter took a turn at talk, and thus could be oriented to as having the floor. If verbalizing held the floor it prevented other demands, such as composing, being made on the inputter.

There was a second possible function of verbalizing, a function which aided solution of the locational requirement at the individual level. This function was served when the inputting task was handled by one party, usually the writer. Verbalizing the letter while looking at it on the page of the dictionary loaded the sound of the letter into both auditory and visual memory so that the inputter had a better chance of remembering what letter needed to be found in a search of the keyboard. During the search, more information was introduced into short term visual memory from the keyboard, perhaps making it more difficult to succeed if memory of the letter were only visual.

B. Searching. Inputter verbalizing at times operated in conjunction with two other inputting practices: searching and checking. The inputter who used a searching practice to find a key usually verbalized the letter prior to depressing the key, or the verbalizing was an accompaniment to the search, with the letter being repeated or sounded in an elongated form.

In calling searching a practice I am referring to something having the character of a strategy. I observed the same students at the beginning of first grade, when they were working through the *Write/One* keyboard familiarization programs which require the student to find and depress the key corresponding to the letter presented on the screen. Some students in my study appeared to use the same strategies during their word processing efforts at the end of the first grade.

One strategy worth noting was used by the students whose response time was the fastest, and who seemed to experience the least frustration. Those who did not use this strategy simply let their eyes roam over the keyboard. Those who did use the strategy roamed the terrain with a finger providing guidance for their eyes. The movement of the finger was not random, and was remarkably consistent between students. Students usually began with a finger at the left side of the bottom row of keys, sweeping to the right along that row. At the right end of the row, the finger moved up a row and swept left, then up a row and swept right. The tactic assured that most of the keyboard's terrain was searched. If the letter was not found, the strategy was repeated.

Some students used this strategy to search for letters while inputting during story writing. It seemed to come into play when the letter was one not used repeatedly in their stories. The student who was most frequently asked to be a helper was the student who used this practice most, and most efficiently, when the needed key was not quickly sighted.

C. Checking. The other practice used with verbalizing was checking. As mentioned above, dictators could check what was input. Persons inputting from dictation checked as well. Consistent with the character of inputting from dictation, they typically checked each letter after it had been input. Persons who were inputting directly appeared to check after each letter was input, or not until the entire word was input. Checking after each letter meant that inputting took longer, but it assured that what was displayed on the screen corresponded to the keys depressed, whereas checking after inputting made the process faster, but less safe from error, and more cumbersome to repair.

When inputting was done from dictation, checking on a letter-by-letter basis was the preferred tactic, as both dictator and inputter may have been checking the screen. Again, the presence of another person may have had consequences for how the writer or helper behaved. The concern may have been with being seen to make an error. The students were quick to point out each other's errors.

With the practices of inputting, both writer and helper could be involved, even though only one of them did the actual pressing of display keys. This was clearest in the case of the two forms of the verbalizing practice. It could have been true during the use of the checking practice, since both persons were free to check the screen. The searching practice seems to have been the only practice which was carried out by only one person, but even in the case of this practice, the presence of the other person may have made a difference.

Because a letter had to be input before the next collaborative action could occur, there was possibly the pressure of the sense of the other person waiting. Secondly, there was the possibility that the other person would invade the terrain of the keyboard to "help" in the search, or to take over. Since helpers often knew the keyboard better than writers, they were often ready to take over inputting. It was not unusual to see a writer push away the invading hand of a helper.

While only one person was inputting at a time, both were involved. Through the exercise of the above practices, collaborators achieved a finely calibrated sense of where they were, and what came next in inputting.

3. Arranging Practices

Arranging acts were the least collaborative of the three types of writing acts. Competition between the writer and the helper made visible the claim of equal arranging rights, even though it was the helper's responsibility to see that the screen document's arrangement (its "composition") reflected appropriate formatting conventions. The helper would exercise her or his arranging rights unless the writer solved the arranging requirement. Occasionally helpers instructed writers as to what should be done by way of arranging. When such instruction happened, as when a helper said to the writer: "Put a space," arranging can be spoken of as having been collaborative.

A. Spacing. In printing with a stylus, the stylus is lifted and moved to the next place where a letter will be printed. In cursive writing, usually the stylus is not raised until the entire word is written, when the stylus is lifted to dot "i"s and cross "t"s. In learning to print one is not taught to form a space, one learns to leave a space. In using a keyboard, a space between words is not left, it is put. One must depress the space bar in order to "create" a space.

In that the use of the space bar was the most prevalent arranging act which I observed, it shaped the character of arranging's relation to inputting and composing. The relation was one where arranging (spacing) could be said to be interleaved between inputting and composing acts.

The space bar was used between words in continuous acts of inputting, and continuous acts of inputting were usually done by writers, with the writer doing her or his own spacing. But much inputting could not be said to be continuous. It was done more as "one word at a time," and between words it was usually the helper who did the spacing, or reminded the writer that spacing must be done.

In that arranging was mostly interleaved and was concerned with the document (signs), it stands in a different relation to the two production requirements in the writing process. One does not need to know where one is in the text (meaning) to know that a space is needed after a word. Arranging acts, like spacing, do not visibly solve for participants where they are in the text (as the meaning of the document). Rather, collaborators have to know where they are, collectively, in producing the text in order to know that a space is required. If the arranging act is one of deletion, collaborators still need to know where they are in the text (meaning) such that they could see that the screen document (signs) does not represent what they want as text.

As to the directional requirement, the situation is much the same. Spacing is a precondition to inputting whatever is next, but it does not decide what is next. Vince and Norm argue about candidate cloze parts within one compositional sequence.

> V: The sun is:::/
> 30 N: (/old the sun costs colda hurryup) *hot*/
> V: /is::

32 N: 'hot'
33 ?: (p is maught)
34 N: */
35 V: /'bright'/
36 N: /*/
37 V: /no: 'bright'
    N: 'hot'!
    V: 'bur*right*'
40 N: (ho:::t)
    V: 'bright and hot', how's that? yeah

Look at lines 32 to 37. After Norm, the helper, offered "hot" for a second time, and after some student off camera said something like "p is maught," Norm depressed the space bar (indicated by the * at line 34). Latching this move, on line 35 Vince rolled out his candidate cloze part. Latched to this offering was Norm's use of the space bar on line 36. This was done, as on line 34, in a staccato manner. Both Norm and Vince were sitting back in their chairs, and on both line 34 and 36 Norm turned from facing sideways in his seat, orienting to Vince, and reached over to the keyboard and tapped the space bar. (Why Norm cleared two spaces is unclear.)

Note the oriented-to difference between Norm's two spacing acts. The spacing act on line 34 seems merely inserted into the argument between the two boys. It is interleaved. It seems only coincidental that Vince's offering on line 35 latches Norm's move. This is not how the latched turn seems on line 37. Convention required that only one space be placed after "is" in the screen-story part "The sun is." By expressing his candidate cloze part on line 35, Vince already had registered his disagreement with Norm's candidate, "hot," offered on line 32. I would argue that the latched "no" on line 37 could be a response to (and formulation of) Norm's second spacing act as an apparently unlicensed inputting move.

The first spacing act, on line 34, had the appearance of an arranging act. Thus, it carried no potential for resolving the collaborators' directional problem of "what next?" The initiation of the second act, on line 36, had the appearance of an inputting act. Interpreted in this way, Norm's second keyboard act appeared to have potential for resolving the directional problem. And the resolution was not one yet authorized or accepted by the writer. In my terms, the second act did not look like it was an interleaved act in the writing process. It looked like an act of writing. It should be added that the onset of Vince's "no" was a bit too soon to argue strongly that the "no" was a response to Norm's keyboard action rather than a response to Norm's candidate cloze part "hot."

B. Control. Under the general heading of arranging, some further types of interaction should be mentioned. If we understand arranging to be concerned with control, then it is not stretching usage too far if we consider interaction which was prevalent, and concerned with control.

Issues of control arose around seating at the computer. The students vied to use the "driver's seat,"[6] directly in front of the computer. A second seat was placed to the right of the driver's seat. Occasionally, a third seat was placed to the left of the driver's seat. Whoever got to the computer center first would slide into the driver's seat. At the arrival of the designated writer, the helper usually moved over to the right side seat. Often the helper sat on the left edge of the right side seat, almost sitting on the right edge of the driver's seat. When the writer got up the helper sometimes slid left into the driver's seat. On the writer's return, the helper usually moved back to the right side seat. In disputes over who had the right to sit where, the children formulated to each other what the rules for seating were. Often a student sought to have the teacher ratify her or his version of the rules.

Such disputes sometimes arose because of there being three chairs but only two students. When there were three chairs, the left chair tended to overlap the space normally taken by the driver's chair. Confusion arose if the writer took the left chair and tried to "drive" from it, with the helper too well positioned for the writer successfully to resist invasions of display-key terrain. Or trouble arose if the helper sat on the left side chair. Use of the delete key required the helper to cross the display-key terrain. This in itself became a problem only when the writer was engaged in inputting.

As the above makes evident, access to and use of the keyboard was at times a contentious issue. The writer faced the most trouble when there were two helpers, one on each side. In such terrain disputes, which were mainly inputting and punctuation disputes, a

---

[6] This usage was adopted in my field observations during May, 1984. In January, 1985, I spent time at Xerox Palo Alto Research Center (PARC) and discovered a grammatically related usage. When asking another person if he or she would like to operate the computer as it ran a certain program, personnel at PARC would say something like "Would you like to drive?" When I inquired into the genesis of this usage, I was told that it was picked up from researchers working at Massachusetts Institute of Technology who had visited PARC fairly recently. Driving seems an appropriate metaphor for user controlled software, as opposed to designer controlled software such as computer assisted instruction, which can be said to drive the user.

writer occasionally grabbed a helper's hand. The helper's hand would be lifted from a key, shoved away, held immobile, or, more rarely, sometimes directed to a specific key.

What these struggles reveal is the importance to students of control over the text production process. The practices of composing, inputting, and arranging presuppose solutions to the problem of who will control what happens next. The problem of control is entwined with the problem of communicating what they doing and what needs to be done. The problem of control is endemic to collaboration. It is easier to arrange text than it is to arrange collaboration.

4. Production, Coordination, and Collaboration

The social organization of writing collaboratively at a computer consisted of three levels of rights and responsibilities articulated with three sets of practices: composing, inputting, and arranging.

In the ways in which collaborative writing was constituted, production and coordination requirements "at the point of transcription" were solved. Collaborators had to engage in four operations while composing and inputting. They had to (1) orient to locational and directional requirements, (2) display orientation to locational and directional requirements, (3) grasp the other person's apparent orientation and solutions to locational and directional requirements, and (4) solve the locational and directional requirements of collaborative composition and inputting. While I have laid out these actions as four separate actions, practices were multioperational and multifunctional. In solving production requirements through talking, speakers carried out the first two operations. In order to coordinate actions, to collaborate, speakers had to listen in order to grasp the other person's apparent orientation and solutions as displayed in talk and behavior. Production requirements and social coordination requirements were solved simultaneously through composing and inputting practices.

Arranging practices were not carried out with displayed orientation to the locational and directional production requirements of writing. I observed that they were done as moves interleaved in the inputting process and in some compositional sequences, and as such, they had to be coordinated in a double sense. They had to be coordinated to occur between other writing moves, but also they had to be coordinated so as to be done by only one person. Where composing and inputting were often done as social acts, that is, acts begun by one person and completed by another (Mead, 1934), arranging was mostly done as an individual act inserted between social acts. This feature, and its placement in writing, gave arranging its noncollaborative, but nonetheless coordinated, character.

PART VI: CONCLUDING OBSERVATIONS

In that I have formulated how writing was done collaboratively by novices at a computer, the question can be asked as to the practical, pedagogical advantages of turning writing into a coordinated, collaborative effort at the early Primary Level. I believe there to be many possible advantages, and some disadvantages as well (see Heap, 1985).

I want to draw attention to the advantage and relevance of collaborative writing. To appreciate this relevance I look at the medium of expression which makes collaborative writing attractive and feasible: the computer.

Use of the computer has the obvious and important advantages (over using a stylus and paper) of allowing writers to input and arrange their screen documents with ease, to alter those documents and to read them. What observation has revealed, however, is that the computer adds to and compounds these advantages when used collaboratively. Through differentiating "transcribing" into inputting and arranging, the computer (as hardware and software) makes possible a multitude of collaborative keying arrangements, only a few of which were enacted in the class which I observed.

In that the use of the keyboard had to be coordinated, verbal and non-verbal communication was required between collaborators. The computer can be said to have compounded the advantages it otherwise provided in its word processing mode by allowing and requiring students writing together to use all of the language arts. During my observations, students spoke. They listened. They wrote, and as the oral reading practice made clear, they read what they had verbally composed and input. The use of the computer had a value that transcended development of the single language art which computer writing would otherwise appear to serve. This may be especially valuable in classrooms where the heritage language of students is other than English, as in Mrs. Purdy's class where all but three students had Italian or Portuguese as the first language of their parents.

What I hope can be appreciated from this research is that consideration of the place of computers in education must focus not on the context-independent features of hardware and software, but on the social, situated, and task-specific use of computers. In this chapter I have unfolded the micro-organization of one type of computer usage. The account provided here of collaborative computer writing can be understood as an example of what it means to focus on the situated, task-specific use of computers.

REFERENCES

Austin, J.L. (1970). *Philosophical papers.* New York: Oxford University Press.

Bereiter, C. (1980). Development in writing. In L. Gregg & E. Steinberg (Eds.), *Cognitive processes in writing.* Hillsdale, NJ: Erlbaum.

Bereiter, C., & Scardamalia, M. (in press). Cognitive coping strategies and the problem of 'inert knowledge.' In S.S. Chipman, J.W. Segal & R. Glaser (Eds.), *Thinking and learning skills: Current research and open questions* (Vol. 2). Hillsdale, NJ: Erlbaum.

Daiute, C. (1985). *Writing and computers.* Don Mills, Ontario: Addison-Wesley.

Dickinson, D. (1985). *Collaborative writing at the computer.* Paper presented at the annual meeting of the American Educational Research Association, Chicago.

Flower, L., & Hayes, J. (1981). A cognitive process theory of writing. *College Composition and Communication, 32*(4), 365–387.

Garfinkel, H. (1967). *Studies in ethnomethodology.* Toronto: Prentice-Hall.

Hayes, J.R., & Flower, L.S. (1980). Identifying the organization of writing processes. In L.W. Gregg & E.R. Steinberg, (Eds.), *Cognitive processes in writing.* Hillsdale, NJ: Erlbaum.

Heap, J.L. (1975). Non-indexical action. *Philosophy of the Social Sciences, 5*(4), 393–409.

Heap, J.L. (1977). Toward a phenomenology of reading. *Journal of Phenomenological Psychology, 8*(1), 105–114.

Heap, J.L. (1980). Description in ethnomethodology. *Human Studies, 3*(3), 87–106.

Heap, J.L. (1983). *On task in discourse: Getting the right pronunciation.* Paper presented at the annual meeting of the American Educational Research Association, Montreal.

Heap, J.L. (1984). Ethnomethodology and education: Possibilities. *Journal of Educational Thought, 18*(3), 168–171.

Heap, J.L. (1985). *Collaboration in word processing: The impact of technology on education and the evolving role of the student.* Final report to the Ontario Ministry of Education.

Husserl, E. (1962). *Ideas: General introduction to pure phenomenology.* New York: Collier Books.

Levin, J., & Boruta, M. (1983). Writing with computers in classrooms: "You get *exactly* the right amount of space." *Theory into Practice, 22*(4), 291–295.

Matsuhashi, A., & K. Quinn. (1984). Cognitive questions from discourse analysis: A review and a study. *Written Communication, 1*(3), 307–339.

Mead, G.H. (1934). *Mind, self & society.* Chicago: Chicago University Press.

Morrison, K. (1987). Stabilizing the text: The institutionalization of knowledge in historical and philosophic forms of argument. *Canadian Journal of Sociology, 12*(3), 242–274.

Purdy, S., & Purdy, T. (1983). *Write/One.* Toronto: Collier Macmillan.

Riel, M. (1983). Education and ecstasy: Computer chronicles of students writing together. *Quarterly Newsletter of the Laboratory of Comparative Human Cognition, 5*(3), 59–67.

Sacks, H., Schegloff, E., & Jefferson, G. (1974). A simplest systematics for the organization of turn-taking in conversation. *Language, 50*(4), 696–735.

Scardamalia, M., & Bereiter, C. (1985). Written composition. In M.C. Wittrock (Ed.), *Handbook on research on teaching* (3rd ed.). New York: Macmillan.

Scardamalia, M., Bereiter, C., & Goelman, H. (1982). The role of production factors in writing ability. In M. Nystrand (Ed.), *What Writers Know.* New York: Academic Press.

Schegloff, E., Jefferson, G., & Sacks, H. (1977). The preference for self-correction in the organization of repair in conversation. *Language, 53*(2), 361–382.

Schutz, A. (1962). *The collected papers I: The problem of social reality.* The Hague, Netherlands: Martinus Nijhoff.

Sippl, C. (1983). *Microcomputer dictionary* (2nd ed.). Indianapolis: H.W. Sims.

Wittgenstein, L. (1958). *Philosophical investigations.* New York: Macmillan.

CHAPTER ELEVEN

Learning through Sharing: Peer Collaboration in Logo Instruction*

CATHERINE EMIHOVICH
The Florida State University

How children help each other to learn is a well researched topic, one which has been studied from a number of different perspectives. The sociological perspective, exemplified by the work of Slavin (1983), Stodolsky (1984), and Bossert (1979), among many others, examines group processes and instructional arrangements as embedded within the social structure of the classroom. As Stodolsky noted, the *form* of instruction and the settings in which children work produce knowledge *about* learning, along with the planned achievement in content areas. Stodolsky has also distinguished five types of peer instructional work groups: (1) completely cooperative, (2) cooperative, (3) helping obligatory, (4) helping permitted, and, (5) peer tutoring. The contrast among these groups is that each arrangement has a differential effect on learning with reference to specific tasks. Slavin (1986) pointed out that what is *critical* in cooperative learning is the combination of group contingencies and high-quality peer interactions, that is, "students are motivated to engage in elaborated, cognitively involved explanations and discussions if the learning of their groupmates is made important by the provision of group rewards based on individual learning performances" (p. 10). Taking both Stodolsky and Slavin's view into account, the degree of children's cooperation is affected not only by the instructional format of the

---

* This is a revised version of a paper which was first presented at the American Educational Research Association Division G Southeastern Regional Conference, Baton Rouge, LA., February, 1986. The research was funded in part by a Research and Productive Scholarship Grant from the University of South Carolina, although the final interpretations are the responsibility of the author. The author would like to thank Ms. Mary Nichols, former director of the Booker T. Washington Children's Center, and the classroom teachers and the children for their cooperation in this research.

lesson, but also by what children perceive they will gain if each individual works hard to succeed.

A contrasting view is offered by the sociolinguistic perspective, which focuses on the use of language in classroom interaction. Here, attention is paid to the language forms children use in directing or assisting each other's behavior (e.g., requests, directives, etc.), and how these forms function in creating a context for learning. In this perspective, the emphasis is not so much on how the instructional format shapes children's behavior in terms of specific outcomes, but rather on how their behavior functions (as reflected primarily through their language, although nonverbal cues are utilized as well) within that format to make cooperation possible. Important issues which have been examined are the role of peer status in providing information (Garnica, 1981), developmental trends in peer learning exchanges (Ervin-Tripp & Mitchell-Kernan, 1977; Genishi, 1979), and the characteristics of effective peer learning discourse (Cazden, 1986; Cooper, 1980; Cooper, Marquis, & Ayers-Lopez, 1982; Peterson, Wilkinson, Spinelli, & Swing, 1984).

The third perspective is drawn from cognitive psychology, where children are given problem-solving tasks, and their behavior studied in great detail to determine developmental trends in their use of cognitive strategies for solutions. Although most of the literature has been focused on individual children's behavior, attention is now being paid to how paired problem solving enhances the discovery of multiple solutions (Lochhead, 1985). A growing body of literature has evolved which suggests that cooperative learning promotes the development of higher order thinking skills (Skon, Johnson, & Johnson 1981), particularly those studies which are grounded in the Vygotskian perspective that cognitive development unfolds within given social contexts (Forman & Cazden, 1985; Forman & Kraker, 1985). Piaget's ideas are also being revised to take into account the importance of social interaction in mediating cognitive development (Doise & Mackie, 1981; Perret-Clermont, 1980).

The role that various mediating devices (e.g., television, written communication, computers) play in influencing learning is well documented (Greenfield, 1984; Olson, 1976; Salamon, 1982). What is especially intriguing about the computer is that preliminary reports suggest that it facilitates cooperative learning among children (Hungate & Heller, 1984; Klinzing, 1985; Sheingold, 1984; Strand, Gilstad, McCollum, & Genishi, 1986). In some schools, computers are more highly valued for fulfilling this function than for promoting individual achievement on standardized tests. A natural question to ask in this context is whether the increased sociability results in either increased learning, and/or the development of more efficient cognitive strategies.

In answering this question, several parameters need to be defined first: the nature of the setting, the type of task performed on a computer, and the type of students performing the task. What will be discussed in this chapter is how young children learned to collaborate while using Logo, an interactive computer language designed with children in mind (Papert, 1980). The major research question was whether the use of Logo facilitated children's metacognitive development in the area of comprehension and self-monitoring skills. The quantitative analyses revealed that Logo did have such an effect (Miller & Emihovich, 1986), but what needs to be explicated is the role that peer collaboration may have played in producing this effect. A detailed analysis of children's language as they worked in pairs revealed how children progressed from merely copying the teacher's directives to initiating and planning projects together.

THE STUDY

Theoretical Framework

The reference model upon which this research is based is discussed more completely elsewhere (Emihovich & Miller, 1988); an overview of the model is provided in Table 1. The model ties concepts together from three different disciplines: developmental and cognitive psychology, sociolinguistics, and anthropology. From the psychological perspective, the concepts of mediated activity, internalization, and the zone of proximal development, are drawn from Vygotsky's work, which is just now becoming prominent in Western culture (Vygotsky, 1978), while the concept of meta-cognitive strategies enhanced through systematic training surfaced in research on reading as a psychological process (Miller, 1985; Palinscar & Brown, 1983; Paris & Myers, 1983). From sociolinguistics were borrowed the concepts of teaching as a linguistic process (Cazden, 1986; Green, 1983) and the concept of "scaffolding" as described by Wertsch (1979). Finally, the contribution of anthropology in seen in the concepts of contextual levels of learning (Erickson, 1981; Rogoff, 1982) and the concept of a "natural history" of an experiment (Scheflen, 1973). The point made throughout this book is that future studies of learning will require an interdisciplinary perspective to consider more fully the relationship between individual behavior and the social context in which the behavior is embedded. In this chapter, the focus is primarily on the

linguistic aspects of the children's performance, and how that performance informs us not only about the children's communicative
competence, but also of their cognitive capacities in terms of their
programming competence. While the data under analysis are not
taken from an ethnographic study of a naturally occurring event, an
ethnographic perspective is employed in the sense that the meaning
of the child–child and child–teacher interactions were derived from
the context of the lesson which was a mutually negotiated affair.

Method

The data analyzed in this chapter are taken from an experimental
study in which 14 children, ages 4–6, were selected to participate.
Children were pretested on an analogue block building task following
procedure developed by Flavell, Speer, Green, and August (1981) to
assess children's self-monitoring and comprehension processes. The
children were then randomly assigned to either a Logo session or a
CAI session, working in pairs for four, 30-minute sessions a week for
3 weeks. The Logo sessions followed the sequence of lessons employed by Clements and Gullo (1984) in which children first learn
isolated "turtle" commands and then learn to write procedures which
incorporate the commands, using a special support program for young
children developed by Clements (1983). In addition, a set of cognitive
teaching acts were developed for use by the teacher in promoting
metacognitive thinking (see Table 2). Following the conclusion of
training, all children were posttested on alternative form of the
original measures.

   To analyze the discourse structure of the lessons, videotapes of
the Logo lessons for two time periods, one session per week for the
first and last week of instruction, were transcribed for two pairs of
children in terms of verbal and nonverbal behaviors. The transcripts
were then recoded following procedures developed by Sinclair and
Coulthard (1975).

   One important aspect of this study is that the children were actively
encouraged to cooperate in learning Logo. This encouragement took
the form of giving children a checkmark every time they showed
some evidence of cooperative behavior, such as taking turns, giving
each other ideas of what to do next, or help in finding the next key
to be pushed. If children received more than 10 checkmarks in a
session, they were eligible to receive a colored stamp on their hand.
In one sense, this arrangement corresponded to the work group
Stodolsky (1984) labeled "helping obligatory," but since the emphasis

Table 1. Reference Model for Logo Instruction

Psychological Perspective	Sociolinguistic Perspective	Anthropological Perspective
1. Concept of mediated activity	1. Concept of teaching as a linguistic process	1. Concept of contextual levels of learning
2. Concept of internalization	2. Concept of scaffolding	2. Concept of natural history of an experiment
3. Concept of zone of proximal development		
4. Concept that metacognitive strategies can be developed and facilitated through systematic training		

Theoretical premises guiding research

1. The computer embodies both the properties of a tool and sign; both are a function of mediated activity.

2. Learning is mediated through social interaction; children learn through jointly constructed activities with older peers and/or an adult teacher.

3. Language is the primary means of transmission of metacognitive knowledge and strategies; through the child's speech and the language of instruction strategies can be first externalized and later internalized by the child.

4. The primacy of language implies a focus on the teaching-learning process as a linguistic process.

5. The instructional treatment sessions should be treated as contexts in their right; a holistic perspective is needed to see the relationship between this context and other learning contexts.

Table 2. Cognitive Teaching Acts for Logo Training

Name of Act	Description	Examples
Meta-elicit (Mel)	Agent asks receiver to recall information previously learned	Remember what those were for? What is ___ supposed to do? How do we get a new line?
Meta-evaluation (Mev)	Agent asks receiver to evaluate ongoing actions	What happened? What did the turtle just do? What's going to happen when we put _____ ? Do you know why that's there? How far did he go? Did the turtle do what you told him? Did you want him to go that way? Do you know what I am doing?
Meta-prompt (Mp)	Agent is asking receiver to think about or reflect on what they want to do next	What do you want the turtle to do next? Which way do you want him to point? How will you make him go there? What else do you want him to do?
Planning prompt (pp)	Agent indicates there is a next action planned but it has not been in response to reflective thinking	Let's try the other one. Let's make him go forward and put a line up here.
Direct intervention (Di) or	Agent *explains* and *demonstrates* what to do to the receiver	Let me show you something. And now put "d"
Direct (D)	Agent explains or tells what to do to the receiver	Put space and then 70. Tell Kia what she should do.
Self-cuing (Sc)	Agent verbalizes some meta and other direct statements to guide their actions	OK, What am I going to do? Hmmm, I will have to put in a BK. I think I know what happened? How will I make him get there? Did that turtle do what I told him?

was on mutual problem-solving efforts rather than on individual performance, the form was also "completely cooperative" in intent. The main goal was to see if children would spontaneously increase their cooperative efforts without the teacher's prompting. From a Piagetian perspective, we would not expect this to happen, since Piaget felt that young children's communication skills were egocentric in nature. However, more recent studies of children's communicative competence (Cook-Gumperz & Corsaro, 1977; Ervin-Tripp & Mitchell-Kernan, 1977) have suggested that young children can take into account their peers' needs and concerns.

Analysis: Week 1

As noted above, transcripts of two pairs' performance in the Logo sessions across time were made. Pair 1 consisted of Karen, a Black American girl, and Andy, a Black child of Ethiopian origin. Pair 2 consisted of Mike, an Asian-American boy, and Tina, a Black American girl. While watching the two pairs perform, it quickly became obvious that within each pair, one child emerged as the more dominant partner. In Pair 1 this child was Karen; in Pair 2, it was Mike. This fact had important implications in terms of how each child interacted with the teacher, and each other.

Typically, a Logo lesson was segmented into four phases: (1) transition, where the teacher, usually discussed procedural items before beginning the lesson (e.g., setting up the disk, selecting the commands to be taught); (2) review, where commands taught the previous day were reviewed and practiced; (3) new learning, where the teacher introduced the new concept and provided practice time, and, (4) closing, where the teacher summed up the sessions's work and rewarded children for their cooperative efforts. Throughout the discussion which follows, attention is concentrated on children's cooperative behavior in the review and new learning phases.

One important aspect of cooperative behavior is, of course, how often children actually help other out. In our case, the children were rewarded for doing so, so the incentive was clearly there. To study the language of cooperation, we used Sinclair and Coulthard's (1975) concept of exchange, which consists of an interaction organized into three parts: an initiation of some type, a reply, and a follow-up. We created our own category known as a codirect exchange, which essentially followed the same structure, but one which described behavior where activities were jointly constructed by two or more persons to accomplish a task. In these exchanges, no one person really controlled the actions of others; the emphasis was on mutual collaboration to make the turtle perform. Examples 1 and 2 illustrates this behavior for each pair.

EXAMPLE 1: PAIR 1

(Note: the teacher has just asked Andy to delete a letter, a task he is not quite sure how to perform).

98   T: See if you can't take one of those 'm's' off Andy
99   See if you can take one off now
100   Press back

101 (A begins pressing the cursor)

102 K: Back

103 A: This one?

104 T: Yup

105 K: Yeah

106 T: Watch it
107   There you go
108   Now you got it blinking over it
109   Now-

110 K: OK now (takes A's hand to press "d" key)

111 T: Control (leans forward to press control key)

112 A: Let me try

113 [K: Control
114   T: Control]

115 T: Press that down
116   And now "d" (points to "d" key)

117 K: "d" (holds A's hand over the key)

118 T: "d"

119 (A presses both control key and "d" key)

120 K: Take it off

121 T: You have to press control
122   Control . . .
123   Did he do it?

124 A: Yeah

125   K: Yeah

EXAMPLE 2: PAIR 2

(Note: The teacher and the children have been working on the problem of getting the turtle to move to a certain point on the screen)

113   T: And now
114   OK now remember
115   I think-
116   If I had to guess I might guess ten
117   Ten "1" "0"
118   Let's see how far
119   Oh it looks like you can still go up more

120   M: Maybe twenty

121   T: Maybe another ten

122   M: Maybe . . .

123   Ti: I want to do another one

124   T: OK
125   Can you-
126   OK well
127   Can we-
128   Let's try one more to see how far up we can get it
129   One more
130   What do you think?

131   M: Twenty132   Try twenty (addressed to Tina)

133   (Tina begins to type in the command)

134   M: And two two

135   T: Maybe she wanted to try twelve
136   You got it
137   That's perfect you see (points to screen)
138   Cause it's just starting to disappear
139   Perfect
140   So about that far (points) is as far as you can go before it starts disappearing (moves finger up and down the screen)

141   Very good

For both these examples, the exchange was initiated by the teacher, and was not completed until the desired goal concerning the turtle's actions was reached. At this point, the teacher provided a follow-up evaluation, signalling the end of the exchange, and then the children and teacher would then move on to the next task. In terms of frequency of occurrence during phase 2, codirect exchanges happened about the same number of times for both pairs (Pair 1 had two; Pair 2 had three), but the quality of the interaction was quite different (see Table 3).

In Example 1, we see that Karen spends a great deal of time imitating the teacher, and directing Andy's actions, even to the extent of giving him a literal hands-on experience at the computer. Karen in this case is operating like a peer tutor (Steinberg & Cazden, 1979), although it is doubtful that Andy welcomes her assistance. In contrast, Mike was more likely to interact with the teacher directly, providing, in effect, a peer model for Tina to emulate, but he rarely directed Tina as much as Karen did Andy.

By phase 3 within the same lesson, both pairs had increased their number of codirect exchanges (Pair 1 had seven; Pair 2 had nine).

Table 3. Frequency of Exchange Types in Week 1

Exchange Type	Phase 1	Phase 2	n	Phase 1	Phase 2	n
Elicit[a]	17	29	46	19	17	36
Direct[b]	15	17	32	15	16	31
Inform[c]	7	12	19	9	21	30
Initiate[d]	8	9	17	8	11	19
Reinitiate[e]	1	2	3	3	3	6
Check[f]	1	2	3	0	5	5
Repeat[g]	3	2	5	1	1	2
Codirect[h]	2	7	9	3	9	12
	54	80	134	58	83	141

Source: After Sinclair & Coulthard (1975).

[a]An elicit exchange type is headed by an elicitation or question functioning to request a language response.

[b]A direct exchange type is headed by an imperative functioning to request an action, nonlanguage response.

[c]An inform exchange type is headed by utterances designed to be informative, to impart information to listeners.

[d]An initiate exchange type is headed by utterances functioning to get an action under way (Emihovich & Miller, in press).

[e]A reinitiate exchange type is headed by utterances designed to re-establish the line of discourse which a teacher or student feels may have gotten "off the track."

[f]A check exchange type is headed by an actual question seeking unknown information, such as "Are you finished typing now?"

[g]A repeat exchange type is headed by an utterance designed to elicit again an utterance made by someone, such as "What did you say?"

[h]A codirect exchange is headed by an utterance where one person initiates an action and two or more people are needed to complete the transaction (Emihovich & Miller, 1988).

The reasons for the change differed between pairs. With Pair 1, the change occurred because Karen became progressively more interested in obtaining the promised reward, and Andy became tired of Karen always directing his efforts (e.g., "Now let me do it. Let me do the numbers" [pushes K's hand away]). In the case of Pair 2, the change may have occurred because the teacher provided several prompts to effect cooperation. But the qualitative difference between the pairs is not necessarily revealed by comparing frequency of codirect exchanges, since with both pairs, the teacher actively collaborated in moving the turtle. The real difference lies in who is the interactional partner; Karen interacted much more frequently with Andy (albeit in the role of a co-teacher) than did Mike with Tina.

Overall, the number of codirect exchanges for both pairs was relatively small compared with the total number of exchanges in the session (Table 4). Out of a total of 275 exchanges, approximately 8% were exchanges where collaboration was the rule. This low percentage is due to two factors: (1) The age of the children, which decreased the likelihood of cooperative behavior; and (2) The teacher's need to accomplish other tasks in the lesson, such as explaining commands (Inform exchanges), telling them what to do next (Direct exchanges), and asking questions to confirm their understanding of one procedure before moving onto the next one (Elicit exchanges). By the end of the third week of instruction, we would expect the percentage of codirect exchanges to increase, since the children would become more practiced (and reinforced) in cooperating, and the type of procedures being taught would demand more collaborative efforts because of their complexity.

Table 4.   Total Exchange Types for Week 1

Exchange Types	Pair 1		Pair 2		Total	
	n	%	*n*	%	*n*	%
Elicit	46	34	36	26	82	30
Direct	32	24	31	22	63	23
Inform	19	14	30	21	49	18
Initiate	17	13	19	21	36	13
Reinitiate	3	2	6	4	9	3
Check	3	2	5	3	8	3
Repeat	5	4	1	2	7	2
Codirect	9	7	9	12	21	8
	134	100	141	100	275	100

ANALYSIS: WEEK 3

By Week 3, several dramatic changes had taken place. Since the children were being rewarded for cooperating, we expected the number of codirect exchanges featuring mutual collaboration to increase, and in fact, that is exactly what happened. For both pairs, the number of codirect exchanges approximately doubled (Table 5). Out of a possible 240 exchanges, 15% were co-direct exchanges.

What was most interesting about this change was that individual differences between pairs were more clearly differentiated. As Table 6 indicates, Pair 1 spent more time in phase 2, reviewing previous material, than Pair 2 did. Pair 2, in fact, spent most of its time on learning new procedures, which they combined into long sequences for the turtle to perform.

This difference arose because Mike was the most apt pupil among the four children, and by the third week, he was proposing more and more ideas for the turtle, which entailed the learning of more complicated procedures. In contrast, Karen and Andy took longer

Table 5.   Total Exchange Types in Week 3

Exchange Types	Pair 1		Pair 2		Total	
	n	%	n	%	n	%
Elicit	33	28	33	26	66	28
Direct	20	16	25	21	45	19
Inform	23	19	21	18	44	18
Initiate	17	14	13	11	30	13
Reinitiate	0	0	0	0	0	0
Check	7	6	2	2	9	4
Repeat	2	2	7	6	9	3
Codirect	18	15	19	16	37	15
	120	100	120	100	240	100

Table 6.   Frequency of Exchange Types in Week 3

Exchange Type	Pair 1			Pair 2		
	Phase 2	Phase 3	n	Phase 2	Phase 3	n
Elicit	26	7	33	9	24	33
Direct	13	7	20	2	23	25
Inform	12	11	23	4	17	21
Initiate	9	8	17	3	10	13
Reinitiate	0	0	0	0	0	0
Check	4	3	7	1	1	2
Repeat	2	0	2	3	4	7
Codirect	9	9	18	5	14	19
	75	45	120	27	93	120

to relate the learning of new procedures to old ones, so the teacher spent more time practicing old commands first with them before presenting new material.

Another significant change was that the less dominant partner within each pair became more assertive in proposing new ideas. In Example 3, we see how Andy takes charge of setting up the next task and then working with Karen.

EXAMPLE 3: PAIR 1

(Note: The children have been working on constructing a house by combining a series of procedures)

961 A: OK now
962   Give me one

963 K: OK
964   Chimney

965 A: [Chimney?
966   "J"
967 K: OK
968   OK now you press the-]

969 K: No you press the one that's for chimney
970 K: I did two
971   K: I did two now # now it's your turn to do two

972 T: Nice sharing
973   Nice sharing Karen

974 A: "c" "c"

975 K: (echoes) "c"

976 A: "c"

977 K: "h"

978 A: "h"
979   I call it "h" (gives sound a different stress)
980   I don't call it "h" (sound heard in English)
981   I call it-

982 K: "h-h-h-h-h"
983   I need two (inaudible)
984   What?

985 (Andy laughs)

986 K: "i"

987   A: "i"

988   K: "m"

989   A: "m"
990   The last one's "m"?

991   K: Yeah

992   T: Neat
993   The last one
994   Don't forget
995   Don't forget in between the words-

996   K: Spaces
997   K: OK
998   "b"

999   A: "b"

1000 K: "u"
1001 A: "u"

1002 K: "u" is up on top (Andy is searching for the key)
1003   high
1005   "u"

1006 T: Nice helping you guys

1007 K: "h"

1008 A: "h" (looks for key)

1009 K: "h" is over there (points)
1010   Third line
1011   Third line
1012   OK (Andy presses key)

1013 K: [OK space space
1014   A: No this is] the second line space

1016 K: Space
1017   Return (presses key)

Although in this sequence Andy is still following Karen's lead, throughout the lesson he consistently comes up with ideas for both of them to try. He also monitors more closely Karen's behavior, and doesn't hesitate to correct her when she makes a mistake. A similar situation existed with Tina, as seen in Example 4.

EXAMPLE 4: PAIR 2

(Note: Tina has just proposed to Mike that they make a window on the house they are building)

466 Ti: Win
467   Win

468 T: Remember
469   We're still working on the word "flo"
470   "f" "l" "o"
471   OK?
472   So-

473 M: "w"
474   My turn after your's
475

         We are going to take turns

477 T: Nice working together again you guys
478 M: "w" "i"

479 Ti: "n"

480 M: "n" (sings "n" seven times)
481 M: "o"
482 Ti: Not "o"
483   "d"

484   (Mike laughs)

485 Ti: Then "o"

486 M: "r"

485 T: Mhm-uh

488 M: "w"

489 T: Boy have you guys worked together nice

490 M: OK

491   My turn now

492 T: Nice you guys

493 M: "i"

494   "n"

495   Return (presses return)

In this little sequence, Mike makes an error in spelling "window" (line 481), which Tina immediately corrects. She does miss his next mistake (line 486), which the teacher notices but doesn't correct. What this little sequence indicates is that Tina is more closely monitoring Mike's behavior, something she did not do in the first week of lessons. By the third week, Andy was also more closely monitoring Karen's behavior, even admonishing her to "be careful with those papers" (referring to the sheets on which the commands were printed), and to insert "spaces" when necessary before pressing "return".

Another change which occurred for both pairs was that the co-direct sequences were more extended than in the first week, and the teacher spent less time telling the children what to do next (because they told each other), and more time on evaluating or explaining the outcomes of their actions. Even though the total number of exchanges in the lesson decreased from Week 1 to Week 3, the children's content of talk became less telegraphic and more concentrated on providing substantive information on what to do next. There was also a greater recognition of error on each other's part, again an indication that the children were beginning to monitor each other's behavior.

DISCUSSION

Two issues which arise from this data are germane for discussion: (1) The degree of peer collaboration actually taking place; and, (2) The children's use of cognitive strategies in helping in each other. Regarding the first issue, Parten (1932) identified three levels of social interaction among children, which apply to this situation. The three levels are: (1) Parallel play, where children share materials and exchange comments about the task, but make few, if any, attempts to monitor the work of the other or to inform the other of their own thoughts and actions; (2) Associative play, where children try to exchange information about some of the tasks each one has selected, and, (3) Cooperative play, where children constantly monitor each other's work and play coordinated roles in performing tasks.

Using these criteria, the interaction between the pairs of children most closely resembles associative play. The children are monitoring each other's behavior in detecting and correcting errors, but each child waits for his or her turn impatiently, not seeing the other as a resource in creating new ideas for the turtle. The teacher still has to play a substantive role in ensuring that cooperation will take place. The fact that preschool children were able to cooperate in a limited way is encouraging, however, since research on older children's cooperative efforts in problem-solving tasks with or without a computer has not demonstrated that true collaboration is the norm in the absence of adult supervision (Forman & Cazden, 1985; Leron, 1985; Pea & Kurland, 1984; Webb, 1984).

A second issue is whether the children have make any use of cognitive strategies in helping each other. McBride (1985) has identified a set of strategy rules that young children (ages 7–8) use while programming with Logo. These rules are: (1) The random rule, where children select whatever inputs come to mind, without any visible relation to the current problem; (2) The repetition rule, where children select inputs that they have used in past examples or problems, and use these repeatedly until the object (e.g., a "bush" created through other procedures) is placed; and, (3) The maximum rule, where a child chooses the largest possible input to the "forward" command without overshooting the goal, and does so recursively until the goal is reached.

In this study, the children either typed commands at random, or they repeatedly used the same commands they had used before in previous sessions. Although they were encouraged to plan their ideas by drawing pictures of what they wanted the turtle to do next, true planning in terms of the identification and selection of programming commands (Newell & Simon, 1972) did not really take place in a meaningful way. In fact, most of the strategies originated with the teacher; they did not emanate from the children in a collaborative effort.

The issue of strategy use raises a further question as to whether there are developmental prerequisites in order for children to understand what programming means. Examining this issue in detail, Pea and Kurland (1984) state emphatically:

> In light of the lack of research on the development of computer programming knowledge and strategies, two reasons lead us to reject a formulation of the computer skill problem in terms of the concept of Piagetian "developmental level" as inappropriate. First, the development and display of Piagetian-defined logical abilities is importantly tied to context domain, to the eliciting context, and to the particular experiences of individuals. Since it is not apparent why and how different materials affect the "developmental level" of children's performances within Piagetian experimental tasks, it is not feasible to predict what relationships might inhere between computer programming experience and performance on Piagetian tasks. Our second concern . . . is that the task of learning to program has not thus far been subjected to developmental analysis or characterized in terms of its component skills. . . . We thus reject a general developmental level formulation as useful for articulating the cognitive demands of specific

programming skill development, and embrace in its stead an approach that is more concept based. (1984, p. 48–49)

Pea and Kurland further stated that "what is needed are methods to identify the limits of knowledge use. Cognitive supports in programming environments that permit a child to seemingly go beyond his or her current level of logical development are as yet poorly understood . . . but may allow programming performance that would be unexpected given current knowledge of children's abilities as measured in other task environments" (p. 49). Their comments are very relevant in view of the fact that most of the children who participated in the study, especially the two pairs of children (with the exception of Mike), were children who scored poorly on standardized tests and for whom school success was not easily predicted. Yet these same children were able to perform tasks with the turtle that would not have been imagined prior to the study.

How then is the children's performance to be explained? One explanatory concept which may account for the children's ability to engage in limited programming is Vygotsky's (1978) concept of the zone of proximal development. In his definition:

It is the distance between the actual developmental level as determined by independent problem solving and the level of potential development as determined through problem solving under adult guidance or in *collaboration with more capable peers.* (p. 86) [Italics mine]

If the word "programming" is substituted for "problem solving," then what children accomplish with Logo in collaboration with others is a precursor to what they will accomplish independently later in development. The key concept is collaboration with others. Cole (1983) noted that the concept allows us to understand that children (or more generally novices) can be participants in events they do not fully understand and which they are incapable of accomplishing as individual activities. His view implies that learning is a mutually constructed activity in which the child carries out those actions he or she is capable of performing alone while becoming coordinated with new aspects of the interaction that can be used later in new situations. While it may be too much to expect preschool children to become true collaborators in programming, providing them with opportunities to practice giving assistance in a structured situation may be a good place for them to begin honing the skills they can use later to become more effective peer tutors.

As computers become more prevalent in the schools, an important implication for practice is that teachers will need to rethink their teaching methods with regard to computer instruction. The old model of direct instruction to a whole group of passively listening children who compete for the teacher's attention may give way to a model where children work in pairs or small groups at computer work stations, helping each other jointly master the concepts. Such a model would free the teacher to take on the role of facilitator, moving around the room and lending assistance where needed. Collaborative writing on the computer is already being studied (see Heap in the previous chapter and the work of Levin, Boruta, & Vasconcellos, 1983; Riel, 1983), but it is too soon to tell what effect this learning arrangement will have on the development of children's writing skills. Undoubtedly, the major research effort of the next decade will be to examine the effects of this new technology on children's learning in a multitude of contexts and subject areas.

Given the limited state of knowledge of the relationship between computer programming and children's cognitive development within particular types of social interaction or learning arrangements, considerable research will be needed to sort out the dynamics of such relationships. The research reported in this chapter is a step forward in this direction, but much work remains to be done. A critical component is the theoretical approach which will direct future efforts. An approach which views children's cognitive development as mediated within the context of mutually negotiated learning frameworks is more likely to yield significant information that just a focus on the outcomes of computer programming experience alone.

REFERENCES

Bossert, S.T. (1979). *Tasks and social relationships in classrooms.* New York: Cambridge University Press.

Cazden, C. (1986). Classroom discourse. In M.C. Wittrock (Ed.), *Handbook of research on teaching* (3rd ed.). New York: MacMillan.

Clements, D.H. (1983). Supporting young children's Logo programming. *Computing Teacher, 11*(5), 24–30.

Clements, D.H., & Gullo, D.G. (1984). Effects of computer programming on young children's cognition. *Journal of Educational Psychology, 76*(6), 1051–1058.

Cole, M. (1983). The child and other cultural inventions. In F.S. Siegal & A.W. Siegal (Eds.), *Houston Symposium Series on Psychology and Society,* (Vol. 4). New York: Praeger.

Cook-Gumperz, J., & Corsaro, W.A. (1977). Social-ecological constraints on children's communicative strategies. *Sociology, 11,* 411–434.

Cooper, C.R. (1980). Development of collaborative problem solving among preschool children. *Developmental Psychology, 16,* 433–440.

Cooper, C.R., Marquis, A., & Ayers-Lopez, S. (1982). Peer learning in the classroom. In L.C. Wilkinson (Ed.), *Communicating in the classroom.* New York: Academic Press.

Doise, W., & Mackie, D. (1981). On the social nature of cognition. In J.P. Forgas (Ed.), *Social cognition.* New York: Academic Press.

Emihovich, C., & Miller, G.E. (1988). Learning Logo: The social context of cognition. *Journal of Curriculum Studies, 20*(1), 57–70.

Emihovich, C., & Miller, G.E. (1988). Show me the turtle: A discourse analysis of Logo instruction. *Discourse Processes, 11,* 183–201.

Erickson, F. (1981). Taught cognitive learning in its immediate environments: A neglected topic in the anthropology of education. *Anthropology & Education Quarterly, 13,* 149–180.

Ervin-Tripp, S., & Mitchell-Kernan, C. (1977). *Child discourse.* New York: Academic Press.

Flavell, J.H., Speer, J.R., Green, F.L. & August, D.L. (1981). The development of comprehension monitoring and knowledge about communication. *Monographs of the Society for Research in Child Development.* Serial #192.

Forman, E.A., & Cazden, C.B. (1985, April). Exploring Vygotskian perspectives in education: The cognitive value of peer interaction. In J.V. Wertsch (Ed.), *Culture, communication and cognition: Vygotskian perspectives.* New York: Cambridge University Press.

Forman, E.A., & Kraker, M. (1985). *The cognitive benefits of collaborative problem solving: Piagetian and Vygotskian perspectives.* Paper presented at the annual meeting of the American Educational Research Association, Chicago.

Garnica, O.K. (1981). Social dominance and conversational interaction: The Omega child in the classroom. In J.L. Green & C. Wallat (Eds.), *Ethnography and language in educational settings.* Norwood, NJ: Ablex.

Genishi, C. (1979). Young children communicating in the classroom: Selected research. *Theory into Practice, 18,* 244–250.

Green, J. (1983). Research on teaching as a linguistic process: A state of the art. *Review of Research in Education, 10,* 151–252.

Greenfield, P. (1984). *Mind and media: The effects of television, video games, and computers.* Cambridge, MA: Harvard University Press.

Hungate, H., & Heller, J.I. (1984, April). *Preschool children and microcomputers.* Paper presented at the annual meeting of the American Educational Research Association, New Orleans.

Klinzing, D.G. (1985, April). *A study of the behavior of children in a preschool equipped with computers.* Paper presented at the annual meeting of the American Educational Research Association, Chicago.

Leron, U. (1985). Logo today: Vision and reality. *Computing Teacher, 12*(5), 26–32.

Levin, J., Boruta, M., & Vasconcellos, M. (1983). Microcomputer-based environments for writing: A writer's assistant. In A.C. Wilkinson (Ed.), *Classroom computers and cognitive science.* New York: Academic Press.

Lochhead, J. (1985). Teaching analytic reasoning skills through paired problem solving. In J.W. Segal, A.F. Chapman, & R. Glaser (Eds.), *Thinking and learning skills* (Vol. 1). Hillsdale, NJ: Erlbaum.

McBride, S.R. (1985). *A cognitive study of children's computer programming.* (Tech. Rept. No. 8502). Cognitive Science Program, University of Delaware.

Miller, G.E. (1985). The effects of general and specific self-instruction training on children's comprehension monitoring performances during reading. *Reading Research Quarterly, 20,* 616–628.

Miller, G.E., & Emihovich, C. (1986). The effects of mediated programming instruction on preschool children's self monitoring. *Journal of Educational Computing Research, 2,* 283–297.

Newell, A., & Simon, H.A. (1972). *Human problem solving.* Englewood Cliffs, NJ: Prentice-Hall.

Olson, D.R. (1985). Computers as tools of the intellect. *Educational Researcher, 14*(5), 5–7.

Palinscar, A.S., & Brown, A.L. (1983). *Reciprocal teaching of comprehension monitoring activities.* (Tech. Rept. No. 269). Urbana: University of Illinois, Center for Study of Reading.

Papert, S. (1980). *Mindstorms.* New York: Basic Books.

Paris, S.G., & Myers, M. (1981). Comprehension monitoring, memory, and study strategies of good and poor readers. *Journal of Reading Behavior, 13,* 7–22.

Parten, M. (1932). Social participation among preschool children. *Journal of Abnormal & Social Psychology, 27,* 243–269.

Pea, R.D., & Kurland, D.M. (1984). *On the cognitive prerequisites of learning computer programming.* (Tech. Rept. No. 18). New York: Center for Children and Technology, Bank Street College of Education.

Perret-Clermont, A. (1980). *Social interaction and cognitive development in children.* New York: Academic Press.

Peterson, P.L., Wilkinson, L.C., Spinelli, F., & Swing, S.R. (1984). Merging the process-product and sociolinguistic paradigms: Research on small-group processes. In P.L. Peterson, L.C. Wilkinson, & M. Hallinan (Eds.), *The social context of instruction.* Orlando, FL: Academic Press.

Riel, M. (1983). Education and ecstasy: Computer chronicles of students writing together. *Quarterly Newsletter of the Laboratory of Comparative Human Cognition, 5,* 59–67.

Rogoff, B. (1982). Integrating context and cognitive development. In M.E. Lamb & A.L. Brown (Eds.), *Advances in developmental psychology* (Vol. 2). Hillsdale, NJ: Erlbaum.

Salamon, G. (1982, March). *The differential investment of mental effort in learning from different sources.* Paper presented at the annual meeting of the American Educational Research Association, New York.

Scheflen, A.E. (1973). *Communicational structure: Analysis of a psychotherapy transaction.* Bloomington: Indiana University Press.

Sheingold, K. (1984). *The microcomputer as a medium for young children.* (Tech. Rept. No. 26). New York: Center for Children and Technology, Bank Street College of Education.

Sinclair, J., & Coulthard, R.M. (1975). *Toward an analysis of discourse: The English used by teachers and pupils.* London: Oxford University Press.

Skon, L., Johnson, D., & Johnson, R. (1981). Cooperative peer interaction versus individual competition and individualistic efforts: Effects of the acquisition of cognitive reasoning strategies. *Journal of Educational Psychology, 73,* 83–92.

Slavin, R.E. (1983). *Cooperative learning.* New York: Longman.

Slavin, R.E. (1986, April). *Cooperative learning: Where behavioral and humanistic approaches to classroom motivation meet.* Paper presented at the annual meeting of the American Educational Research Association, San Francisco, CA.

Steinberg, Z.D., & Cazden, C.B. (1979). Children as teachers, of peers and ourselves. *Theory into Practice, 18*(4), 258–266.

Stodolsky, S.S. (1984). Frameworks for studying instructional processes in peer-work groups. In P.L. Peterson, L.C. Wilkinson, & M. Hallinan (Eds.), *The social context of instruction.* New York: Academic Press.

Strand, E., Gilstad, B., McCollum, P., & Genishi, C. (1986, April). *A descriptive study comparing preschool and kindergarten Logo interaction.* Paper presented at the annual meeting of the American Educational Research, San Francisco, CA.

Vygotsky, L.S. (1978). *Mind in society: The development of higher psychological processes.* Cambridge, MA: Harvard University Press.

Webb, N.M. (1984, April). *Cognitive requirements of learning computer programming in group and individual settings.* Paper presented at the annual meeting of the American Educational Research Association, New Orleans.

Wertsch, J.V. (1979). From social interaction to higher psychological processes: A clarification and application of Vygotsky's theory. *Human Development, 22,* 1–22.

CHAPTER TWELVE

Microcomputers, Maieutics and Education: Policy Implications

GEORGE PAPAGIANNIS
Florida State University

MICROCOMPUTERS AS AN EDUCATIONAL INNOVATION

Since the 1970s, information technology has been heralded as a "transforming" technology, supposedly with profound implications for education. Mainframe-based computer education programs such as Plato and TICCIT had already been introduced but with varying success (House, 1974; Maddison, 1983). It was the introduction of microcomputers in the late 1970s, however, that provided educators with the means to apply widely the purported educational potential of "computing power" to the educational process. The first clue that this technological innovation was different was that unlike innovations of the past, resistance by educators, particularly by teachers, has been conspicuously modest. Indeed, it should be noted that teachers were among the first in the educational establishment to recognize the educational potential of microcomputers and were the first to spearhead their introduction into schools, at least in the initial period of microcomputer diffusion (Becker, 1983, 1984; Meister, 1984). While there was considerable developmental work and evaluation research conducted on the use of mainframe and minicomputers for computer-assisted learning (CAI) in education prior to the appearance of the microcomputer (Chen, 1985; Chen & Paisley, 1985; House, 1974; Roblyer, 1985; Suppes, 1979), the introduction of microcomputers into schools was not "research" or "expert" driven or the result of policy "fiats from above." (see Becker, 1984)

Indeed, unlike previous innovations, a number of important factors and trends external to the educational enterprise occurred simultaneously which contributed to this receptivity and facilitated the acceptance of microcomputers into educational environments. First and foremost among these factors and influences was the upsurge of acceptance of "computing power" into the workplace, initially with mainframes, followed by minicomputers and then with the microcomputer, in almost every major commercial, industrial, professional, and service sector. Computers in the workplace, especially the microcomputer, experts argued, were a necessity, if we as a nation were to improve our efficiency and improve our work productivity. One only has to recall the national panic concerning our declining productivity, the runaway inflation and rising unemployment of the late 1970s and early 1980s which made industrial leaders ripe for technological solutions.[1] Computerization and robotics were seen as the way by which we would begin to restructure our economy and recover our world position as the most advanced technological nation in the world.[2]

Second, the common perception arose that we were entering a new era characterized by an information explosion. There was a rapidly growing need to manage and analyze this information, as well as to be able to transmit or communicate this data and information within and across nations, if we were to profit or benefit from this information "opportunity." The implicit assumption was that a citizenry of a democratic nation needs to be able to access, manage, and use information in order to enhance (not only for economic reasons) the quality of their lives.

Third, the prior revolution of radio, television, and audiovisual technology (Paisley, 1985) had already stimulated the belief that we were moving into a new postindustrial stage, the "information society." Fourth, the spread of telecommunications—the combining of microelectronics and computing power with data transmission in all its possible forms—was beginning to influence our culture and the cultural definitions of ourselves and how we relate to each other.[3] Finally, the media inspired the belief among laypersons, educators,

---

[1] See Grubb 1984, for a description of America's cultural inclination to search for technological quick fixes to complex societal problems.

[2] For an interesting analysis of the public's perception of the consequences of microelectronics on the labor market, see Russell W. Rumberger's analysis and contention that this perception is unfounded. (Rumberger, 1984a). Also, as Cuban (1986) and others have pointed out, this was and is reminiscent of the Sputnik decade, which also spawned nationwide educational reforms.

[3] For an interesting discussion of the computer as a "defining" technology, see Bolter (1984) and Turkle (1984); the latter has described the computer as a "subjective machine" and as a cultural object. For a more radical interpretation of computers as culture, see Tony Solomonides and Les Levidow, *Compulsive Technology: Computers as Culture* (1985).

parents, and the business community that our children and youth needed to be introduced to microcomputers if they were to be adequately prepared for the computer-based work world of the future.

MICROCOMPUTERS IN EDUCATION: THE FIRST PHASE

This social and economic context, with its emerging trends, has had a profound impact on education. For instance, educational policy makers, already concerned about the state of education in the United States, began to see the need to reform and revitalize our educational enterprise. The growing concern over decline in SAT scores, the rapidly increasing dropout rates and high teacher turnover, and ever-decreasing educational budgets pushed policy makers to seek out legislative solutions such as establishing more stringent certification requirements for teachers, more frequent administration of statewide tests for students and teachers alike, and the development of new accountability measures for personnel performance.

In addition, limited federal and state funds for education created a climate that dovetailed with the growing cry in the business world that we needed to become more productive and more efficient. In education, new technology was seen as one solution to this "troubled" labor-intensive enterprise. While the ramifications of these trends on the educational enterprise are still problematic, these societal shifts have encouraged new thinking about education's aims and how it meets them. New ideas about the role of teachers, how children learn and how education should be organized are only some of the topics now being discussed and debated. It is this context, for instance, that played a major role in preparing the public mind for Papert's (1980) *Mindstorms: Children, Computers, and Powerful ideas,* which has lent support and further legitimation to developmental and cognitive theories on teaching and learning and a rationale for educators to use the computer in the educational process, and of course, more specifically, to promote the adoption of the programming language LOGO as a teaching tool to enhance the development of critical thinking or procedural skills.[4]

---

[4] It has been noted, however, by various observers (Chen & Paisley, 1985; Maddison, 1983; Rowntree, 1982) that Skinner's behavioristic approach to learning and teaching, still closely associated with earlier attempts at computer-based teaching and learning (mainframe-and minicomputer-based learning systems), continues to dominate not only our ideas about technology in general, but our recent efforts to apply and use

Moreover, since the first Apple microcomputer was introduced into the Cupertino school district in 1977, there has been a phenomenal spread and diffusion of information technology into the schools. (Becker, 1983, 1984). Today, few schools are without at least one microcomputer and many have at least five or more. Such a rapid introduction of microcomputers into the schools is a phenomenon in itself, especially when one compares their level of diffusion with the level of penetration of prior innovations such as educational TV, programmed learning, film, and radio.[5]

THE RESEARCH: SOME PRELIMINARY FINDINGS

This diffusion, however, has tended to favor the better-off schools, schools in which groups of teachers strive for improvement, and where the financing of microcomputers is generous and community driven. Moreover, how the microcomputers were introduced, how they are organized for use in schools, what role teachers or administrators play in their implementation, and whether they are at the primary or secondary level determines in part who among the students have access to them. For instance, Becker (1984) found that when only one or two teachers introduced or implemented a computer strategy, there was a tendency for only the very bright students to get exposure. If more teachers were involved, more students across the school were likely to have access. While access to computers at the primary level indicated little or no gender bias, at the

---

microcomputers in current teaching–learning situations as well. Rowntree (p. 16) comments that, "conceiving of the learner as an object to be worked on rather than as a social being whose purposes and strategies are influenced by what he perceives about the people around him and the demands of the institutional setting in which he is operating . . ." is a simplistic conception of classroom realities. Nevertheless, it is this behavioristic theory that still influences the type of software developed and how the computer will be used. The point here is that while Papert represents an alternative theory of learning, one that focuses on the developmental, cognitive, and social situational factors of learning, and has proposed an approach that builds on the interactional features of microcomputers and Logo, most of what has already occurred in education with computers has been strongly shaped by this earlier ancestry of the alliance of educational technology with programmed learning.

[5] Chen and Paisley in their book, *Children and Microcomputers: Research on the Newest Medium,* described this earlier period of innovation as the first electronic revolution and the recent period of computers as the second revolution. Of particular importance here is their paradoxical observation that the second revolution brings with it a new demand for text literacy (pp. 21–22). They also distinguish the second electronic revolution from the first by the strong interactive quality of computers, a quality missing from the first revolution.

secondary level, access and use by male students was much higher than for females. This parallels the predominate use of microcomputers in math and science, where gender bias has long been entrenched. Another observation was that minority children were more likely to be exposed to "electronic page-turning type software while majority culture children were more likely to be exposed to LOGO programming, justifying the term applied several years ago to microcomputer use in schools by the Wall Street Journal, "The Class Machine." How a school district views innovation and change, in general, also seems to play a role as well, suggesting that organizational factors, educational philosophy and "wealth" and the type of organizational setting of schools continue to play their part in either enhancing or mitigating the possible benefits of innovation (Sheingold, Kane, & Endreweit, 1983).[6]

Moreover, this diffusion has been aided by the changes in the work world where information technology is playing a major role in transforming the organization and structure of jobs and employment. Indeed, the notions of High Tech, the Information Society, and industrial revitalization through the use of information technology and robotics serve as a larger sociocultural context that legitimates, perhaps even drives, this new educational technology into the educational environment. As Turkle has suggested, microcomputers have become a cultural phenomenon in and of themselves (Turkle, 1984). Despite the various reasons given for introducing microcomputers into the schools and the various debates about how they should or could transform learning, it is important to examine how microcomputers have been implemented in education and to assess what their impact has been. Similarly, in Europe and the Third World, the microcomputer has made its appearance, with many nations already quite advanced in their introduction and application in education. The patterns of use, however, vary according to level of economic development, contextual and historical factors (Papagiannis, 1985).

Some effort has also been made to assess to what extent computer-based instruction (CAI) is cost-effective, compared with other innovations (Levin, Glass, & Meister, 1984). Finally, there have been studies to assess the impact of microcomputers on achievement, which include studies of CAI based on the mainframe and minicomputer (Roblyer, 1985). There is also a rapidly growing literature of actual descriptions of techniques, approaches and strategies involving

---

[6] For a critical review of the relationship of teachers and educational innovation, see Cuban (1986); for a more general review, see Papagiannis, Klees, & Bickel (1982).

the pedagogic use of microcomputers in the classroom.[7] Systematic evaluation of these materials or the activities they describe, including "horror stories," such as reports of unused computers in school storerooms, are becoming available, but they are usually anecdotal (Hatch, 1986; Tucker, 1985).

Overall, the findings are mixed, and while it is not wise to make judgments about this technology too early, the results fall far short of the original educational promise, requiring that we rethink or reframe our purposes and our hopes for the microcomputer in education. Briefly, despite the fact that almost 15 million students and 500,000 teachers used computers, the ratio of students to computers remained high. Becker points out, for instance, that the ratio of students enrolled to computers available in k-6 was 60:1; in middle-junior high school, it was 41:1. He says, "To provide even 30 minutes of computer time per day to all students enrolled, a school would need to have one computer for every 12 students—and that assumes that the computers are in constant use" (CREMS, 1986, p. 3). On the other hand, when compared with previous educational innovations such as instructional TV or the film and radio, the level of diffusion is impressive. Cuban (1986) reports very modest acceptance of these previous innovations.

Another major finding of this survey was that the major use of microcomputers in elementary schools involved working with a drill-and-practice type of learning programs. Only about 12% of student time is spent on writing computer programs, presumably LOGO. While microcomputers can be located in the classroom, the library

---

[7] In addition to the countless books on computers in education that have been published recently, there have also emerged several journals, such as *Computers in the Schools, Computers & Education* and *Education & Computing,* to name a few that encourage the publication of articles on practice, theory and applied research. Philosophical works discussing the implications of computers for curricular reform, and more specifically, philosophical analyses focusing on the implications of the emergent "information society," telecommunications, and computing for educational aims and goals have also been published. Then there is a genre of publications that focus on the pitfalls and dangers of computers for society, education, and human freedom. While the concerns expressed in this type of critical literature go beyond the immediate topic of this book, many of the issues raised have implications for the how and why of microcomputers in education. Nevertheless, this type of literature or these types of questions usually trouble and perplex American educators, accustomed to viewing education and curriculum as a strictly technical and professional activity rather than a complex and dynamic human and social process, influenced by assumptions of values, economics and politics. Most of the literature was, and continues to be, promotional. The conditions in the larger societal context and the public's ready and almost uncritical acceptance of the microcomputer as a possible cure for many of our educational ills promises a steady market for this type of literature.

or a special laboratory, the middle schools in the study had led the way in having "mobilized" them into laboratories (62%). This is important since the study shows that computers located in a laboratory setting are more likely to be used (Becker, 1986). Other studies (Ascher, 1984; Hess & Miura, 1984; Lockheed, Nielson, & Stone, 1983; Miura, 1986) show further differences in access, interest and use as determined by diffuse status characteristics such as race, gender and class. Males used computers more, particularly in math and science, and students from well-off schools did more LOGO type work and students from less well-off schools did much more drill and practice (that is, electronic page turning).

It has been a decade since the microcomputer first entered the classroom (keeping in mind, however, that Plato, the mainframe computer learning system, arrived much earlier but was never widely implemented) and the research of its impact has begun. A national survey (Becker, 1983) of 1,082 computer-using schools has already been carried out to assess the level and kind of use of microcomputers in schools. Concurrently, there have been efforts to assess to what extent microcomputers have been integrated into the core curriculum (Meister, 1984) and what effects they have had on the quality of education (Sheingold, Kane, & Endreweit, 1983) Other studies have focused on equity of access and type of use questions: To what extent is there differential access based on status characteristics such as race, gender, and class? To what extent do microcomputer curricular strategies differ across these characteristics? And, to what extent are there other unintended consequences or side-effects, positive or negative?

Impact on acheivement is also problematic. Using several review approaches, including meta-analysis, on sets of CAI type studies, Roblyer (1985) found mixed results. For instance, she found that effect sizes on achievement for computer-based learning, compared with more traditional approaches, were high at the elementary level. At higher educational levels, the effect sizes were low to moderate. Supplemental computer-based instruction produces higher effects than "replacement" CAI. In general, math study benefited more than reading/language arts. At the college level, the opposite was found, she reported. Lower-ability students seemed to learn comparatively better from drill while high-ability students seemed to do better using tutorial CAI (p.20). Roblyer (see also Tucker, 1985, p. 15, who makes much of this point as well) also reports that several researchers found other noncomputer learning strategies, such as instructional television or improved reading/study skills, more effective. It should also be noted that the results of her review of studies that did not lend themselves to meta-analysis found no significant difference between computer and noncomputer treatments. One final finding was that there was a clear reduction on learning time using the computer but that traditional learning contributed to better retention. In a more recent synthesis effort (Samson, Niemiec, Weinstein, & Walberg, 1985), findings were reported from 43 studies conducted in natural settings which indicated, on the average, small but significant improvements in achievement scores. Clear causal connections may be confounded, the authors suggest, since most of the studies suffered methodological shortcomings. The achievement gains may be as much the result of the instructional method, novelty effect, or content differences (p.8).

Mixed and ambiguous findings also characterize the study of the microcomputer on cognitive development. Pea and Kurland (1984) found that LOGO programming did not have an effect on problem-solving skills. Indeed, they found that after a year, students did not even have a full command of programming skills. Studying the effect of LOGO on generalizability, Gaffney (1984) found little evidence that what was learned in LOGO (or BASIC) generalized to other content areas. In his study to determine whether LOGO could enhance higher order learning skills, Pogrow (1985) found that it did under certain conditions. Because LOGO lacks "concrete links" between subject matter and the LOGO process, teachers must develop lessons that integrate the two. Cramer (1984), Al-Orainy (1984), and Pea and Kurland (1984) all found evidence in their respective studies that there are skills which must be developed prior to learning programming in order to derive significant benefits. In other LOGO related studies, such as one in this book (see the chapter by Emihovich), mixed findings concerning the power of LOGO to enhance learning-related skills, such as peer collaboration, are the norm. Whether LOGO-based activities contribute to writing ability, peer collaboration, planning (Pea, 1983), and procedural or higher-order thinking is still unclear.

One final area of interest in the emerging research on microcomputers is that of its cost-effectiveness. If the use of CAI or other computer-based teaching-learning strategy improves or at least maintains learning at acceptable levels but at reduced cost, then the microcomputer can be heralded as an innovation that delivers instruction more efficiently. This could allow teachers to do other important teaching or remedial work, often left undone. Or, students would have additional time to participate in enrichment activities or to pursue their studies in greater depth. At the very least, educational budgets could be stabilized and more efficient allocation of both funds and human resources would obtain. This certainly has been one of the promises of technology in education, and most recently, the promise of the computer, whether it be mainframe, mini or microcomputer. Levin and Meister (1985) summarize the arguments that advocates of computers routinely make:

> Microcomputers promise to be the most cost-effective and adaptable instructional vehicles. They are highly flexible in use and configuration. They can be operated singly or in a network; they can employ both visual and audio stimuli and they can integrate interactive video-cassettes or videodisc components. They can be used for a wide variety of instructional applications, subjects, and approaches including games, simulations, drill and practice, topics within a course, or a complete course. Students can learn by following prescribed routines or be challenged with written, artistic, or mathematical assignments or problems in which the computer provides an individualized response and assistance to the learner.(p.5)

The research on past educational innovations has almost always shown that costs were underestimated. All too often in the early phases of investment, the focus has been on the cost of the hardware, not on the actual cost of implementation, or on the opportunity costs. While little research has been found that assesses the cost effectiveness of microcomputers, in one study using the tools of meta-analysis and cost-effectiveness analysis (Levin, 1984; Levin, Glass, & Meister, 1984) to compare four educational interventions, peer and adult tutoring approaches were found to be more cost-effective than reducing class size, increasing the length of the schoolday, or using computer-assisted instruction. This preliminary finding and the past history of technology costs suggests caution in accepting this promise as well (Levin & Meister, 1985).

While much more research is being conducted and more developmental work with computers is taking place, the results of this first phase are fairly clear. Computers may be in schools but the promised revolution has yet to take place (Tucker, 1985). The diffusion of computing power into schools has certainly taken hold, unlike previous innovations. Nevertheless, the preliminary information on who uses them and how they are used, what the impact has been on achievement or other valued educational goals, and their presumed cost savings, compared with other teaching-learning strategies, can only suggest that the "decisive influence" of computers on education has yet to occur (see Kirst & Meister, 1984, pp. 21–22, for a discussion as to why impact is modest).

NEW QUESTIONS AND ISSUES

Given the lack of clear evidence for the effectiveness of computers in schools, why then have they so successfully entered the schools? First, external factors supporting their introduction have been powerful, particularly the fact that it is a cultural phenomenon (Pogrow, 1985; Turkle, 1984). This is, in my estimation, the critical difference between innovation of the past and this one. It explains, in part, why earlier technological innovations, computer-based or otherwise, while fully integrated into other societal institutions, were never widely diffused throughout the educational systems of the United States (Cuban, 1986). Despite the fact that some of these earlier innovations had public support, they were not rooted in perceived changes in the workplace nor did they have the cultural pervasiveness of the microcomputer. Rather, while seen by their advocates as improving the quality of education and the efficiency of instructional delivery, they were also seen by the ultimate users, the teachers, as "irrelevant to their practice; [that they] . . . increased[d] their burdens without adding benefits to their students' learning, or . . . weaken [ed] their control of the classroom" (Cuban, 1986, p. 71).[8]

The relatively successful diffusion and acceptance of microcomputers in education, despite some of its negative side-effects and thus far limited benefits, may be best understood as a result of not only these current trends, but also of those found in earlier periods as well, which did not lead to enduring changes in education. However, because of an explicit cultural ideology of personal use and empowerment, their obvious interactive capability and their implicit promise of revitalizing the role of teachers and the restructuring of the learning environment within the school, microcomputers have been perceived as the new panacea for educational ills. It is this cultural metaphor, more than formal or informal philosophies of educating, Papert's or anyone else's, that has played a key enabling role in the rapid expansion of microcomputers in education. I contend that Papert's vision of LOGO and learning, its current salience to

---

[8] See Michael Apple (1982), *Education and Power,* who argues that efforts to produce instructional approaches that separate execution and control of the instructional materials, so-called teacher-proof materials, have the potential to deskill our teachers and to shift control of the learning process in the classroom away from the teacher (a deprofessionalization process). Because they work against our broad-aimed democratic educational goals, teachers often resist these types of innovations, even though the implications of these types of "reforms" may not be fully understood. Contrast this to Cuban's argument that teachers tend to resist innovations that are not "organizationally realistic" or are not attentive to organizational development issues.

educators, is partly the result of this metaphor, even though their actual practice may not reflect it. If my contention is correct, microcomputers have more potential to serve as a stimulus for the reexamination of our educational methods and ends than they have as electronic mediums for specific techniques such as LOGO for effective microcomputer use in the classroom.[9]

INFORMATION, KNOWLEDGE, AND UNDERSTANDING

The key to the successful use of "computing power" in the educational process, however, will depend upon the extent to which it is able to demonstrate its educational worth.[10] In this sense, our attempts to assess the microcomputer's impact on achievement, for example, while it may be important to policy makers, parents, and educators alike, may not be the only question that we should be asking. Even the current questions concerning the impact of programming, or other specific uses of microcomputers on the cognitive development of children and youth, fall short of adding up to the multiple aims we have established for education. "Teaching the microcomputer" (programming), being taught by it (CAI and CMI), using it for "productivity" purposes (word processing, data management, both quantitative and qualitative, spreadsheeting, etc.), may all have some role in educating our children and youth, but we have not looked at whether these specific tactical uses of computing power contribute to the overall quality of the educational process. Indeed, most of the current criteria of educational or learning success may distort the questions and issues that we ought to be asking.

---

[9] In response to criticism about Logo, Papert addressed this issue by stating that many research studies were flawed by what he called "technocentric thinking," in that there is a tendency to think of computers and Logo as "agents that act directly on thinking and learning . . . the context for human development is always a culture, never an isolated technology" (1987, p. 23). He further suggested that the true value of Logo will not be realized until computer criticism extends beyond technocentrism to describe the beginnings of a new computer culture (see Davy, 1984, for a critical review of Papert's book *Mindstorms*).

[10] See Scheffler (1986) for a critical analysis and discussion of the notion of information and how its "technicist" character works against education, 1986; see also Manfred Stanley's (1978) *The Technological Conscience: Survival and Dignity in an Age of Expertise,* for a full discussion of danger of creeping technicism in education.

TOWARD A NEW POLICY AND RESEARCH AGENDA

What have we learned from this first phase and the preliminary research that has been conducted? First, we may have learned that we allowed old innovative type metaphors such as programmed learning to dominate our thinking about how computers could best serve teaching and learning (Note that the key word here is dominate. Programmed learning and drill-and-practice for many learning activities are not only appropriate but desirable. That they should not serve as the guiding principle in education, however, is the point). Second, in our efforts to break away from older approaches, we may have embraced too quickly approaches such as Logo without carefully assessing their assumptions about the learning process. Third, we may have rushed too quickly toward computers as a panacea when other, less glamorous innovations were available. Fourth, we may have overlooked some of the lessons of past attempts at educational innovation. And finally, in our efforts to implement this innovation, we may have forgotten how complex the educational enterprise is and of what it is comprised. Indeed, in our efforts to implement a microcomputer strategy in education and to assess its impact on education, we may have relied too much on the narrow goals and questions of cost-efficiency and achievement to guide its development and its evaluation, when in fact the computer's value in education may lie elsewhere. As once said by a sage professor of mine, "The right answer to the wrong question is still the wrong answer to the right question." Now, with the first phase of computer penetration into education coming to an end, it is time to rethink our goals and questions concerning computing power and education.

Another reason for re-examining our questions is that we have often formed our research and evaluation questions, which typically result from public, political, or popular concerns, and have substituted them for complex and thorny "policy questions" or our broad-aimed educational goals that we must continually address if we are to continue to improve our educational enterprise and have it contribute to the improvement of our lives, in general, not just in a particular occupation or in the workplace. Another reason is that because of our tendency to focus solely on learning outcomes of computing, we may underplay or miss entirely other kinds of impacts as suggested in several recent studies of microcomputers and those who use them. I suggest, for instance that while we have begun to examine extensively the impact of computing on achievement scores, cognitive development, skill development in various subject-matter areas, and efficiency in the learning of information, we have given all too little attention to the qualitative aspects of this microelectronic device. They include the observations that social context and interaction (both the interactiveness of user and computer and interaction among the users, pupils with pupils, pupils with teachers) are key mediating factors in the learning process, and several researchers have noted that those who advocate the introduction of the microcomputer but don't take these facts into account may doom the technology to failure, despite its promise and potential (Anderson, Welch, & Harris, 1983; Emihovich & Miller, 1988; Heap, 1985; Lockheed, 1985; Sheingold, Kane, & Endreweit, 1983; Turkle, 1984).

As a preliminary research agenda, then, we need to pose questions that do not foucs on achievement outcomes alone but rather on current uses of computers in schools, and in the workplace, to see how they might be used more effectively in schools. Concurrently, we need to examine in context those current experiments in education that focus on computers as tools. These approaches are already being conducted (see, e.g., Levin, Riel, Rowe, & Boruta, 1984). Drawing on naturalistic and ethnographic approaches, we should examine to what extent these productivity tools stimulate the development of learning experiences that contribute to problem posing, problem solving, and critical understanding. In this regard, it is my contention that if teachers can design lessons that embody these goals, the use of microcomputer productivity tools will enhance the learning of those skills. On the other hand, if lessons are not developed that embody those goals or ideas, computers will not make a difference either. No innovation, regardless of its potential, can substitute for the thoughtful, critically thinking, well-prepared, well-educated teacher. Therefore, we need to study how teachers work, under what conditions, and how they understand the curricular development process in practice.

Next, we need to assess to what extent using the microcomputer as a productivity and information tool affects the concept and process of teacher training and retraining costs, which should be less. This is because training teachers in the use of applications software in the form of productivity tools that can be used across subject areas is easier, less costly, and less time consuming than training them in programming, for instance. Moreover, generic applications such as word processing, spreadsheeting, data management, telecommunications and bibliographic management can be used across subject areas. Building and using educational telecommunications networks and/or using nationwide commercial information services for learning and teaching are other avenues that need to be implemented and researched. Note that the capacity to access and analyze large amounts of information is developed from a curriculum that would be increasingly focused on problem posing and problem solving, knowledge creation, management, analysis, synthesis and evaluation of information, and understanding. To accomplish the task of developing these skills, the present curriculum and textbooks would need to undergo considerable change; even what we would evaluate would undergo change. This suggested strategy, however, would require a more thorough examination of the curriculum and would require reorganization of the structures and culture of the learning place itself. Conditions would need to be created that enabled teachers to continue to play a leadership role in the development of a new curriculum and the organizational setting to support this reform.

Given this perspective, then, we need to study the impact of using computers as productivity tools on the educational context, on the attitudes of teachers toward their work, and on the student attitudes toward education and learning. Here the argument is that if computers can make the workplace a better place to be, if effective use of computers in the learning process helps teachers regain their sense of professional efficacy and restores students' appreciation of learning as synthesis and analysis rather than information and memorization, then we will have taken a major step toward accomplishing our goal of preparing students for lifelong learning in the information society. Finally, we need to do the type of policy research that proposes what kinds of organizational environments are required to facilitate this kind of curricular activity and how many and what kind of computers and software are needed, how to finance them and how to make sure that all students are armed with this tool.

Interestingly enough, Papert (1980) himself supports this approach. Early in his book he speaks to the issue and problem of innovation in education, the role of the teacher and educational purpose by observing that "the educator must be an anthropologist" (p. 32) if the teacher is to understand what cultural materials and societal trends may contribute to intellectual development. I add that the teacher as anthropologist must also understand how these new cultural artifacts are being used. Papert as educator may not be altogether right about Logo's power to transform one's mind, but Papert as insightful advocate of educational reform is absolutely right. This means beginning to understand microcomputers as productivity tools, as electronic assistants, not, as Tucker warns, as "electronic teachers administering instruction" (1985, p. 19).

This approach is much more consistent with what is possible in education; training teachers to use generic application programs with subject matter specialization is much easier than teaching them to program or to use authoring systems, and immediately opens up opportunities for the teacher and the student to establish telecommunication networks, to have access to new databases, bibliographic sources, and to practice using tools designed to input, manage, analyze and evaluate information.[11] Again, if we return to Papert, we note that he views the ultimate value of the microcomputer as a "cultural machine" in its role as revitalizer or enabler of change. He says, "Today what is offered in the education market is largely determined by what is acceptable to a sluggish and conservative system. But this is where the computer presence is in the process of creating an environment for change" (p.37).

This brings us back to our earlier comments on the enduring goals of education. I maintain that the link between these goals and what is practiced, using the various database management programs—word and concept-processing (outlining) programs, spreadsheeting, quantitative and qualitative data-management programs—within the various subject-area specialties, are precisely the skills in which we urge our teachers to prepare students. In other words, our traditional educational aims of improving problem solving, problem posing, and critical understanding, through the use of productivity tools and creative programs in the subject areas, could become a reality in practice, especially if we realize the "maieutic"[12] potential of the computer and interactive applications software programs; the development of new learning needs and the rediscovery of old ones; and that the possible stratifying tendencies of the current "access to quality education" strategies currently being employed in the educational enterprise have also stimulated solutions for these access problems. And perhaps most important of all, that the microcomputer may be most important as a "subjective machine" (Turkle, 1984), a defining technology that influences and shapes our ideas and views of ourselves and increases or renews our sense of personal efficacy. For instance, for teachers, the microcomputer may be more important

---

[11] Already universities have paved the way for defining the use of microcomputers from this perspective. Tucker notes with irony how few professors use the microcomputer as part of their instructional delivery system.

[12] Maieutics refers to the educational process and practice of the dialectical or socratic mode. "The Socratic mode of teaching, a mode of teaching called meiotic because it helps the student bring ideas to birth. It is teaching by asking questions, by leading discussions, by helping to raise their minds up from a state of understanding or appreciating less to a state of understanding or appreciating more." (Adler, 1982, p. 29).

as a tool that revitalizes the school workplace and the place of the teacher in it.

CONCLUSIONS: THE NEED FOR A SECOND PHASE

The computer symbolizes both the problem and the solution related to information overload and bureaucratization of our work lives. The exponential growth of information and the galloping standardization, routinization, and fragmentation of the workplace promotes alienation and loss of personal efficacy. In this sense, the computer promotes the production and saving of information in a context not suited to the management and effective use of its information management and analytical capability. On the other hand, if the computer is used thoughtfully, it can spearhead the breaking down of traditional ways of organizing work and knowledge in education and work, and actually increase our awareness of the need to be mindful of the distinctions between information, knowledge, and critical understanding, and the skills necessary to teach them to our youth. These are, after all, the educational goals for which educators strive but have rarely accomplished. A fitting last comment is given by Tucker, who summarizes the possible future of computers in education:

> The key to the future use of the computer in education . . . lies not in its history in schools as an instructional delivery system but in its evolving use in the society at large, as a tool to get work done—not as an extension of the teacher but as an intellectual companion for the student. (1985, p. 22)

REFERENCES

Adler, M. (1982). *The paideia proposal*. New York: Macmillan.

Al-Orainy, A.S. (1984). *The effect of computer literacy on problem solving in mathematics: An analysis of NAEP data*. Unpublished doctoral dissertation, University of Denver.

Anderson, R.E., Welch, W.W., & Harris, L.J. (1983). *Computer inequities in opportunities for computer literacy*. University of Minnesota, Minnesota Research and Evaluation Center.

Apple, M. (1982). *Education and power*. Boston: Routledge & Kegan Paul.

Ascher, C. (1984). *Microcomputers: Equity and quality in education for urban disadvantaged students*. ERIC/CUE Digest No. 19. ERIC Clearinghouse on Urban Education, New York.

Becker, H.J. (1983, June). *School uses of microcomputers.* Baltimore: Center for Social Organization of Schools, Johns Hopkins University.

Becker, H.J. (1984, February). *School uses of microcomputers.* Baltimore: Center for Social Organization of Schools, Johns Hopkins University.

Bolter, J.D. (1984). *Turing's man: Western culture in the computing age.* Chapel Hill, NC: University of North Carolina Press.

Chen, M. (1985). Microworlds of research. In M. Chen & W. Paisley (Eds.), *Children and microcomputers: Research on the newest medium* (pp. 276–296). Beverly Hills, CA: Sage.

Chen, M., & Paisley, W. (Eds.). (1985). *Children and microcomputers: Research on the newest medium.* Beverly Hills, CA: Sage.

Cramer, S.E. (1984). *Cognitive processing variables as predictors of student performance in learning a computer programming language.* Unpublished doctoral dissertation, University of Georgia.

CREMS. Center for Research on Elementary and Middle Schools Newsletter. (1986, June). Baltimore, MD: Johns Hopkins University.

Cuban, L. (1986). *Teachers and machines: The classroom use of technology since 1920.* New York: Teachers College Press.

Davy, J. (1984). Mindstorms in the lamplight. *Teachers College Record, 85*(4), 549–558.

Emihovich, C., & Miller, G.E. (1988). Learning Logo: The social context of cognition. *Journal of Curriculum Studies, 20,* 57–70.

Gaffney, C.R. (1984). *Computing languages: Tools for problem solving?* Arlington, TX: Unpublished doctoral dissertation, University of Texas at Austin.

Grubb, W.N. (1984). *The bandwagon once more: Vocational preparation for high-tech occupations.* (Program Report No. 84–B6). Stanford, CA: Institute for Research on Educational Finance and Governance.

Hatch, C.W. (1986, February). *Computers in classrooms—An innovation at risk, an American assessment.* Paper presented at the American Educational Research Division G: The Social Context of Education, Southeastern Regional Conference, Baton Rouge, LA.

Heap, J.L. (1985). *Collaboration in word processing and the impact of technology on education: The evolving role of the student.* Ontario, Canada: Ministry of Education.

Hess, R.D., & Miura, I.T. (1984). *Issues in training teachers to use microcomputers in the classroom.* (Policy Paper No. 84-C2). Stanford, CA: Institute for Research on Educational Finance and Governance.

House, E.R. (1974). *The politics of educational innovation.* Berkeley, CA: McCutchan.

Kirst, M., & Meister, G.R. (1985). Turbulence in American secondary schools: What reforms last? *Curriculum Inquiry, 15*(1), 169–186.

Levin, H.M. (1984). *Cost-effectiveness of four educational innovations.* (Project Rep. No. 84-A11). Stanford, CA: Institute for Research on Educational Finance and Governance.

Levin, H.M., & Glass, G., & Meister, G.R. (1984). *Cost-effectiveness of four educational interventions.* (Project Rep. No. 84-A11). Stanford, CA: Institute for Research on Educational Finance and Governance.

Levin, H.M., & Meister, G.R. (1985). *Educational technology and computers: Promises, promises, always promises.* (Project Rep. No. 85-A13). Stanford, CA: Institute for Research on Educational Finance and Governance.

Levin, J.A., Riel, M.M., Rowe, R.D., & Boruta, M.J. (1984). Muktuk meets jacuzzi: Computer networks and elementary school writers. In S.W. Freedman (Ed.), *The acquisition of written language: Revision and response.* Norwood, NJ: Ablex.

Lockheed, M. (1985). Women, girls, and computers: A first look at the evidence. *Sex Roles, 13,* 115–122.

Lockheed, M., Nielson, A., & Stone, M.K. (1983). Sex differences in microcomputer literacy. In D. Bonnette (Ed.), *Proceedings of NECC/5, national Educational Computing Conference.* Silver Spring, MD: IEEE Computer Society Press.

Maddison, J. (1983). *Education in the microelectronics era.* Milton Keynes, England: Open University Press.

Meister, G.R. (1984). *Successful integration of microcomputers in an elementary school.* (Project Rept. No. 80-A23). Stanford, CA: Institute for Research on Educational Finance and Governance.

Miura, I.T. (1984). *Understanding gender differences in middle-school computer interest use.* Paper presented at the annual meeting of the American Educational Research Association, San Francisco.

Paisley, W. (1985). Children, new media, and microcomputers: Continuities of research. In M. Chen & W. Paisley (Eds.), *Children and microcomputers: Research on the newest medium.* Beverly Hills, CA: Sage.

Papagiannis, G. (1985). *The Nairobi Aga Khan computers in education project: A review.* (Unpublished report). Geneva: Aga Khan Foundation.

Papagiannis, G., Klees, S., & Bickel, R. (1982). Toward a political economy of educational innovation. *Review of Educational Research, 52*(2), 245–290.

Papert, S. (1980). *Mindstorms: Children, computers and powerful ideas.* New York: Basic Books.

Papert, S. (1987). Computer criticism and technocentric thinking. *Educational Researcher, 16*(1), 22–30.

Pea, R.D. (1983). *Logo programming and problem solving.* (Tech. Rept. No. 12). New York: Bank Street College of Education.

Pea, R.D., & Kurland, D.M. (1984). *Logo programming and the development of planning skills.* (Tech. Rept. No. 15). New York: Bank Street College of Education.

Pogrow, S. (1983). *Education in the computer age: Issues of policy, practice and reform.* Beverly Hills, CA: Sage.

Pogrow, S. (1985). Helping student become thinkers. *Electroni Learning, 4*(7), 25–29.

Roblyer, M.D. (1985). *Measuring the impact of computers in instruction: A non-technical review of research for educators.* Washington, DC: Association for Educational Data Systems.

Rowntree, D. (1982). *Educational technology in the curriculum.* London: Harper & Row.

Rumberger, R.W. (1984a). *High technology and job loss.* (Project Rept. No. 84-A12). Stanford, CA: Institute for Research on Educational Finance and Governance.

Rumberger, R.W. (1984b). *The potential impact of technology on the skill requirements of future jobs.* (Project Rept. No. 84-A24). Stanford, CA: Institute for Research on Educational Finance and Governance.

Samson, G.E., Niemiec, R., Weinstein, T., & Walberg, J. (1985). *Effects of computer-based instruction of secondary school achievement: A quantitative synthesis.* Paper presented at the annual meeting of the American Educational Research Association, Chicago.

Scheffler, T. (1986). Computers at school? *Teachers College Record, 87*(4), 513–544.

Sheingold, K., Kane, J.H., & Endreweit, M.E. (1983). Microcomputer use in schools: Developing a research agenda. *Harvard Elementary Review, 53*(4), 412–432.

Solomonides, T., & Levidow, L. (1985). *Compulsive technology: Computers as culture.* London: Free Association Press.

Stanley, M. (1978). *The technological conscience: Survival and dignity in an age of expertise.* Chicago: University of Chicago Press. Suppes, P. (1979). *Current trends in computer-assisted instruction.* New York: Academic Press.

Tucker, M. (1985). Computers in the schools: What revolution? *Journal of Communication, 35*(4), 12–33.

Turkle, S. (1984). *The second self: Computers and the human spirit.* New York: Simon & Schuster.

Author Index

Subject Index

DATE DUE

APR 2 7 1990		OCT 2001
AUG 3		
AUG 1991		
OCT 8		
JAN 5 1999		
XXXX		
GAYLORD		PRINTED IN U.S.A.